Vol. 6

Story & Art by
Kiyo Fujiwara

Wild Ones
アラクレ

Volume 6

CONTENTS

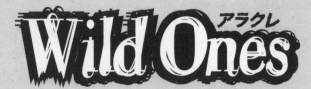

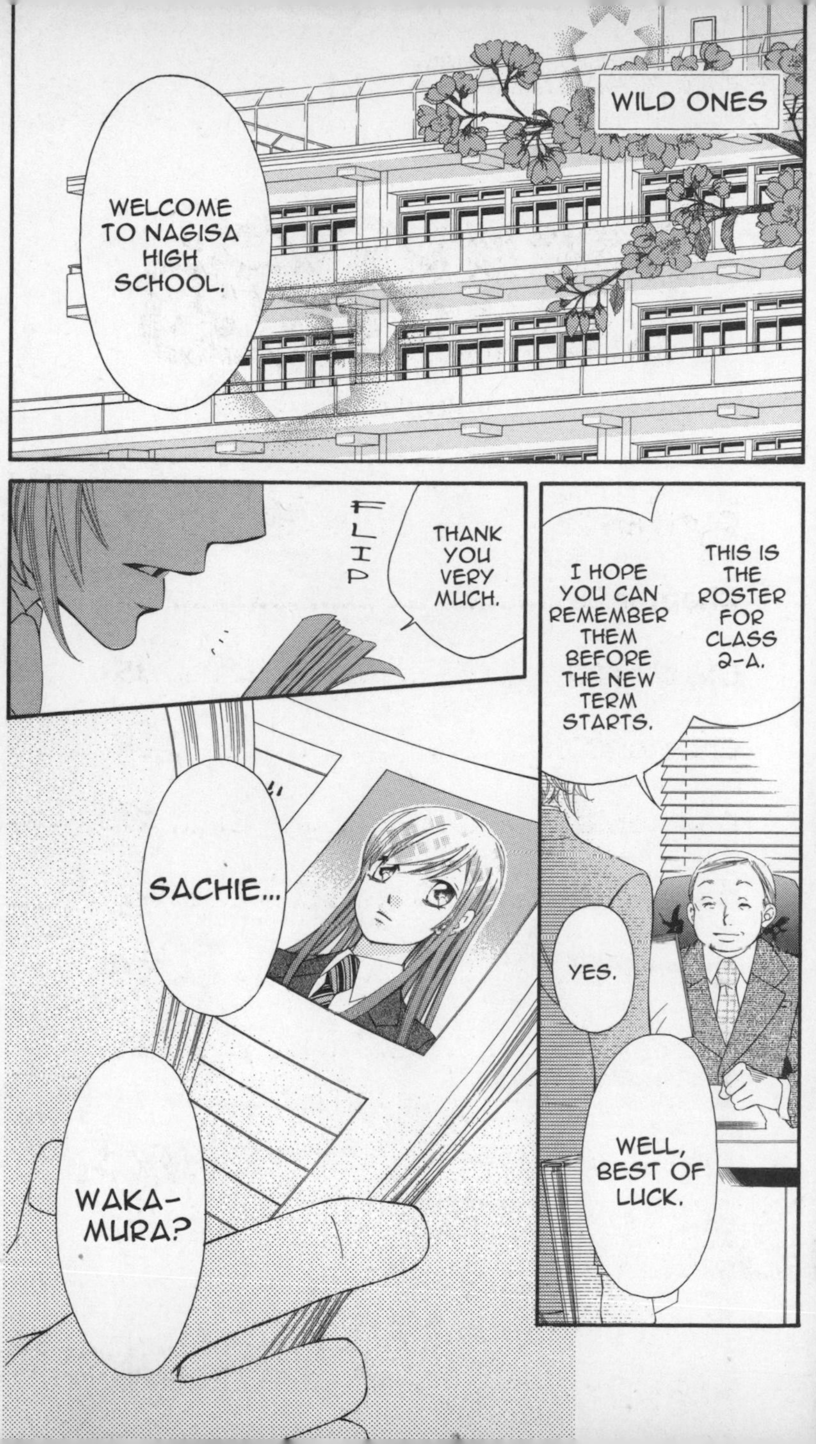
WILD ONES
WELCOME TO NAGISA HIGH SCHOOL.
THIS IS THE ROSTER FOR CLASS 2-A.
I HOPE YOU CAN REMEMBER THEM BEFORE THE NEW TERM STARTS.
YES.
WELL, BEST OF LUCK.
THANK YOU VERY MUCH.
FLIP
SACHIE...
WAKA-MURA?

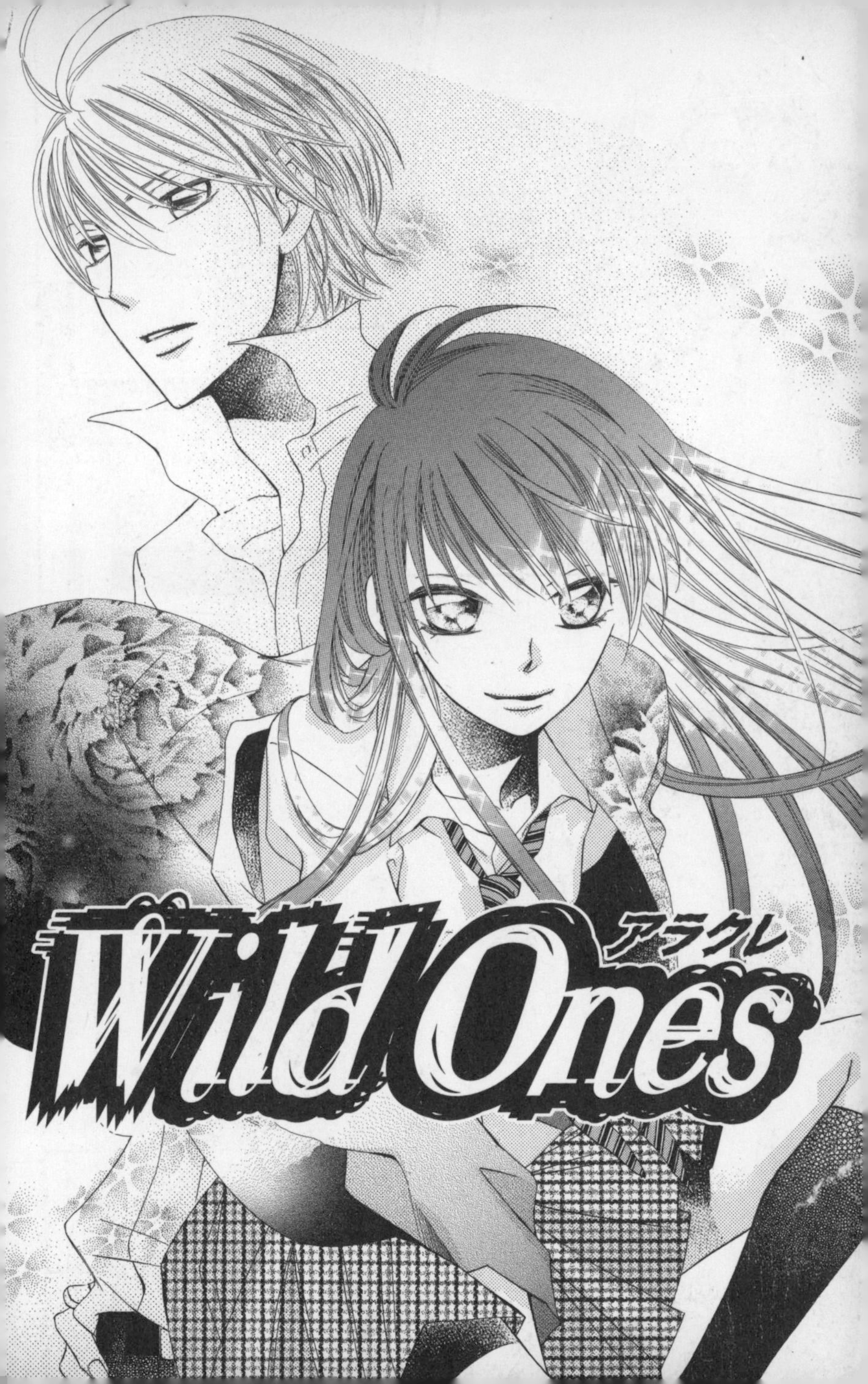
Wild Ones
アラクレ

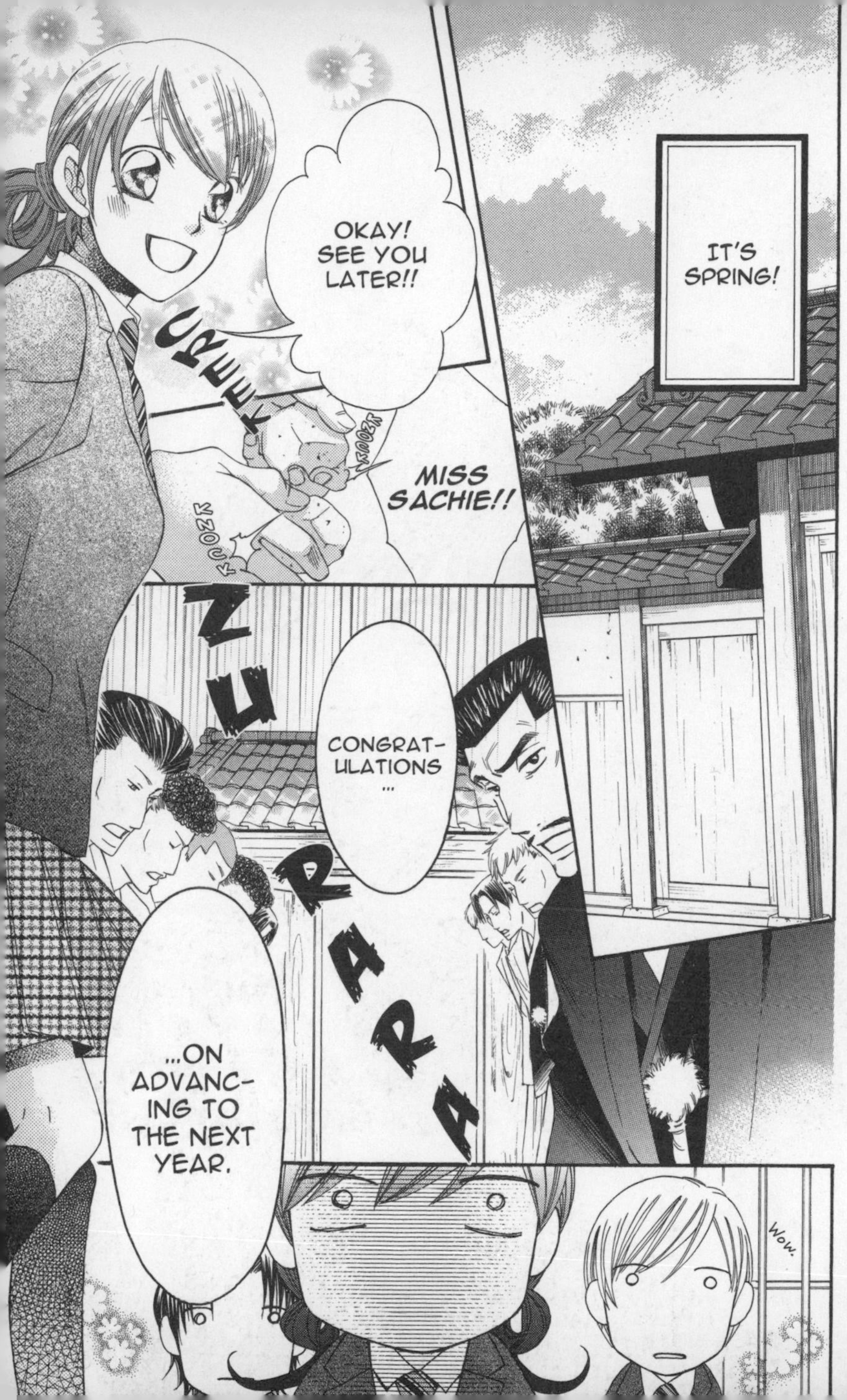
IT'S SPRING!
OKAY! SEE YOU LATER!!
MISS SACHIE!!
KNOCK
KNOCK
CREEK
ZURARARA
CONGRAT-ULATIONS ...
...ON ADVANC-ING TO THE NEXT YEAR.
Wow.

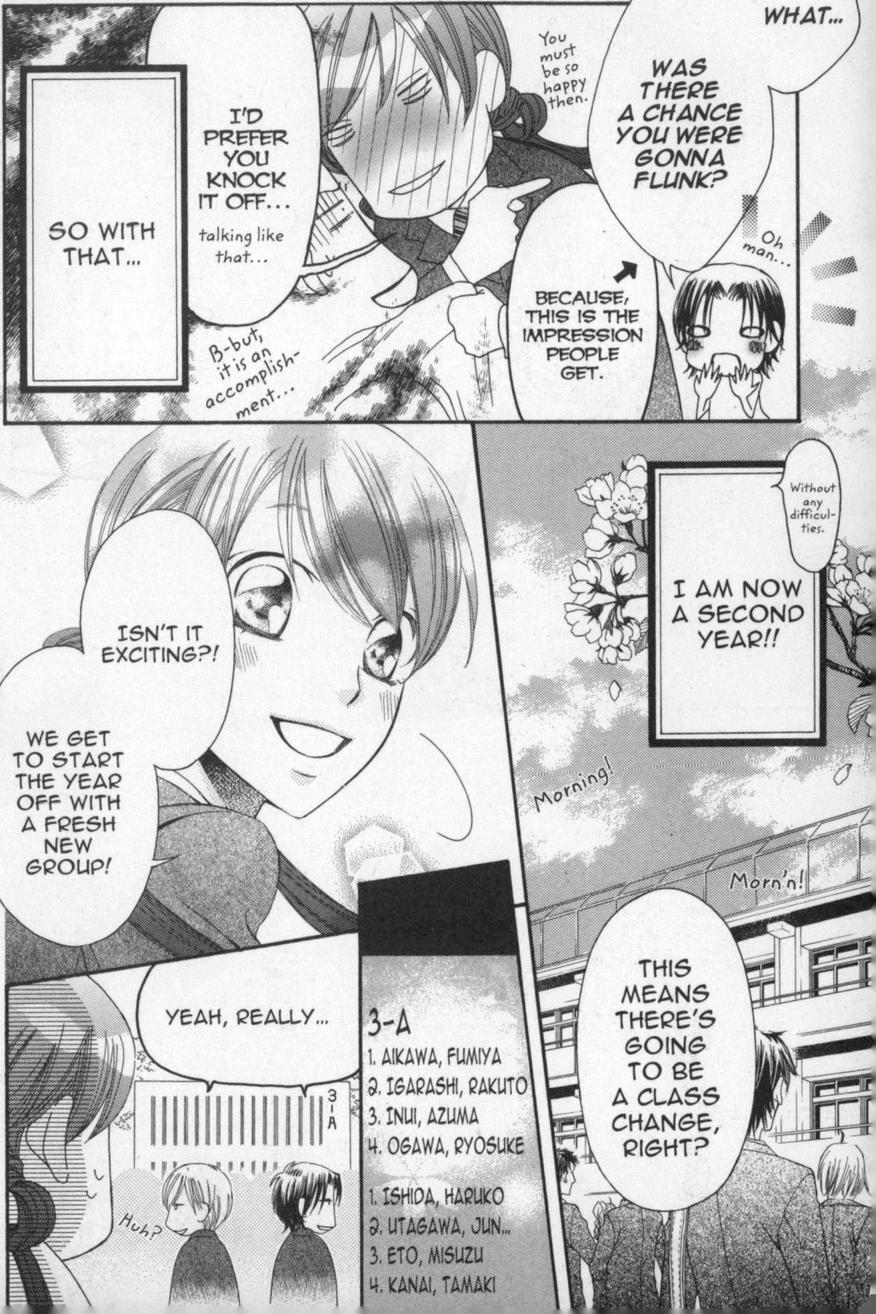
WHAT... WAS THERE A CHANCE YOU WERE GONNA FLUNK?
You must be so happy then.
Oh man...
BECAUSE, THIS IS THE IMPRESSION PEOPLE GET.
I'D PREFER YOU KNOCK IT OFF... talking like that...
B-but, it is an accomplishment...
SO WITH THAT...
Without any difficulties.
I AM NOW A SECOND YEAR!!
Morning!
Morn'n!
THIS MEANS THERE'S GOING TO BE A CLASS CHANGE, RIGHT?
ISN'T IT EXCITING?!
WE GET TO START THE YEAR OFF WITH A FRESH NEW GROUP!
3-A
1. AIKAWA, FUMIYA
2. IGARASHI, RAKUTO
3. INUI, AZUMA
4. OGAWA, RYOSUKE
1. ISHIDA, HARUKO
2. UTAGAWA, JUN...
3. ETO, MISUZU
4. KANAI, TAMAKI
YEAH, REALLY...
3-A
Huh?

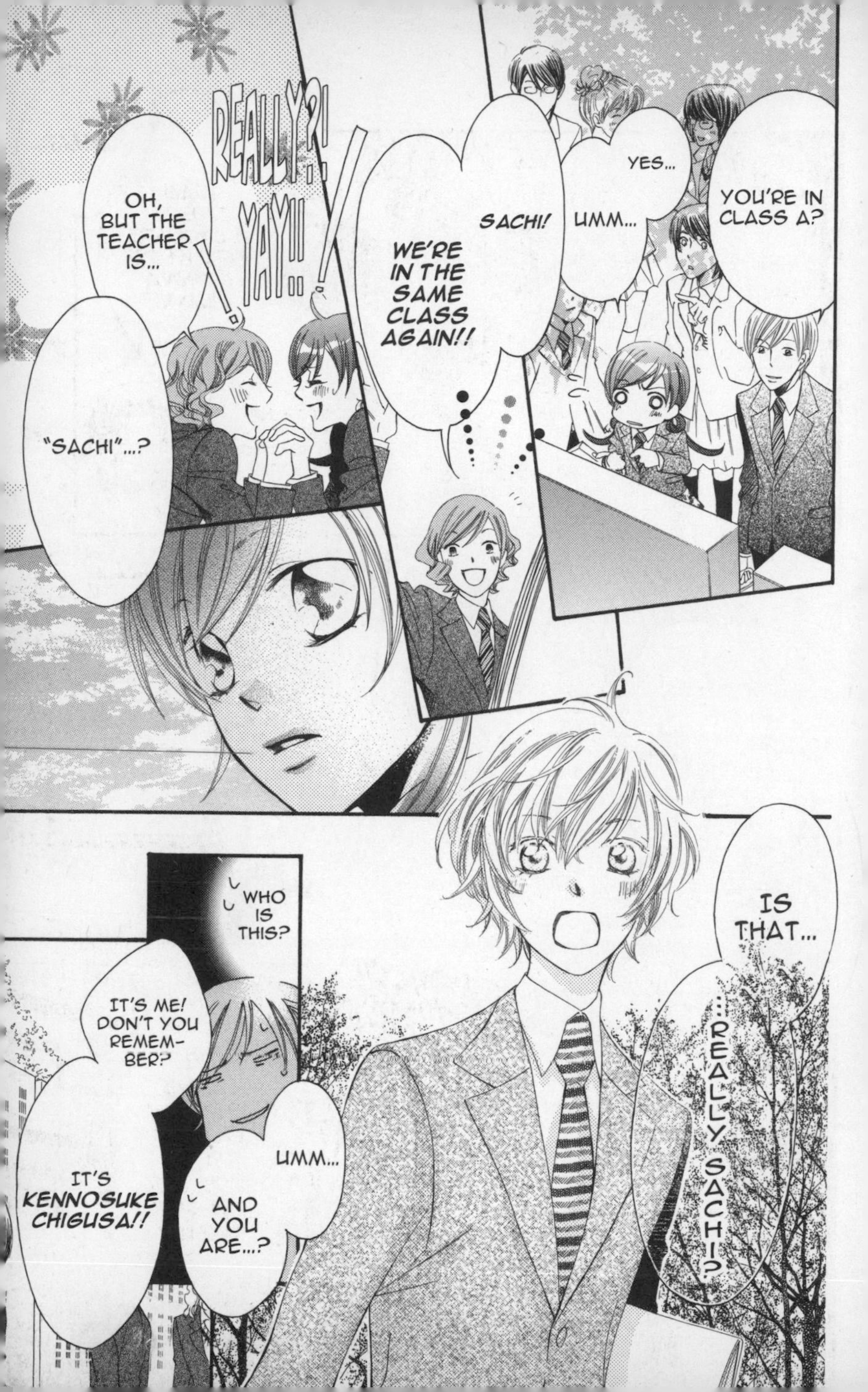
YOU'RE IN CLASS A?
YES...
UMM...
SACHI!
WE'RE IN THE SAME CLASS AGAIN!!
REALLY?! YAY!!
OH, BUT THE TEACHER IS...
"SACHI"...?
IS THAT...
...REALLY SACHI?
WHO IS THIS?
IT'S ME! DON'T YOU REMEM-BER?
UMM...
AND YOU ARE...?
IT'S KENNOSUKE CHIGUSA!!

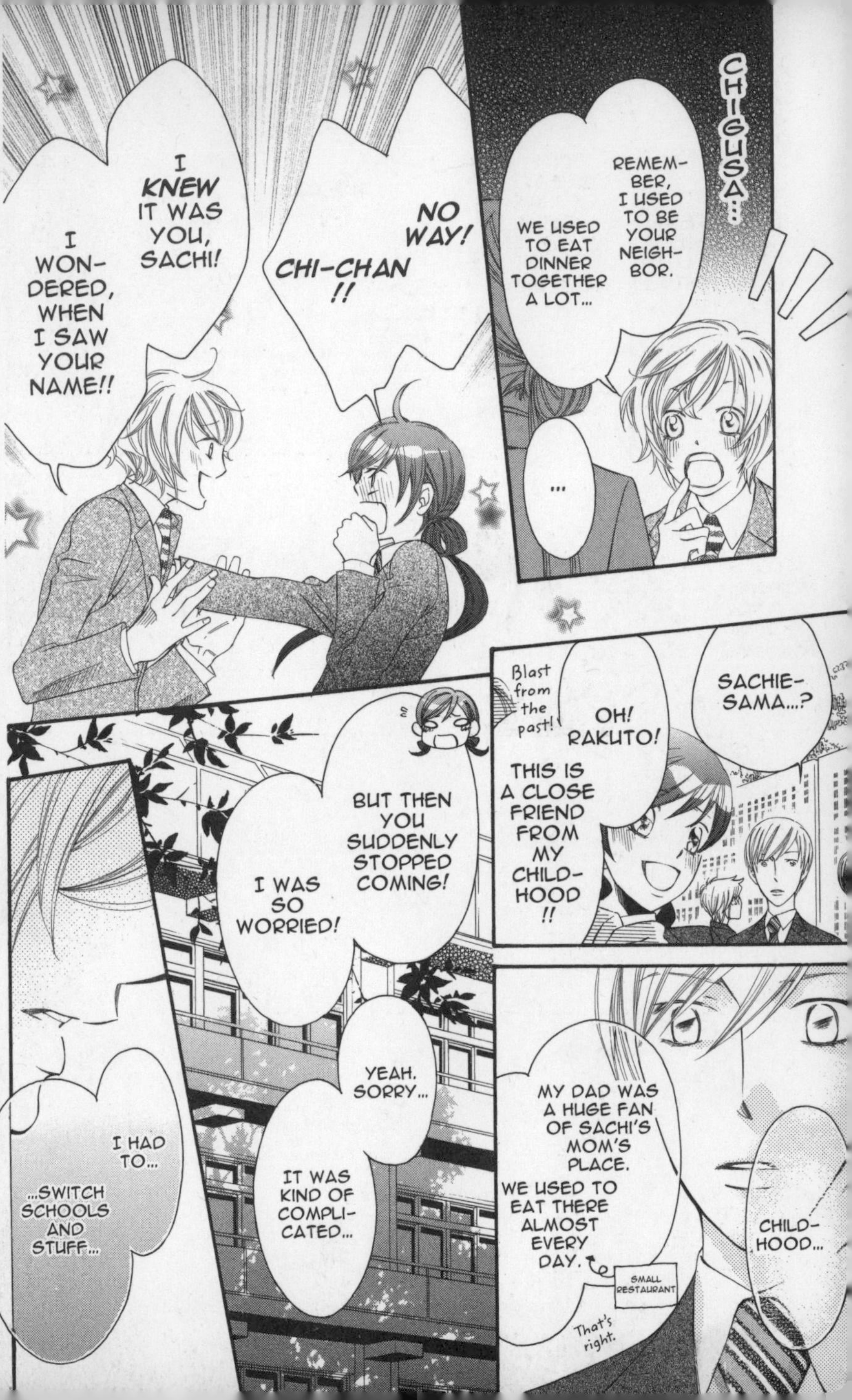
CHIGUSA...
REMEMBER, I USED TO BE YOUR NEIGHBOR.
WE USED TO EAT DINNER TOGETHER A LOT...
...
NO WAY! CHI-CHAN!!
I KNEW IT WAS YOU, SACHI!
I WONDERED, WHEN I SAW YOUR NAME!!
SACHIE-SAMA...?
OH! RAKUTO!
THIS IS A CLOSE FRIEND FROM MY CHILDHOOD!!
Blast from the past!
CHILDHOOD...
MY DAD WAS A HUGE FAN OF SACHI'S MOM'S PLACE.
WE USED TO EAT THERE ALMOST EVERY DAY.
SMALL RESTAURANT
That's right.
BUT THEN YOU SUDDENLY STOPPED COMING!
I WAS SO WORRIED!
YEAH. SORRY...
IT WAS KIND OF COMPLICATED...
I HAD TO...
...SWITCH SCHOOLS AND STUFF...

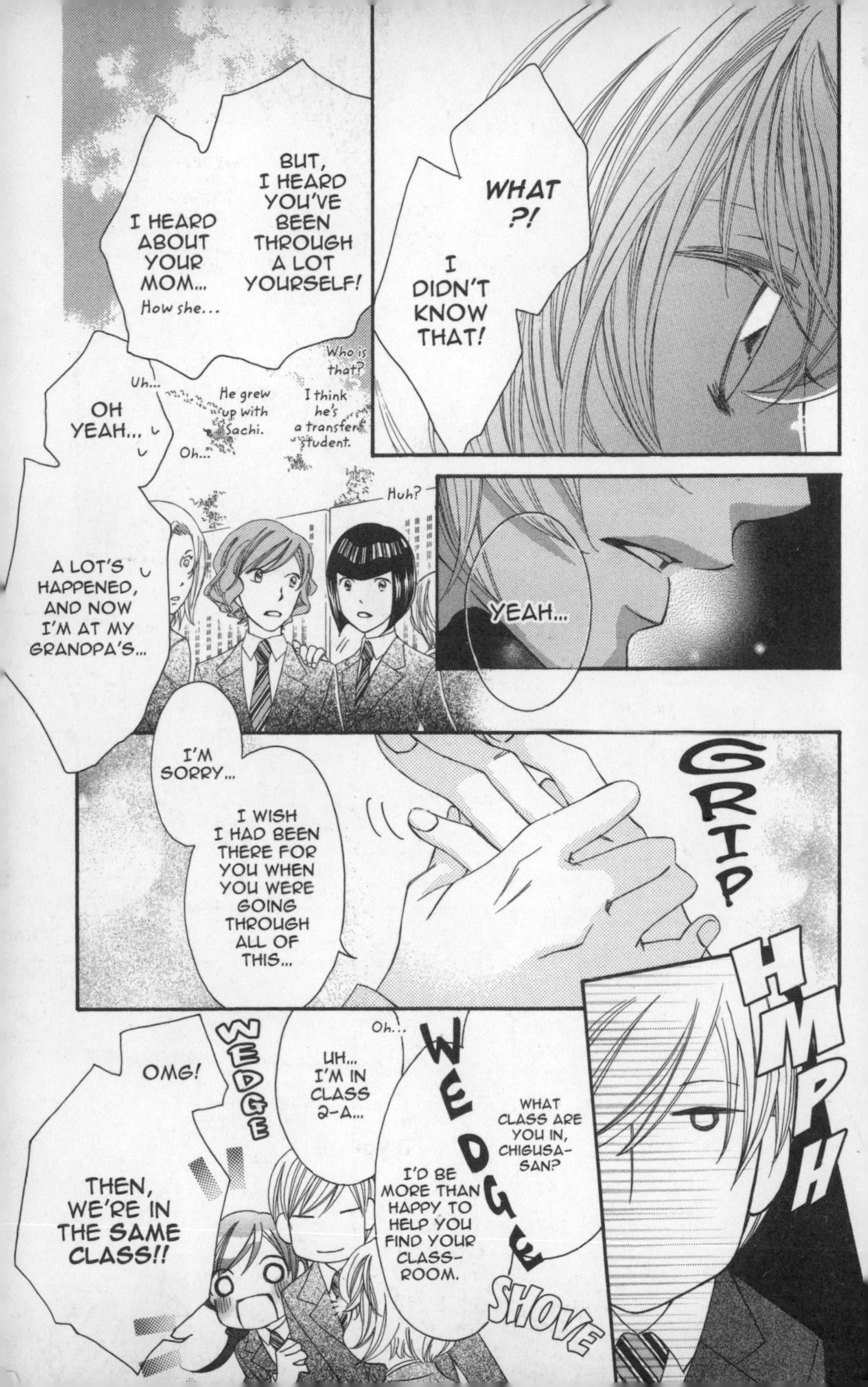
WHAT ?!
I DIDN'T KNOW THAT!
YEAH...
BUT, I HEARD YOU'VE BEEN THROUGH A LOT YOURSELF!
I HEARD ABOUT YOUR MOM... How she...
Who is that?
I think he's a transfer student.
He grew up with Sachi.
Uh...
OH YEAH...
Oh...
Huh?
A LOT'S HAPPENED, AND NOW I'M AT MY GRANDPA'S...
GRIP
I'M SORRY...
I WISH I HAD BEEN THERE FOR YOU WHEN YOU WERE GOING THROUGH ALL OF THIS...
HMPH
WHAT CLASS ARE YOU IN, CHIGUSA-SAN?
WEDGE
I'D BE MORE THAN HAPPY TO HELP YOU FIND YOUR CLASS-ROOM.
SHOVE
Oh...
UH... I'M IN CLASS 2-A...
WEDGE
OMG!
THEN, WE'RE IN THE SAME CLASS!!

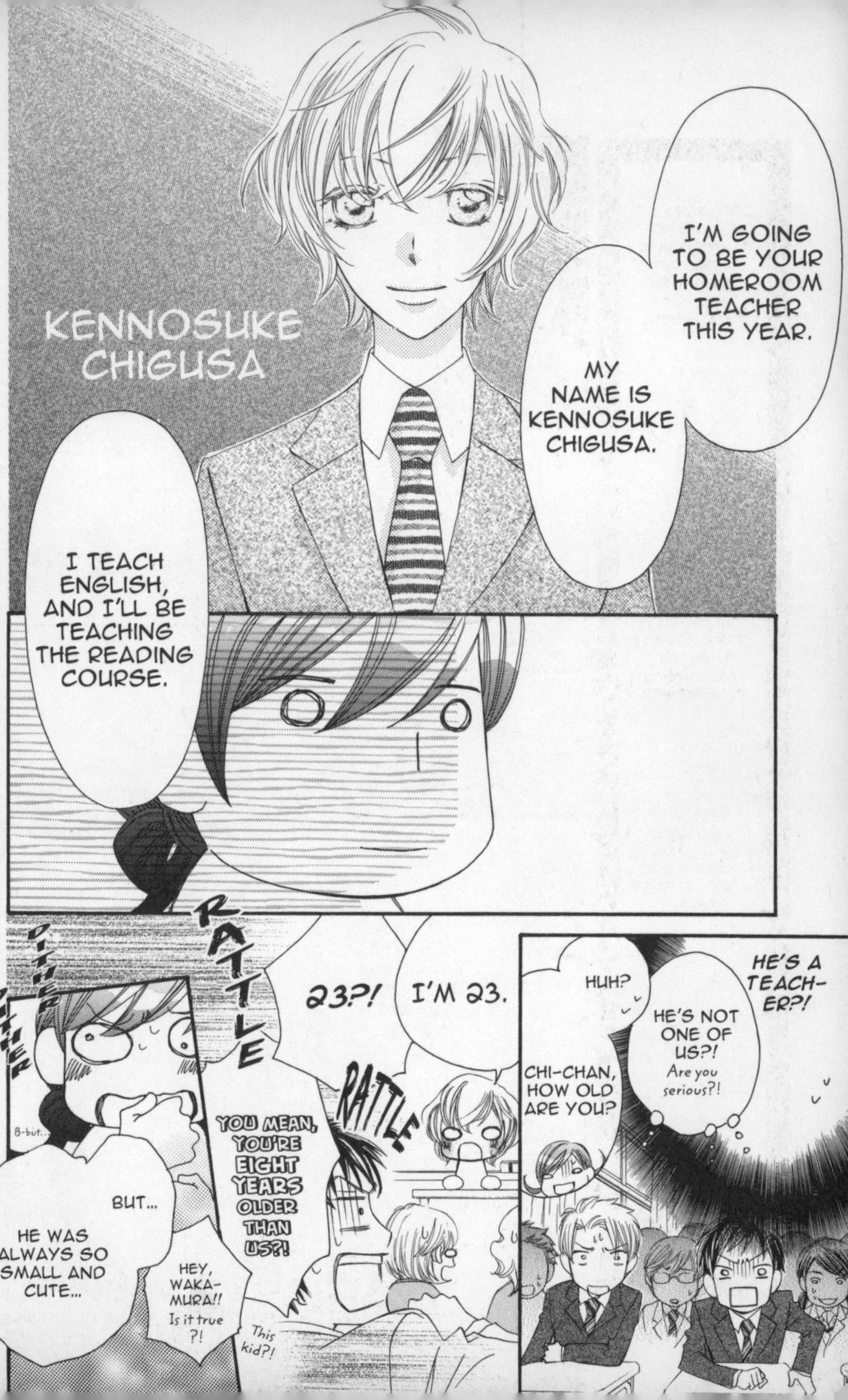
I'M GOING TO BE YOUR HOMEROOM TEACHER THIS YEAR.
MY NAME IS KENNOSUKE CHIGUSA.
KENNOSUKE CHIGUSA
I TEACH ENGLISH, AND I'LL BE TEACHING THE READING COURSE.
HE'S A TEACHER?!
HE'S NOT ONE OF US?! Are you serious?!
HUH?
CHI-CHAN, HOW OLD ARE YOU?
I'M 23.
23?!
RATTLE
RATTLE
YOU MEAN, YOU'RE EIGHT YEARS OLDER THAN US?!
HEY, WAKAMURA!! Is it true?!
This kid?!
DITHER DITHER
B-but...
BUT...
HE WAS ALWAYS SO SMALL AND CUTE...

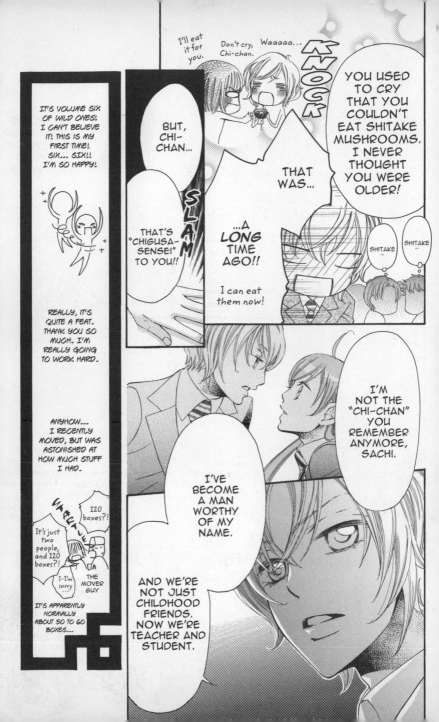

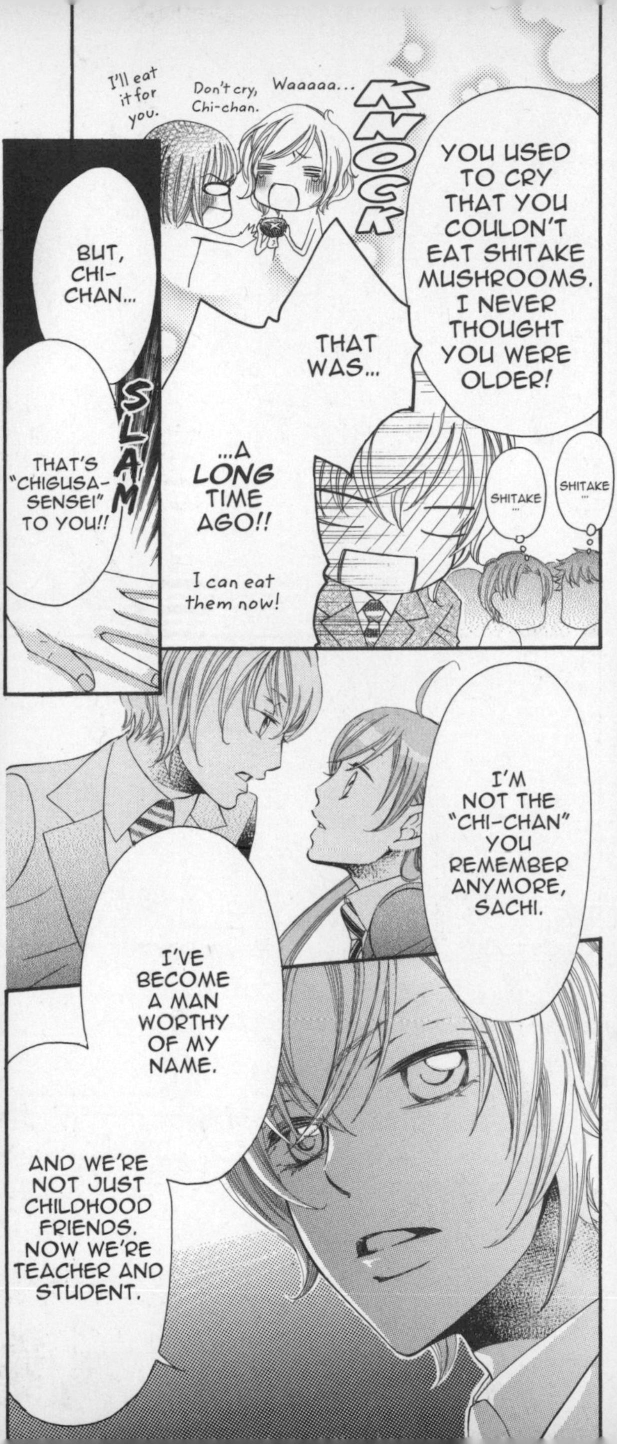
Waaaaa...
Don't cry, Chi-chan.
I'll eat it for you.
KNOCK
YOU USED TO CRY THAT YOU COULDN'T EAT SHITAKE MUSHROOMS. I NEVER THOUGHT YOU WERE OLDER!
THAT WAS...
...A LONG TIME AGO!!
I can eat them now!
SHITAKE...
SHITAKE...
BUT, CHI-CHAN...
THAT'S "CHIGUSA-SENSEI" TO YOU!!
SLAM
I'M NOT THE "CHI-CHAN" YOU REMEMBER ANYMORE, SACHI.
I'VE BECOME A MAN WORTHY OF MY NAME.
AND WE'RE NOT JUST CHILDHOOD FRIENDS. NOW WE'RE TEACHER AND STUDENT.

IT'S VOLUME SIX OF WILD ONES! I CAN'T BELIEVE IT! THIS IS MY FIRST TIME! SIX... SIX!! I'M SO HAPPY!

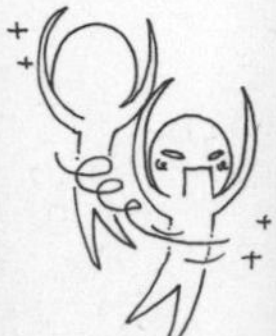

REALLY, IT'S QUITE A FEAT. THANK YOU SO MUCH. I'M REALLY GOING TO WORK HARD.

ANYHOW... I RECENTLY MOVED, BUT WAS ASTONISHED AT HOW MUCH STUFF I HAD.

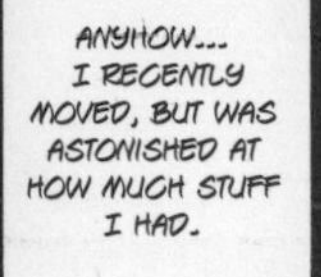
120 boxes?!
It's just two people, and 120 boxes?!
I-I'm sorry...
THE MOVER GUY

IT'S APPARENTLY NORMALLY ABOUT 50 TO 60 BOXES...

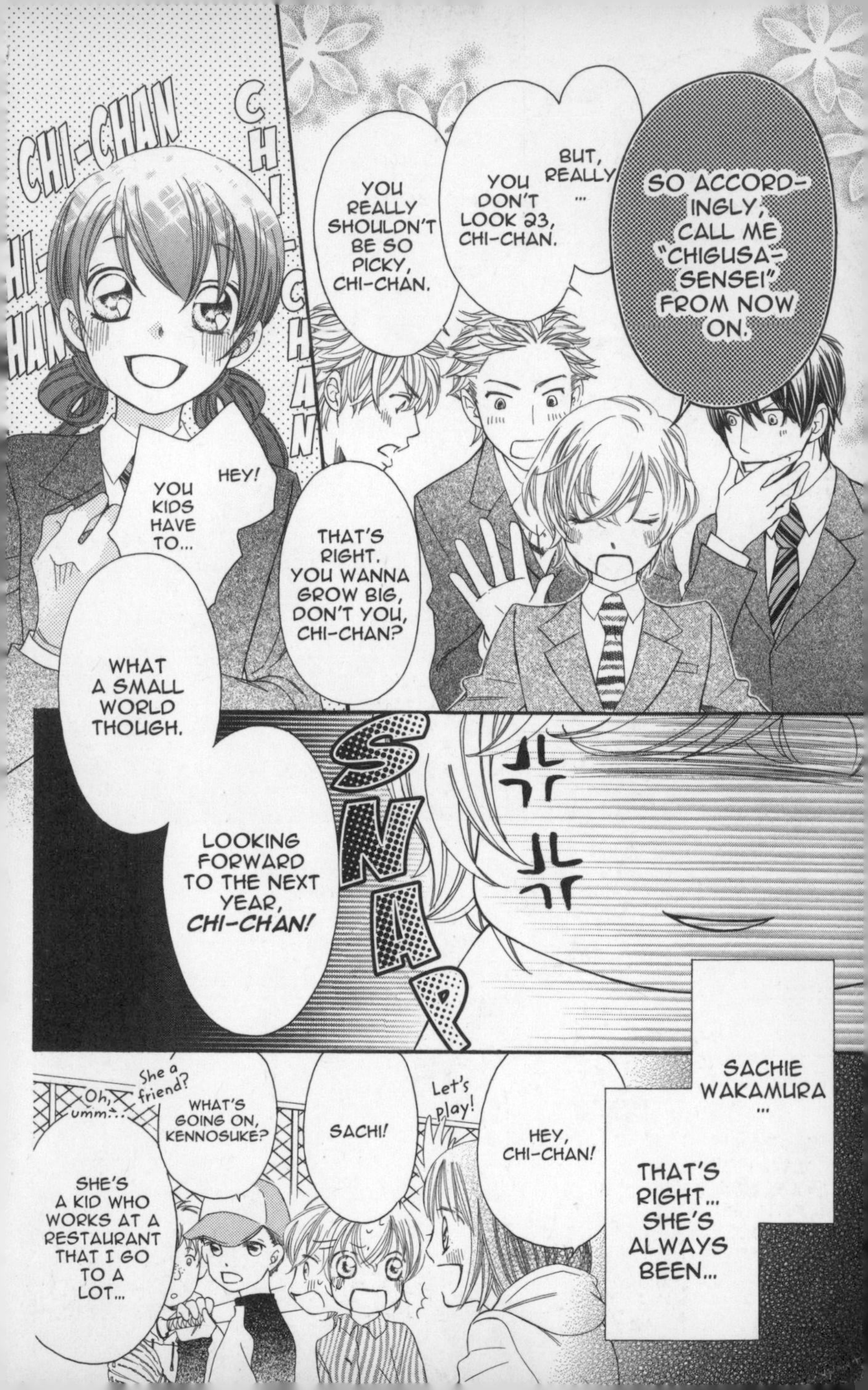
SO ACCORD-INGLY, CALL ME "CHIGUSA-SENSEI" FROM NOW ON.
BUT, REALLY...
YOU DON'T LOOK 23, CHI-CHAN.
YOU REALLY SHOULDN'T BE SO PICKY, CHI-CHAN.
THAT'S RIGHT. YOU WANNA GROW BIG, DON'T YOU, CHI-CHAN?
CHI-CHAN
CHI-CHAN
CHI-CHAN
HEY!
YOU KIDS HAVE TO...
WHAT A SMALL WORLD THOUGH.
SNAP
LOOKING FORWARD TO THE NEXT YEAR, CHI-CHAN!
SACHIE WAKAMURA...
THAT'S RIGHT... SHE'S ALWAYS BEEN...
HEY, CHI-CHAN!
Let's play!
SACHI!
WHAT'S GOING ON, KENNOSUKE?
She a friend?
Oh, umm...
SHE'S A KID WHO WORKS AT A RESTAURANT THAT I GO TO A LOT...

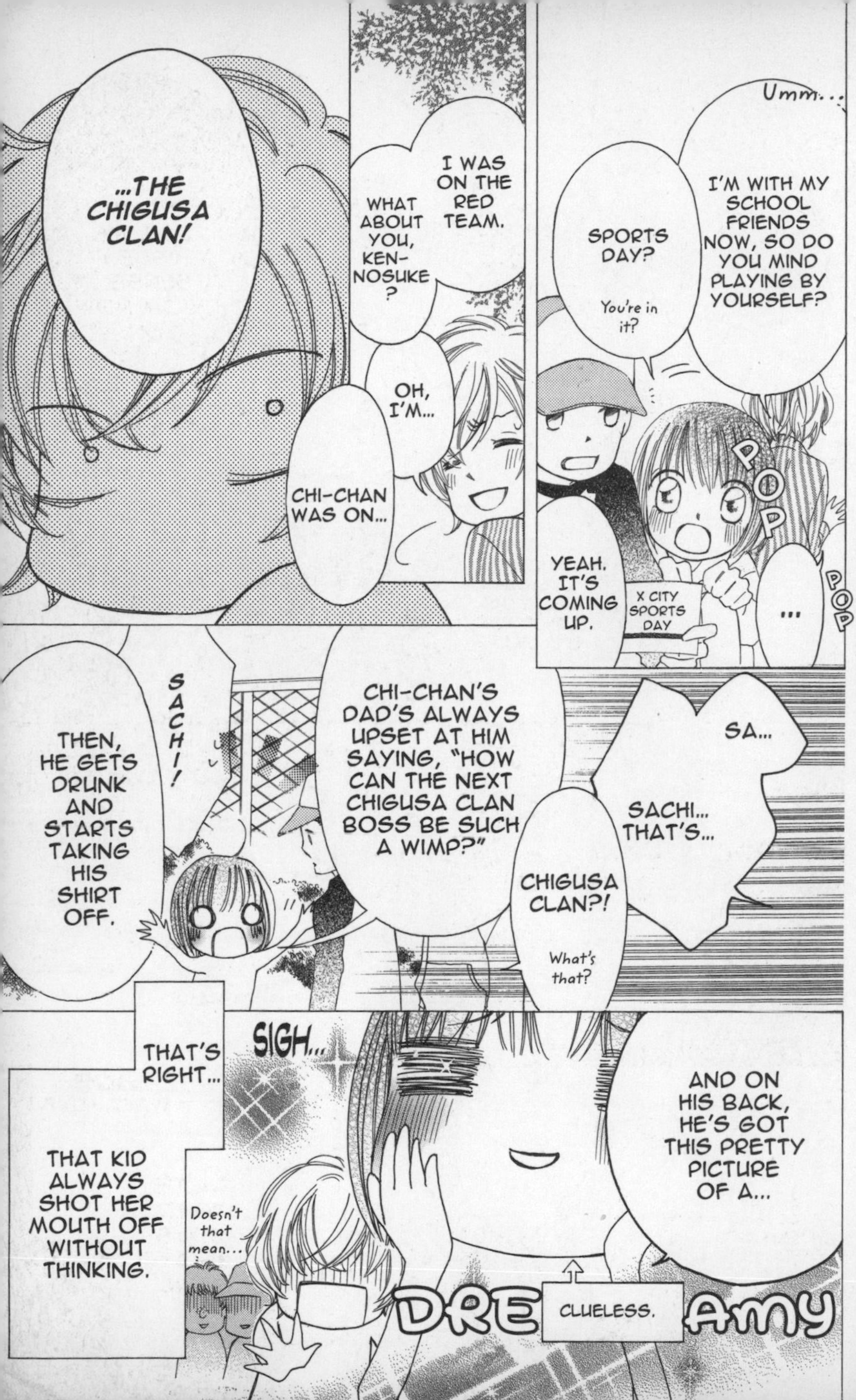
Umm...
I'M WITH MY SCHOOL FRIENDS NOW, SO DO YOU MIND PLAYING BY YOURSELF?
SPORTS DAY?
You're in it?
YEAH. IT'S COMING UP.
X CITY SPORTS DAY
POP POP
...
POP
I WAS ON THE RED TEAM.
WHAT ABOUT YOU, KEN-NOSUKE?
OH, I'M...
CHI-CHAN WAS ON...
...THE CHIGUSA CLAN!
SA...
SACHI... THAT'S...
CHIGUSA CLAN?!
What's that?
CHI-CHAN'S DAD'S ALWAYS UPSET AT HIM SAYING, "HOW CAN THE NEXT CHIGUSA CLAN BOSS BE SUCH A WIMP?"
SACHI!
THEN, HE GETS DRUNK AND STARTS TAKING HIS SHIRT OFF.
AND ON HIS BACK, HE'S GOT THIS PRETTY PICTURE OF A...
DREAMY
CLUELESS.
THAT'S RIGHT...
SIGH...
THAT KID ALWAYS SHOT HER MOUTH OFF WITHOUT THINKING.
Doesn't that mean...

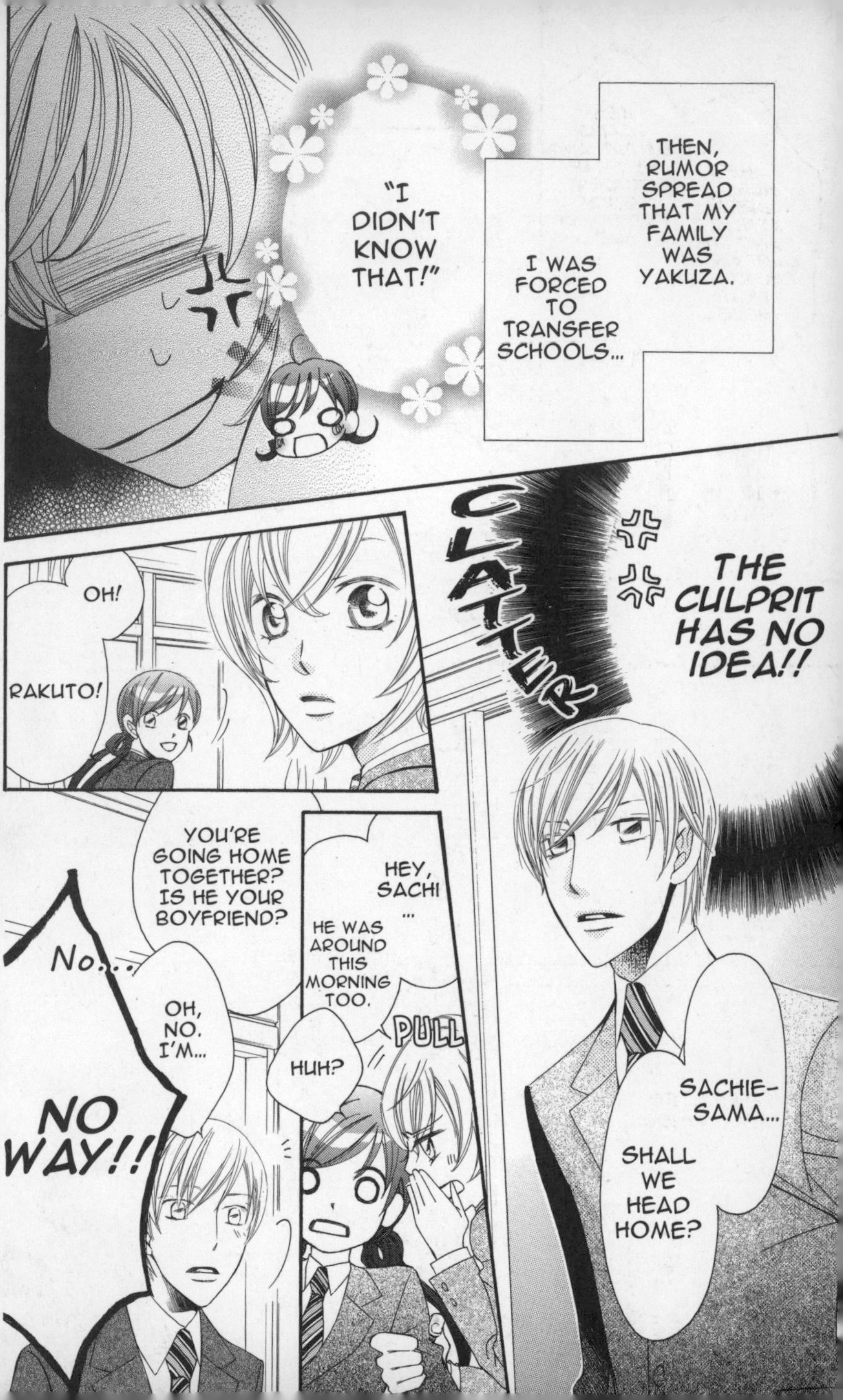
THEN, RUMOR SPREAD THAT MY FAMILY WAS YAKUZA.
I WAS FORCED TO TRANSFER SCHOOLS...
"I DIDN'T KNOW THAT!"
CLATTER
THE CULPRIT HAS NO IDEA!!
SACHIE-SAMA...
SHALL WE HEAD HOME?
OH!
RAKUTO!
HEY, SACHI...
HE WAS AROUND THIS MORNING TOO.
PULL
HUH?
YOU'RE GOING HOME TOGETHER? IS HE YOUR BOYFRIEND?
No...
OH, NO. I'M...
NO WAY!!

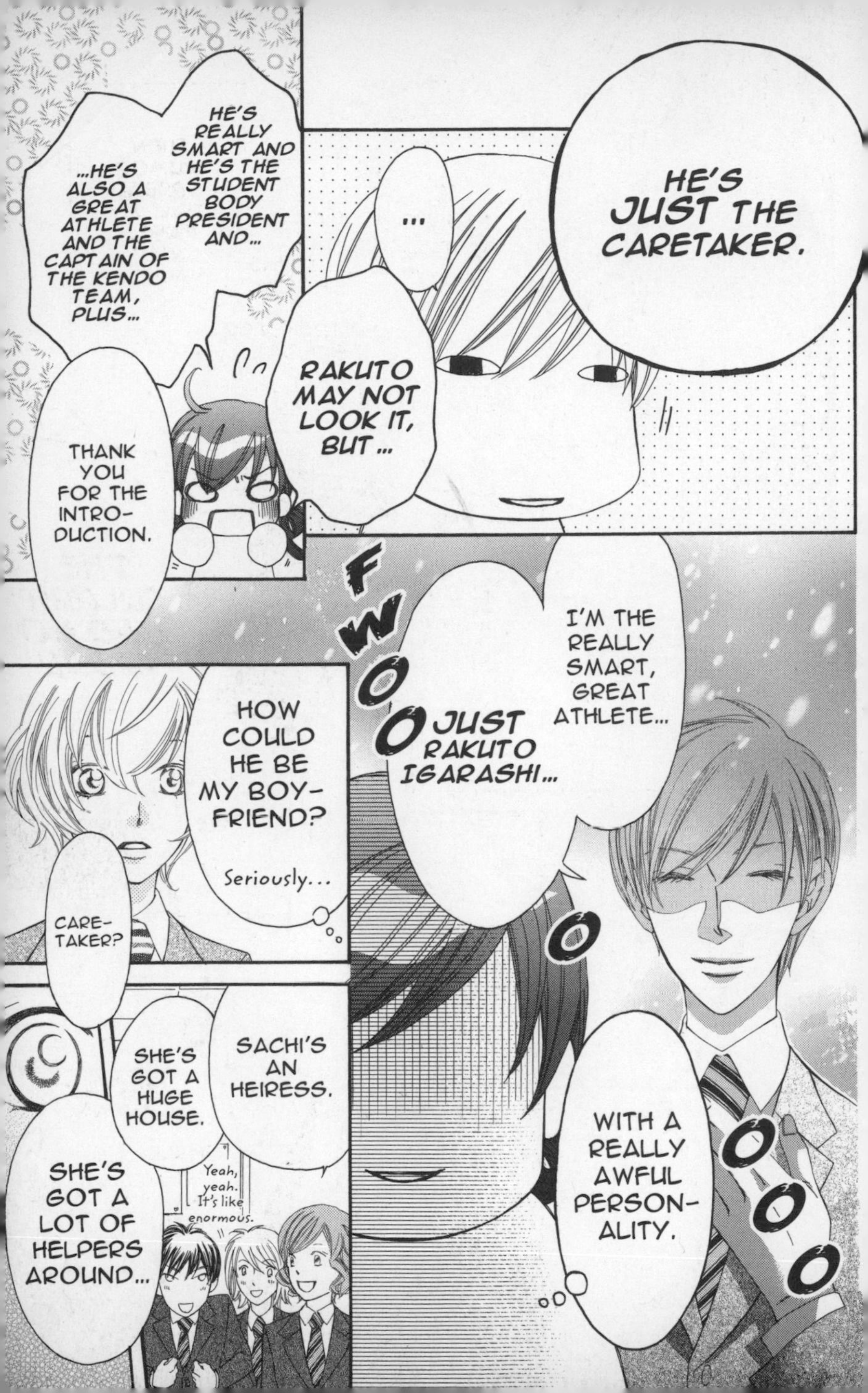
HE'S JUST THE CARETAKER.
...
RAKUTO MAY NOT LOOK IT, BUT ...
HE'S REALLY SMART AND HE'S THE STUDENT BODY PRESIDENT AND...
...HE'S ALSO A GREAT ATHLETE AND THE CAPTAIN OF THE KENDO TEAM, PLUS...
THANK YOU FOR THE INTRO-DUCTION.
FWOOOOOOOOO
I'M THE REALLY SMART, GREAT ATHLETE...
JUST RAKUTO IGARASHI...
WITH A REALLY AWFUL PERSONALITY.
HOW COULD HE BE MY BOY-FRIEND?
Seriously...
CARE-TAKER?
SACHI'S AN HEIRESS.
SHE'S GOT A HUGE HOUSE.
SHE'S GOT A LOT OF HELPERS AROUND...
Yeah, yeah. It's like enormous.

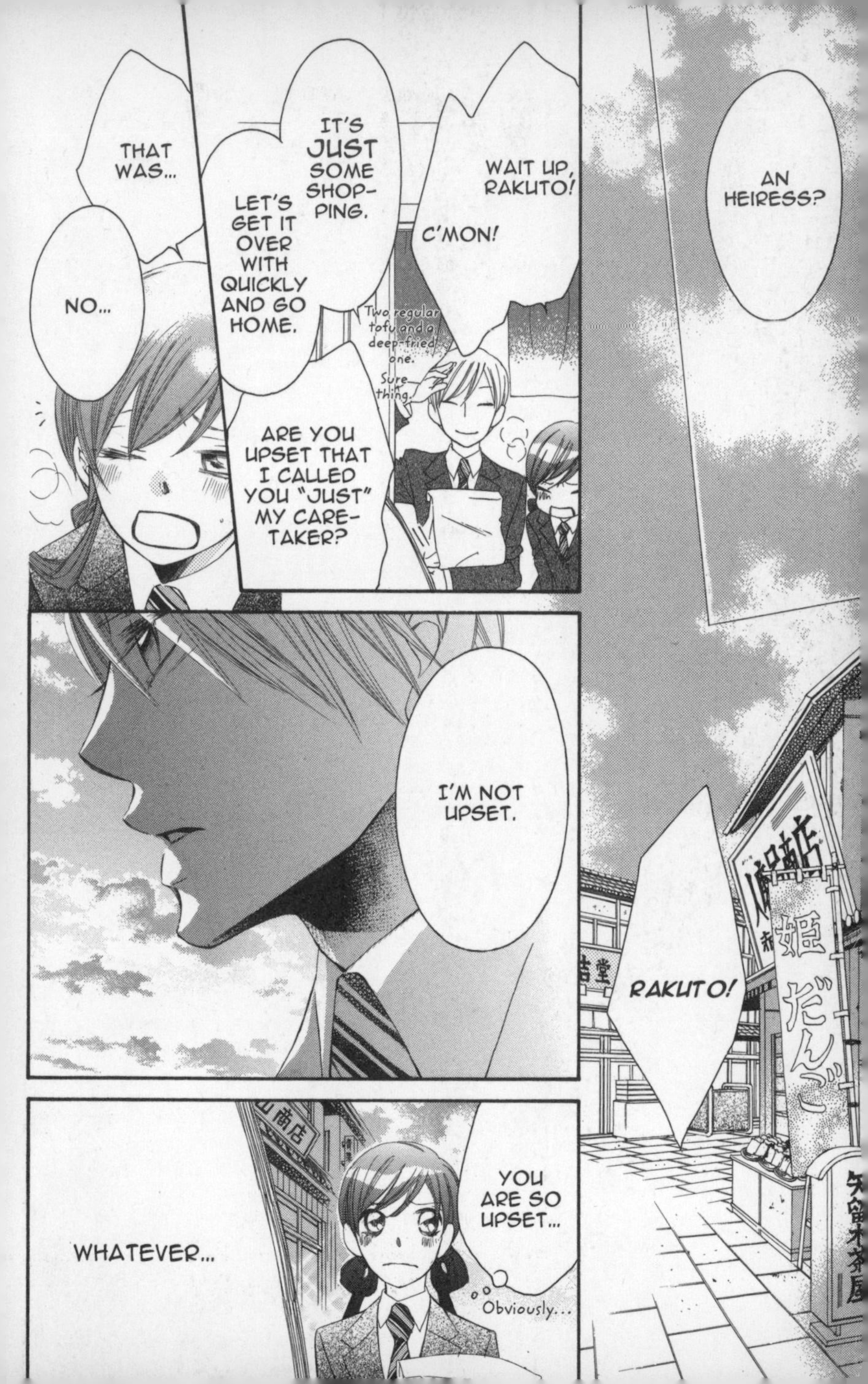
AN HEIRESS?
RAKUTO!
WAIT UP, RAKUTO!
C'MON!
IT'S JUST SOME SHOP-PING.
LET'S GET IT OVER WITH QUICKLY AND GO HOME.
Two regular tofu and a deep-fried one.
Sure thing.
ARE YOU UPSET THAT I CALLED YOU "JUST" MY CARE-TAKER?
THAT WAS...
NO...
I'M NOT UPSET.
YOU ARE SO UPSET...
Obviously...
WHATEVER...

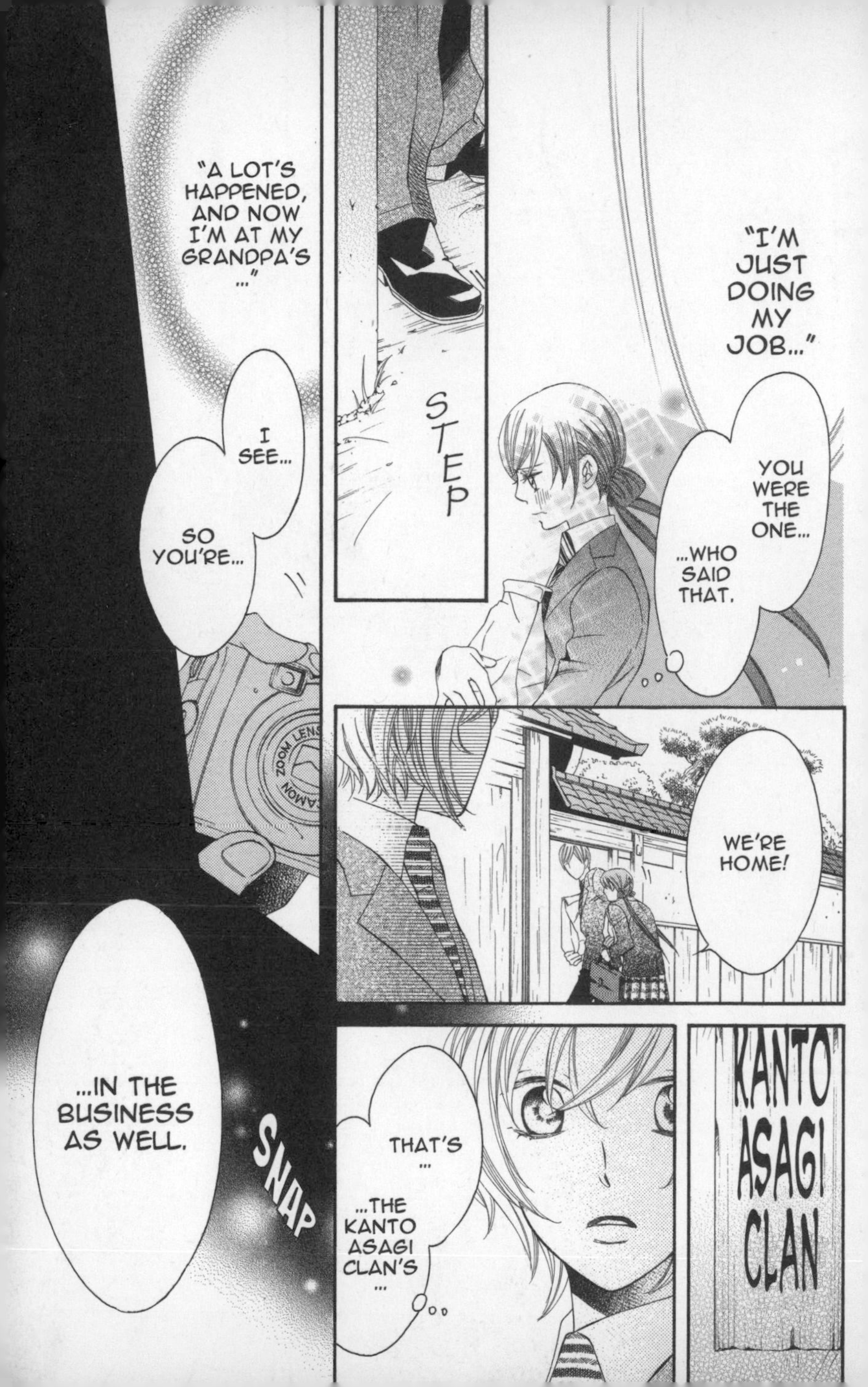

"I'M JUST DOING MY JOB..."
YOU WERE THE ONE...
...WHO SAID THAT.
STEP
WE'RE HOME!
KANTO ASAGI CLAN
THAT'S ...
...THE KANTO ASAGI CLAN'S ...
"A LOT'S HAPPENED, AND NOW I'M AT MY GRANDPA'S ..."
I SEE...
SO YOU'RE...
...IN THE BUSINESS AS WELL.
SNAP

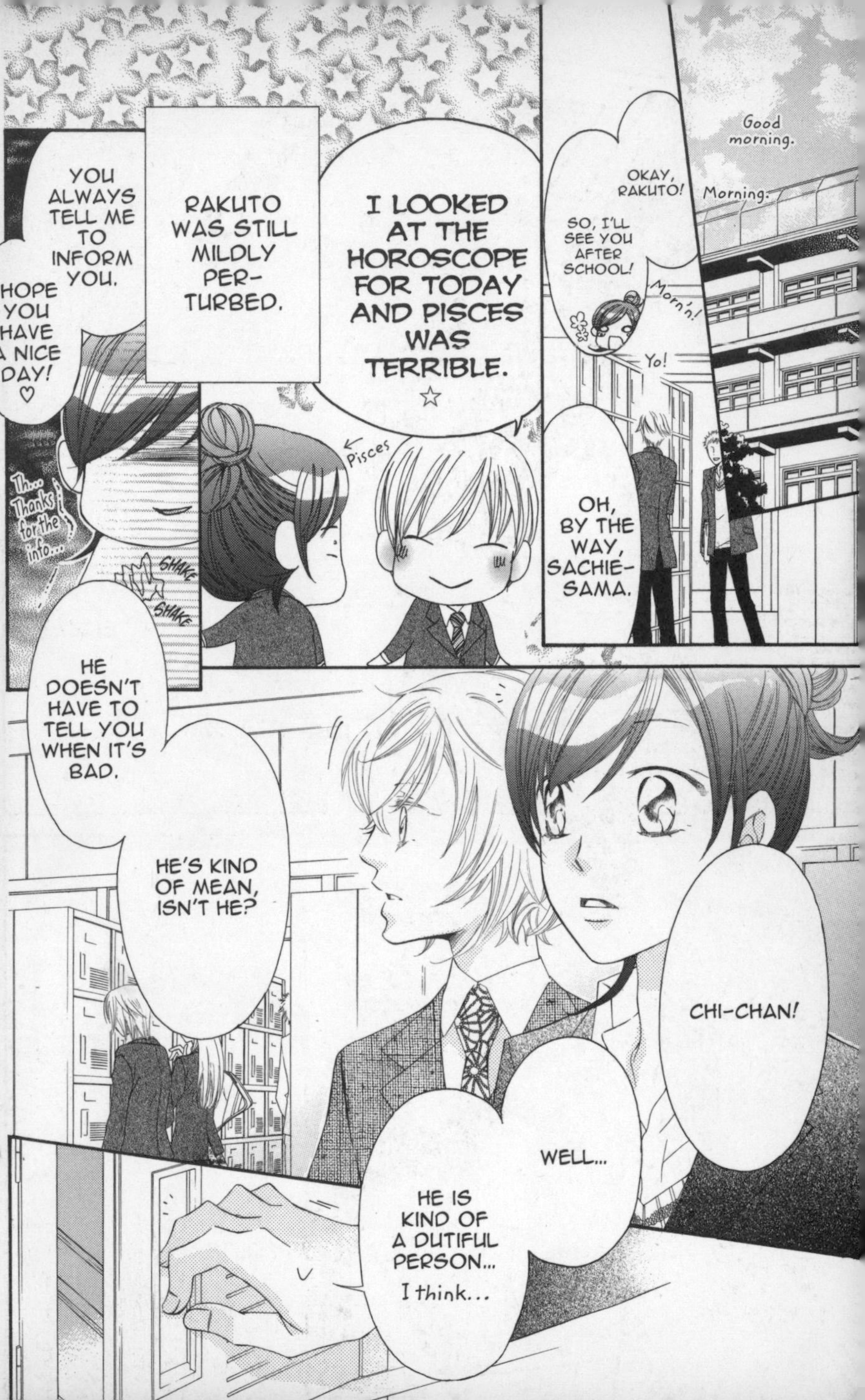

Good morning.
Morning.
OKAY, RAKUTO!
SO, I'LL SEE YOU AFTER SCHOOL!
Morn'n!
Yo!
OH, BY THE WAY, SACHIE-SAMA.
I LOOKED AT THE HOROSCOPE FOR TODAY AND PISCES WAS TERRIBLE. ☆
Pisces
RAKUTO WAS STILL MILDLY PER-TURBED.
YOU ALWAYS TELL ME TO INFORM YOU.
HOPE YOU HAVE A NICE DAY! ♡
Th... Thanks for the info...
SHAKE
SHAKE
CHI-CHAN!
HE DOESN'T HAVE TO TELL YOU WHEN IT'S BAD.
HE'S KIND OF MEAN, ISN'T HE?
WELL...
HE IS KIND OF A DUTIFUL PERSON...
I think...

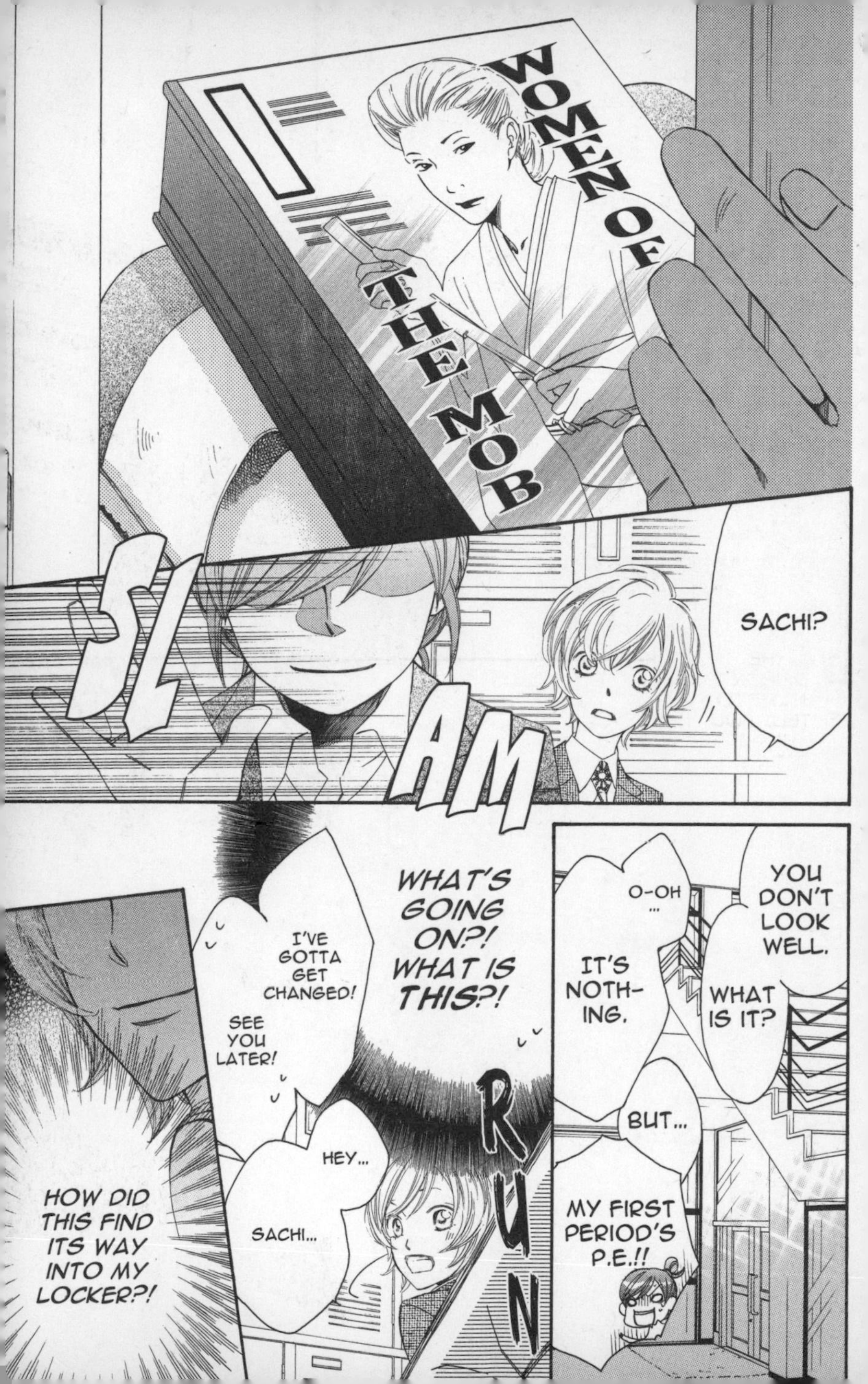
WOMEN OF THE MOB
SACHI?
SLAM
YOU DON'T LOOK WELL.
O-OH ...
WHAT IS IT?
IT'S NOTH-ING.
BUT...
MY FIRST PERIOD'S P.E.!!
WHAT'S GOING ON?! WHAT IS THIS?!
I'VE GOTTA GET CHANGED!
SEE YOU LATER!
RUN
HEY...
SACHI...
HOW DID THIS FIND ITS WAY INTO MY LOCKER?!

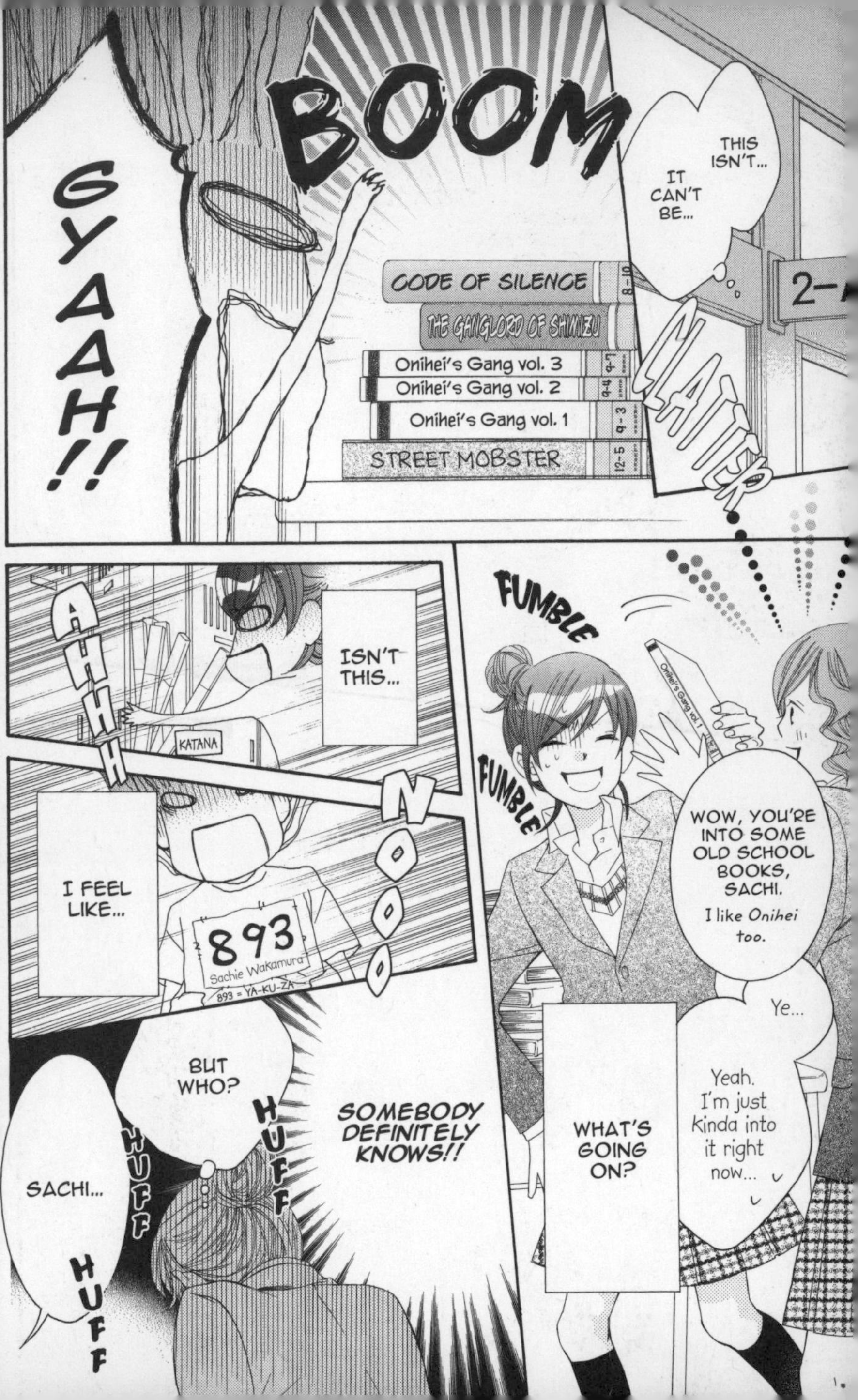
THIS ISN'T...
IT CAN'T BE...
2-
BOOM
GYAAH!!
CODE OF SILENCE
THE GANGLORD OF SHIMIZU
Onihei's Gang vol. 3
Onihei's Gang vol. 2
Onihei's Gang vol. 1
STREET MOBSTER
CLATTER
FUMBLE
FUMBLE
Onihei's Gang vol. 1
WOW, YOU'RE INTO SOME OLD SCHOOL BOOKS, SACHI.
I like Onihei too.
Ye...
Yeah. I'm just kinda into it right now...
WHAT'S GOING ON?
ISN'T THIS...
AHHHH
KATANA
I FEEL LIKE...
NOOOO
893
Sachie Wakamura
893 = YA-KU-ZA
BUT WHO?
SACHI...
SOMEBODY DEFINITELY KNOWS!!
HUFF
HUFF
HUFF

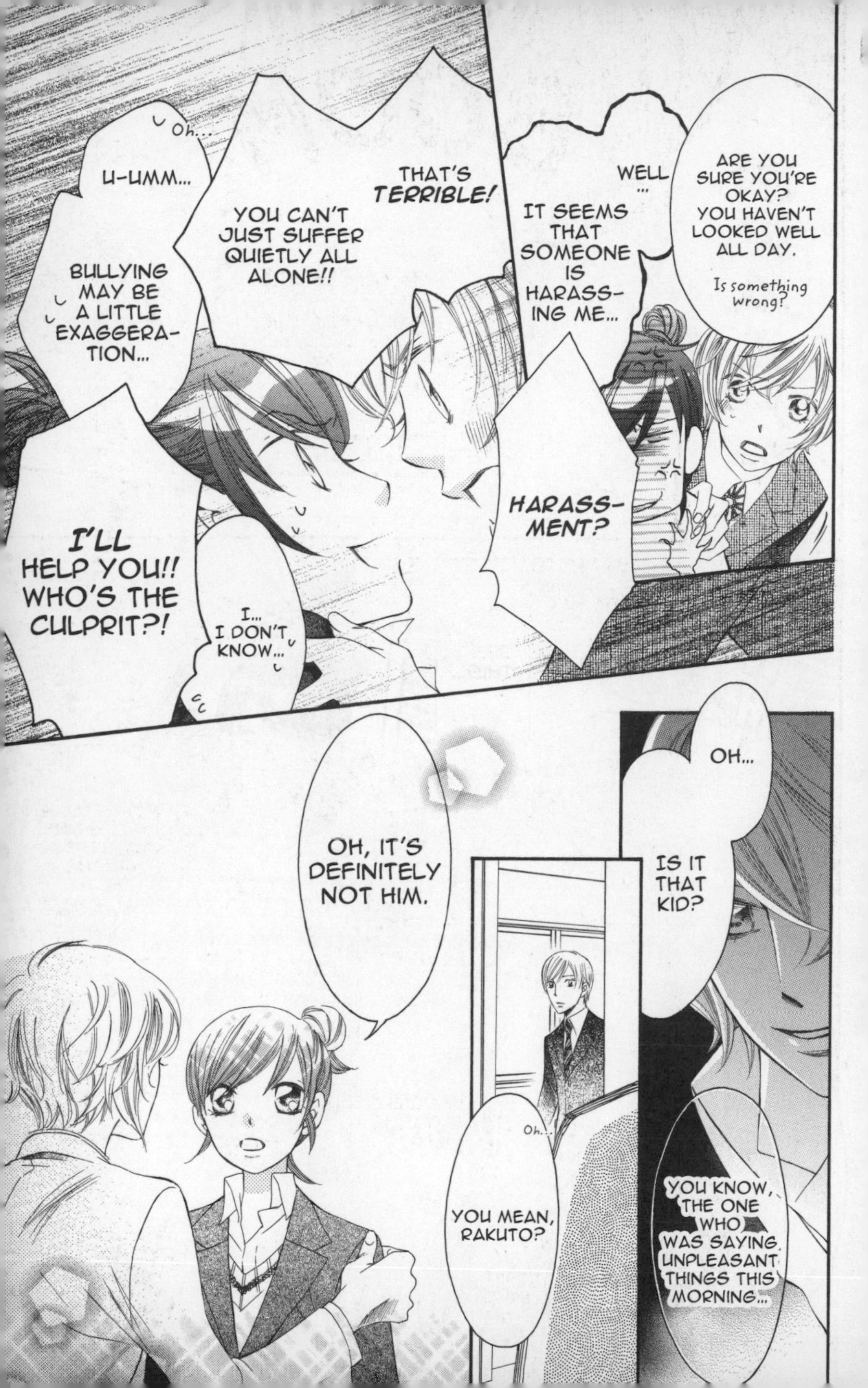
ARE YOU SURE YOU'RE OKAY? YOU HAVEN'T LOOKED WELL ALL DAY.
Is something wrong?
WELL...
IT SEEMS THAT SOMEONE IS HARASSING ME...
HARASSMENT?
THAT'S TERRIBLE!
YOU CAN'T JUST SUFFER QUIETLY ALL ALONE!!
Oh...
U-UMM...
BULLYING MAY BE A LITTLE EXAGGERATION...
I'LL HELP YOU!! WHO'S THE CULPRIT?!
I... I DON'T KNOW...
OH...
IS IT THAT KID?
YOU KNOW, THE ONE WHO WAS SAYING UNPLEASANT THINGS THIS MORNING...
Oh...
YOU MEAN, RAKUTO?
OH, IT'S DEFINITELY NOT HIM.

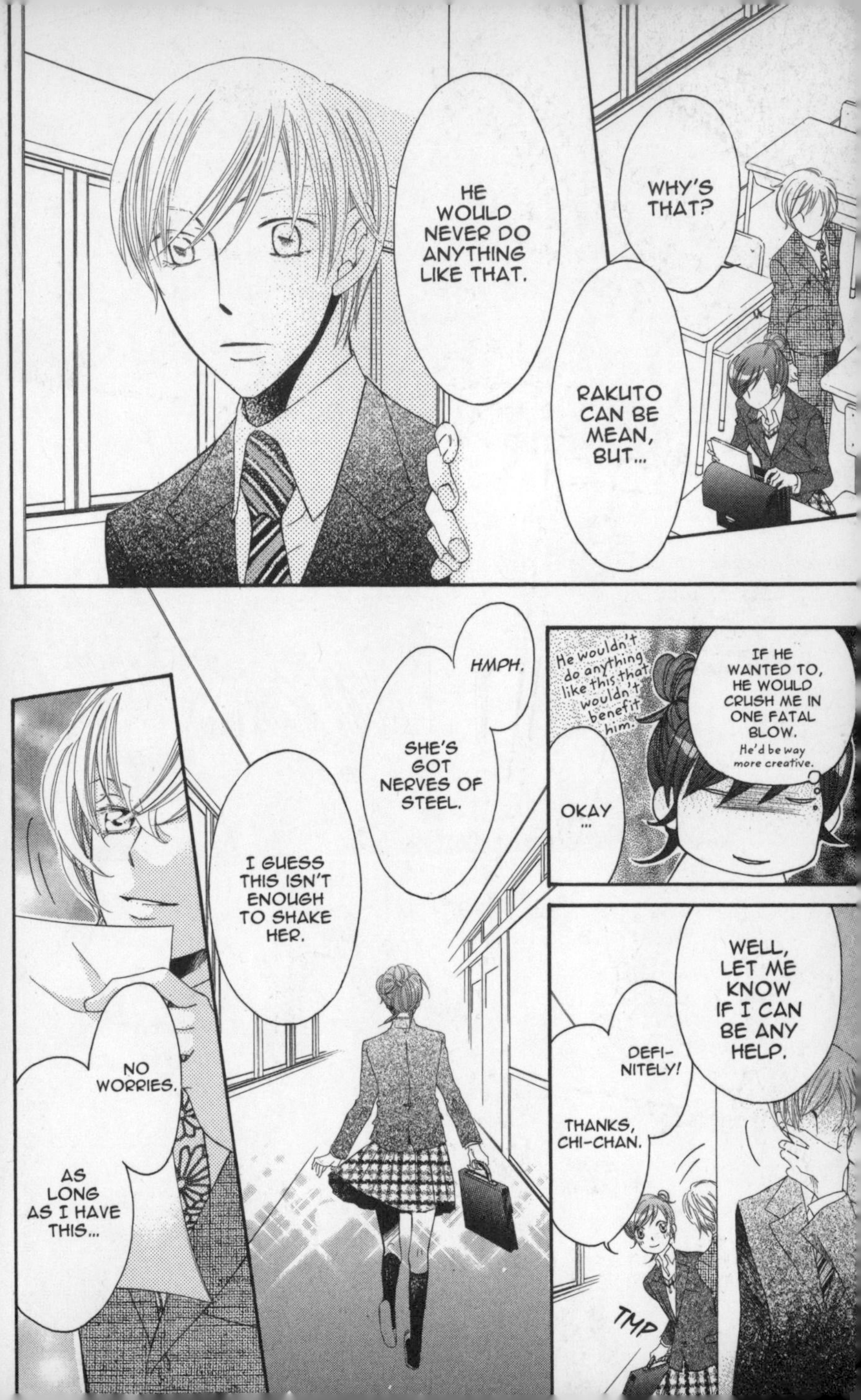
WHY'S THAT?
RAKUTO CAN BE MEAN, BUT...
HE WOULD NEVER DO ANYTHING LIKE THAT.
IF HE WANTED TO, HE WOULD CRUSH ME IN ONE FATAL BLOW.
He'd be way more creative.
He wouldn't do anything like this that wouldn't benefit him.
OKAY...
WELL, LET ME KNOW IF I CAN BE ANY HELP.
DEFI-NITELY!
THANKS, CHI-CHAN.
TMP
HMPH.
SHE'S GOT NERVES OF STEEL.
I GUESS THIS ISN'T ENOUGH TO SHAKE HER.
NO WORRIES.
AS LONG AS I HAVE THIS...

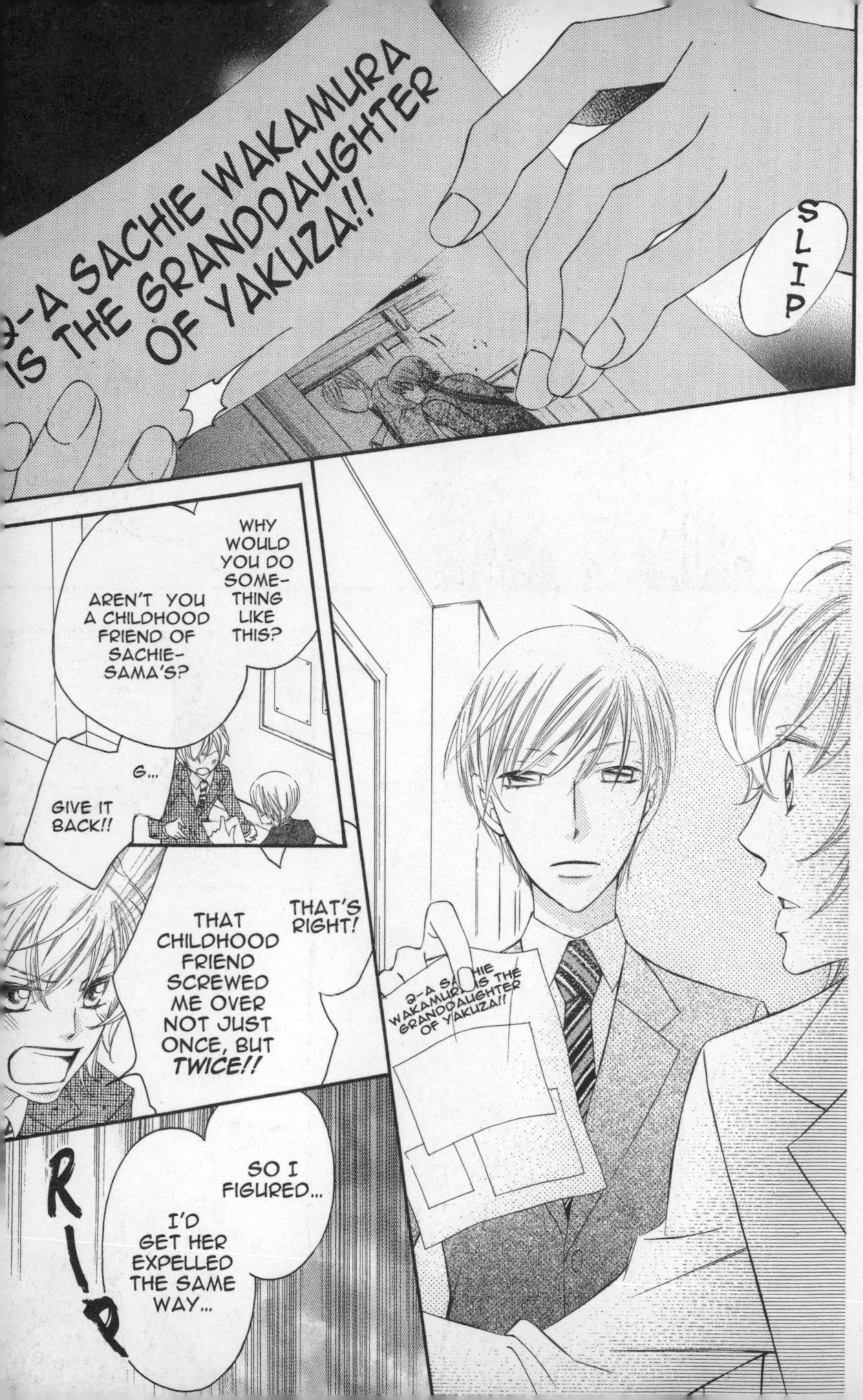

SLIP
Q-A SACHIE WAKAMURA IS THE GRANDDAUGHTER OF YAKUZA!!
Q-A SA HIE WAKAMUR S THE GRANDDAUGHTER OF YAKUZA!!
WHY WOULD YOU DO SOMETHING LIKE THIS?
AREN'T YOU A CHILDHOOD FRIEND OF SACHIE-SAMA'S?
G...
GIVE IT BACK!!
THAT'S RIGHT!
THAT CHILDHOOD FRIEND SCREWED ME OVER NOT JUST ONCE, BUT *TWICE!!*
SO I FIGURED...
I'D GET HER EXPELLED THE SAME WAY...
RIP

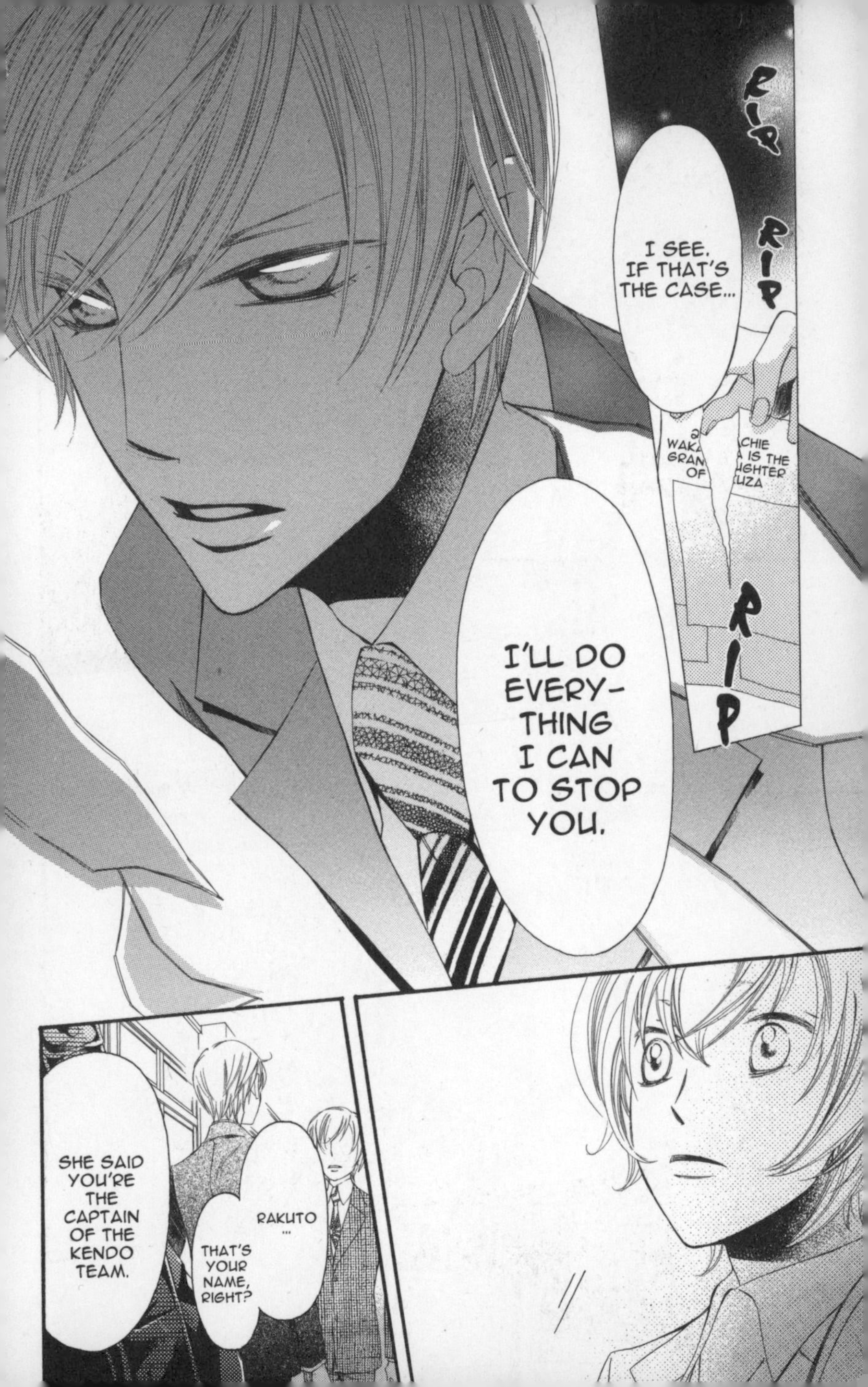
RIP
RIP
I SEE. IF THAT'S THE CASE...
RIP
I'LL DO EVERY-THING I CAN TO STOP YOU.
RAKUTO ...
THAT'S YOUR NAME, RIGHT?
SHE SAID YOU'RE THE CAPTAIN OF THE KENDO TEAM.

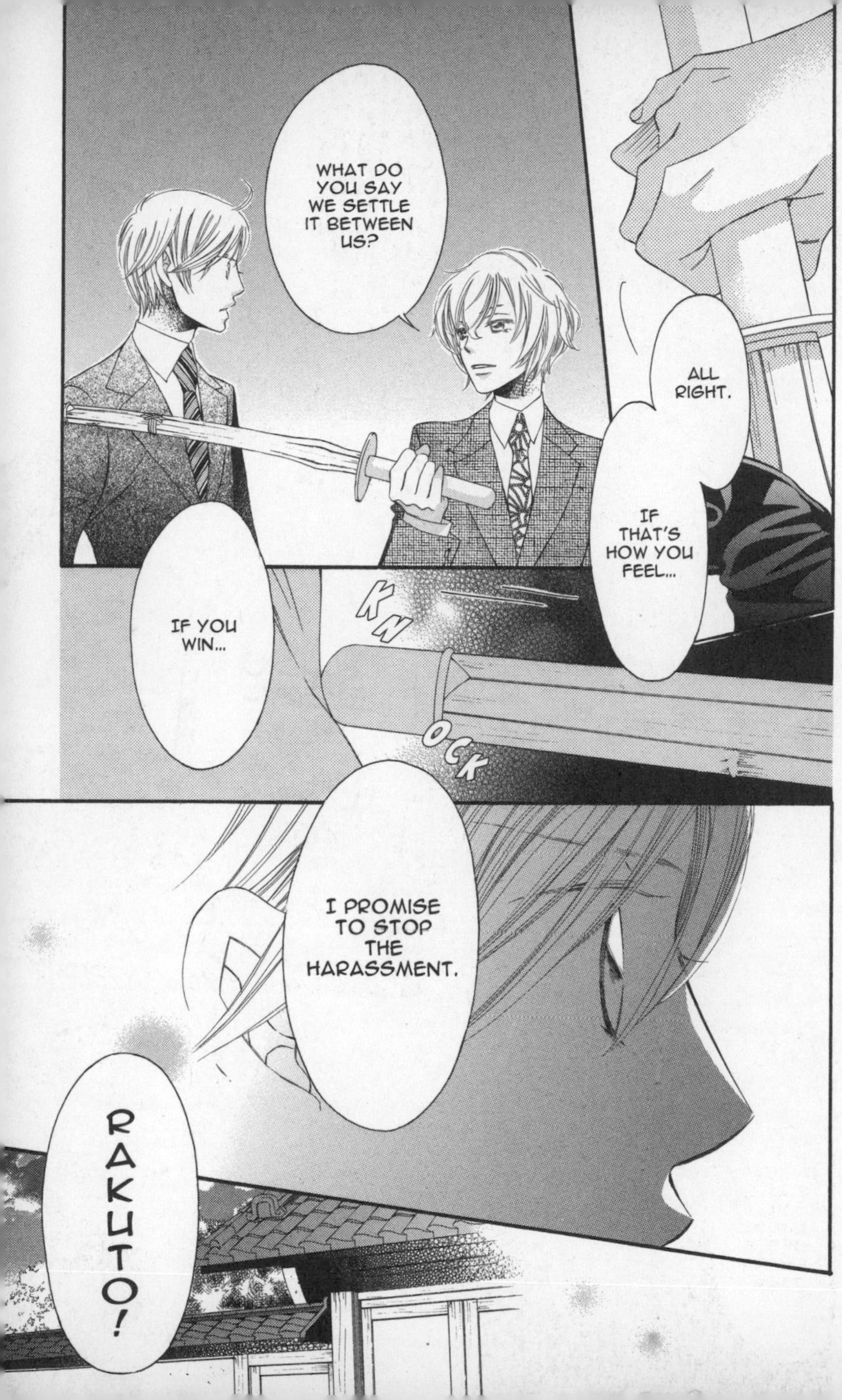
WHAT DO YOU SAY WE SETTLE IT BETWEEN US?
ALL RIGHT.
IF THAT'S HOW YOU FEEL...
KNOCK
IF YOU WIN...
I PROMISE TO STOP THE HARASSMENT.
RAKUTO!

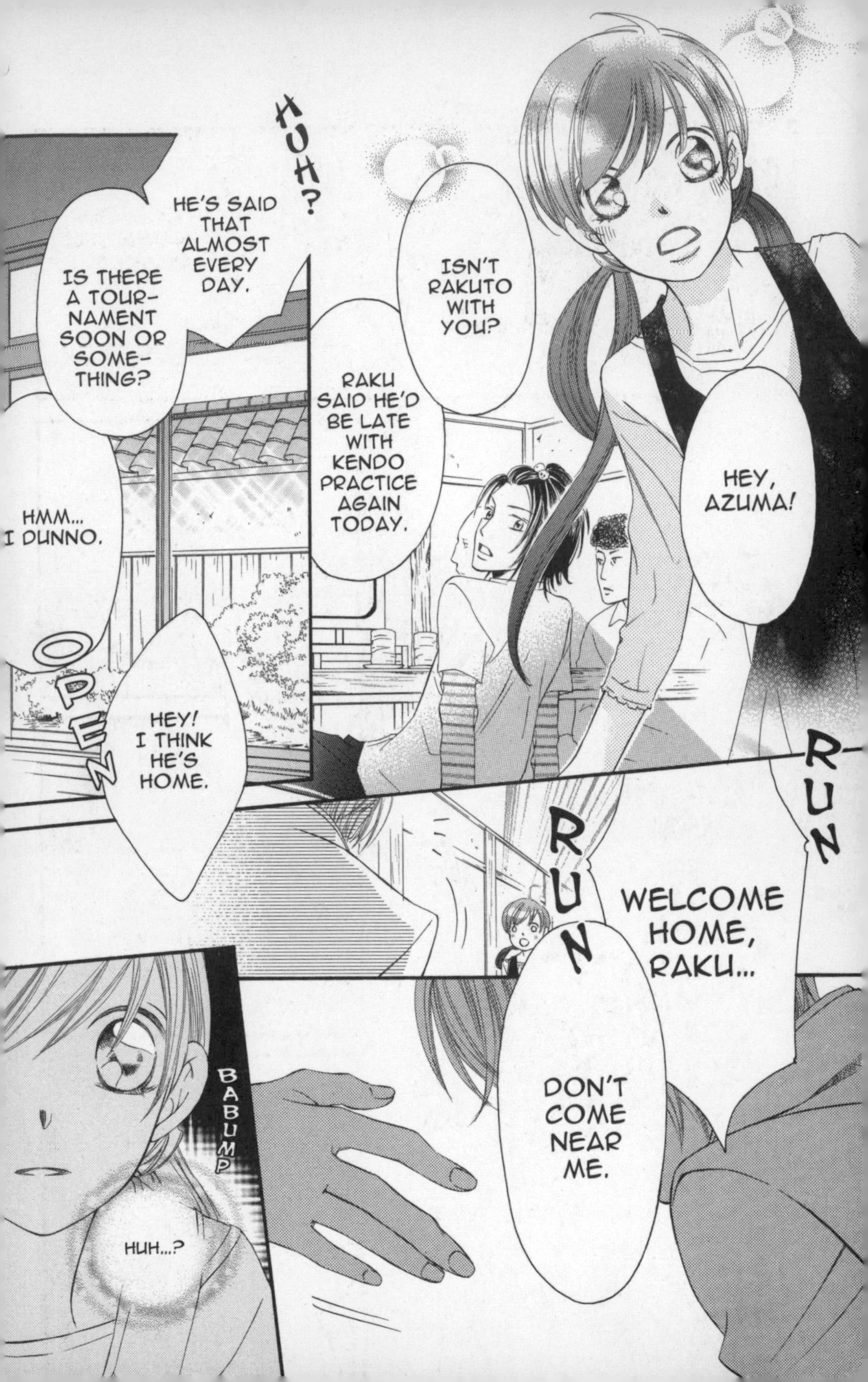
HEY, AZUMA!
ISN'T RAKUTO WITH YOU?
HUH?
RAKU SAID HE'D BE LATE WITH KENDO PRACTICE AGAIN TODAY.
HE'S SAID THAT ALMOST EVERY DAY.
IS THERE A TOURNAMENT SOON OR SOMETHING?
HMM... I DUNNO.
OPEN
HEY! I THINK HE'S HOME.
RUN
RUN
WELCOME HOME, RAKU...
DON'T COME NEAR ME.
BABUMP
HUH...?

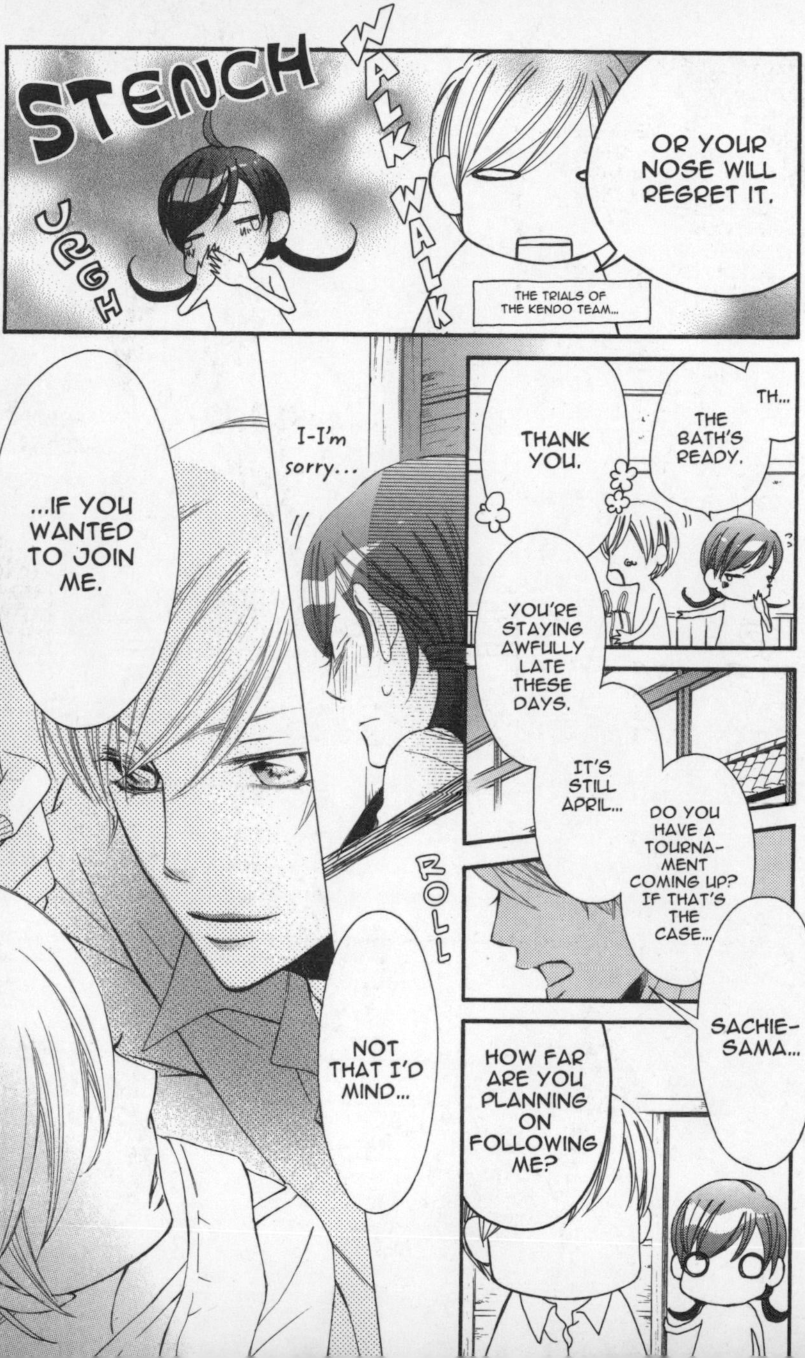
OR YOUR NOSE WILL REGRET IT.
WALK WALK
THE TRIALS OF THE KENDO TEAM...
STENCH
URGH
TH... THE BATH'S READY.
THANK YOU.
YOU'RE STAYING AWFULLY LATE THESE DAYS.
IT'S STILL APRIL...
DO YOU HAVE A TOURNAMENT COMING UP? IF THAT'S THE CASE...
SACHIE-SAMA...
HOW FAR ARE YOU PLANNING ON FOLLOWING ME?
I-I'm sorry...
ROLL
NOT THAT I'D MIND...
...IF YOU WANTED TO JOIN ME.

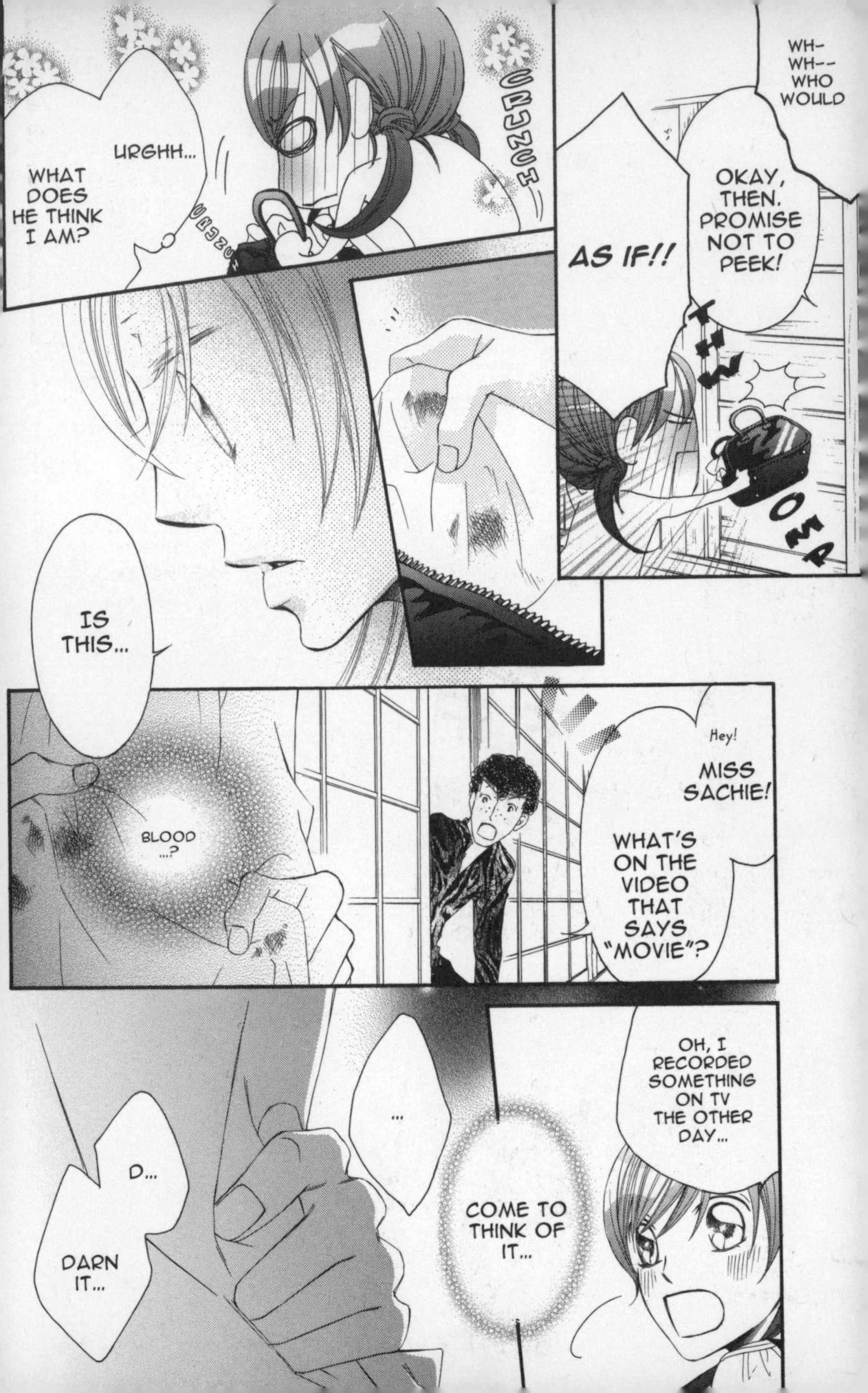
WH- WH-- WHO WOULD
OKAY, THEN. PROMISE NOT TO PEEK!
AS IF!!
URGHH...
WHAT DOES HE THINK I AM?
CRUNCH
IS THIS...
Hey!
MISS SACHIE!
WHAT'S ON THE VIDEO THAT SAYS "MOVIE"?
BLOOD ...?
OH, I RECORDED SOMETHING ON TV THE OTHER DAY...
COME TO THINK OF IT...
...
D...
DARN IT...

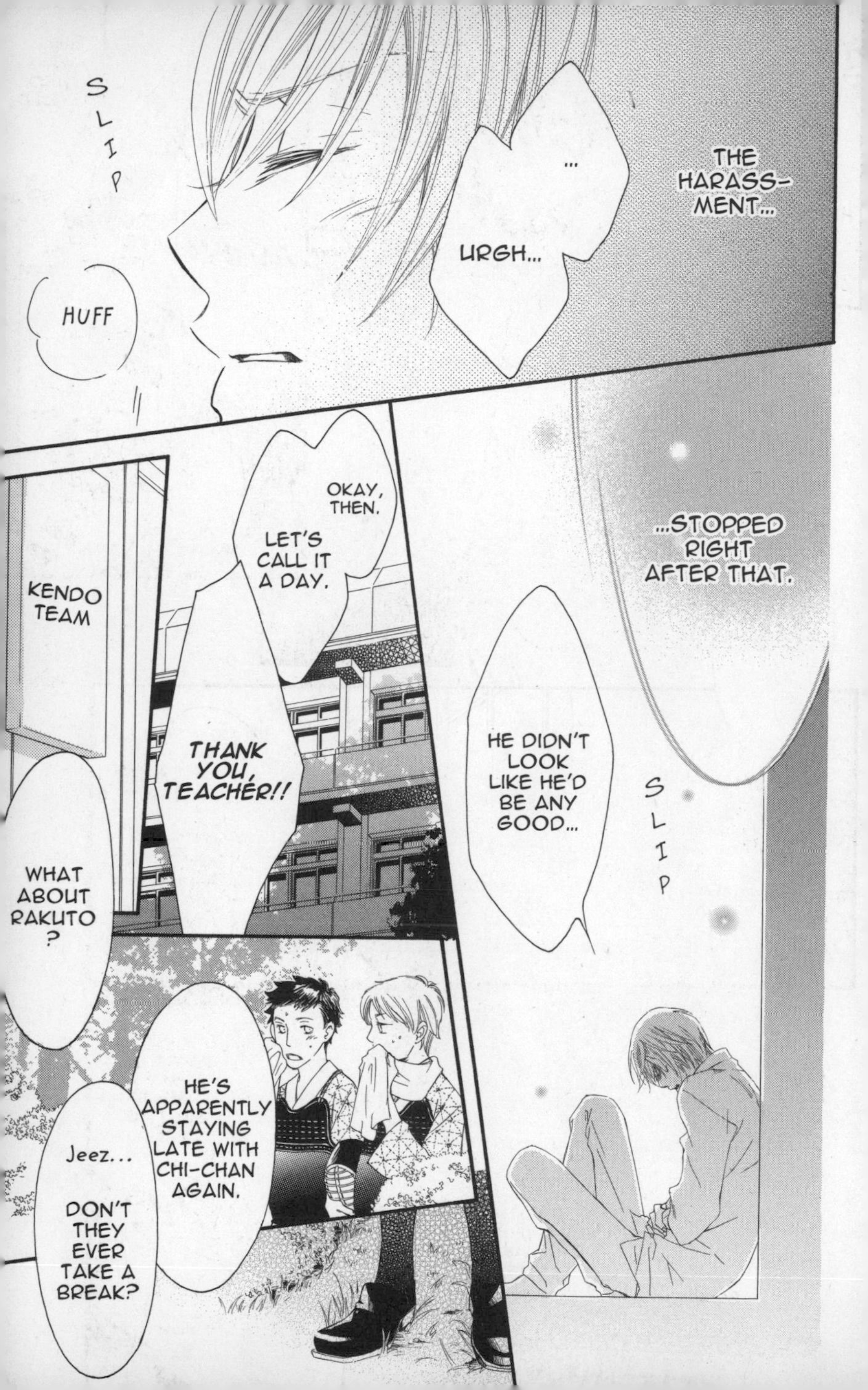
THE HARASSMENT...
...
URGH...
SLIP
HUFF
...STOPPED RIGHT AFTER THAT.
HE DIDN'T LOOK LIKE HE'D BE ANY GOOD...
SLIP
OKAY, THEN.
LET'S CALL IT A DAY.
THANK YOU, TEACHER!!
KENDO TEAM
WHAT ABOUT RAKUTO?
HE'S APPARENTLY STAYING LATE WITH CHI-CHAN AGAIN.
Jeez...
DON'T THEY EVER TAKE A BREAK?

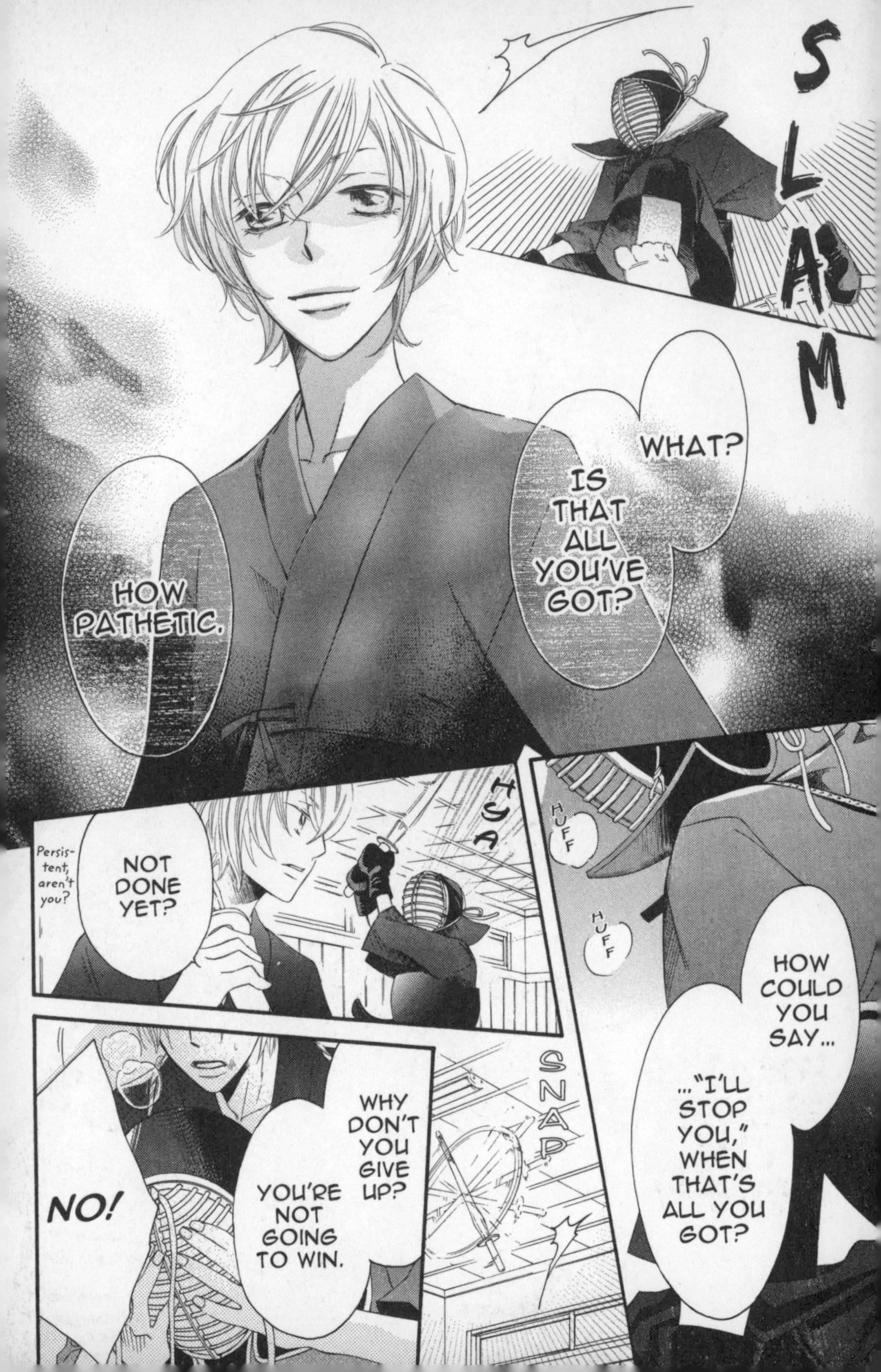
SLAM
WHAT?
IS THAT ALL YOU'VE GOT?
HOW PATHETIC.
HUFF
HUFF
HOW COULD YOU SAY...
..."I'LL STOP YOU," WHEN THAT'S ALL YOU GOT?
HYUA
NOT DONE YET?
Persistent, aren't you?
SNAP
WHY DON'T YOU GIVE UP?
YOU'RE NOT GOING TO WIN.
NO!

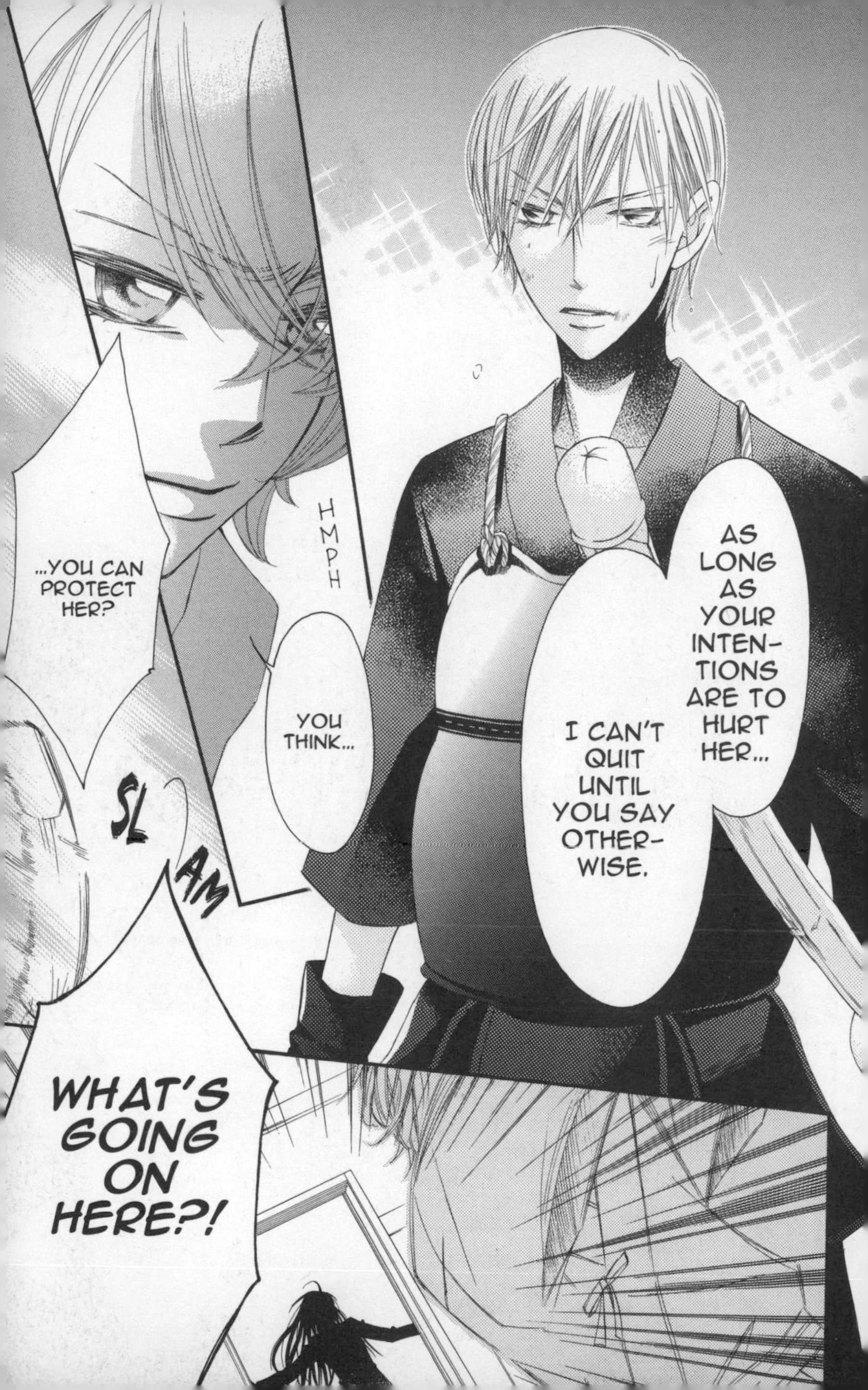
AS LONG AS YOUR INTENTIONS ARE TO HURT HER...
I CAN'T QUIT UNTIL YOU SAY OTHERWISE.
HMPH
YOU THINK...
...YOU CAN PROTECT HER?
SLAM
WHAT'S GOING ON HERE?!

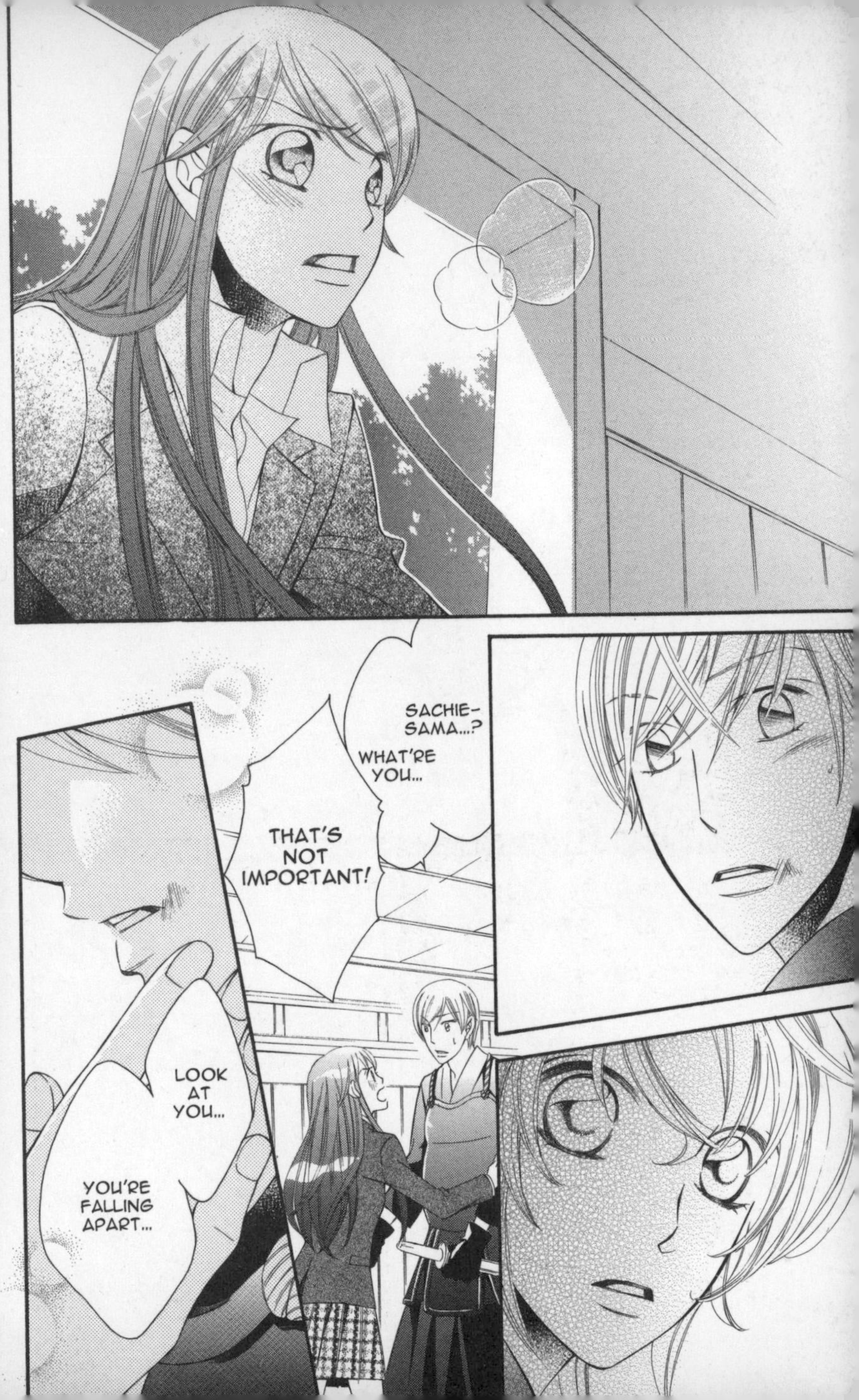
SACHIE-SAMA...?
WHAT'RE YOU...
THAT'S NOT IMPORTANT!
LOOK AT YOU...
YOU'RE FALLING APART...

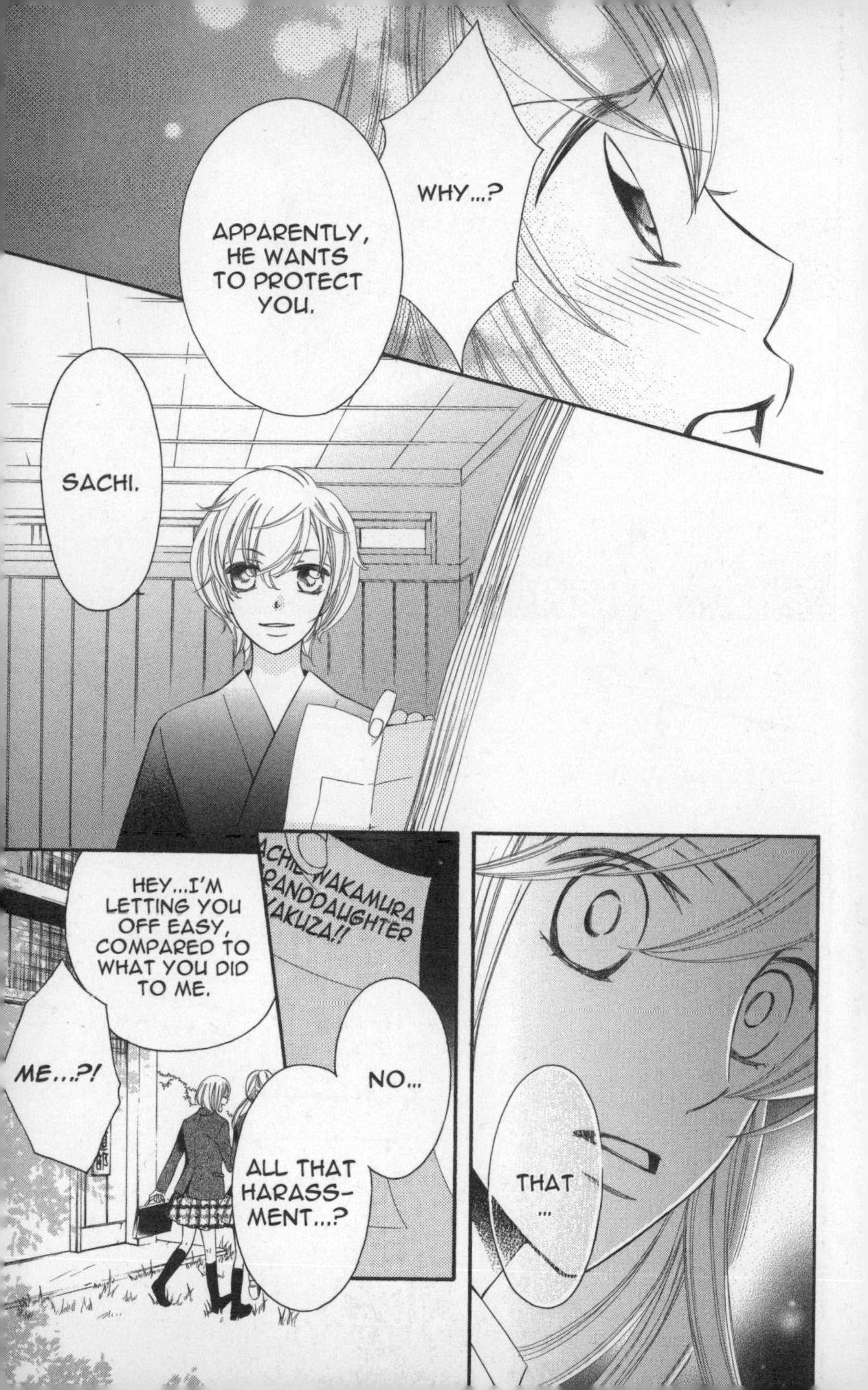
WHY...?
APPARENTLY, HE WANTS TO PROTECT YOU.
SACHI.
THAT...
ACHI WAKAMURA RANDDAUGHTER AKUZA!!
HEY...I'M LETTING YOU OFF EASY, COMPARED TO WHAT YOU DID TO ME.
NO...
ALL THAT HARASS-MENT...?
ME...?!

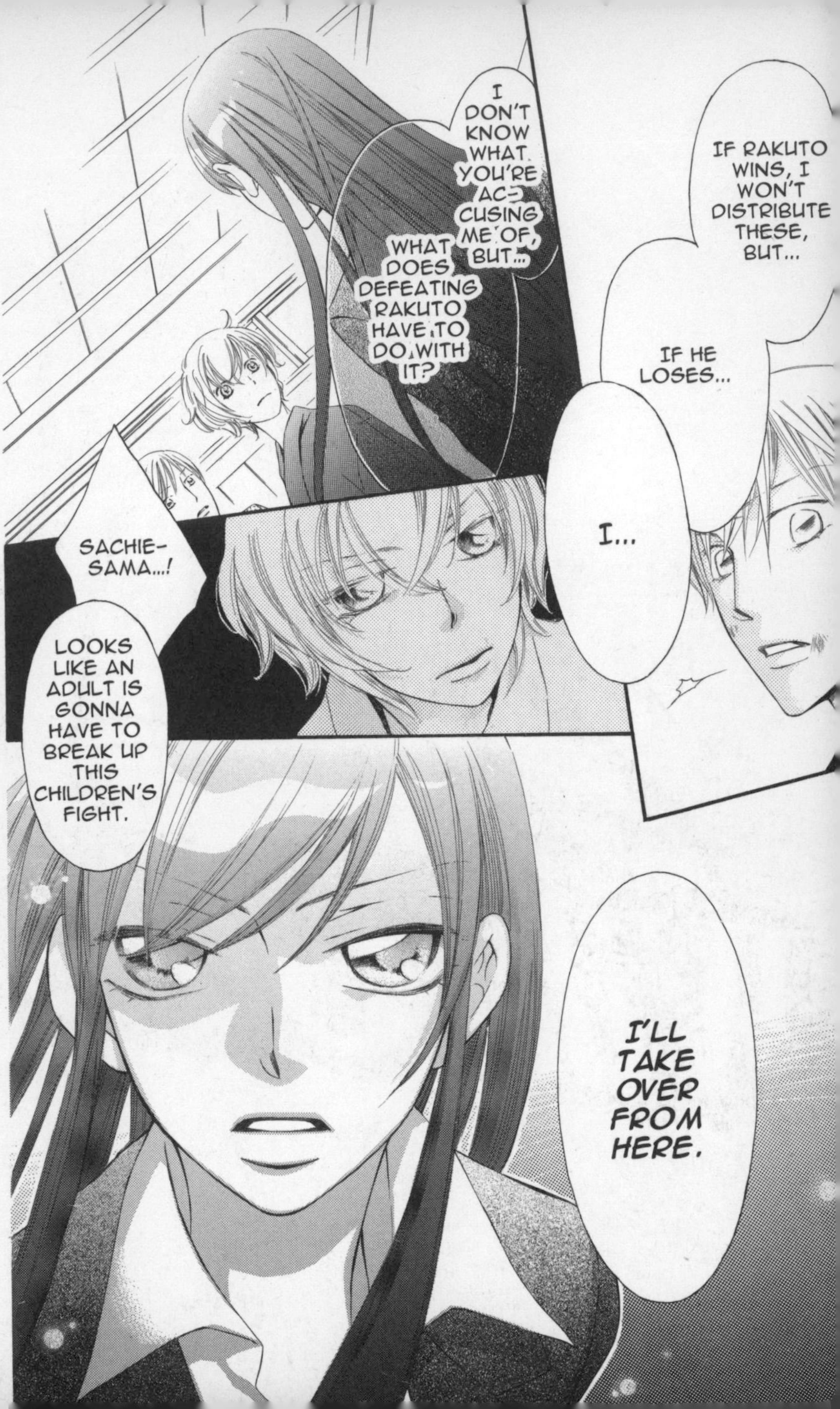
IF RAKUTO WINS, I WON'T DISTRIBUTE THESE, BUT...
IF HE LOSES...
I...
I DON'T KNOW WHAT YOU'RE AC-CUSING ME OF, BUT...
WHAT DOES DEFEATING RAKUTO HAVE TO DO WITH IT?
SACHIE-SAMA...!
LOOKS LIKE AN ADULT IS GONNA HAVE TO BREAK UP THIS CHILDREN'S FIGHT.
I'LL TAKE OVER FROM HERE.

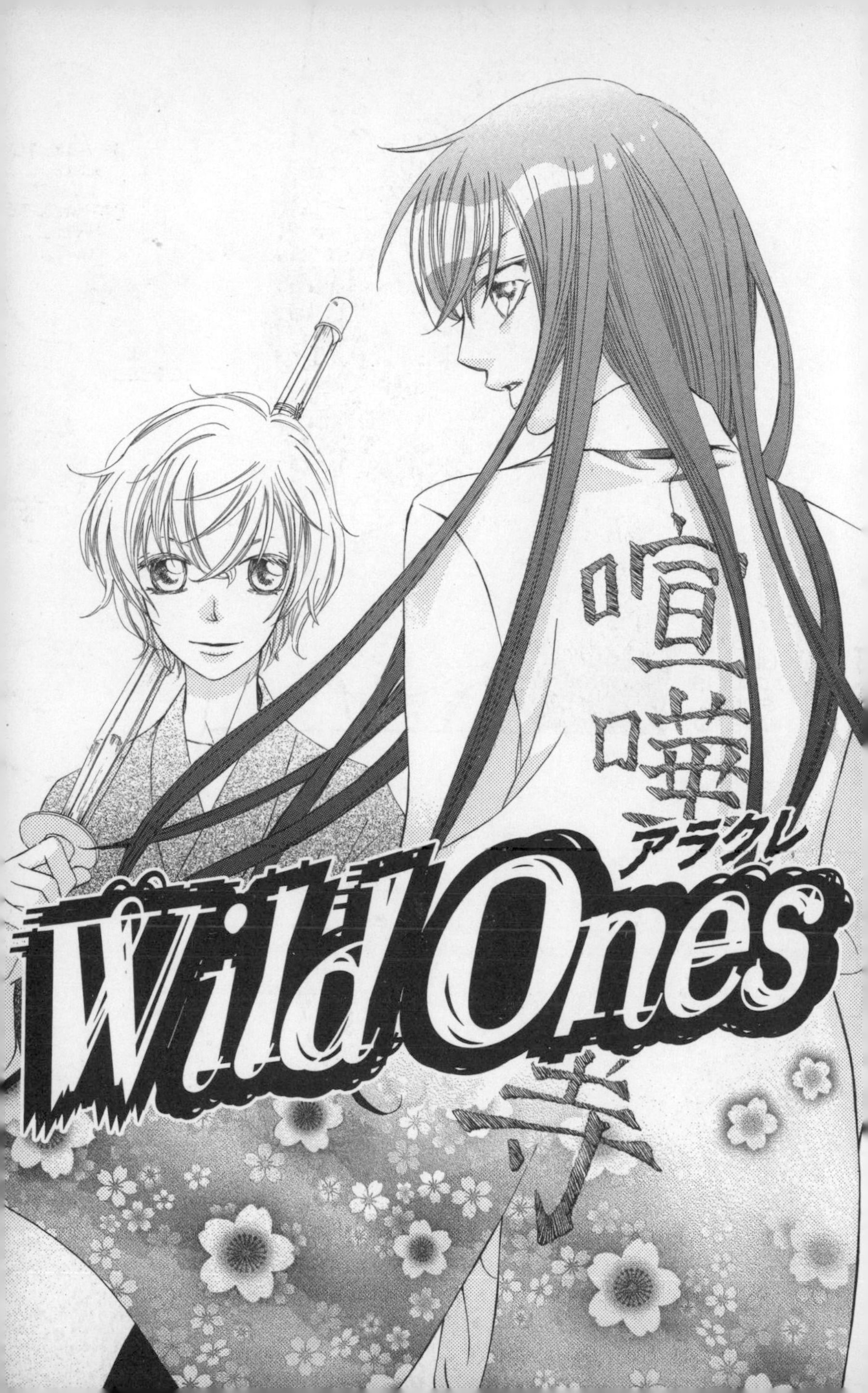

Wild Ones
アラクレ
喧嘩上等

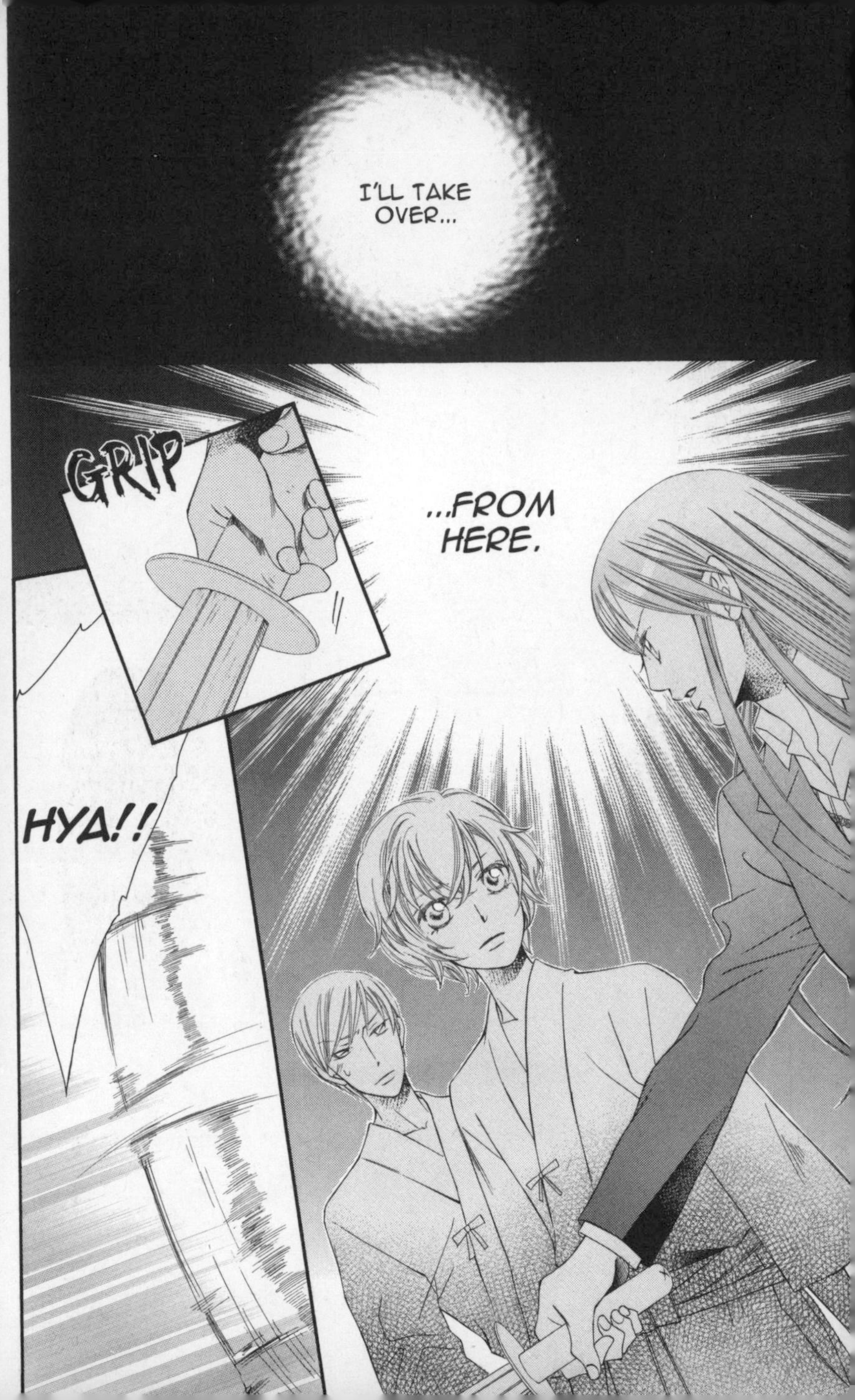
I'LL TAKE OVER...
...FROM HERE.
GRIP
HYA!!

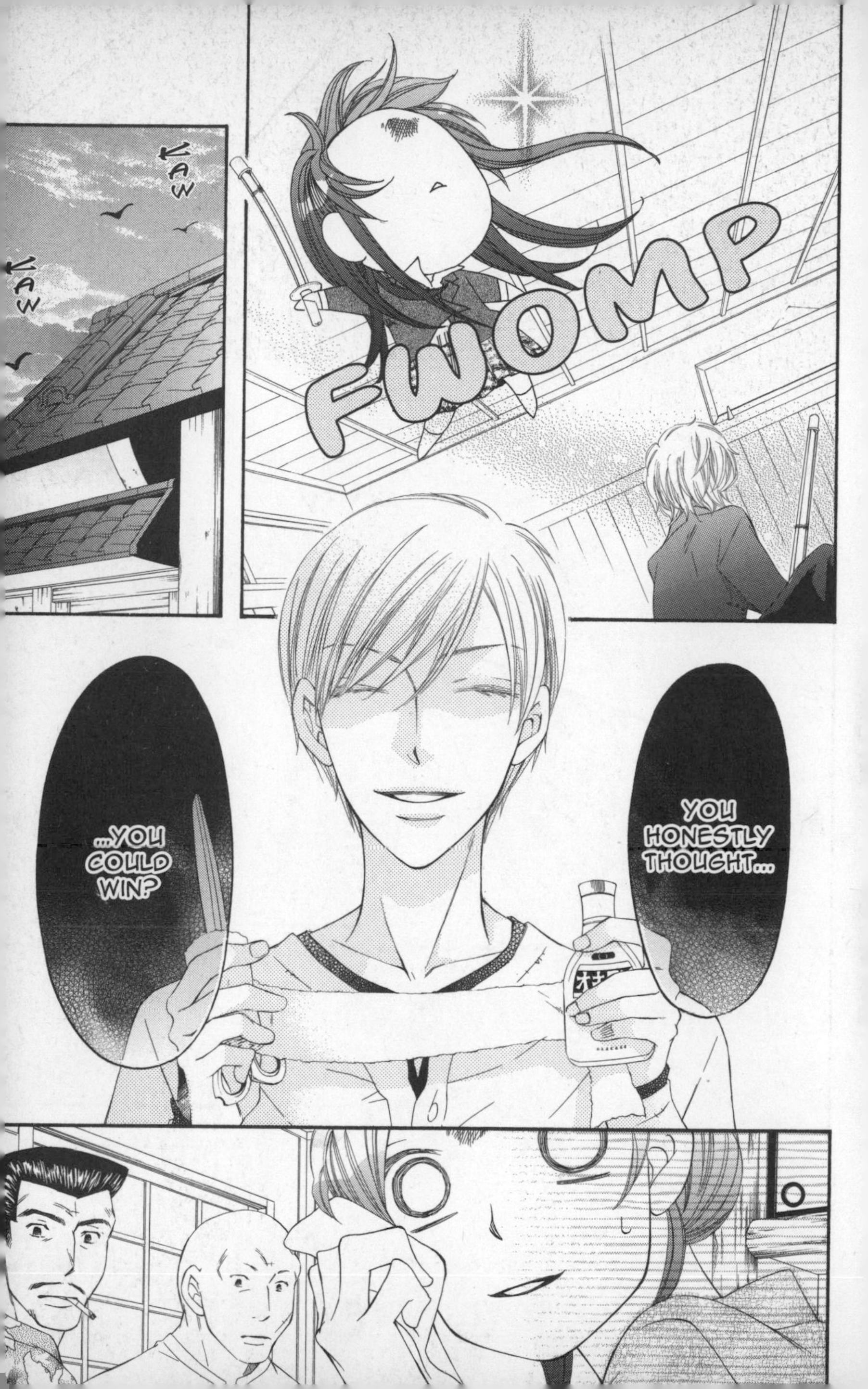
FWOMP
KAW
KAW
YOU HONESTLY THOUGHT...
...YOU COULD WIN?

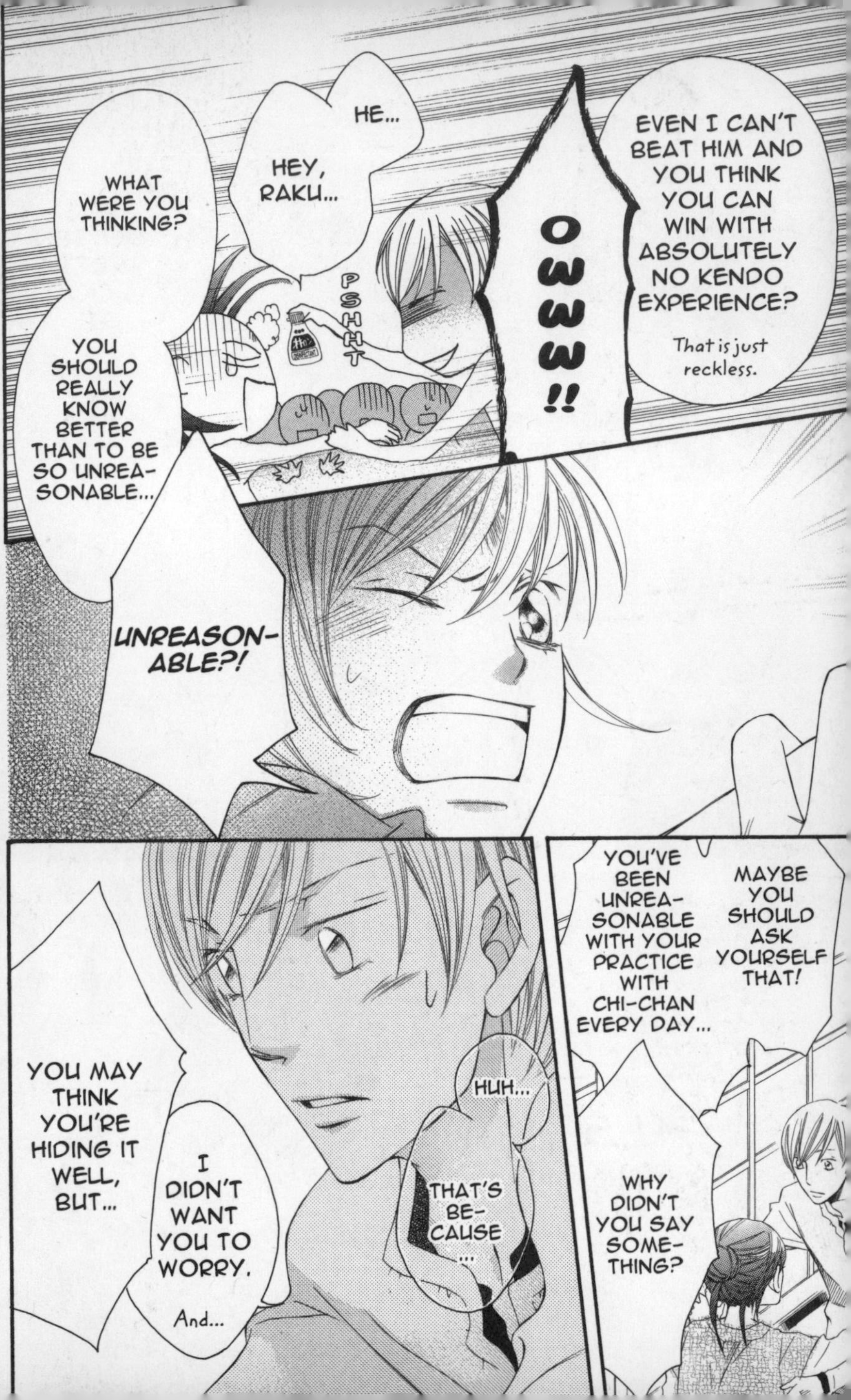
EVEN I CAN'T BEAT HIM AND YOU THINK YOU CAN WIN WITH ABSOLUTELY NO KENDO EXPERIENCE?
That is just reckless.
OWWW!!
HE...
HEY, RAKU...
PSHHT
WHAT WERE YOU THINKING?
YOU SHOULD REALLY KNOW BETTER THAN TO BE SO UNREA-SONABLE...
UNREASON-ABLE?!
MAYBE YOU SHOULD ASK YOURSELF THAT!
YOU'VE BEEN UNREA-SONABLE WITH YOUR PRACTICE WITH CHI-CHAN EVERY DAY...
WHY DIDN'T YOU SAY SOME-THING?
HUH...
THAT'S BE-CAUSE ...
I DIDN'T WANT YOU TO WORRY.
And...
YOU MAY THINK YOU'RE HIDING IT WELL, BUT...

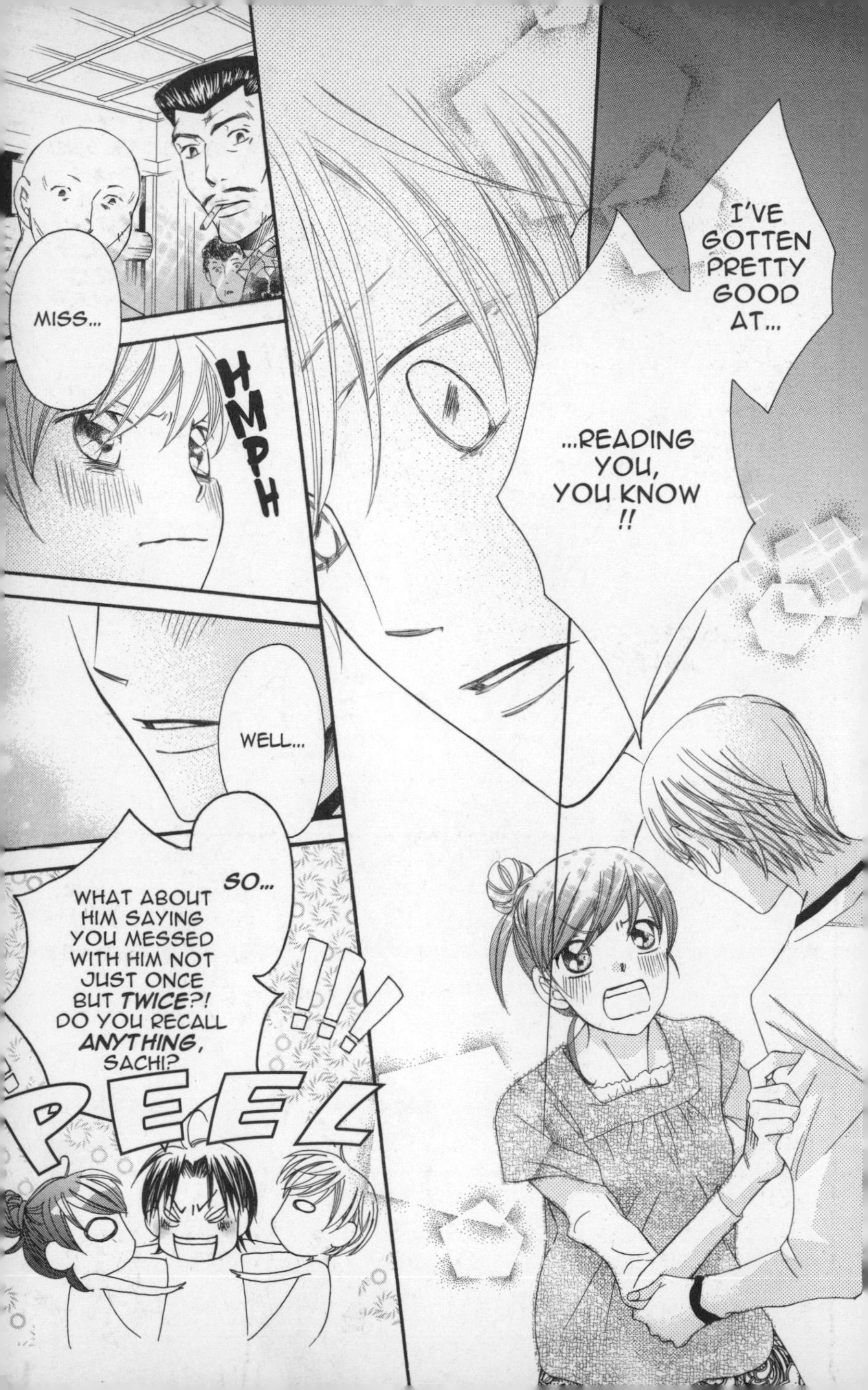
I'VE GOTTEN PRETTY GOOD AT...
...READING YOU, YOU KNOW !!
MISS...
HMPH
WELL...
SO...
WHAT ABOUT HIM SAYING YOU MESSED WITH HIM NOT JUST ONCE BUT TWICE?! DO YOU RECALL ANYTHING, SACHI?
!!!
PEEL

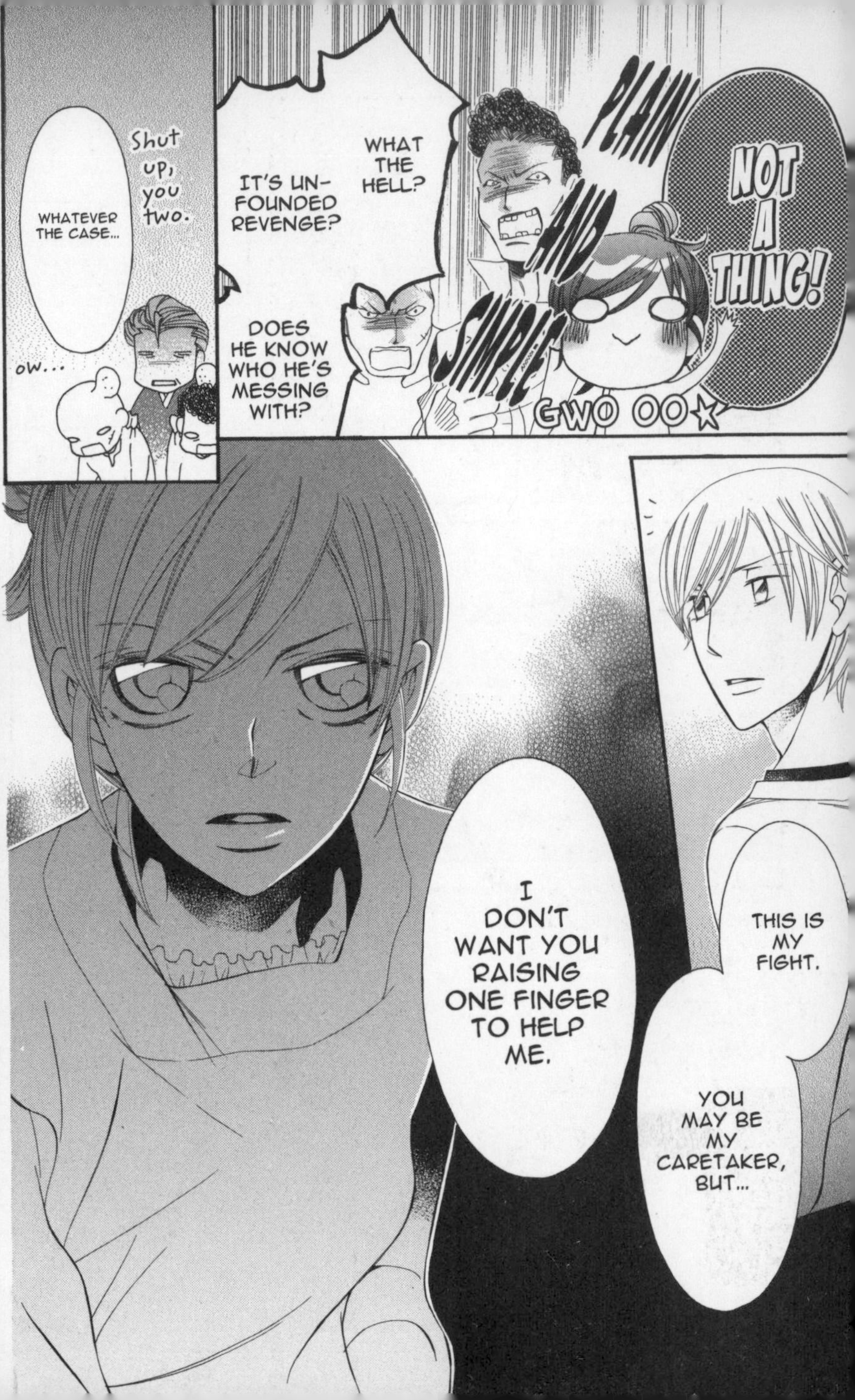
NOT A THING!
PLAIN AND SIMPLE
WHAT THE HELL?
IT'S UN-FOUNDED REVENGE?
DOES HE KNOW WHO HE'S MESSING WITH?
GWO OO★
Shut up, you two.
WHATEVER THE CASE...
OW...
THIS IS MY FIGHT.
YOU MAY BE MY CARETAKER, BUT...
I DON'T WANT YOU RAISING ONE FINGER TO HELP ME.

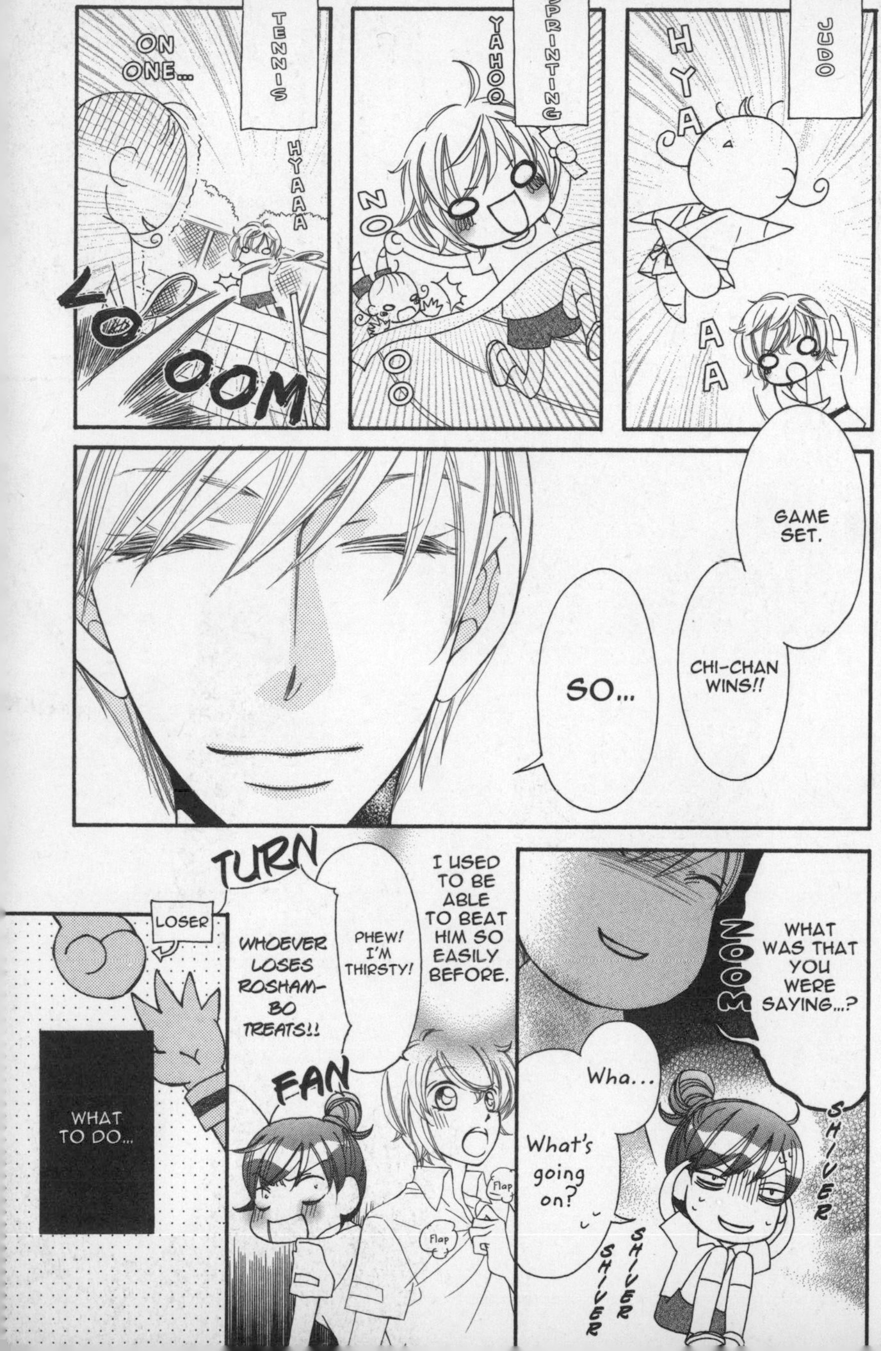
JUDO
HYA
AA
SPRINTING
YAHOO
NOOOO
TENNIS
ON ONE...
HYAAAA
VOOOM
GAME SET.
CHI-CHAN WINS!!
SO...
ZOOM
WHAT WAS THAT YOU WERE SAYING...?
Wha...
What's going on?
SHIVER
SHIVER SHIVER
I USED TO BE ABLE TO BEAT HIM SO EASILY BEFORE.
PHEW! I'M THIRSTY!
TURN
WHOEVER LOSES ROSHAMBO TREATS!!
FAN
Flap
Flap
LOSER
WHAT TO DO...

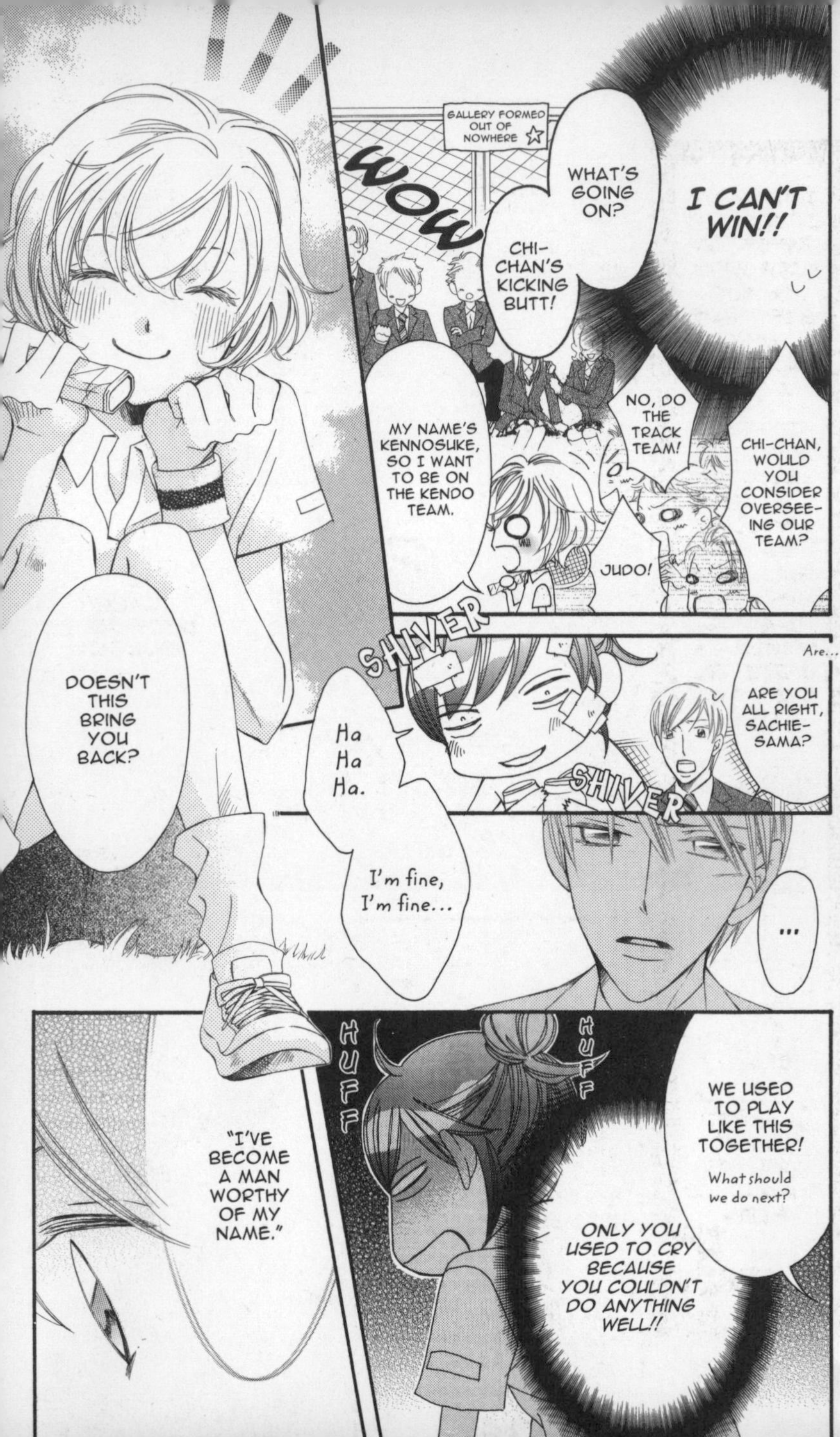
I CAN'T WIN!!
WHAT'S GOING ON?
GALLERY FORMED OUT OF NOWHERE ☆
WOW
CHI-CHAN'S KICKING BUTT!
CHI-CHAN, WOULD YOU CONSIDER OVERSEEING OUR TEAM?
NO, DO THE TRACK TEAM!
JUDO!
MY NAME'S KENNOSUKE, SO I WANT TO BE ON THE KENDO TEAM.
Are...
ARE YOU ALL RIGHT, SACHIE-SAMA?
SHIVER
Ha Ha Ha.
SHIVER
I'm fine, I'm fine...
...
DOESN'T THIS BRING YOU BACK?
HUFF
HUFF
WE USED TO PLAY LIKE THIS TOGETHER!
What should we do next?
ONLY YOU USED TO CRY BECAUSE YOU COULDN'T DO ANYTHING WELL!!
"I'VE BECOME A MAN WORTHY OF MY NAME."

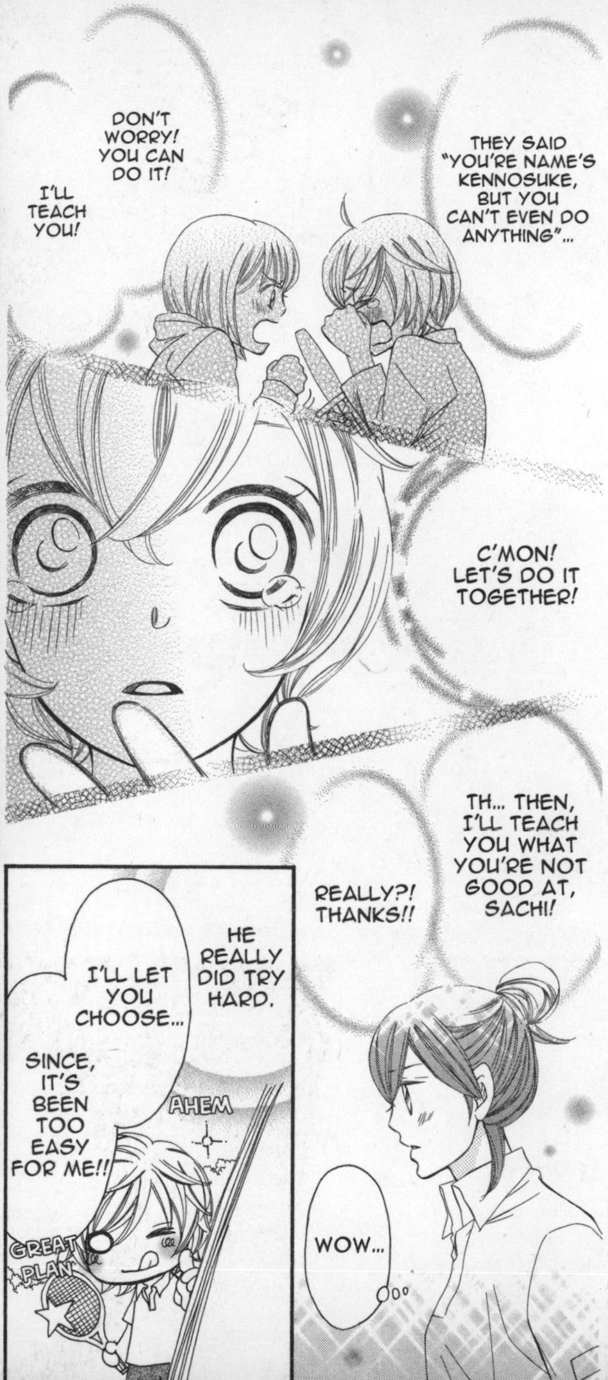
THEY SAID "YOU'RE NAME'S KENNOSUKE, BUT YOU CAN'T EVEN DO ANYTHING"...
DON'T WORRY! YOU CAN DO IT!
I'LL TEACH YOU!
C'MON! LET'S DO IT TOGETHER!
TH... THEN, I'LL TEACH YOU WHAT YOU'RE NOT GOOD AT, SACHI!
REALLY?! THANKS!!
HE REALLY DID TRY HARD.
I'LL LET YOU CHOOSE...
SINCE, IT'S BEEN TOO EASY FOR ME!!
AHEM
WOW...
GREAT PLAN

I HAVE A LOT OF STUFF, OR RATHER I'VE GOT A LOT OF EXCESS STUFF. NONE OF IT NECESSARY TO LIVE!!

IT WAS A CHANCE TO REFLECT AND I WAS APPALLED AT MYSELF. BUT... I JUST CAN'T SEEM TO GET RID OF ANYTHING. I JUST FEEL LIKE I MIGHT USE IT...

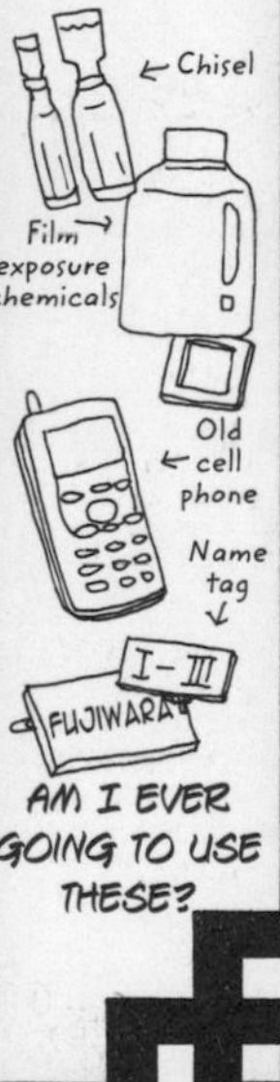
← Chisel
Film → exposure chemicals
Old ← cell phone
Name tag ↓
I–III
FUJIWARA

AM I EVER GOING TO USE THESE?

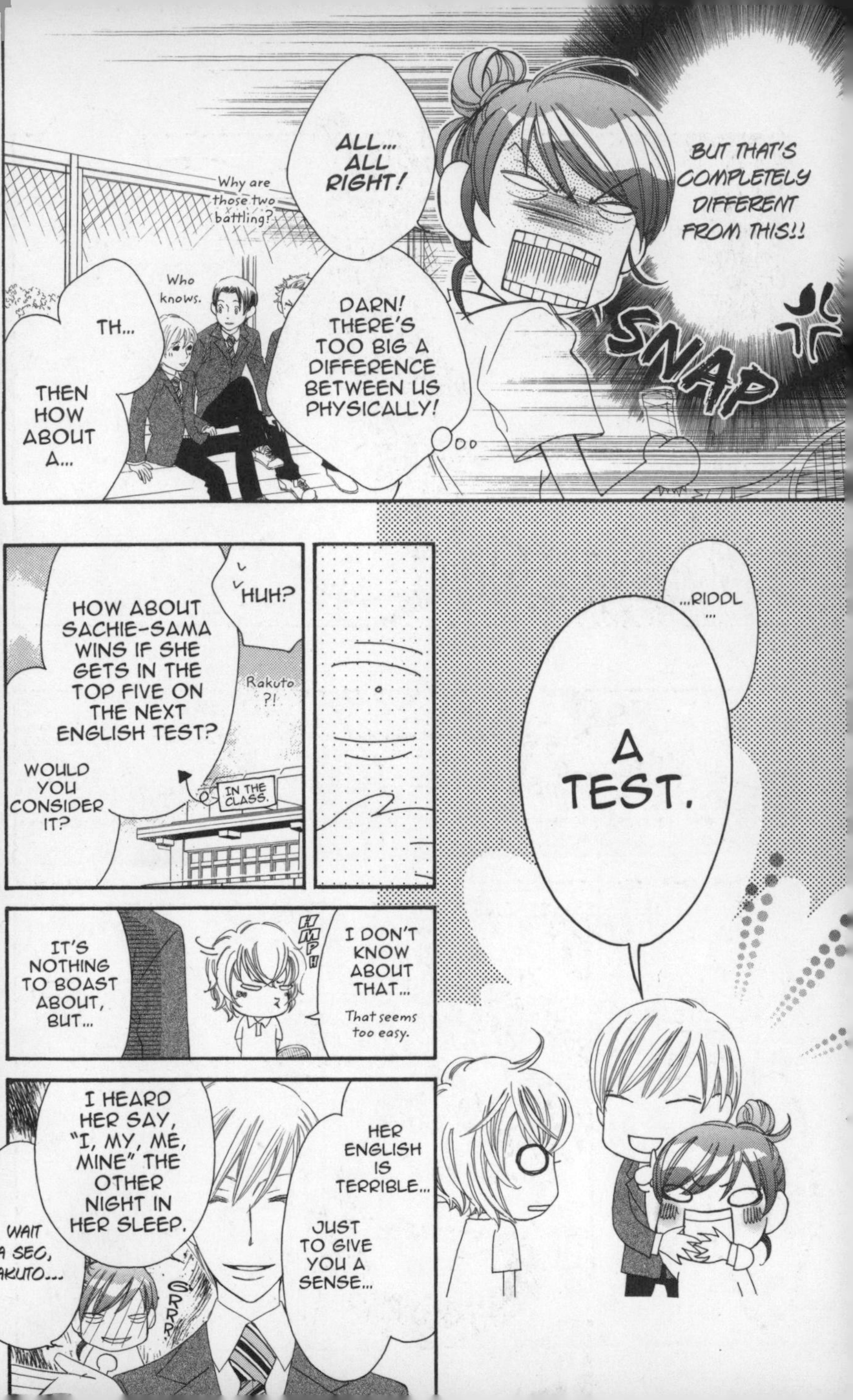
BUT THAT'S COMPLETELY DIFFERENT FROM THIS!!
SNAP
ALL... ALL RIGHT!
DARN! THERE'S TOO BIG A DIFFERENCE BETWEEN US PHYSICALLY!
Why are those two battling?
Who knows.
TH...
THEN HOW ABOUT A...
...RIDDL ...
A TEST.
HUH?
Rakuto ?!
HOW ABOUT SACHIE-SAMA WINS IF SHE GETS IN THE TOP FIVE ON THE NEXT ENGLISH TEST?
IN THE CLASS.
WOULD YOU CONSIDER IT?
I DON'T KNOW ABOUT THAT...
That seems too easy.
HMPH
IT'S NOTHING TO BOAST ABOUT, BUT...
HER ENGLISH IS TERRIBLE...
JUST TO GIVE YOU A SENSE...
I HEARD HER SAY, "I, MY, ME, MINE" THE OTHER NIGHT IN HER SLEEP.
GRRR
WAIT A SEC, RAKUTO...

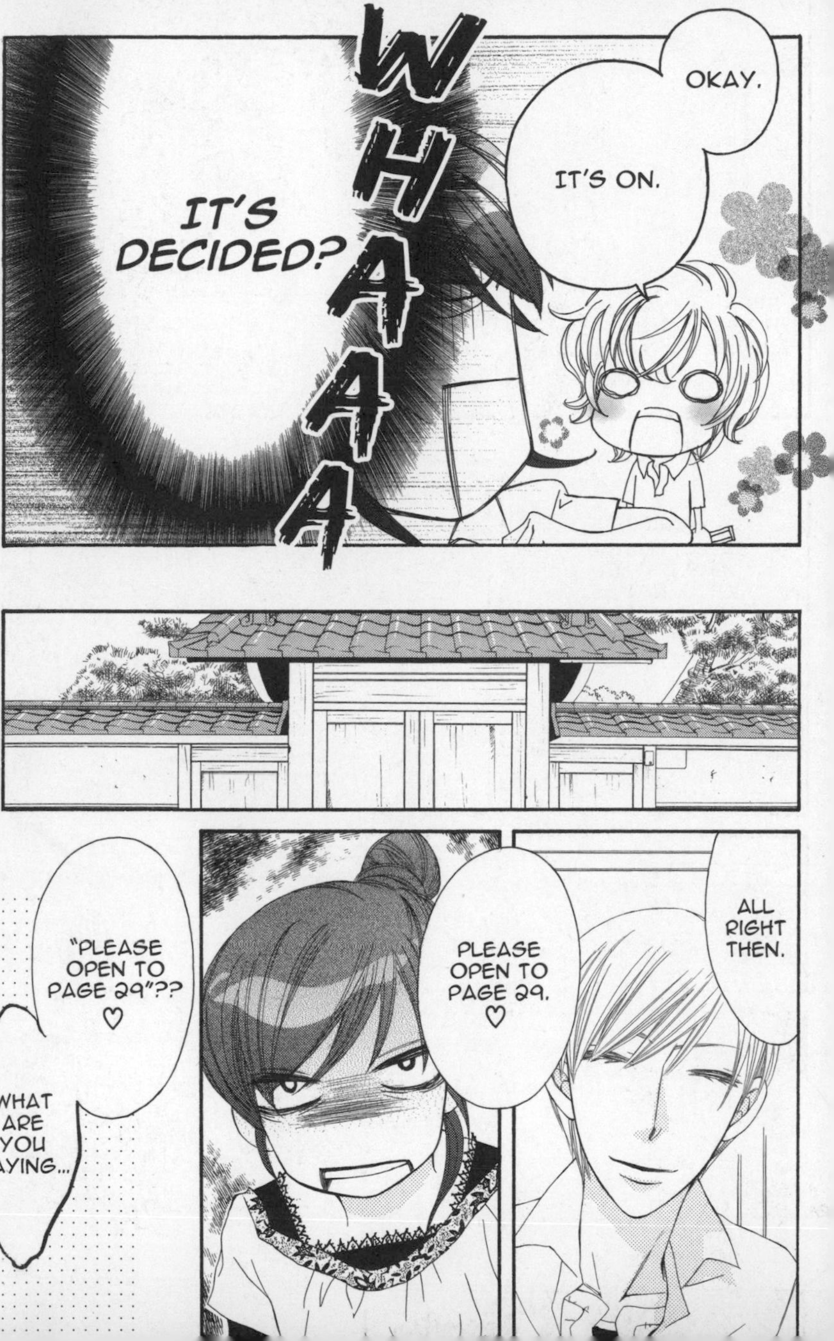
OKAY.
IT'S ON.
WHAAAA
IT'S DECIDED?
ALL RIGHT THEN.
PLEASE OPEN TO PAGE 29. ♡
"PLEASE OPEN TO PAGE 29"?? ♡
WHAT ARE YOU SAYING...

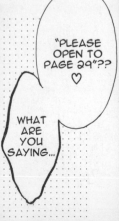

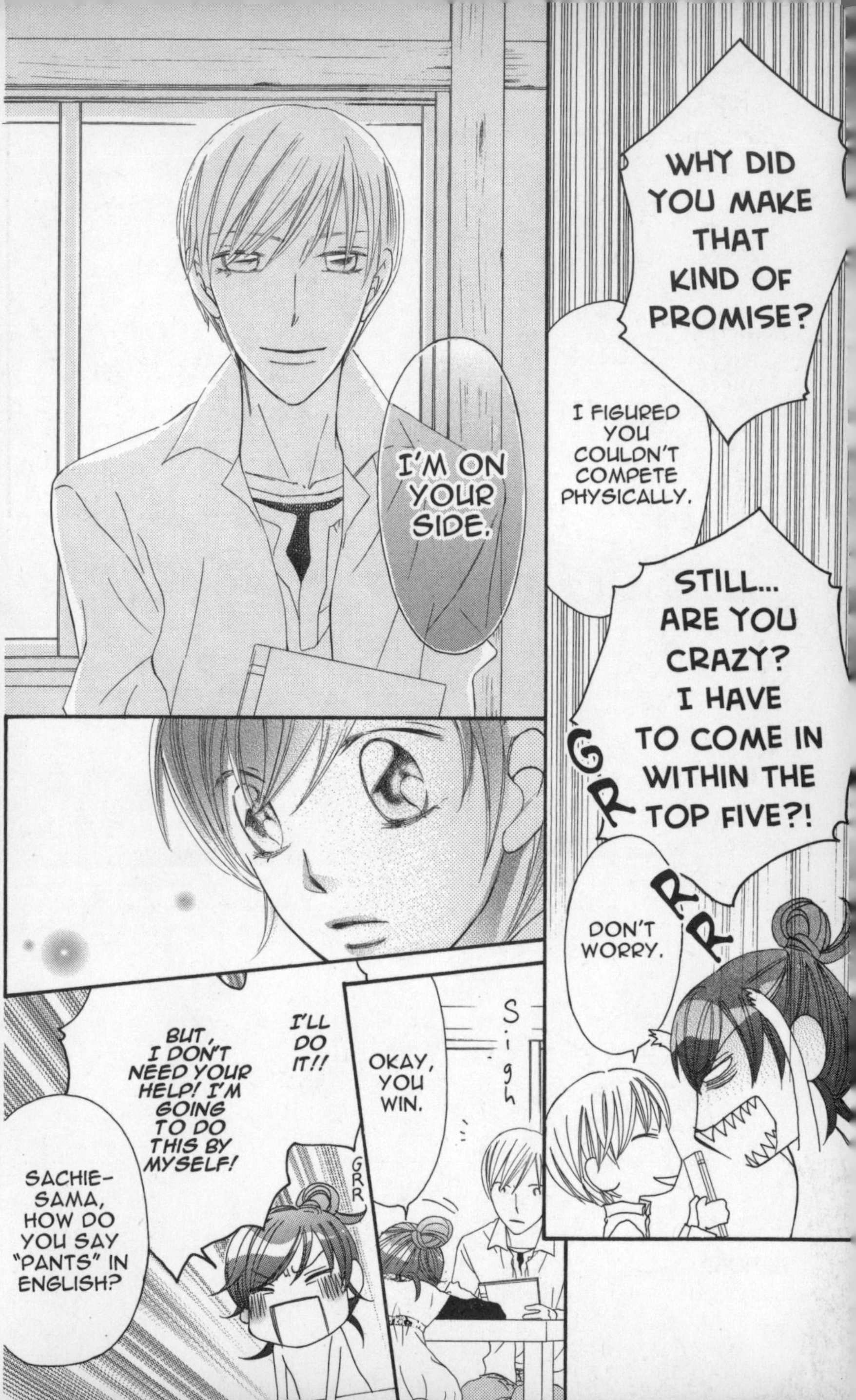
WHY DID YOU MAKE THAT KIND OF PROMISE?
I FIGURED YOU COULDN'T COMPETE PHYSICALLY.
STILL... ARE YOU CRAZY? I HAVE TO COME IN WITHIN THE TOP FIVE?!
GRRRR
DON'T WORRY.
I'M ON YOUR SIDE.
Sigh
OKAY, YOU WIN.
I'LL DO IT!!
BUT, I DON'T NEED YOUR HELP! I'M GOING TO DO THIS BY MYSELF!
GRR
SACHIE-SAMA, HOW DO YOU SAY "PANTS" IN ENGLISH?

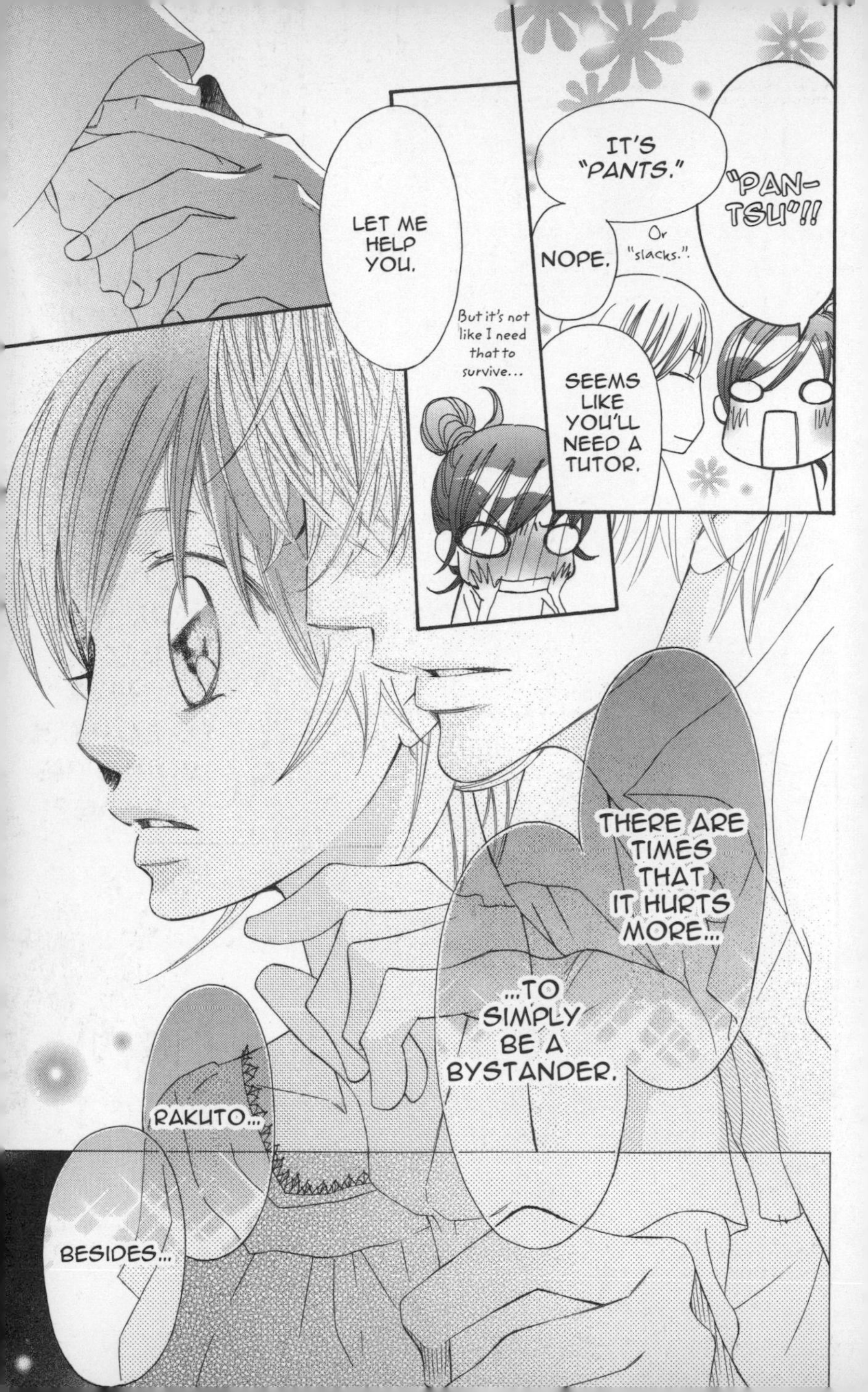
"PAN-TSU"!!
IT'S "PANTS."
Or "slacks."
NOPE.
SEEMS LIKE YOU'LL NEED A TUTOR.
LET ME HELP YOU.
But it's not like I need that to survive...
THERE ARE TIMES THAT IT HURTS MORE...
...TO SIMPLY BE A BYSTANDER.
RAKUTO...
BESIDES...

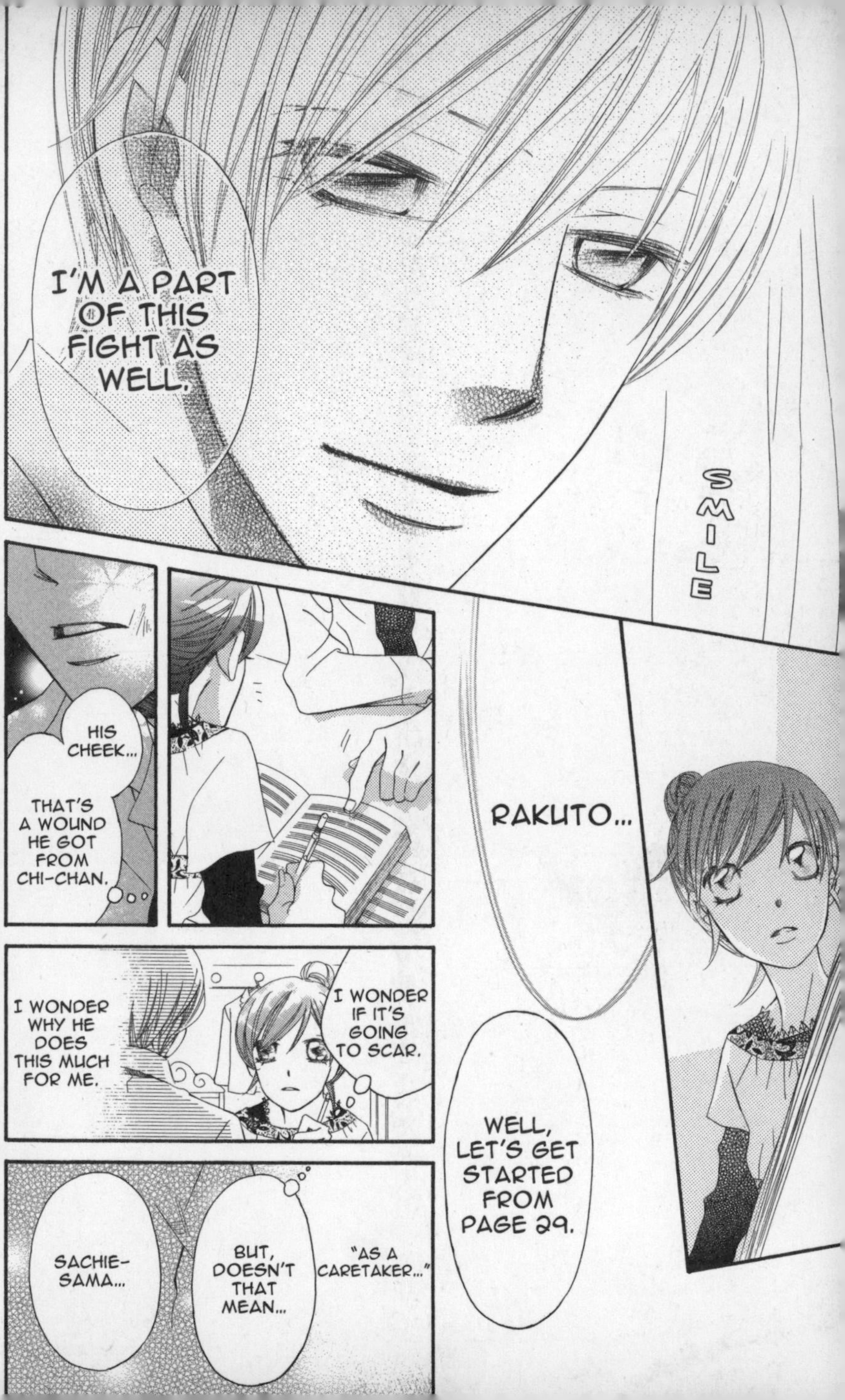
I'M A PART OF THIS FIGHT AS WELL.
SMILE
RAKUTO...
WELL, LET'S GET STARTED FROM PAGE 29.
HIS CHEEK...
THAT'S A WOUND HE GOT FROM CHI-CHAN.
I WONDER IF IT'S GOING TO SCAR.
I WONDER WHY HE DOES THIS MUCH FOR ME.
"AS A CARETAKER..."
BUT, DOESN'T THAT MEAN...
SACHIE-SAMA...

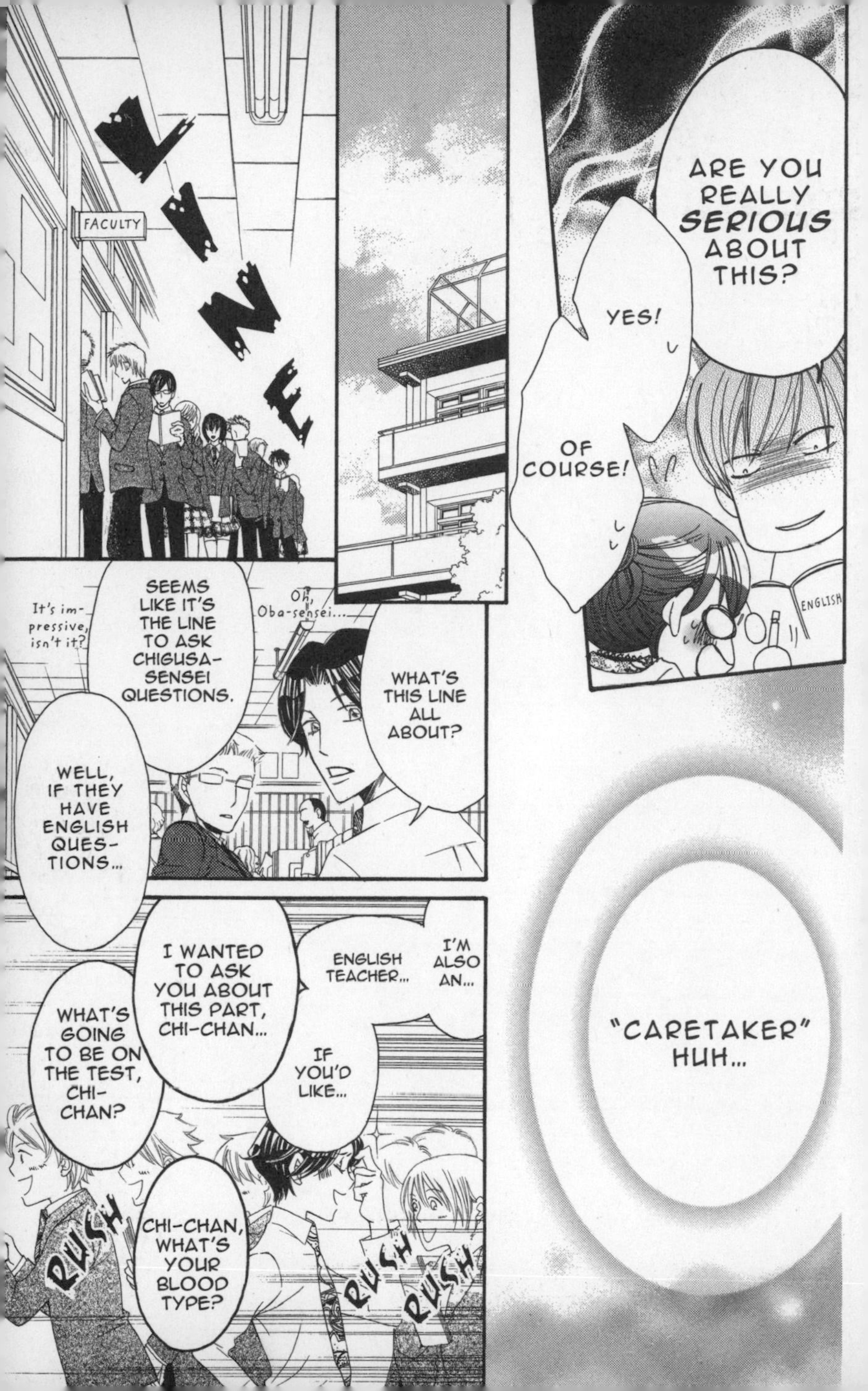
ARE YOU REALLY SERIOUS ABOUT THIS?
YES!
OF COURSE!
ENGLISH
FACULTY
LINE
WHAT'S THIS LINE ALL ABOUT?
Oh, Oba-sensei...
SEEMS LIKE IT'S THE LINE TO ASK CHIGUSA-SENSEI QUESTIONS.
It's impressive, isn't it?
WELL, IF THEY HAVE ENGLISH QUESTIONS...
I'M ALSO AN...
ENGLISH TEACHER...
IF YOU'D LIKE...
I WANTED TO ASK YOU ABOUT THIS PART, CHI-CHAN...
WHAT'S GOING TO BE ON THE TEST, CHI-CHAN?
CHI-CHAN, WHAT'S YOUR BLOOD TYPE?
RUSH
RUSH
RUSH
"CARETAKER" HUH...

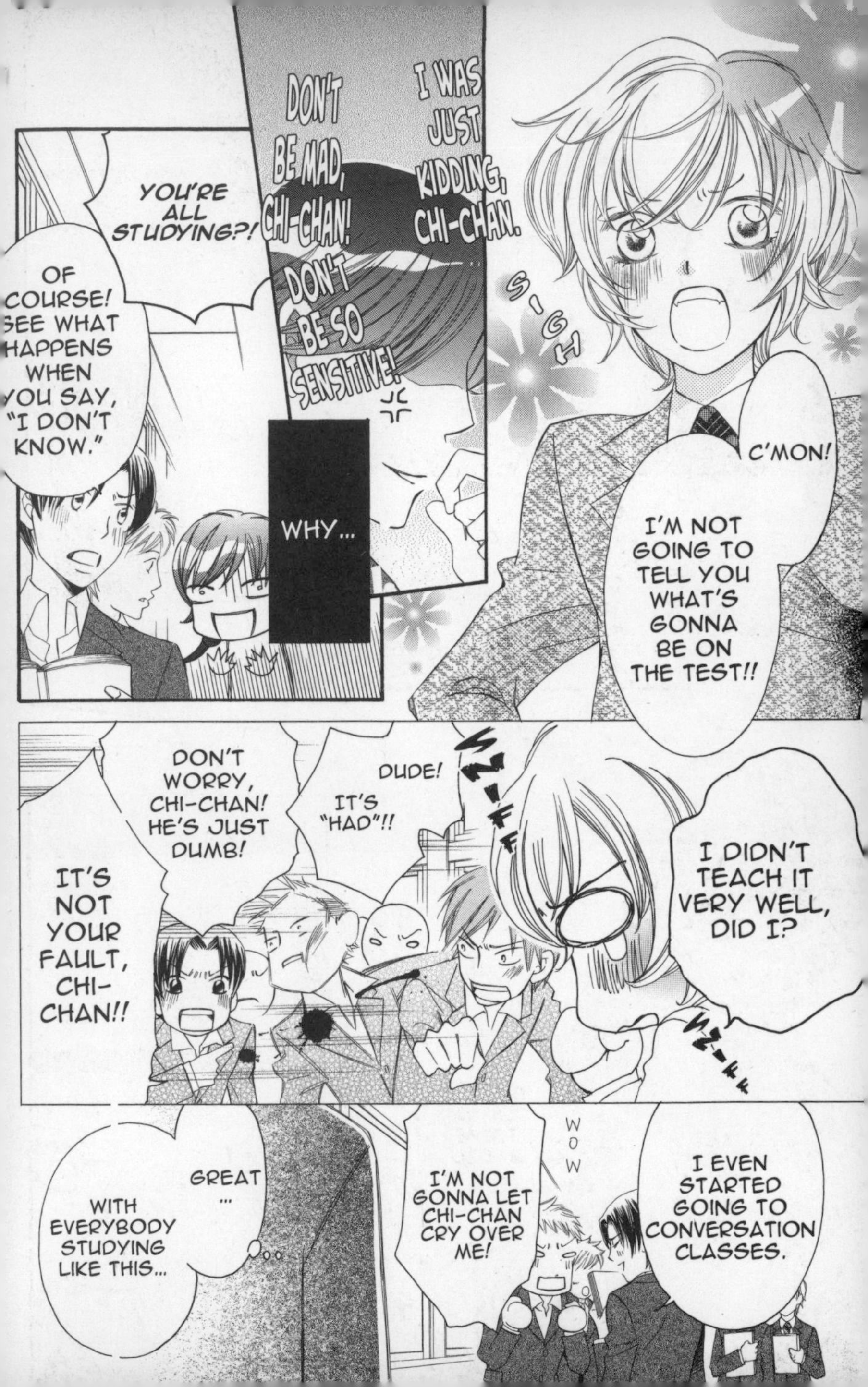
SIGH
C'MON!
I'M NOT GOING TO TELL YOU WHAT'S GONNA BE ON THE TEST!!
I WAS JUST KIDDING, CHI-CHAN.
DON'T BE MAD, CHI-CHAN! DON'T BE SO SENSITIVE!
WHY...
YOU'RE ALL STUDYING?!
OF COURSE! SEE WHAT HAPPENS WHEN YOU SAY, "I DON'T KNOW."
I DIDN'T TEACH IT VERY WELL, DID I?
SNIFF
SNIFF
DUDE! IT'S "HAD"!!
DON'T WORRY, CHI-CHAN! HE'S JUST DUMB!
IT'S NOT YOUR FAULT, CHI-CHAN!!
I EVEN STARTED GOING TO CONVERSATION CLASSES.
WOW
I'M NOT GONNA LET CHI-CHAN CRY OVER ME!
GREAT...
WITH EVERYBODY STUDYING LIKE THIS...

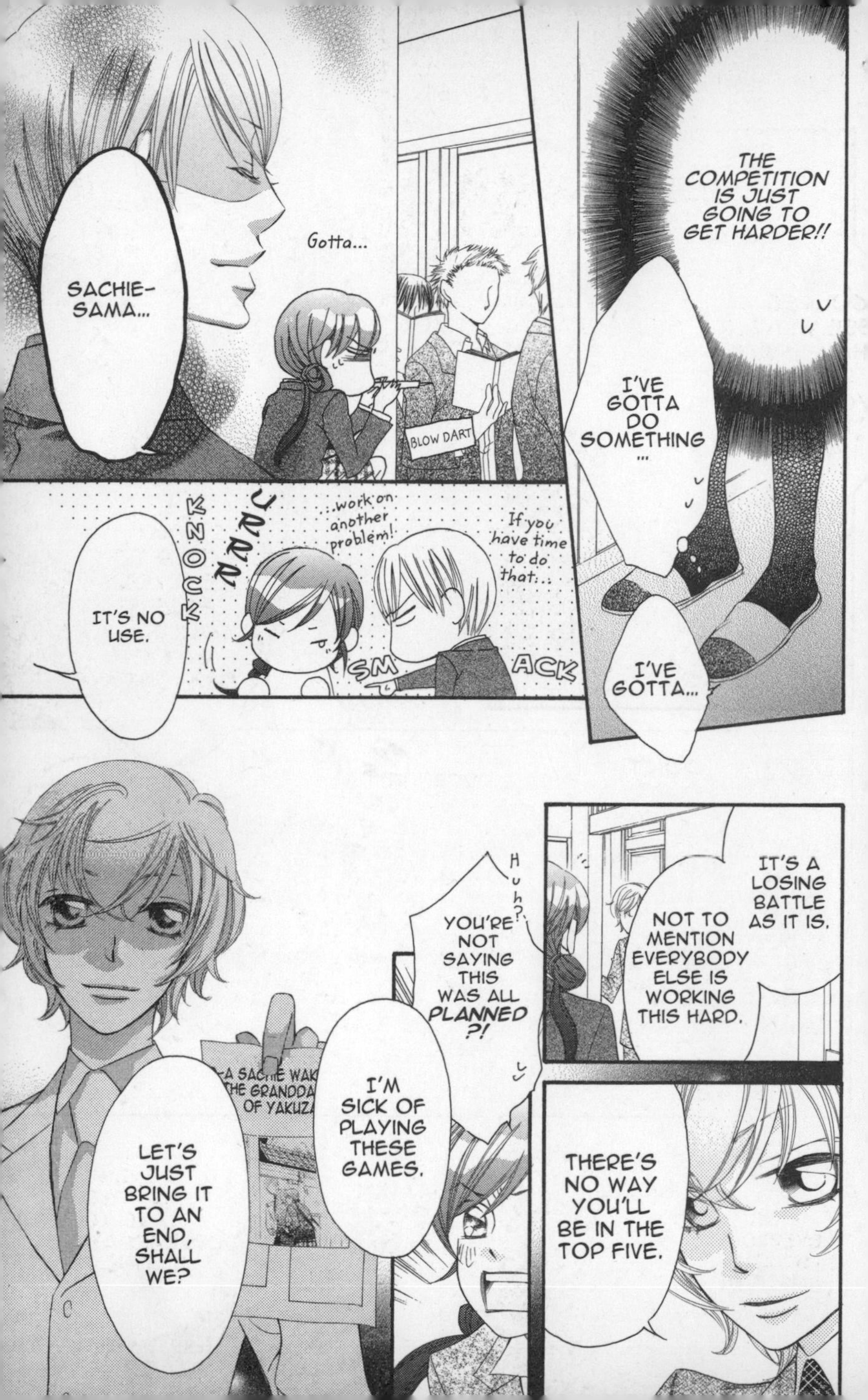
THE COMPETITION IS JUST GOING TO GET HARDER!!
I'VE GOTTA DO SOMETHING ...
I'VE GOTTA...
Gotta...
BLOW DART
SACHIE-SAMA...
If you have time to do that...
...work on another problem!
SMACK
URRR
KNOCK
IT'S NO USE.
IT'S A LOSING BATTLE AS IT IS.
NOT TO MENTION EVERYBODY ELSE IS WORKING THIS HARD.
THERE'S NO WAY YOU'LL BE IN THE TOP FIVE.
Huh?
YOU'RE NOT SAYING THIS WAS ALL *PLANNED* ?!
I'M SICK OF PLAYING THESE GAMES.
LET'S JUST BRING IT TO AN END, SHALL WE?

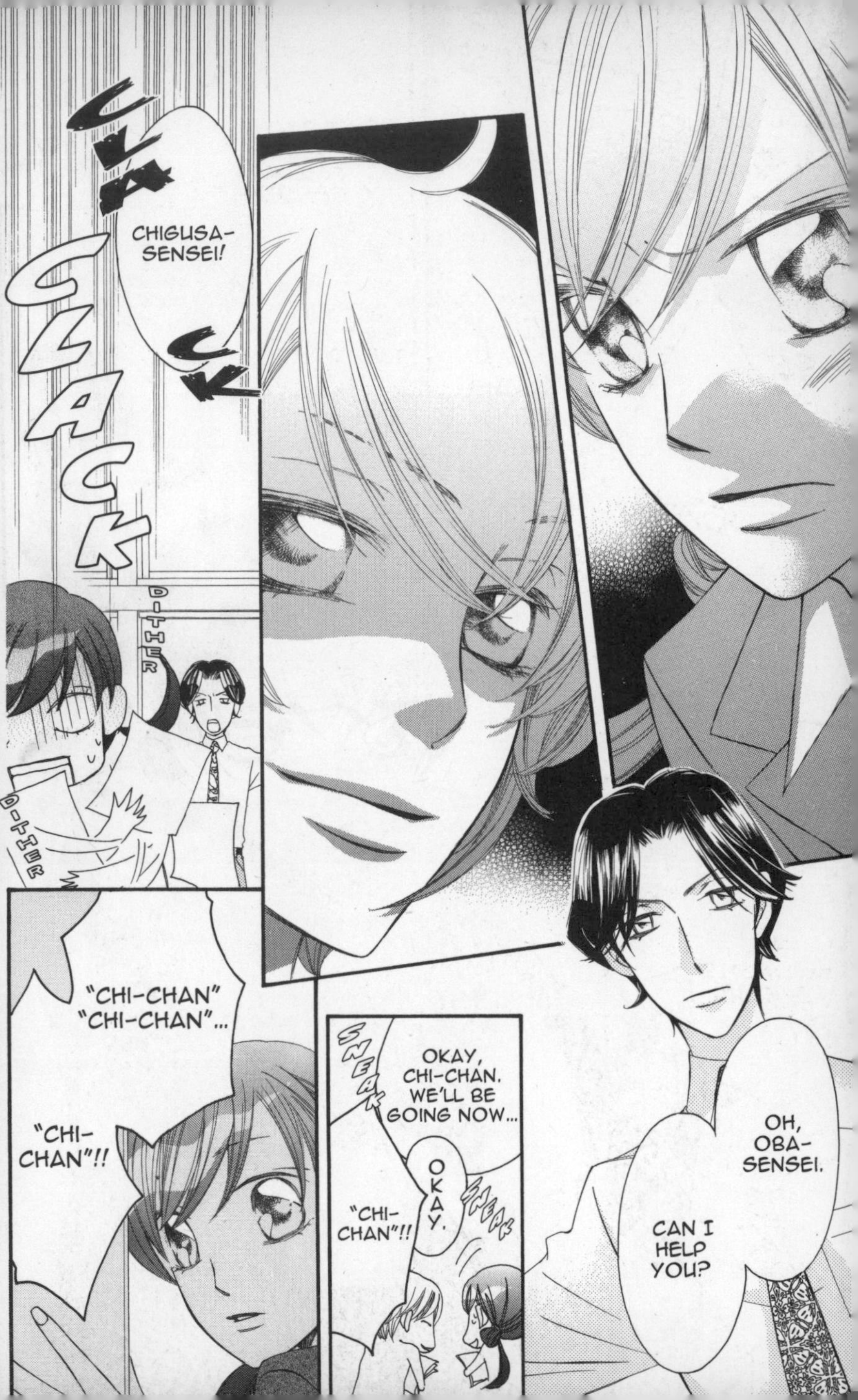
CLACK
CHIGUSA-SENSEI!
CLACK
DITHER
DITHER
OH, OBA-SENSEI.
CAN I HELP YOU?
SNEAK
OKAY, CHI-CHAN. WE'LL BE GOING NOW...
OKAY.
SNEAK
"CHI-CHAN"!!
"CHI-CHAN" "CHI-CHAN"...
"CHI-CHAN"!!

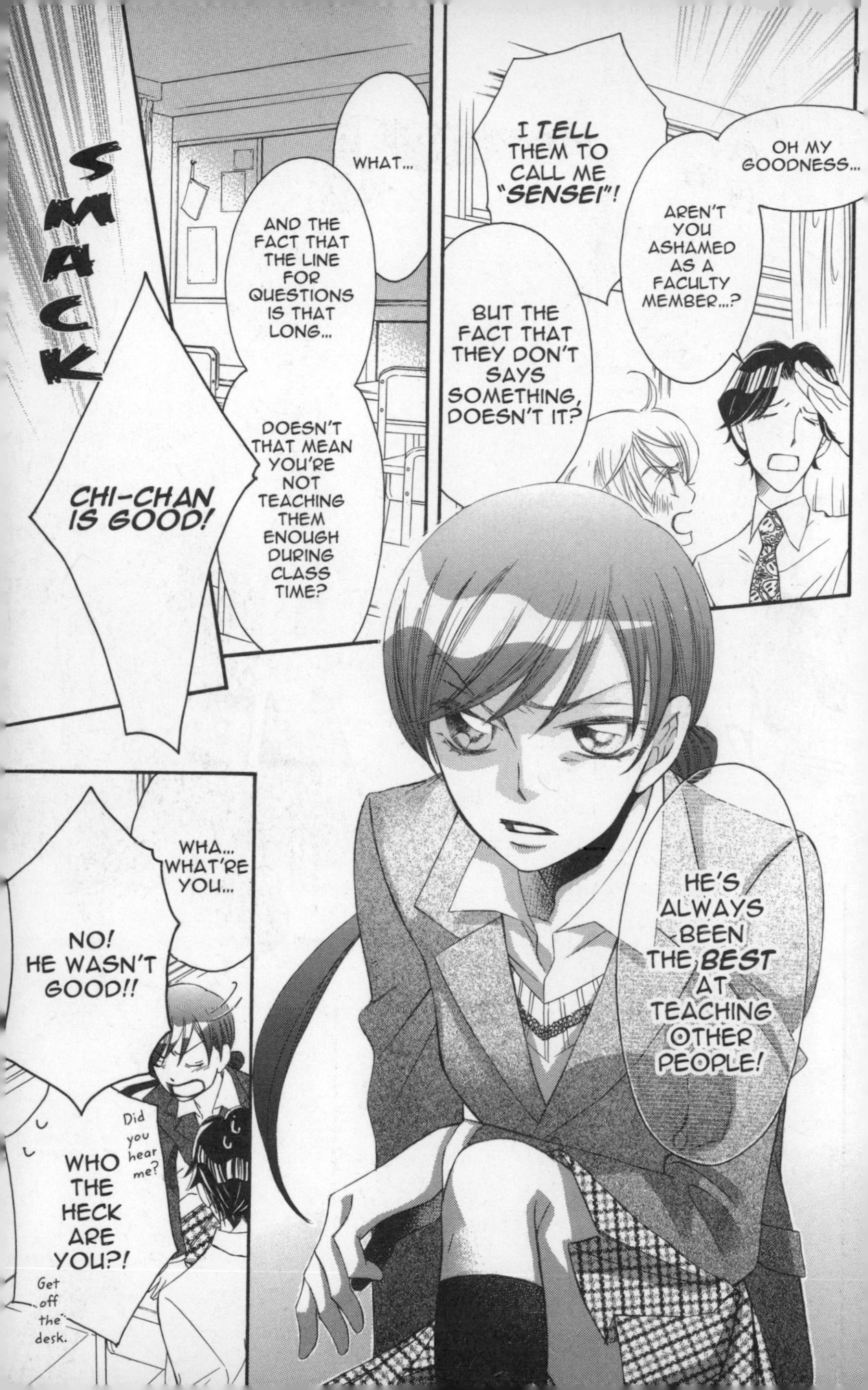
OH MY GOODNESS...
AREN'T YOU ASHAMED AS A FACULTY MEMBER...?
I TELL THEM TO CALL ME "SENSEI"!
BUT THE FACT THAT THEY DON'T SAYS SOMETHING, DOESN'T IT?
WHAT...
AND THE FACT THAT THE LINE FOR QUESTIONS IS THAT LONG...
DOESN'T THAT MEAN YOU'RE NOT TEACHING THEM ENOUGH DURING CLASS TIME?
SMACK
CHI-CHAN IS GOOD!
HE'S ALWAYS BEEN THE BEST AT TEACHING OTHER PEOPLE!
WHA... WHAT'RE YOU...
NO! HE WASN'T GOOD!!
Did you hear me?
WHO THE HECK ARE YOU?!
Get off the desk.

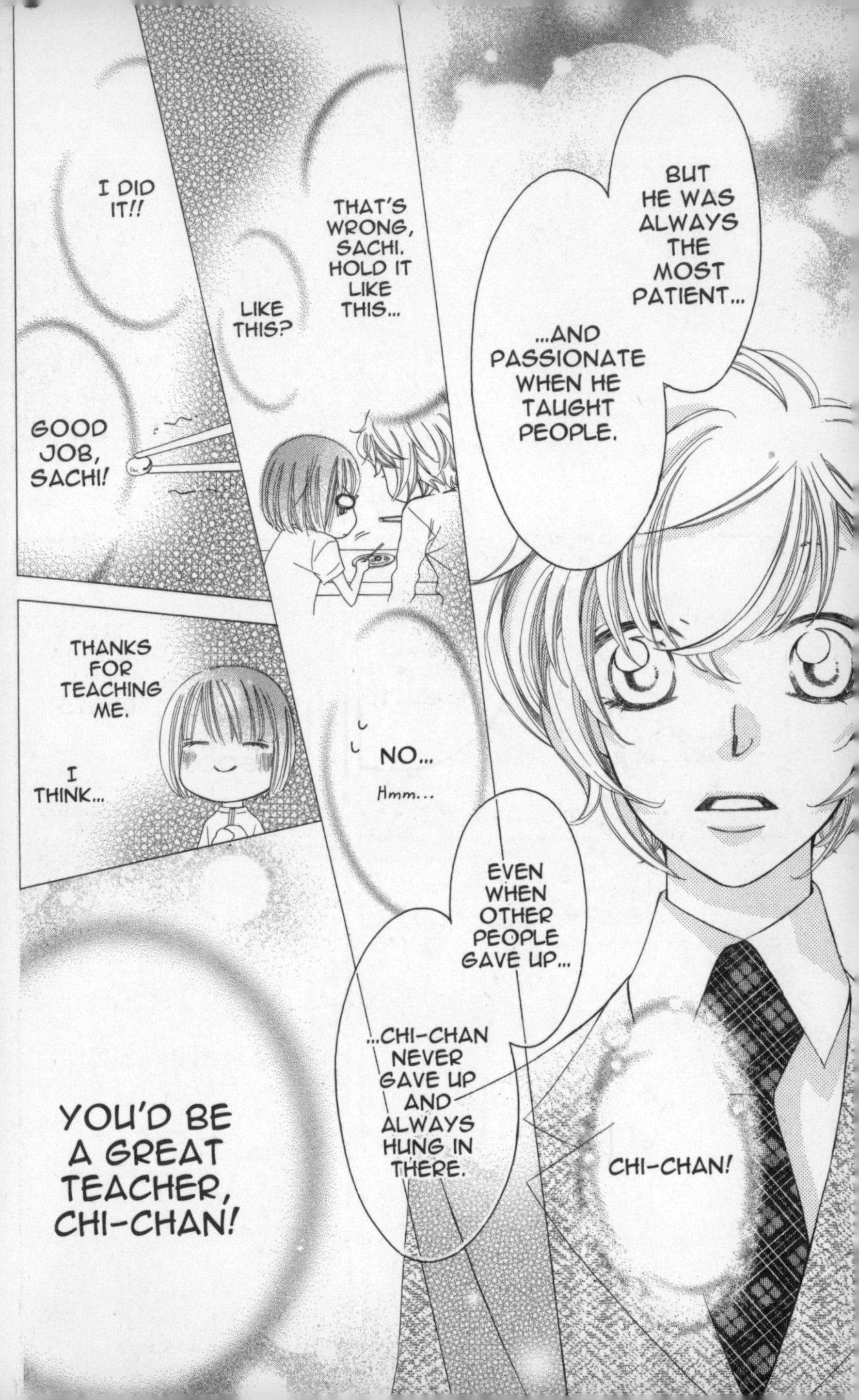
BUT HE WAS ALWAYS THE MOST PATIENT...
...AND PASSIONATE WHEN HE TAUGHT PEOPLE.
THAT'S WRONG, SACHI. HOLD IT LIKE THIS...
LIKE THIS?
NO...
Hmm...
I DID IT!!
GOOD JOB, SACHI!
THANKS FOR TEACHING ME.
I THINK...
EVEN WHEN OTHER PEOPLE GAVE UP...
...CHI-CHAN NEVER GAVE UP AND ALWAYS HUNG IN THERE.
CHI-CHAN!
YOU'D BE A GREAT TEACHER, CHI-CHAN!

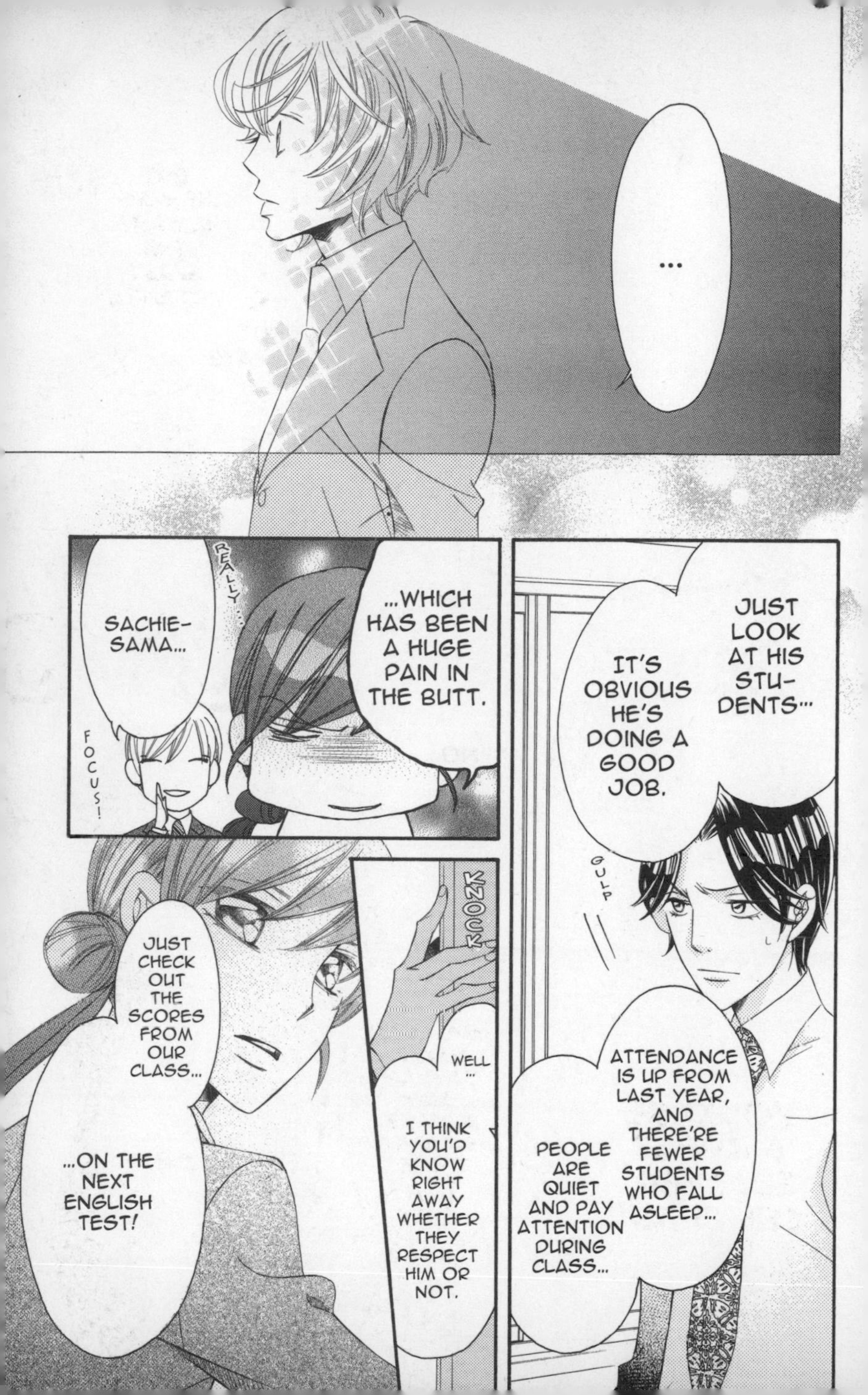
...
JUST LOOK AT HIS STU-DENTS...
IT'S OBVIOUS HE'S DOING A GOOD JOB.
GULP
ATTENDANCE IS UP FROM LAST YEAR, AND THERE'RE FEWER STUDENTS WHO FALL ASLEEP...
PEOPLE ARE QUIET AND PAY ATTENTION DURING CLASS...
...WHICH HAS BEEN A HUGE PAIN IN THE BUTT.
REALLY...
SACHIE-SAMA...
FOCUS!
KNOCK
WELL...
I THINK YOU'D KNOW RIGHT AWAY WHETHER THEY RESPECT HIM OR NOT.
JUST CHECK OUT THE SCORES FROM OUR CLASS...
...ON THE NEXT ENGLISH TEST!

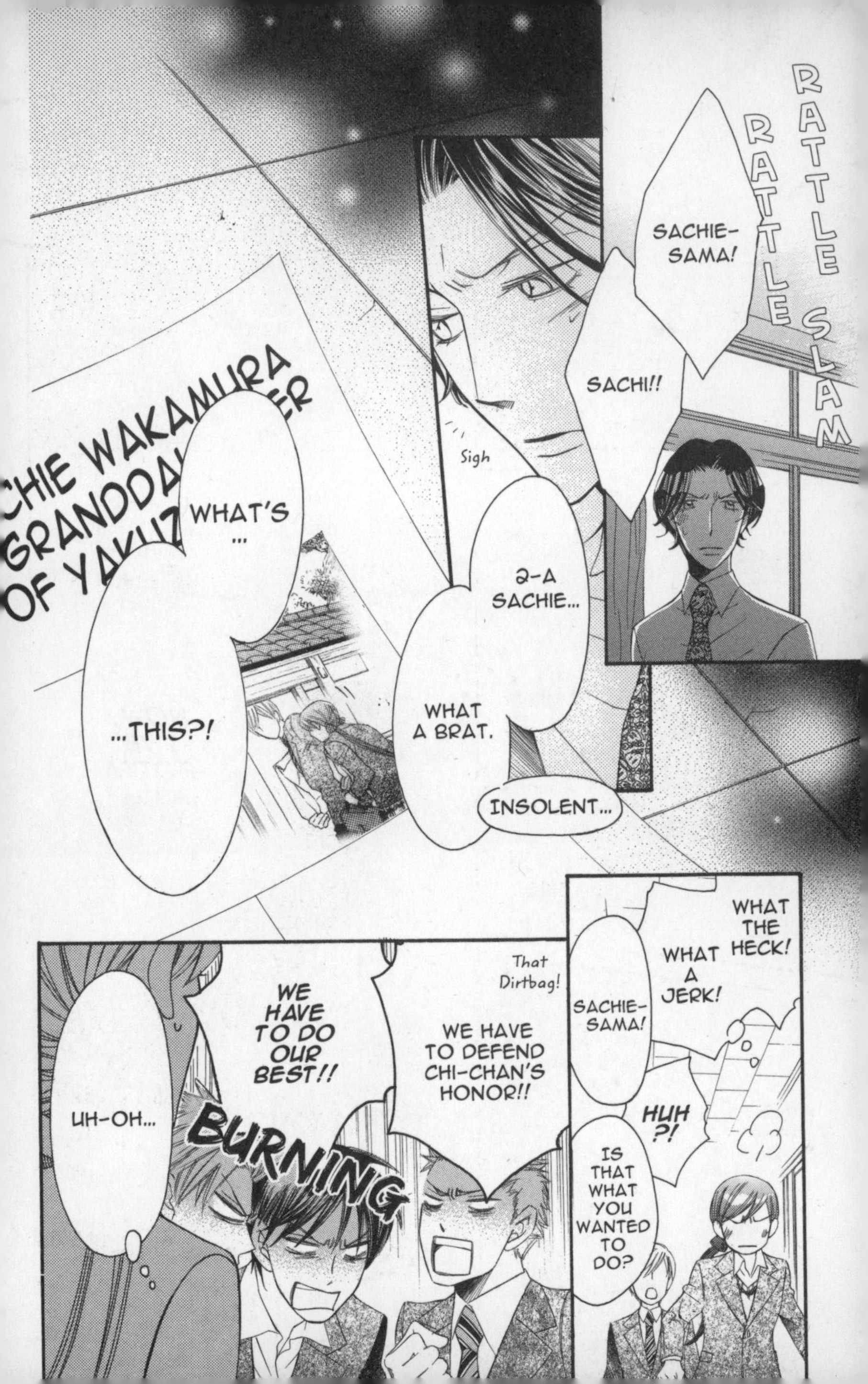
RATTLE RATTLE
SLAM
SACHIE-SAMA!
SACHI!!
Sigh
Q-A SACHIE...
WHAT A BRAT.
INSOLENT...
CHIE WAKAMURA
WHAT'S ...
...THIS?!
WHAT THE HECK!
WHAT A JERK!
SACHIE-SAMA!
HUH?!
IS THAT WHAT YOU WANTED TO DO?
That Dirtbag!
WE HAVE TO DEFEND CHI-CHAN'S HONOR!!
WE HAVE TO DO OUR BEST!!
BURNING
UH-OH...

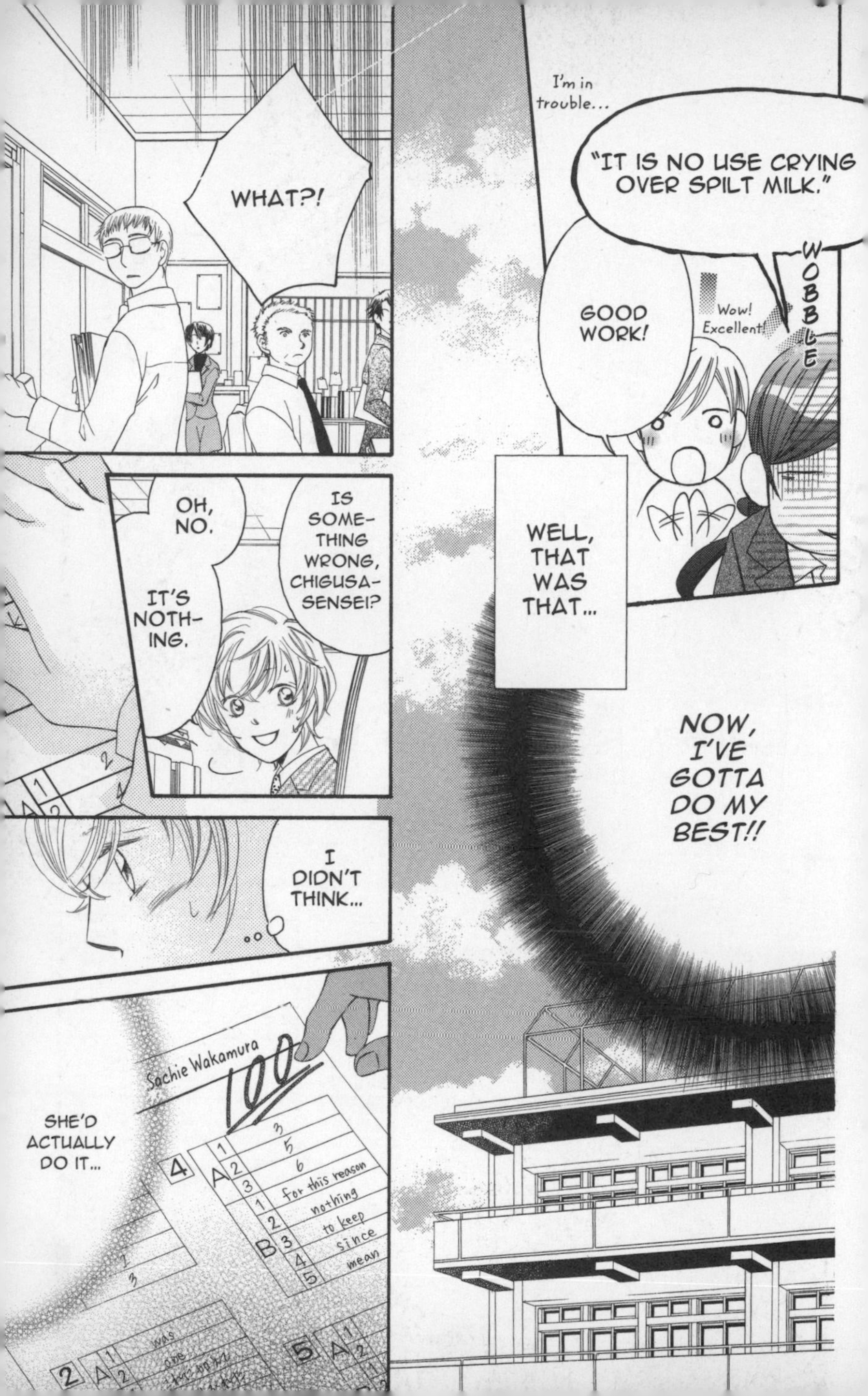

"IT IS NO USE CRYING OVER SPILT MILK."
I'm in trouble...
WOBBLE
Wow! Excellent!
GOOD WORK!
WELL, THAT WAS THAT...
NOW, I'VE GOTTA DO MY BEST!!
WHAT?!
IS SOMETHING WRONG, CHIGUSA-SENSEI?
OH, NO.
IT'S NOTHING.
I DIDN'T THINK...
SHE'D ACTUALLY DO IT...
Sachie Wakamura
100
for this reason
nothing
to keep
since
mean

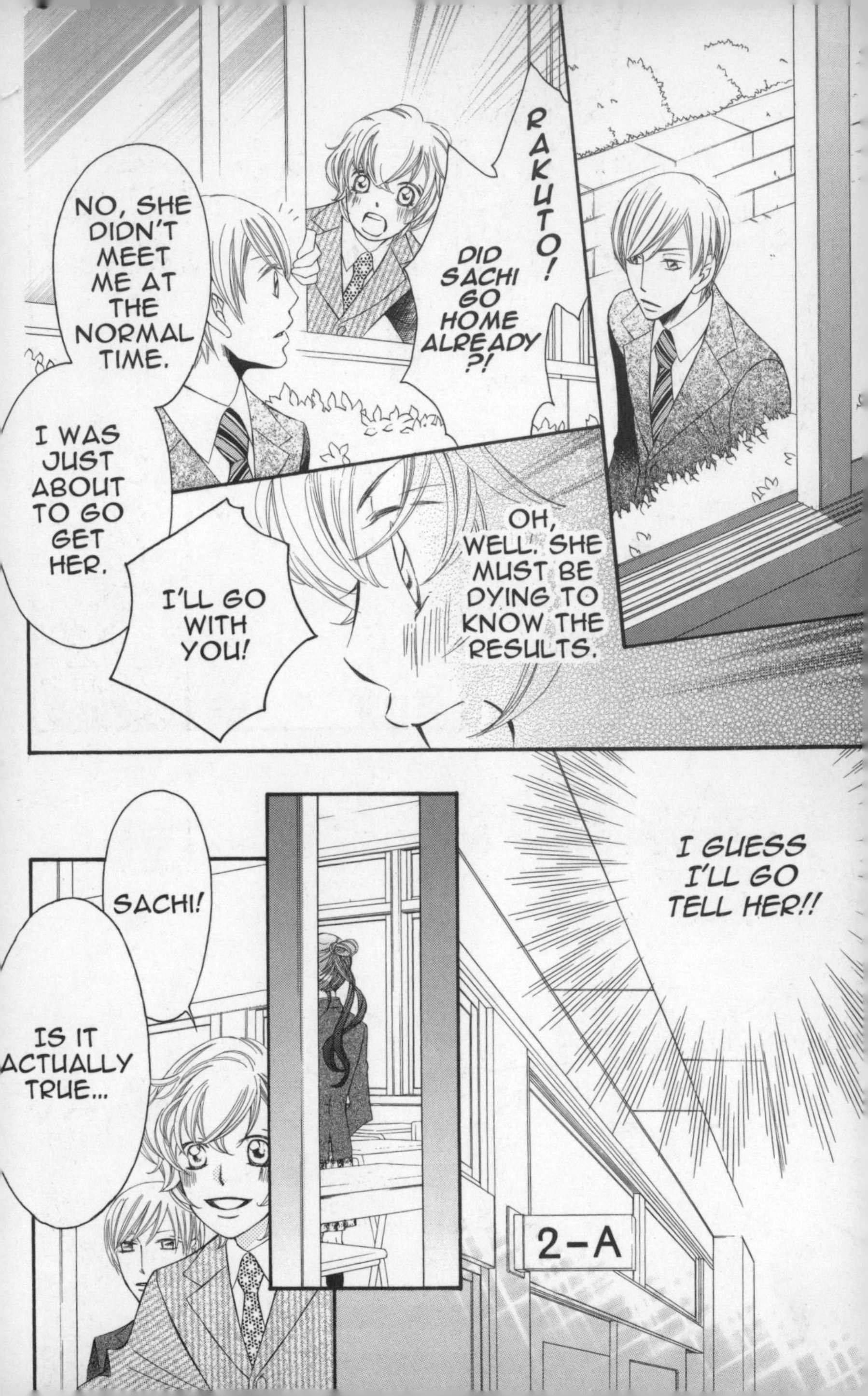
RAKUTO!
DID SACHI GO HOME ALREADY?!
NO, SHE DIDN'T MEET ME AT THE NORMAL TIME.
I WAS JUST ABOUT TO GO GET HER.
OH, WELL. SHE MUST BE DYING TO KNOW THE RESULTS.
I'LL GO WITH YOU!
I GUESS I'LL GO TELL HER!!
2-A
SACHI!
IS IT ACTUALLY TRUE...

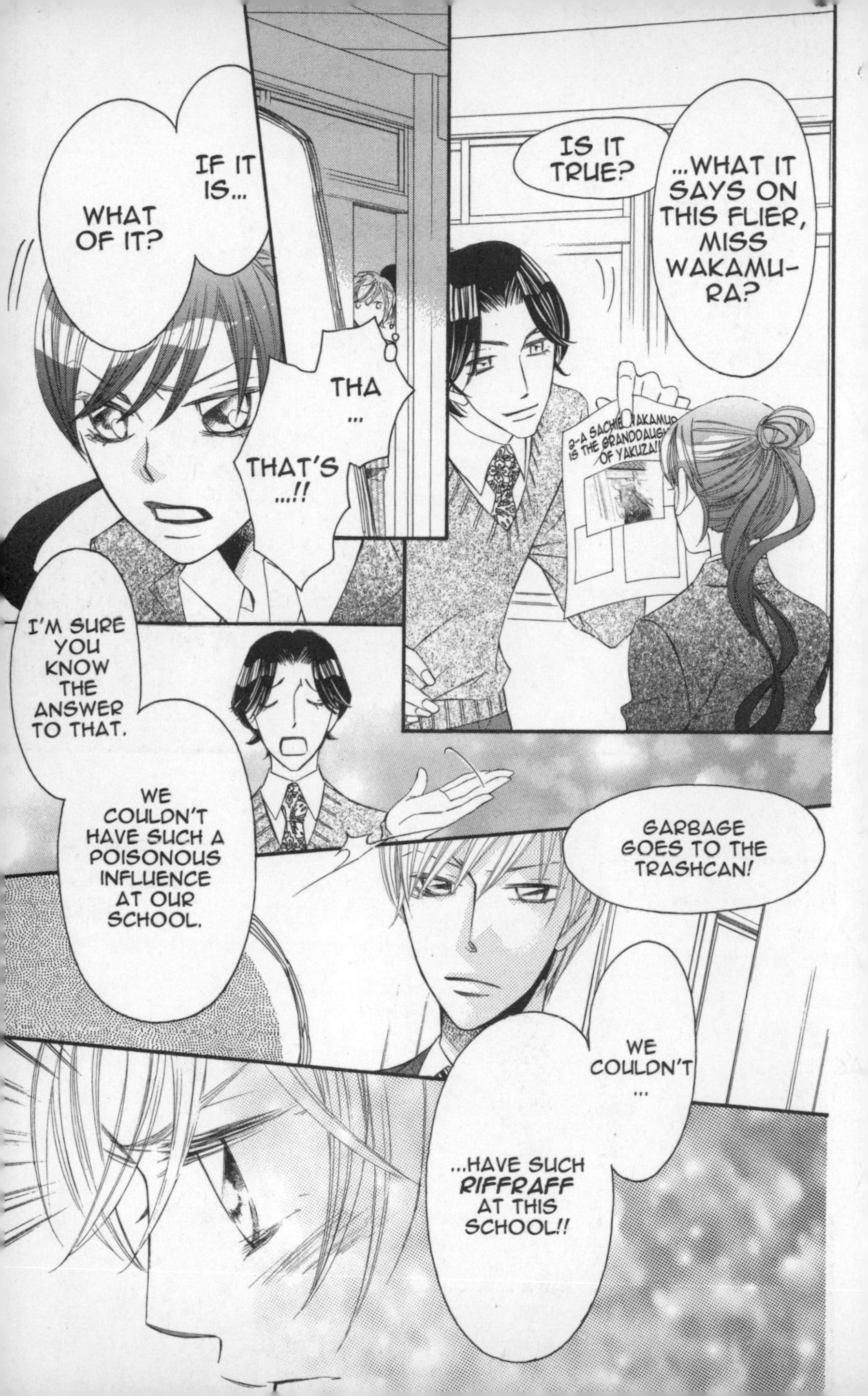
IS IT TRUE?
...WHAT IT SAYS ON THIS FLIER, MISS WAKAMU-RA?
OF YAKUZA!!
IF IT IS...
WHAT OF IT?
THA ...
THAT'S ...!!
I'M SURE YOU KNOW THE ANSWER TO THAT.
WE COULDN'T HAVE SUCH A POISONOUS INFLUENCE AT OUR SCHOOL.
GARBAGE GOES TO THE TRASHCAN!
WE COULDN'T ...
...HAVE SUCH RIFFRAFF AT THIS SCHOOL!!

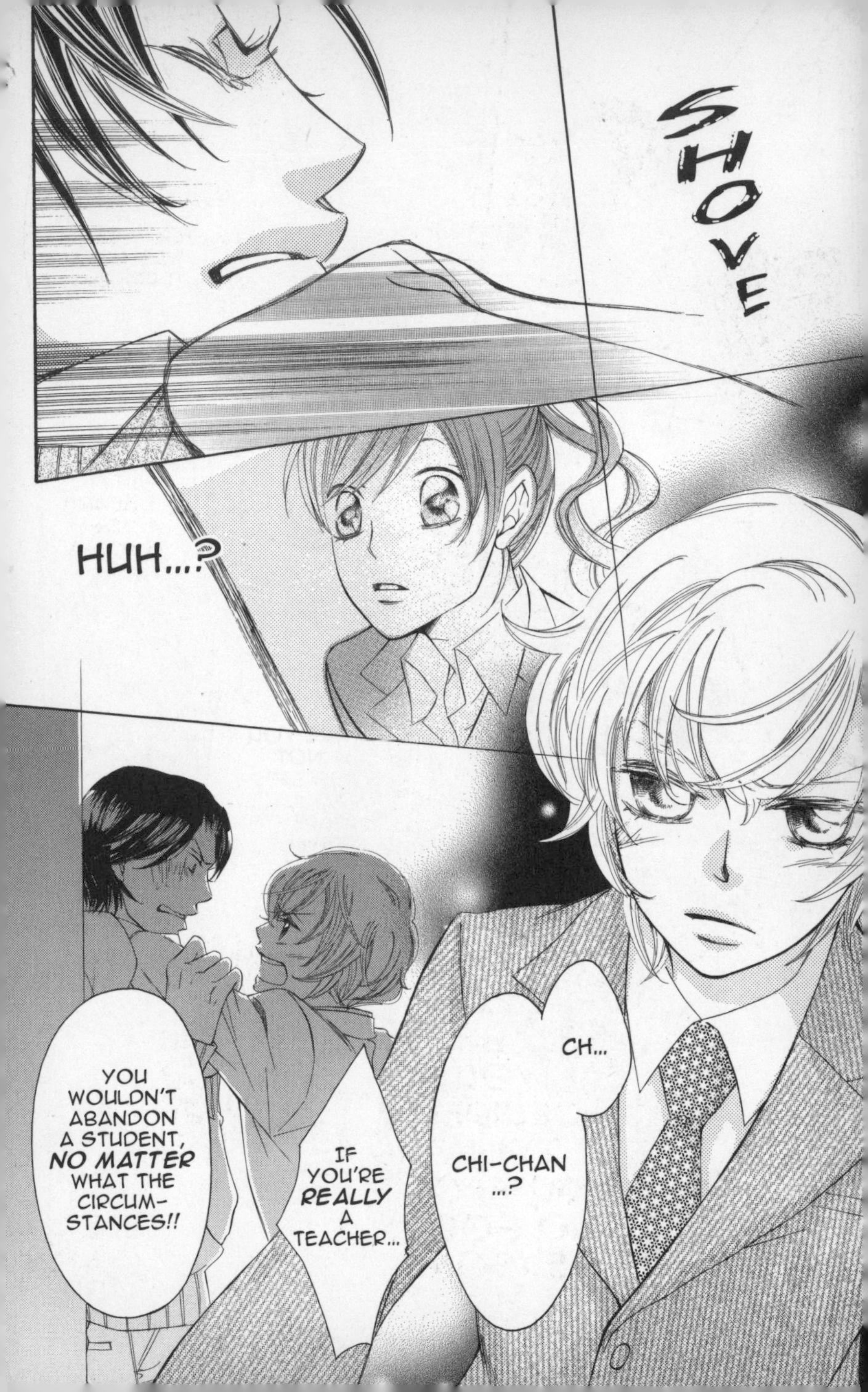
SHOVE
HUH...?
CH...
CHI-CHAN ...?
IF YOU'RE **REALLY** A TEACHER...
YOU WOULDN'T ABANDON A STUDENT, ***NO MATTER*** WHAT THE CIRCUM- STANCES!!

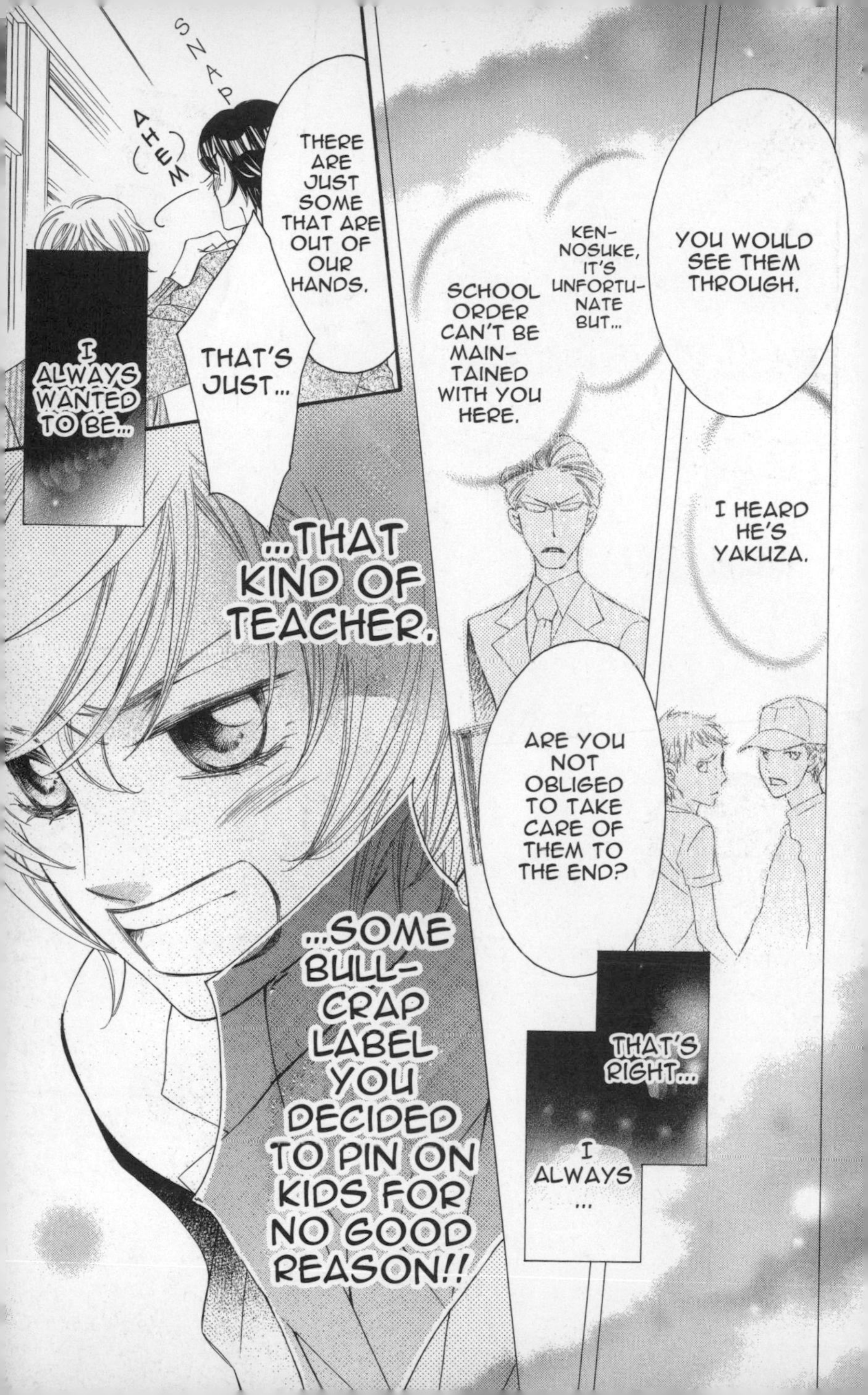
YOU WOULD SEE THEM THROUGH.
I HEARD HE'S YAKUZA.
ARE YOU NOT OBLIGED TO TAKE CARE OF THEM TO THE END?
THAT'S RIGHT...
I ALWAYS ...
KEN-NOSUKE, IT'S UNFORTUNATE BUT...
SCHOOL ORDER CAN'T BE MAINTAINED WITH YOU HERE.
SNAP
AHEM
THERE ARE JUST SOME THAT ARE OUT OF OUR HANDS.
THAT'S JUST...
I ALWAYS WANTED TO BE...
...THAT KIND OF TEACHER.
...SOME BULL-CRAP LABEL YOU DECIDED TO PIN ON KIDS FOR NO GOOD REASON!!

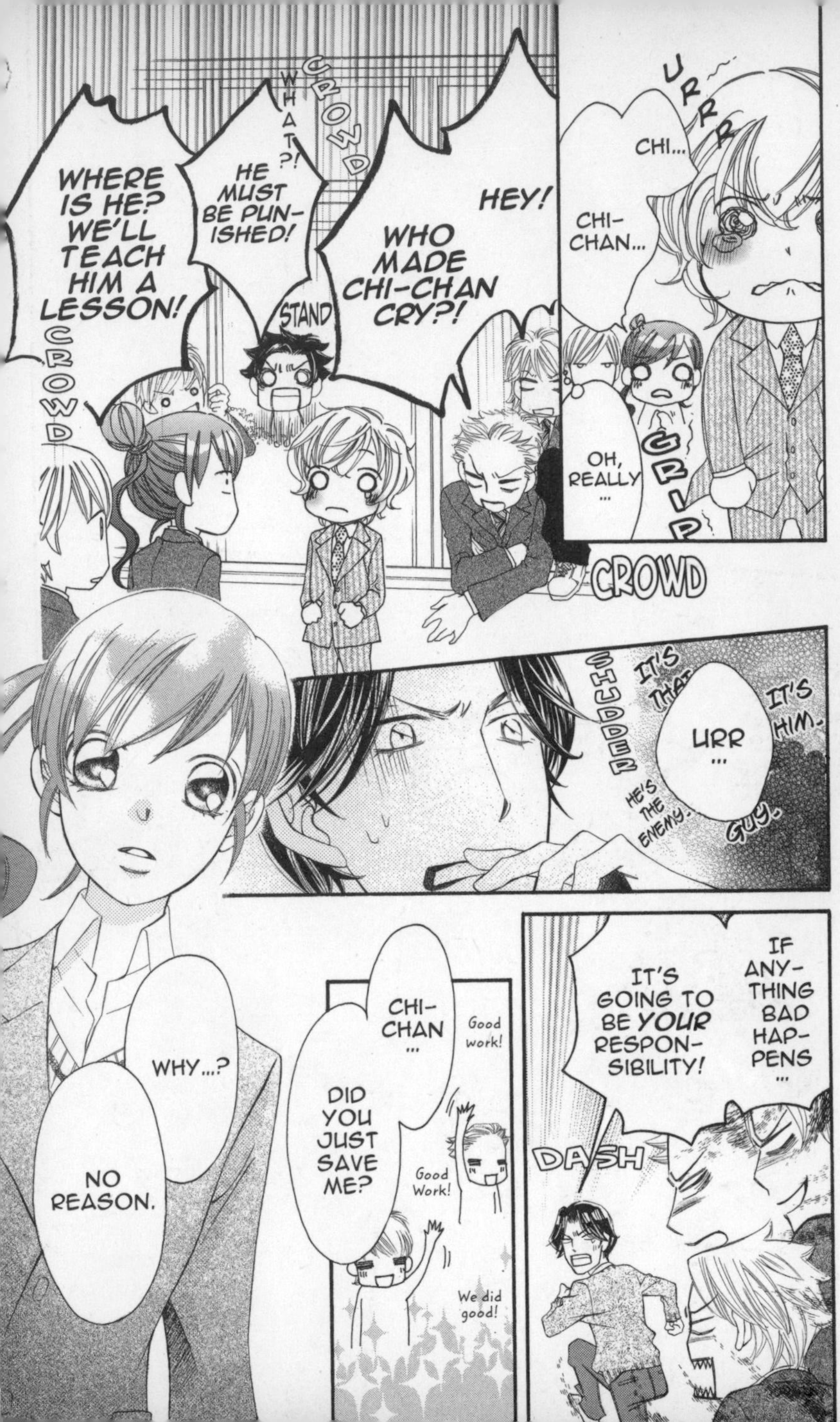
URRR~
CHI...
CHI-CHAN...
OH, REALLY...
GRIP
HEY!
WHO MADE CHI-CHAN CRY?!
CROWD
WHAT?!
HE MUST BE PUN-ISHED!
STAND
WHERE IS HE? WE'LL TEACH HIM A LESSON!
CROWD
CROWD
IT'S HIM.
URR ...
IT'S THAT GUY.
SHUDDER
HE'S THE ENEMY.
IF ANYTHING BAD HAPPENS ...
IT'S GOING TO BE *YOUR* RESPONSIBILITY!
DASH
CHI-CHAN ...
Good work!
DID YOU JUST SAVE ME?
Good Work!
We did good!
WHY...?
NO REASON.

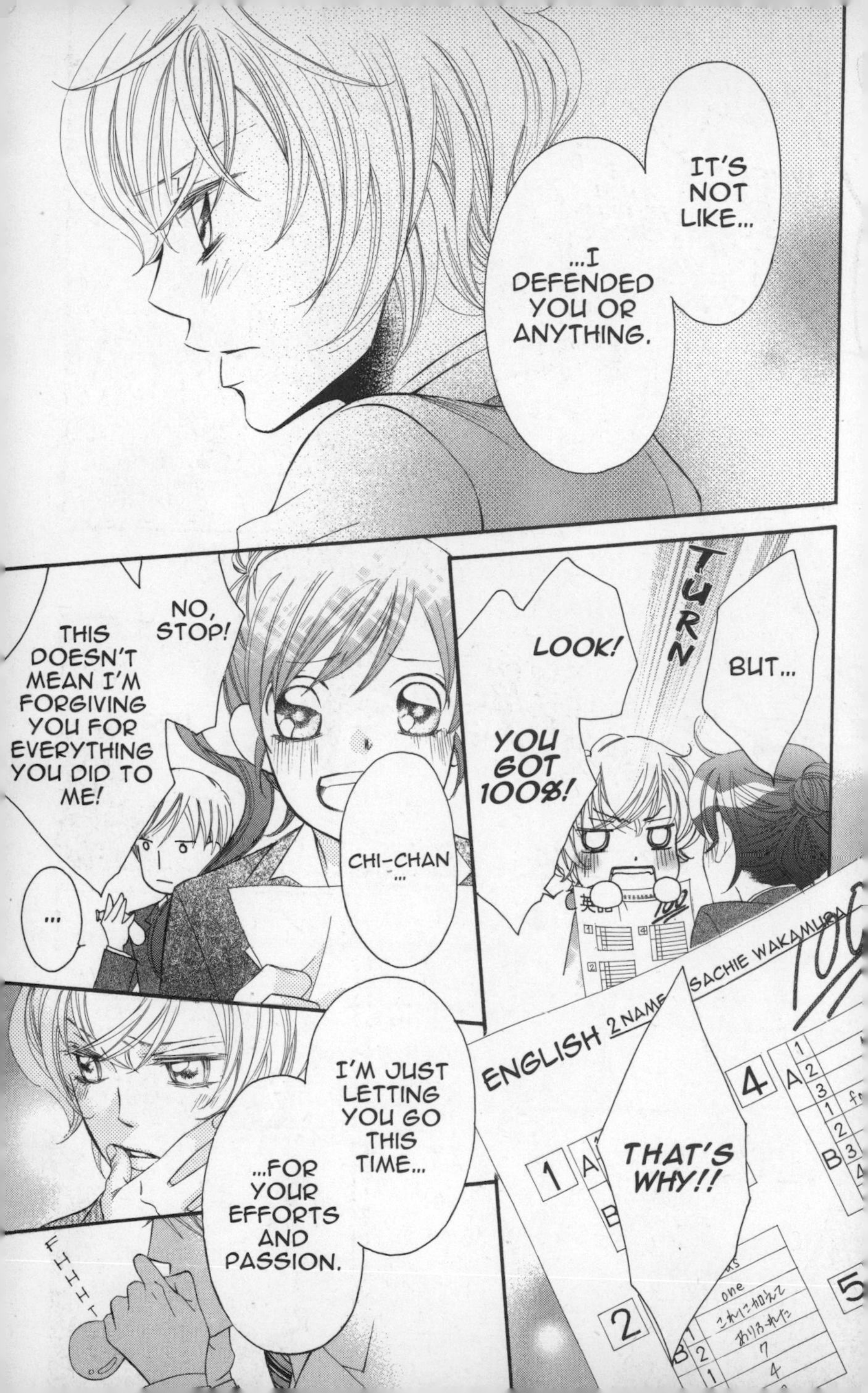

IT'S NOT LIKE...
...I DEFENDED YOU OR ANYTHING.
TURN
BUT...
LOOK!
YOU GOT 100%!
NO, STOP!
THIS DOESN'T MEAN I'M FORGIVING YOU FOR EVERYTHING YOU DID TO ME!
CHI-CHAN...
...
ENGLISH 2 NAME SACHIE WAKAMURA
THAT'S WHY!!
I'M JUST LETTING YOU GO THIS TIME...
...FOR YOUR EFFORTS AND PASSION.
FHHHT

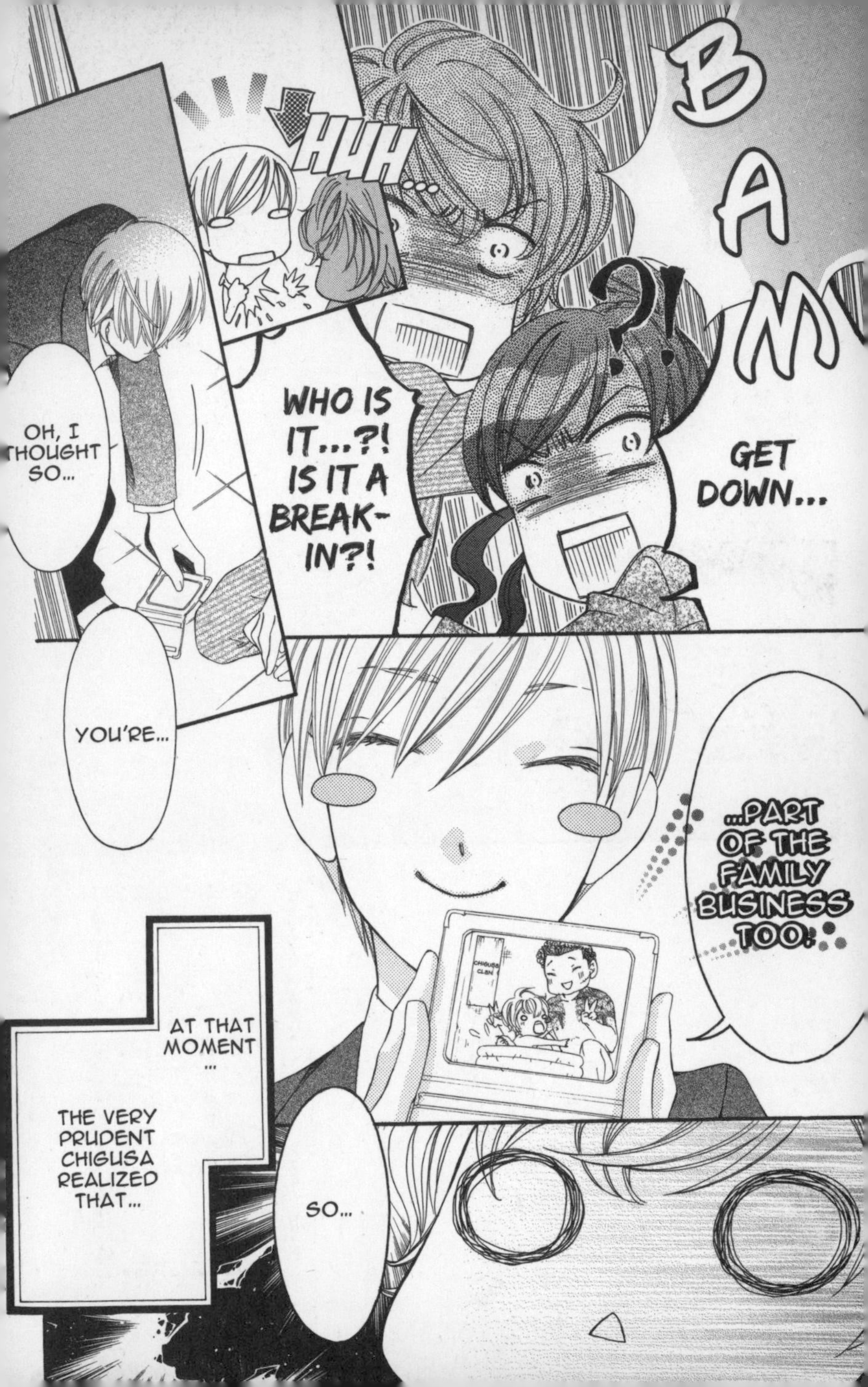
BAM
?!
GET DOWN...
WHO IS IT...?! IS IT A BREAK-IN?!
HUH...
OH, I THOUGHT SO...
YOU'RE...
...PART OF THE FAMILY BUSINESS TOO.
CHIGUSA CLAN
SO...
AT THAT MOMENT...
THE VERY PRUDENT CHIGUSA REALIZED THAT...

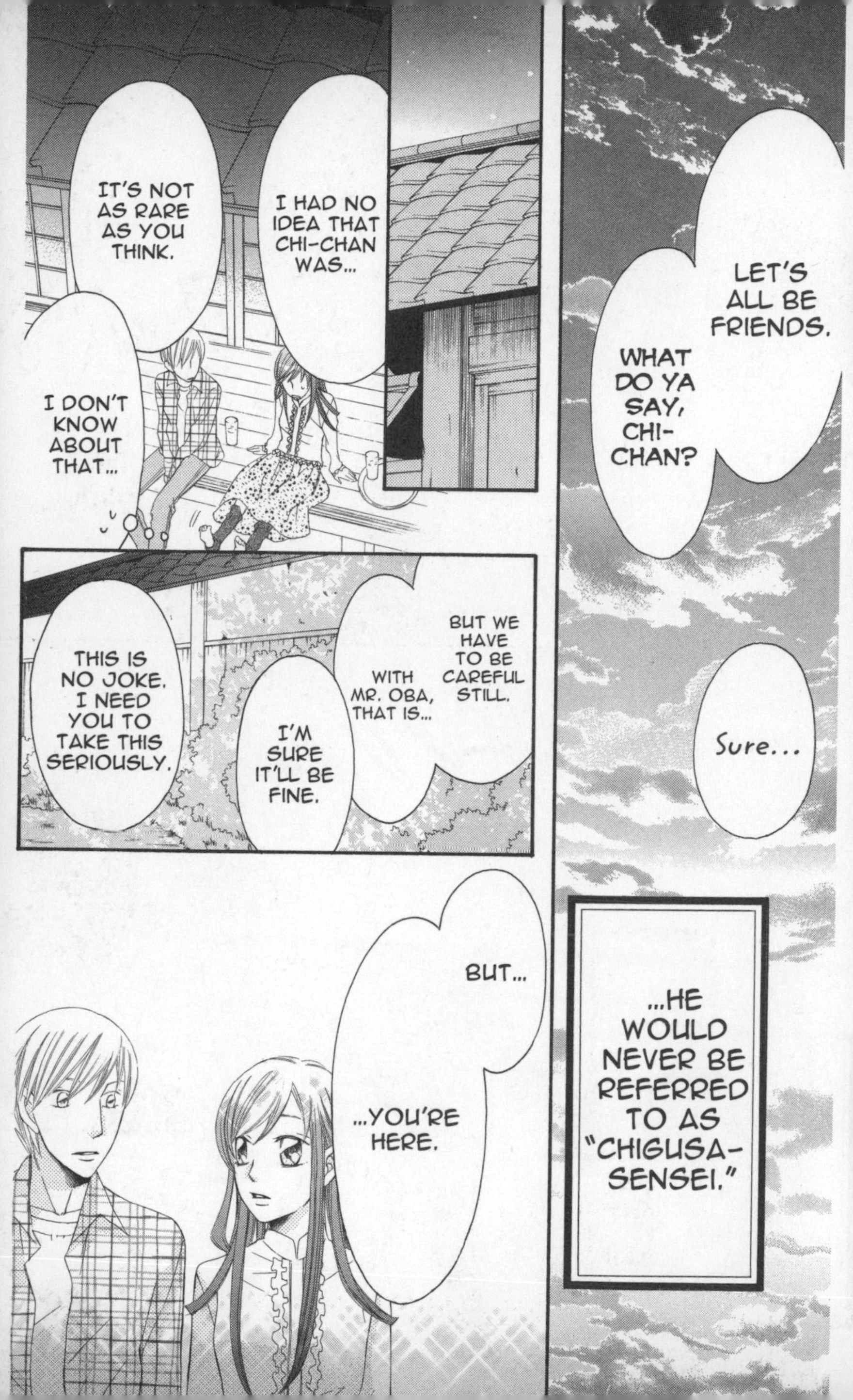
LET'S ALL BE FRIENDS.
WHAT DO YA SAY, CHI-CHAN?
Sure...
...HE WOULD NEVER BE REFERRED TO AS "CHIGUSA-SENSEI."
I HAD NO IDEA THAT CHI-CHAN WAS...
IT'S NOT AS RARE AS YOU THINK.
I DON'T KNOW ABOUT THAT...
BUT WE HAVE TO BE CAREFUL STILL.
WITH MR. OBA, THAT IS...
I'M SURE IT'LL BE FINE.
THIS IS NO JOKE. I NEED YOU TO TAKE THIS SERIOUSLY.
BUT...
...YOU'RE HERE.

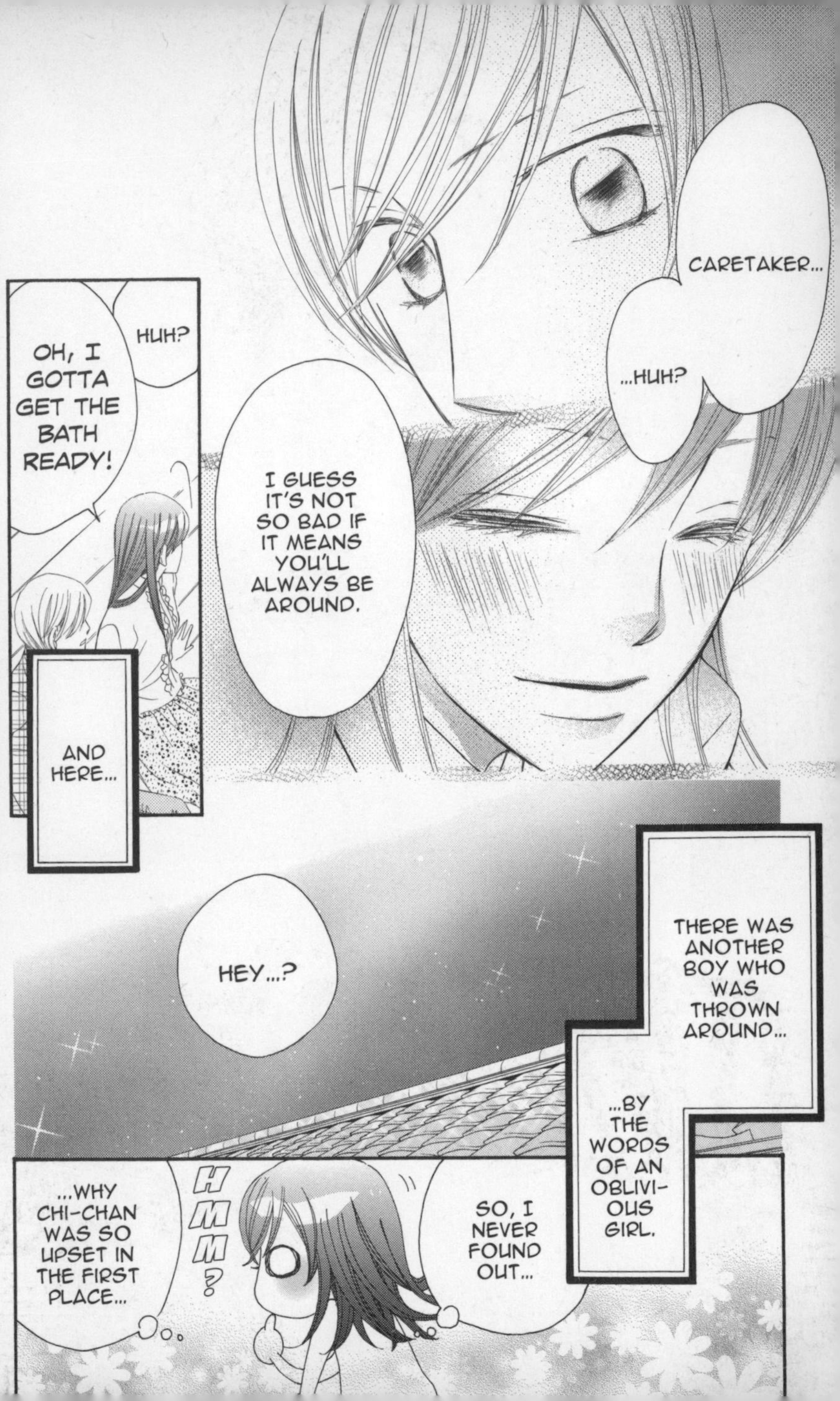
CARETAKER...
...HUH?
I GUESS IT'S NOT SO BAD IF IT MEANS YOU'LL ALWAYS BE AROUND.
HUH?
OH, I GOTTA GET THE BATH READY!
AND HERE...
THERE WAS ANOTHER BOY WHO WAS THROWN AROUND...
HEY...?
...BY THE WORDS OF AN OBLIVIOUS GIRL.
SO, I NEVER FOUND OUT...
HMM?
...WHY CHI-CHAN WAS SO UPSET IN THE FIRST PLACE...

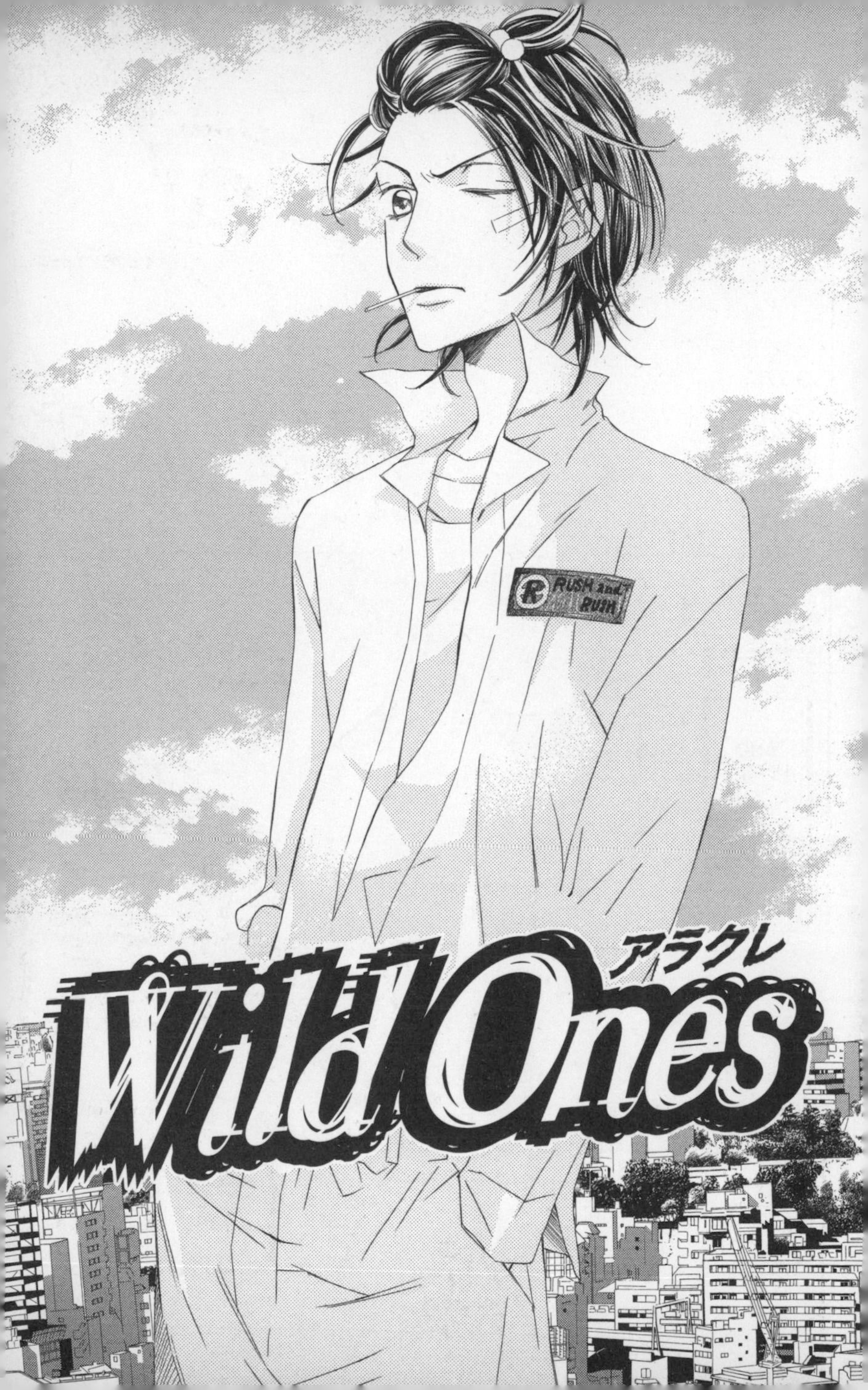
RUSH and RUSH
アラクレ
Wild Ones

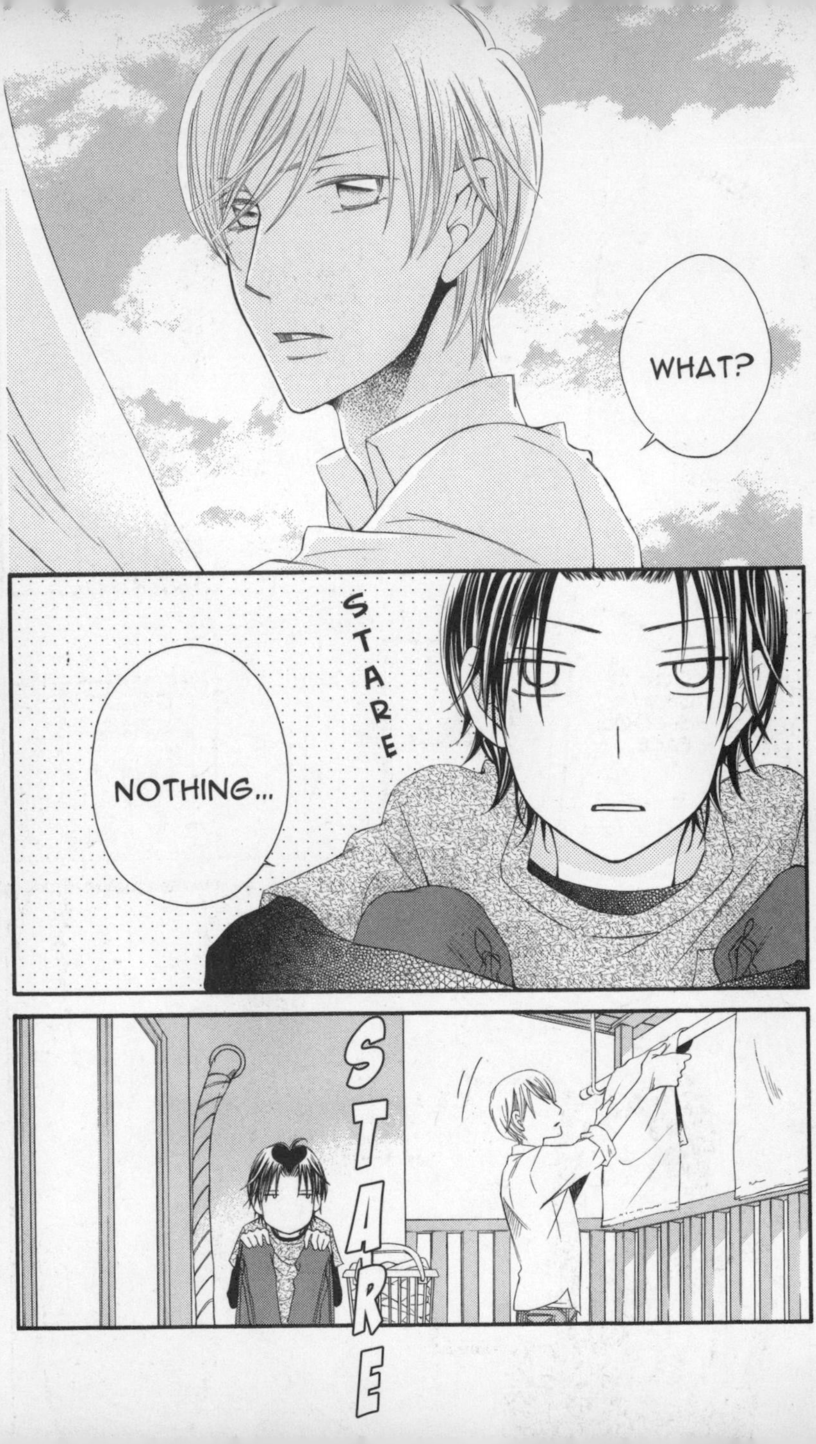
WHAT?
STARE
NOTHING...
STARE

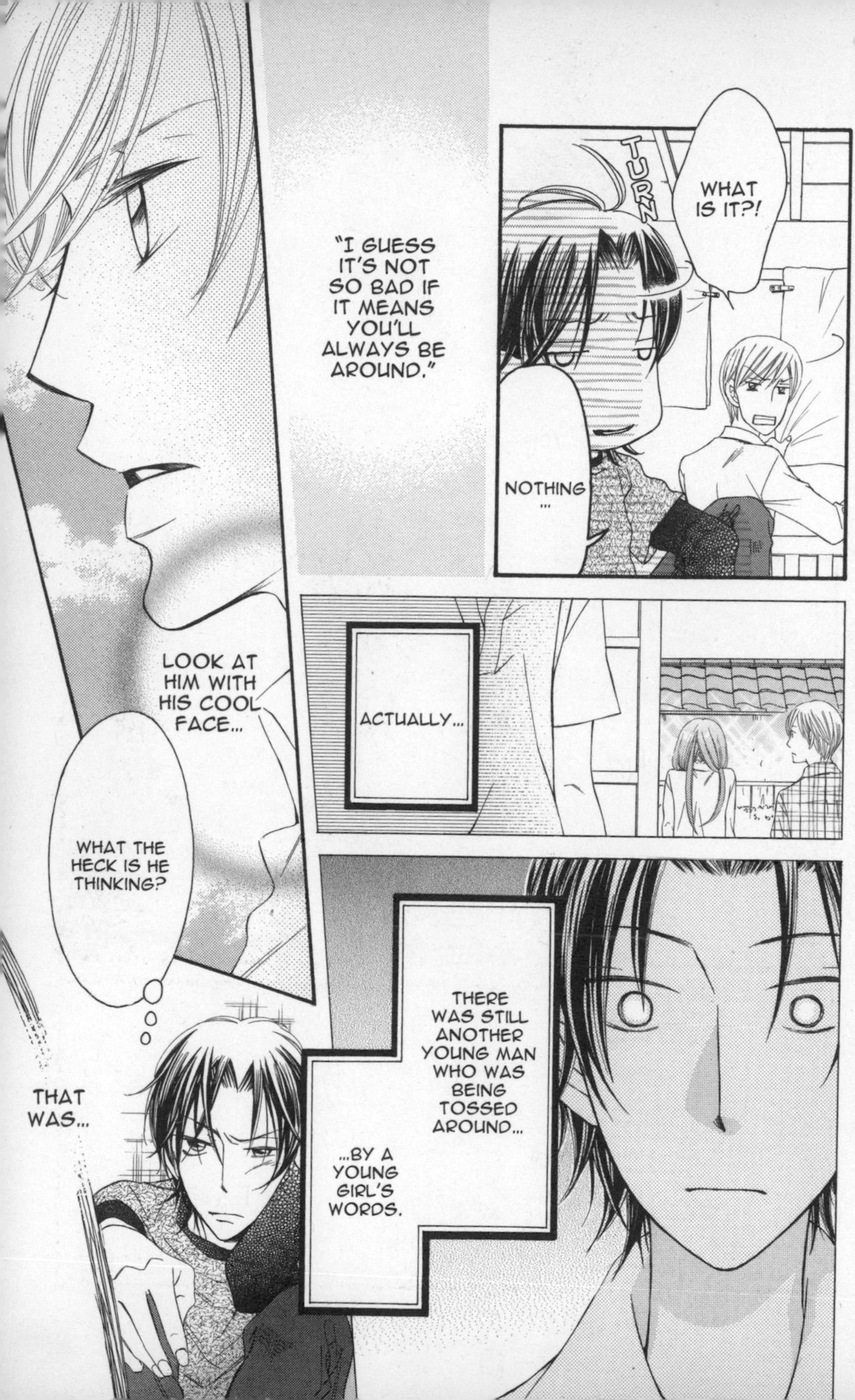
TURN
WHAT IS IT?!
NOTHING...
"I GUESS IT'S NOT SO BAD IF IT MEANS YOU'LL ALWAYS BE AROUND."
LOOK AT HIM WITH HIS COOL FACE...
WHAT THE HECK IS HE THINKING?
THAT WAS...
ACTUALLY...
THERE WAS STILL ANOTHER YOUNG MAN WHO WAS BEING TOSSED AROUND...
...BY A YOUNG GIRL'S WORDS.

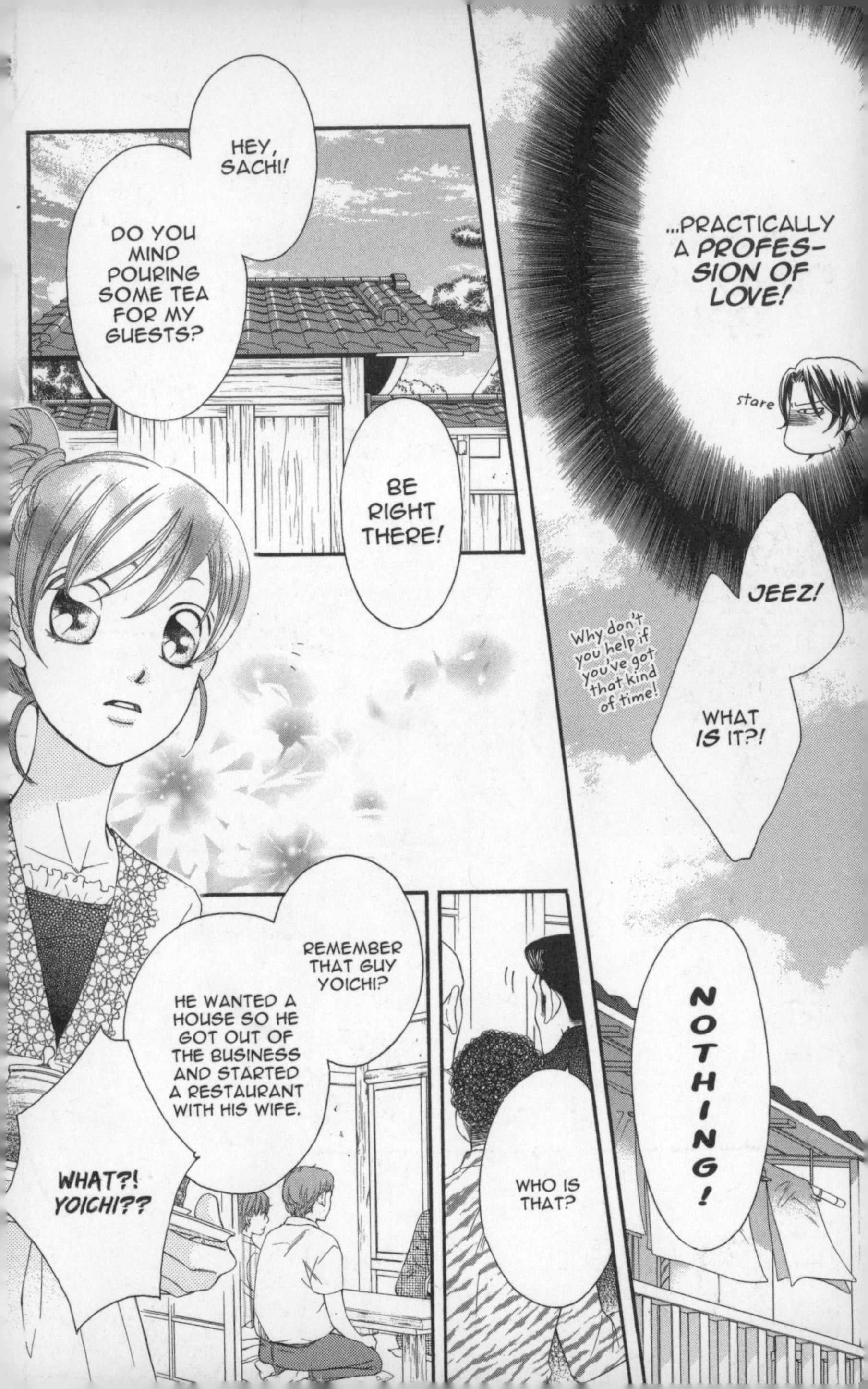
...PRACTICALLY A PROFES- SION OF LOVE!
stare
JEEZ!
Why don't you help if you've got that kind of time!
WHAT IS IT?!
NOTHING!
HEY, SACHI!
DO YOU MIND POURING SOME TEA FOR MY GUESTS?
BE RIGHT THERE!
WHO IS THAT?
REMEMBER THAT GUY YOICHI?
HE WANTED A HOUSE SO HE GOT OUT OF THE BUSINESS AND STARTED A RESTAURANT WITH HIS WIFE.
WHAT?! YOICHI??

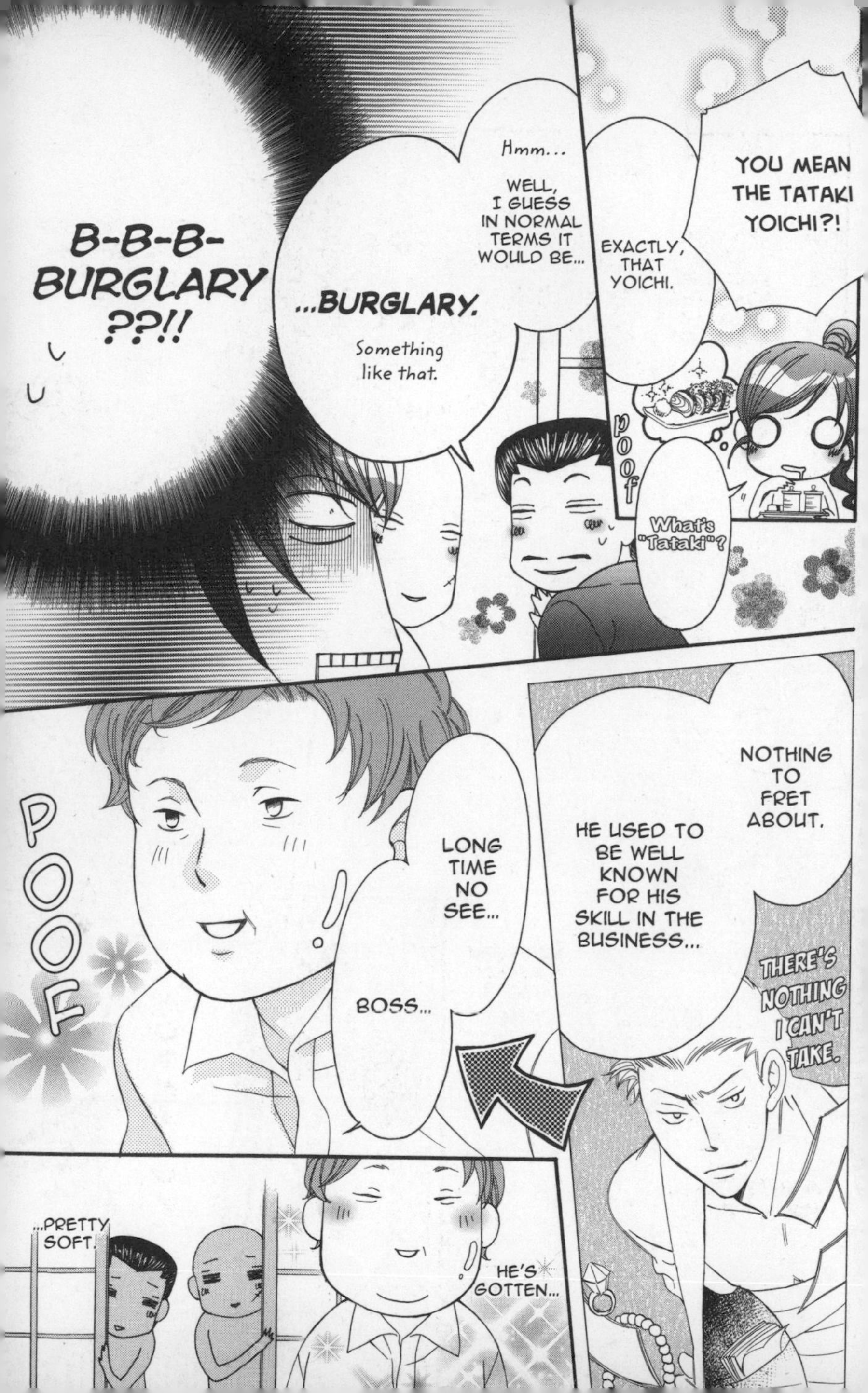
YOU MEAN THE TATAKI YOICHI?!
EXACTLY, THAT YOICHI.
poof
What's "Tataki"?
Hmm...
WELL, I GUESS IN NORMAL TERMS IT WOULD BE...
...BURGLARY.
Something like that.
B-B-B-BURGLARY??!!
NOTHING TO FRET ABOUT.
HE USED TO BE WELL KNOWN FOR HIS SKILL IN THE BUSINESS...
THERE'S NOTHING I CAN'T TAKE.
LONG TIME NO SEE...
BOSS...
POOF
HE'S GOTTEN...
...PRETTY SOFT!

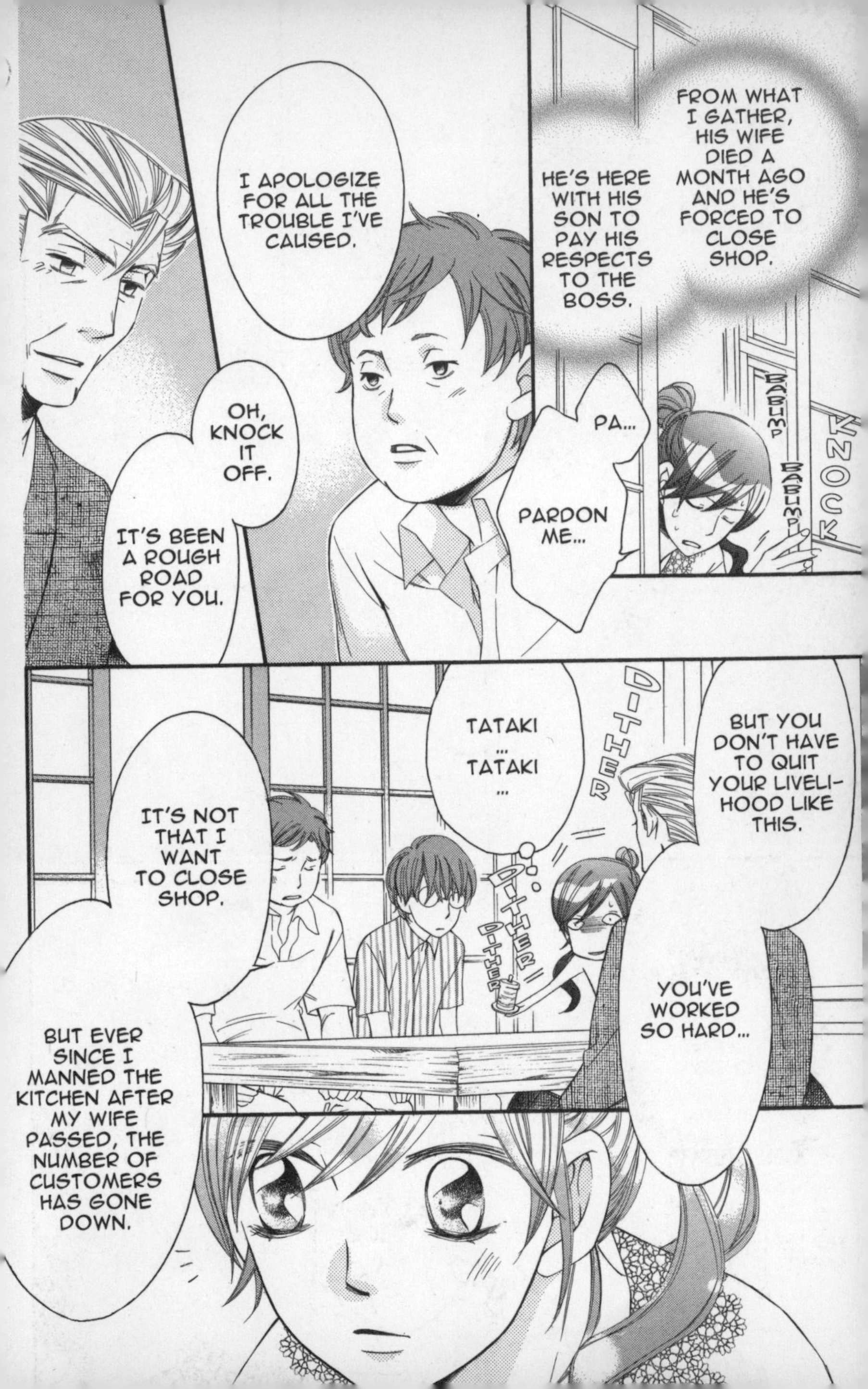
FROM WHAT I GATHER, HIS WIFE DIED A MONTH AGO AND HE'S FORCED TO CLOSE SHOP.
HE'S HERE WITH HIS SON TO PAY HIS RESPECTS TO THE BOSS.
KNOCK
BABUMP
BABUMP
PA...
PARDON ME...
I APOLOGIZE FOR ALL THE TROUBLE I'VE CAUSED.
OH, KNOCK IT OFF.
IT'S BEEN A ROUGH ROAD FOR YOU.
BUT YOU DON'T HAVE TO QUIT YOUR LIVELIHOOD LIKE THIS.
DITHER
TATAKI ... TATAKI ...
YOU'VE WORKED SO HARD...
DITHER
DITHER
IT'S NOT THAT I WANT TO CLOSE SHOP.
BUT EVER SINCE I MANNED THE KITCHEN AFTER MY WIFE PASSED, THE NUMBER OF CUSTOMERS HAS GONE DOWN.

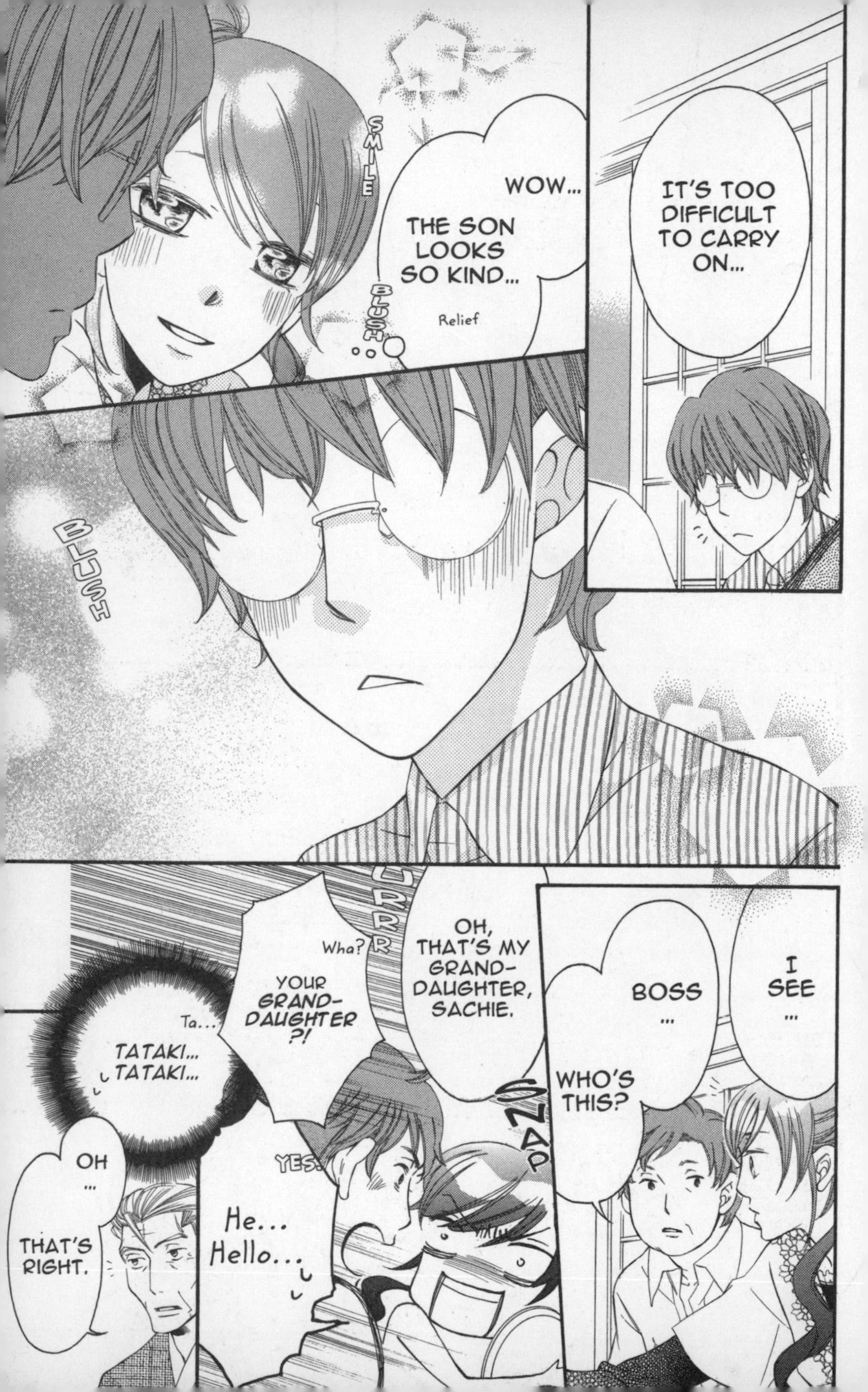
IT'S TOO DIFFICULT TO CARRY ON...
SMILE
WOW...
THE SON LOOKS SO KIND...
BLUSH
Relief
BLUSH
I SEE...
BOSS...
WHO'S THIS?
OH, THAT'S MY GRAND-DAUGHTER, SACHIE.
URRR
SNAP
Wha?
YOUR GRAND-DAUGHTER?!
YES!
He... Hello...
Ta...
TATAKI... TATAKI...
OH... THAT'S RIGHT.

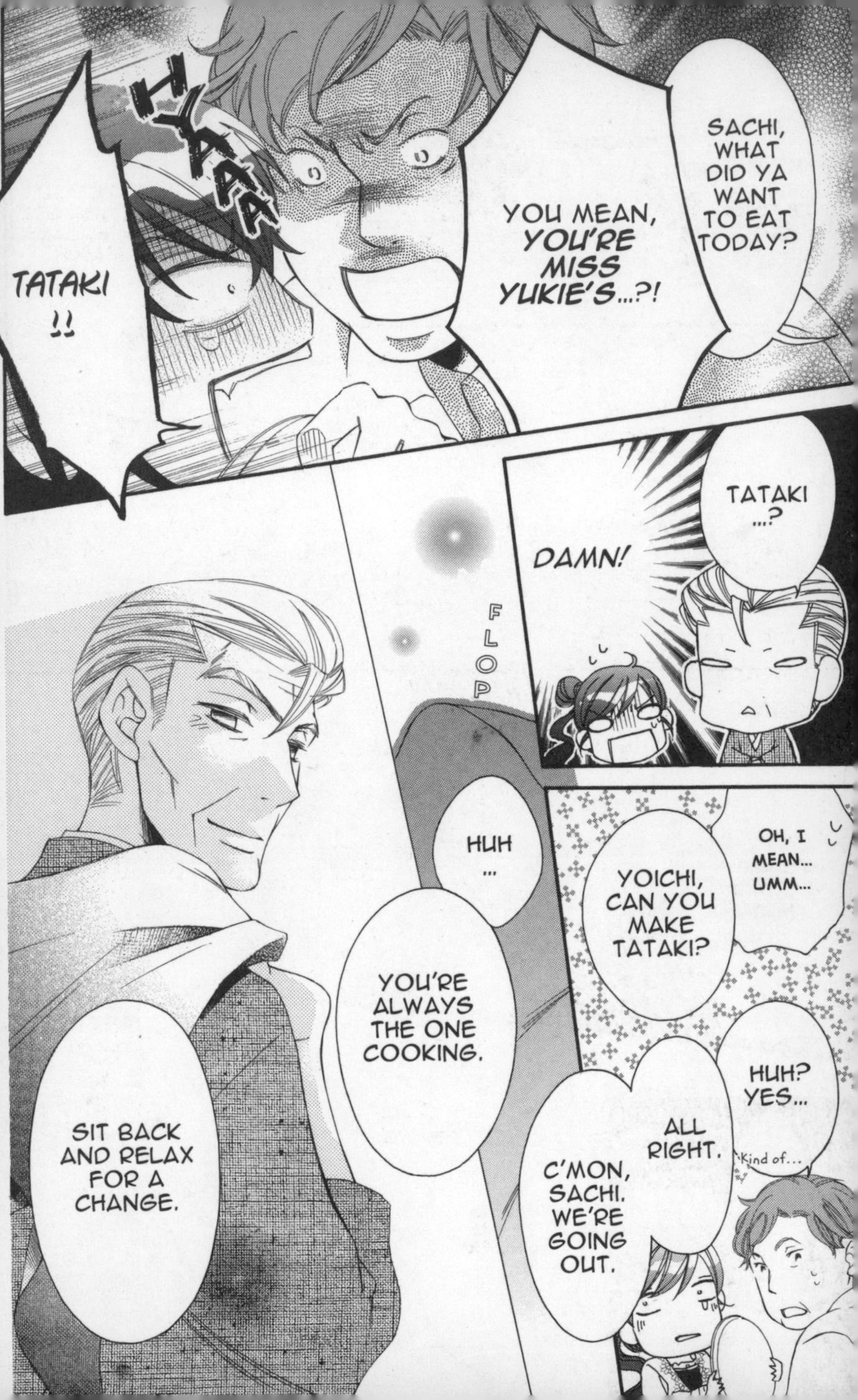
SACHI, WHAT DID YA WANT TO EAT TODAY?
YOU MEAN, YOU'RE MISS YUKIE'S...?!
HYAAA
TATAKI !!
TATAKI ...?
DAMN!
OH, I MEAN... UMM...
YOICHI, CAN YOU MAKE TATAKI?
HUH? YES...
Kind of...
ALL RIGHT.
C'MON, SACHI. WE'RE GOING OUT.
FLOP
HUH ...
YOU'RE ALWAYS THE ONE COOKING.
SIT BACK AND RELAX FOR A CHANGE.

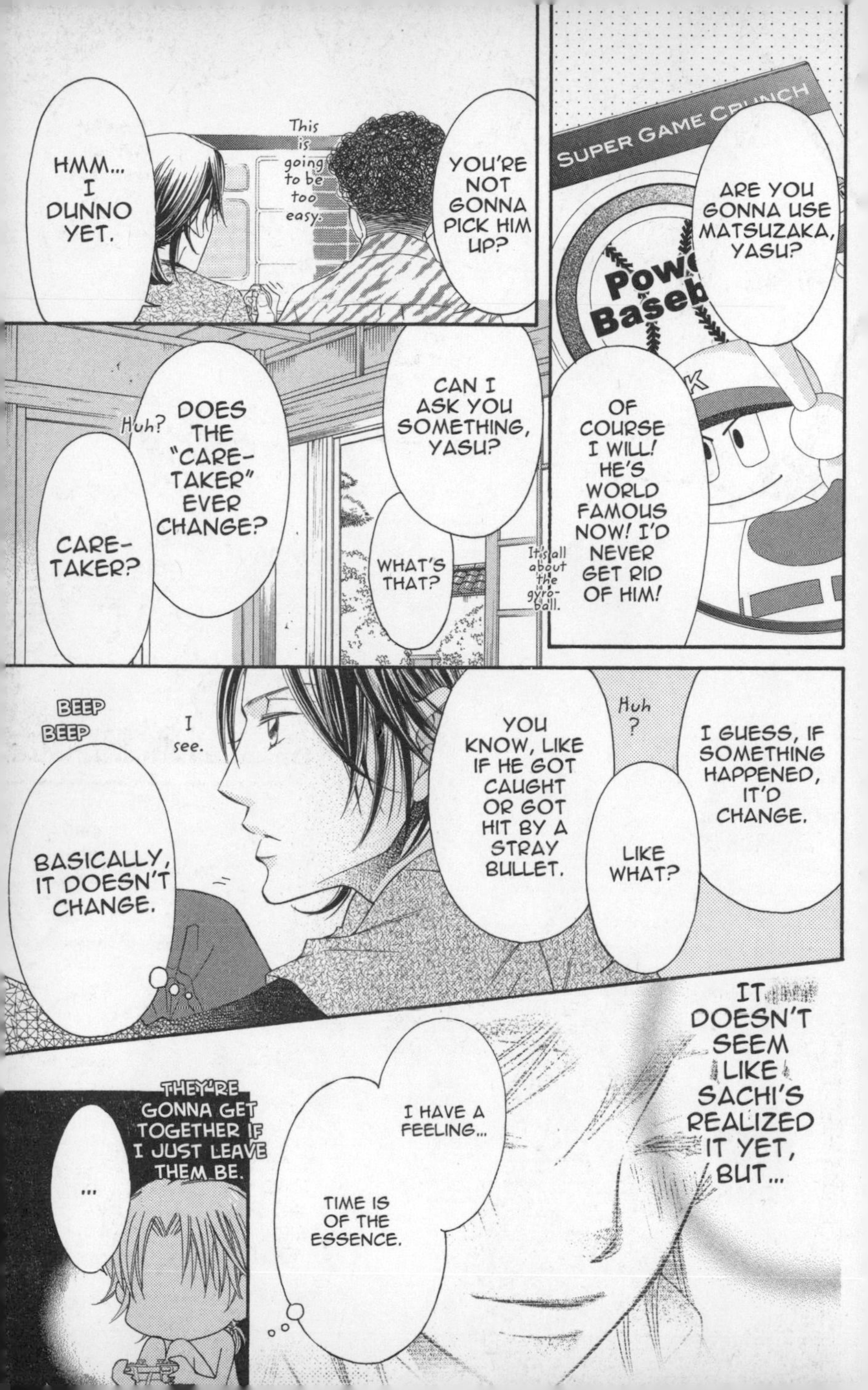
SUPER GAME CRUNCH
ARE YOU GONNA USE MATSUZAKA, YASU?
OF COURSE I WILL! HE'S WORLD FAMOUS NOW! I'D NEVER GET RID OF HIM!
It's all about the gyro-ball.
YOU'RE NOT GONNA PICK HIM UP?
This is going to be too easy.
HMM... I DUNNO YET.
CAN I ASK YOU SOMETHING, YASU?
WHAT'S THAT?
DOES THE "CARE-TAKER" EVER CHANGE?
Huh?
CARE-TAKER?
I GUESS, IF SOMETHING HAPPENED, IT'D CHANGE.
Huh?
LIKE WHAT?
YOU KNOW, LIKE IF HE GOT CAUGHT OR GOT HIT BY A STRAY BULLET.
I see.
BEEP BEEP
BASICALLY, IT DOESN'T CHANGE.
IT DOESN'T SEEM LIKE SACHI'S REALIZED IT YET, BUT...
I HAVE A FEELING...
TIME IS OF THE ESSENCE.
THEY'RE GONNA GET TOGETHER IF I JUST LEAVE THEM BE.
...

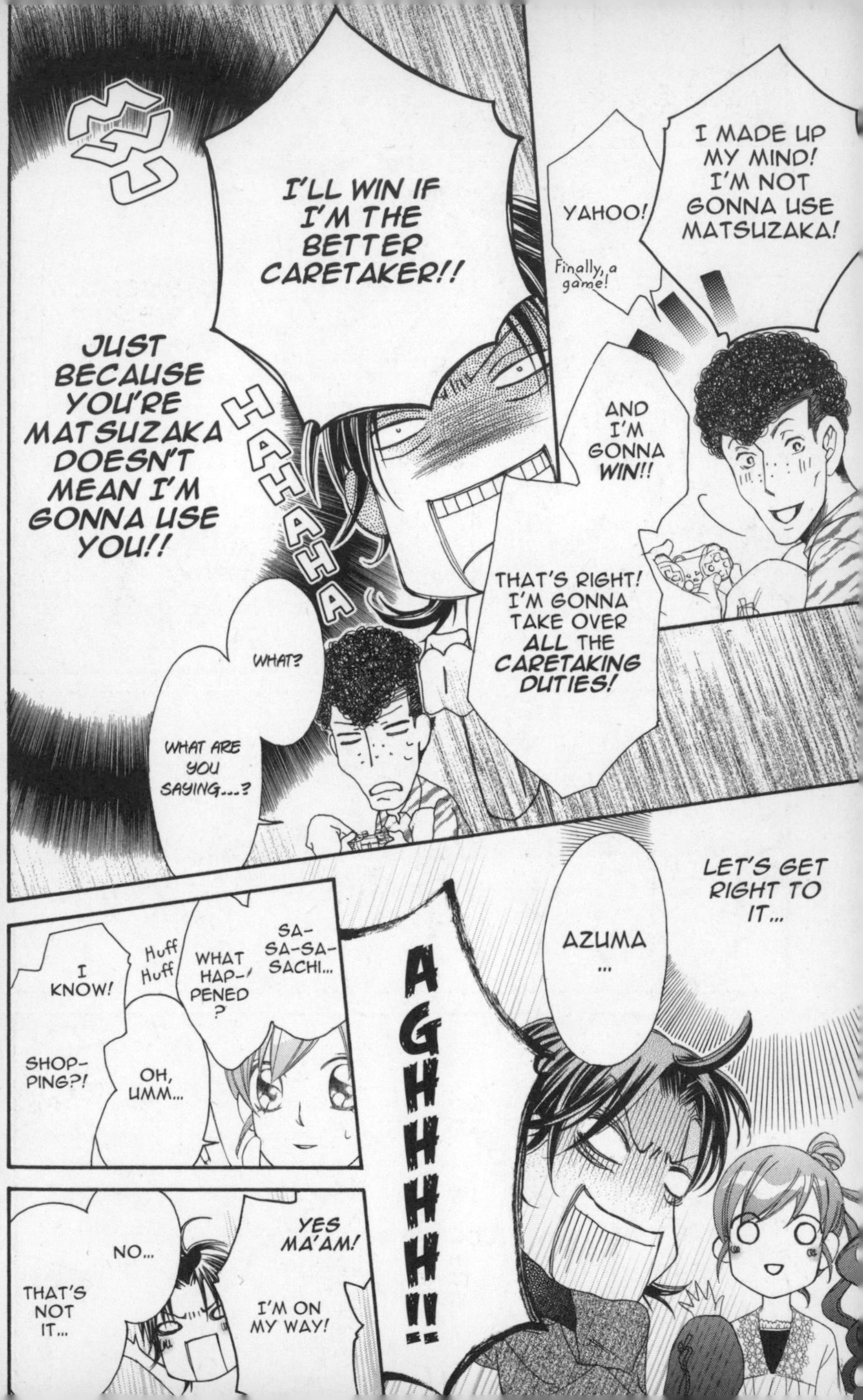
I MADE UP MY MIND! I'M NOT GONNA USE MATSUZAKA!
YAHOO!
Finally, a game!
AND I'M GONNA WIN!!
I'LL WIN IF I'M THE BETTER CARETAKER!!
HAHAHAHA
JUST BECAUSE YOU'RE MATSUZAKA DOESN'T MEAN I'M GONNA USE YOU!!
THAT'S RIGHT! I'M GONNA TAKE OVER ALL THE CARETAKING DUTIES!
WHAT?
WHAT ARE YOU SAYING...?
LET'S GET RIGHT TO IT...
AZUMA...
AGHHHHH!!
SA-SA-SA-SACHI...
WHAT HAPPENED?
Huff Huff
I KNOW!
OH, UMM...
SHOPPING?!
YES MA'AM!
NO...
I'M ON MY WAY!
THAT'S NOT IT...

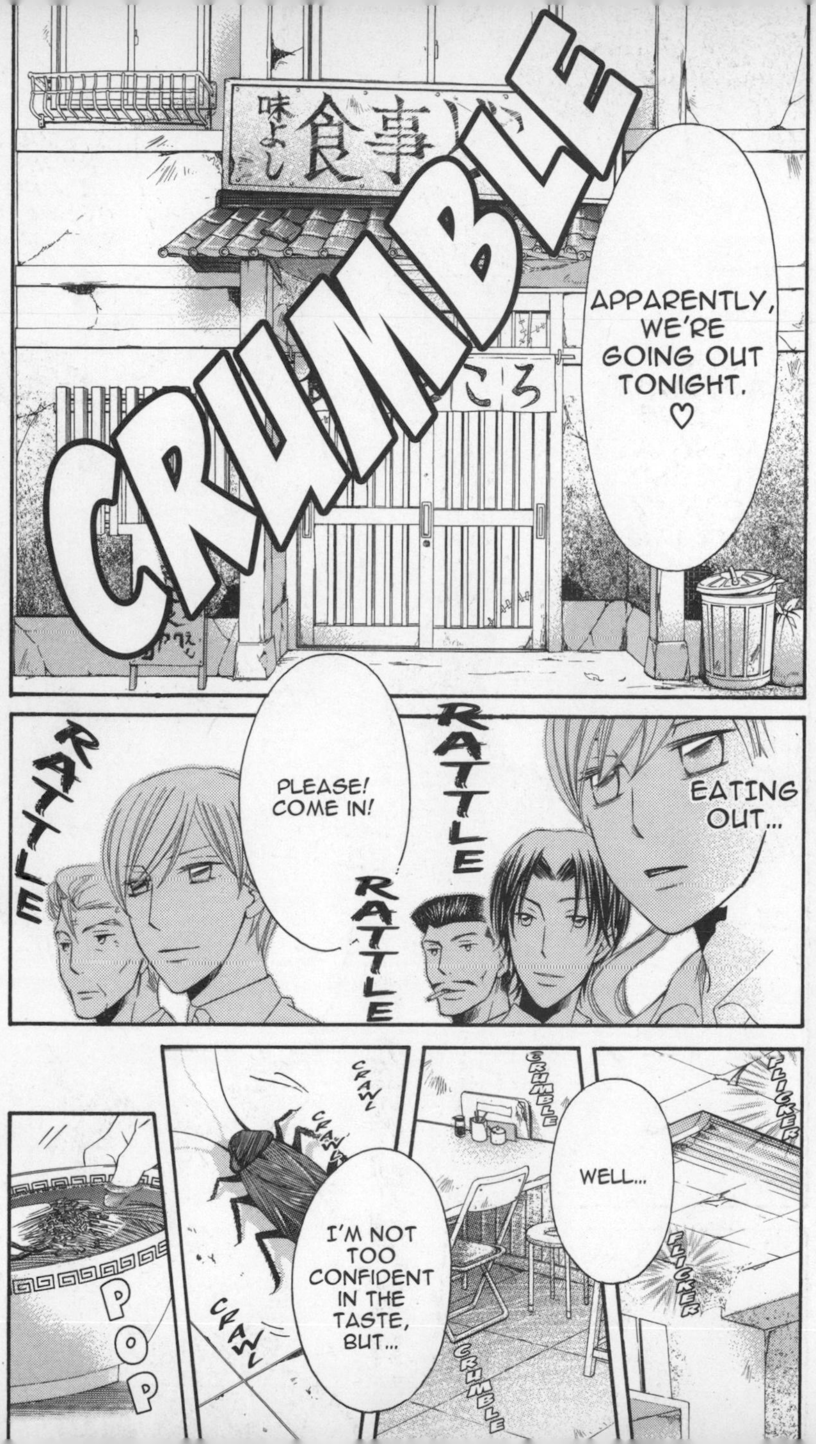
CRUMBLE
APPARENTLY, WE'RE GOING OUT TONIGHT. ♡
EATING OUT...
RATTLE
RATTLE
PLEASE! COME IN!
RATTLE
FLICKER
FLICKER
WELL...
CRUMBLE
CRUMBLE
CRAWL
CRAWL
I'M NOT TOO CONFIDENT IN THE TASTE, BUT...
CRAWL
POP
POP

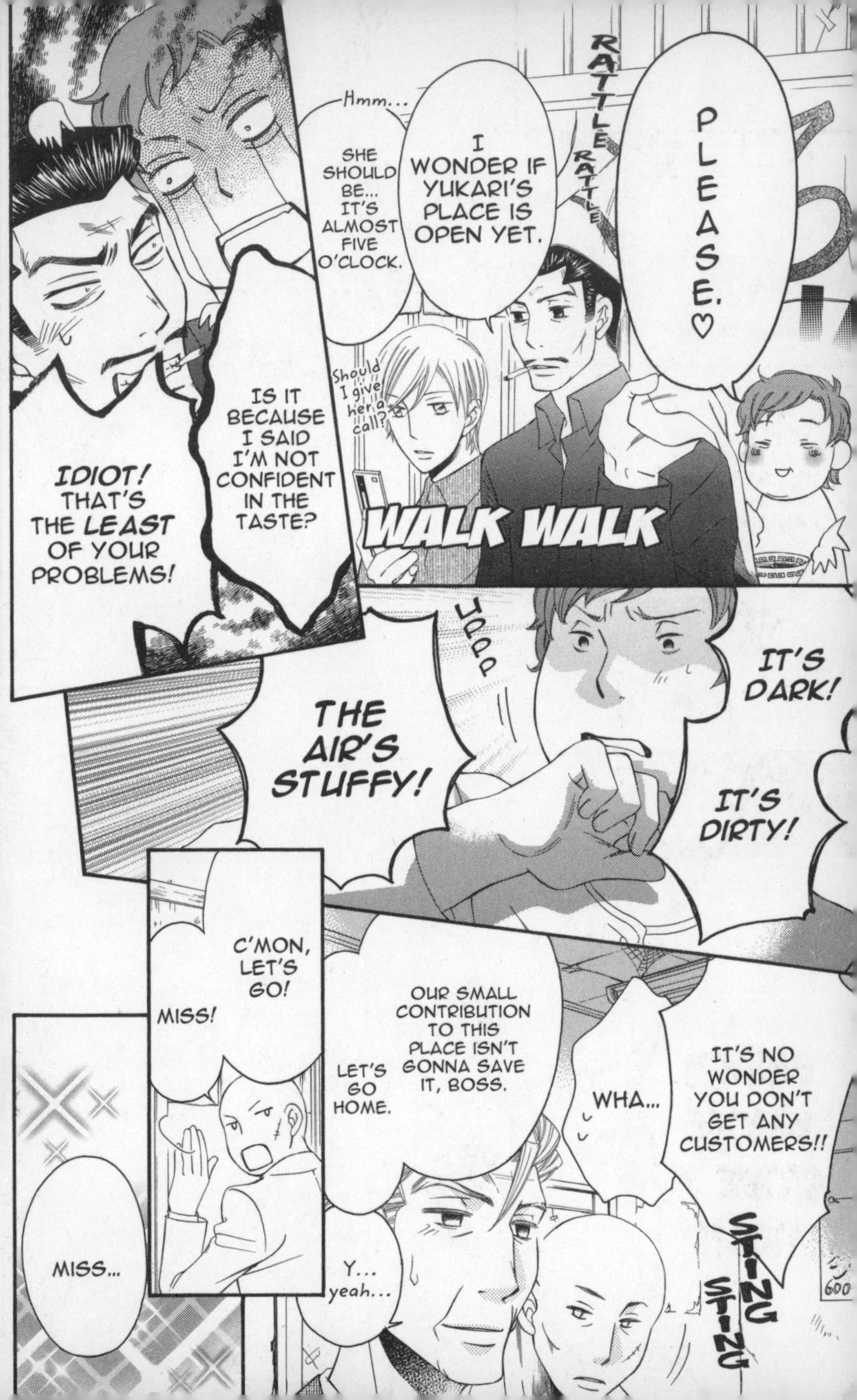
PLEASE.♡
RATTLE RATTLE
I WONDER IF YUKARI'S PLACE IS OPEN YET.
Hmm...
SHE SHOULD BE... IT'S ALMOST FIVE O'CLOCK.
Should I give her a call?
WALK WALK
IS IT BECAUSE I SAID I'M NOT CONFIDENT IN THE TASTE?
IDIOT! THAT'S THE LEAST OF YOUR PROBLEMS!
IT'S DARK!
THE AIR'S STUFFY!
IT'S DIRTY!
IT'S NO WONDER YOU DON'T GET ANY CUSTOMERS!!
STING STING
600
WHA...
OUR SMALL CONTRIBUTION TO THIS PLACE ISN'T GONNA SAVE IT, BOSS.
LET'S GO HOME.
Y... yeah...
C'MON, LET'S GO!
MISS!
MISS...

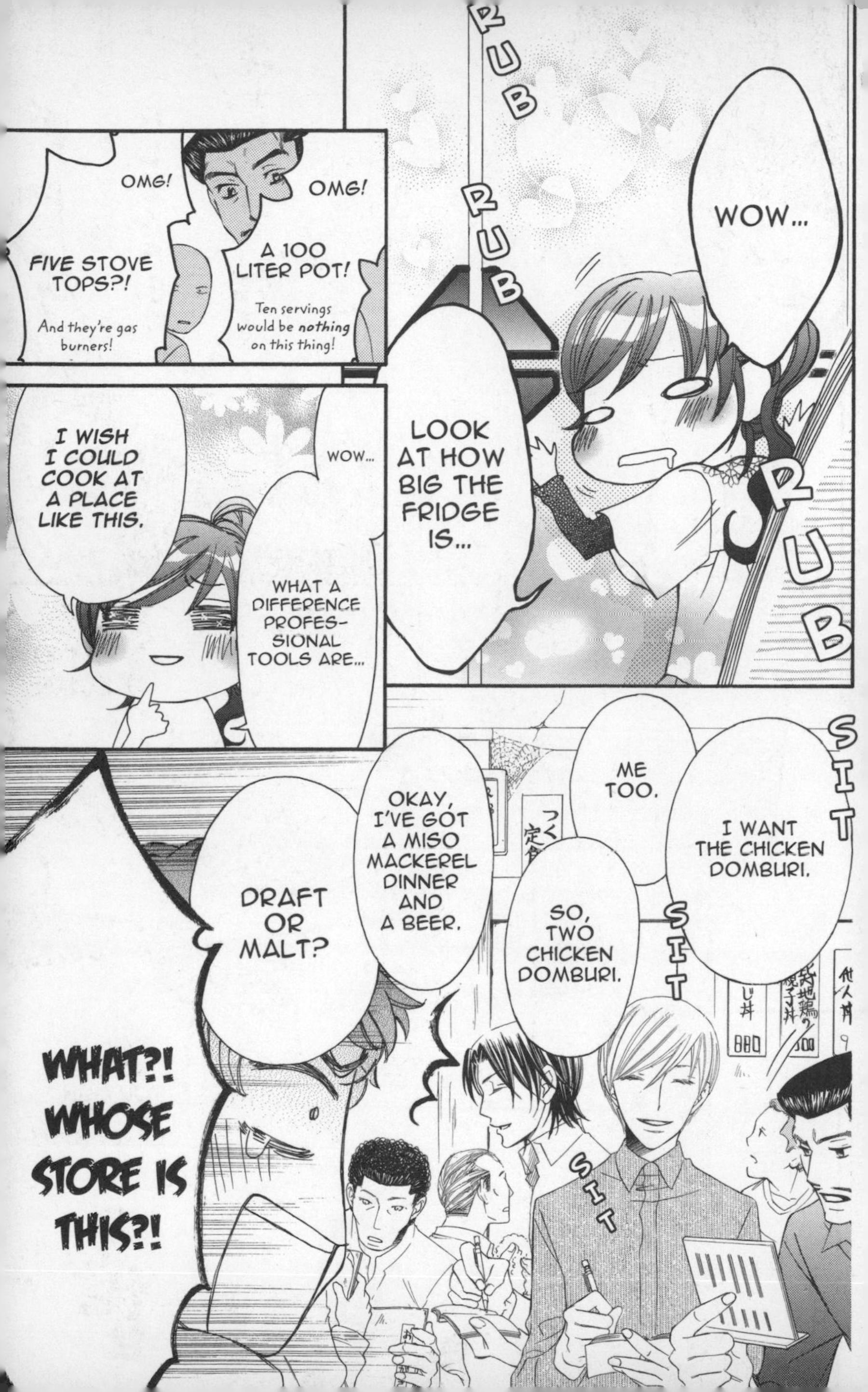
WOW...
RUB
RUB
RUB
RUB
LOOK AT HOW BIG THE FRIDGE IS...
OMG!
A 100 LITER POT!
Ten servings would be *nothing* on this thing!
OMG!
FIVE STOVE TOPS?!
And they're gas burners!
WOW...
WHAT A DIFFERENCE PROFES-SIONAL TOOLS ARE...
I WISH I COULD COOK AT A PLACE LIKE THIS.
SIT
I WANT THE CHICKEN DOMBURI.
ME TOO.
SIT
SO, TWO CHICKEN DOMBURI.
OKAY, I'VE GOT A MISO MACKEREL DINNER AND A BEER.
SIT
DRAFT OR MALT?
WHAT?! WHOSE STORE IS THIS?!

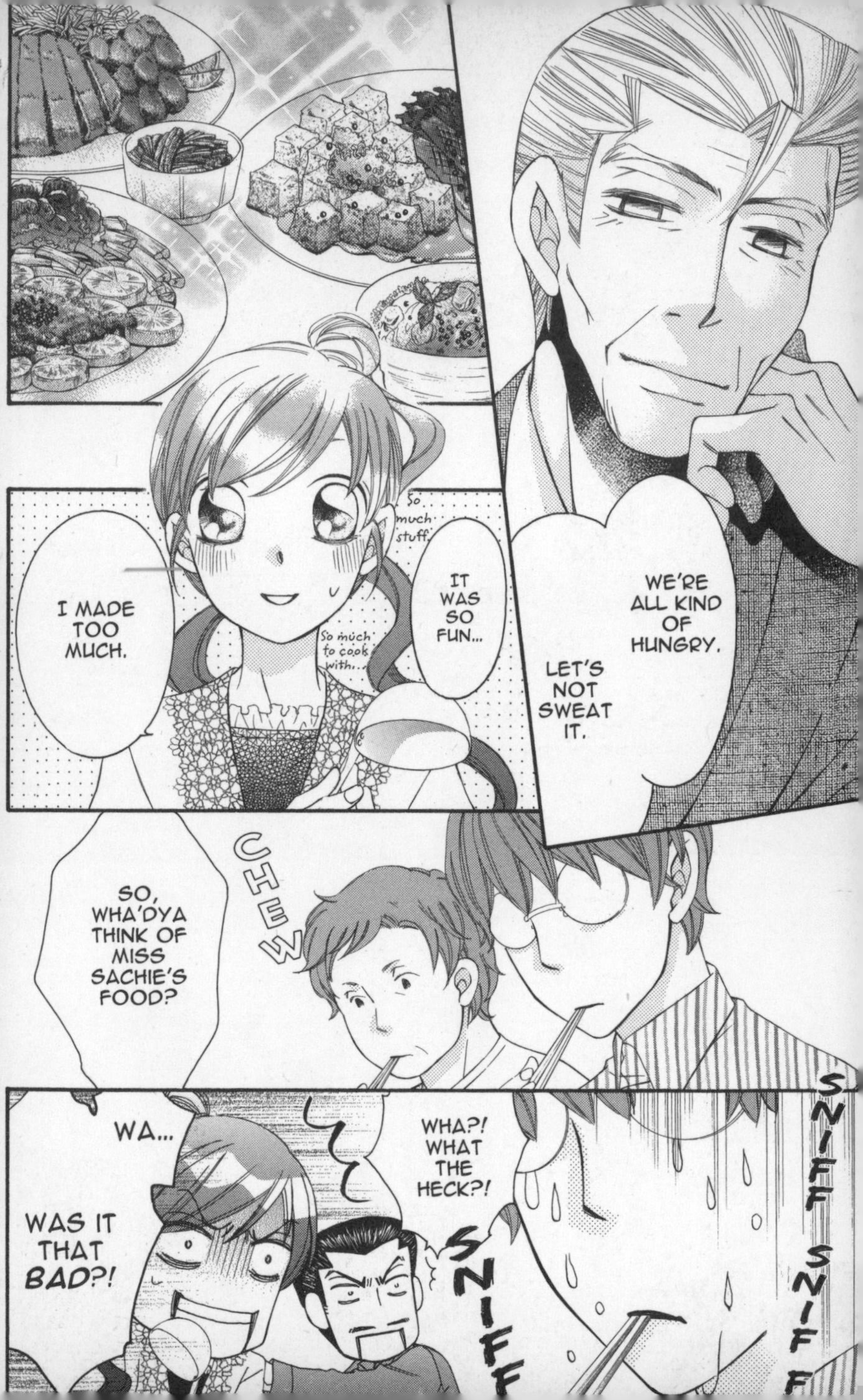
WE'RE ALL KIND OF HUNGRY.
LET'S NOT SWEAT IT.
So much stuff.
IT WAS SO FUN...
So much to cook with...
I MADE TOO MUCH.
CHEW
SO, WHA'DYA THINK OF MISS SACHIE'S FOOD?
SNIFF SNIFF
WHA?! WHAT THE HECK?!
SNIFF
WA...
WAS IT THAT BAD?!

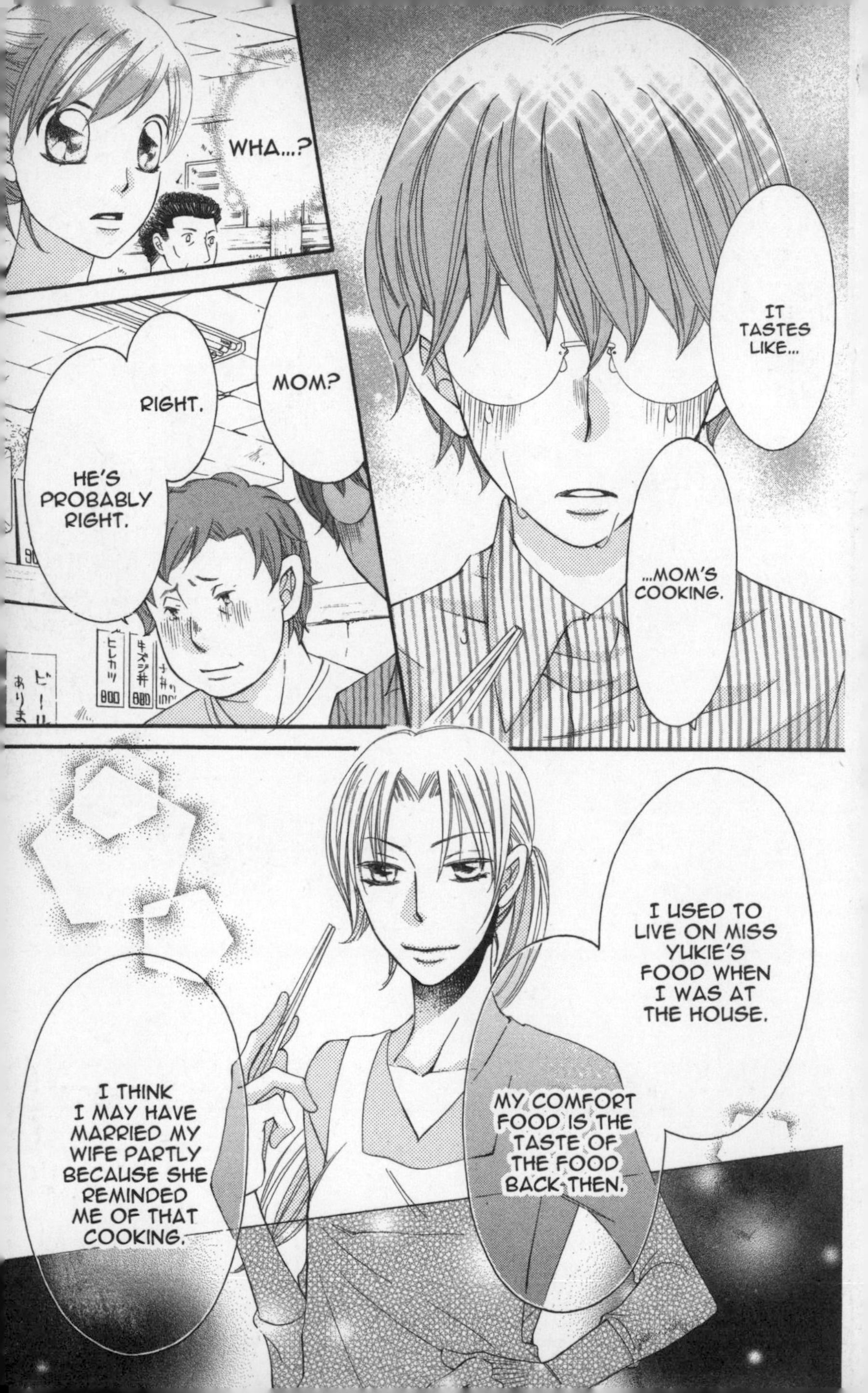
IT TASTES LIKE...
...MOM'S COOKING.
WHA...?
MOM?
RIGHT.
HE'S PROBABLY RIGHT.
I USED TO LIVE ON MISS YUKIE'S FOOD WHEN I WAS AT THE HOUSE.
MY COMFORT FOOD IS THE TASTE OF THE FOOD BACK THEN.
I THINK I MAY HAVE MARRIED MY WIFE PARTLY BECAUSE SHE REMINDED ME OF THAT COOKING.

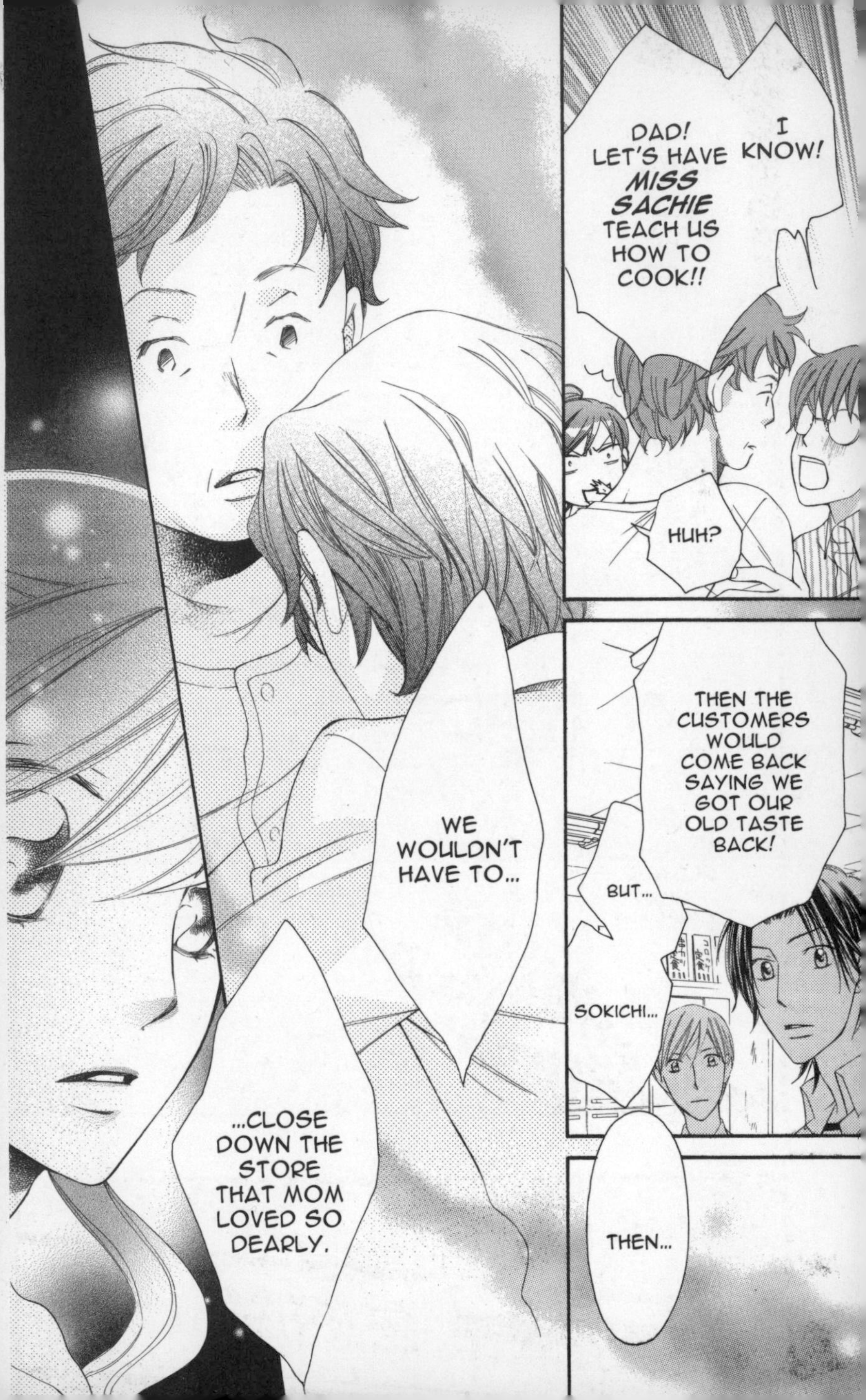
I KNOW!
DAD! LET'S HAVE *MISS SACHIE* TEACH US HOW TO COOK!!
HUH?
THEN THE CUSTOMERS WOULD COME BACK SAYING WE GOT OUR OLD TASTE BACK!
BUT...
SOKICHI...
THEN...
WE WOULDN'T HAVE TO...
...CLOSE DOWN THE STORE THAT MOM LOVED SO DEARLY.

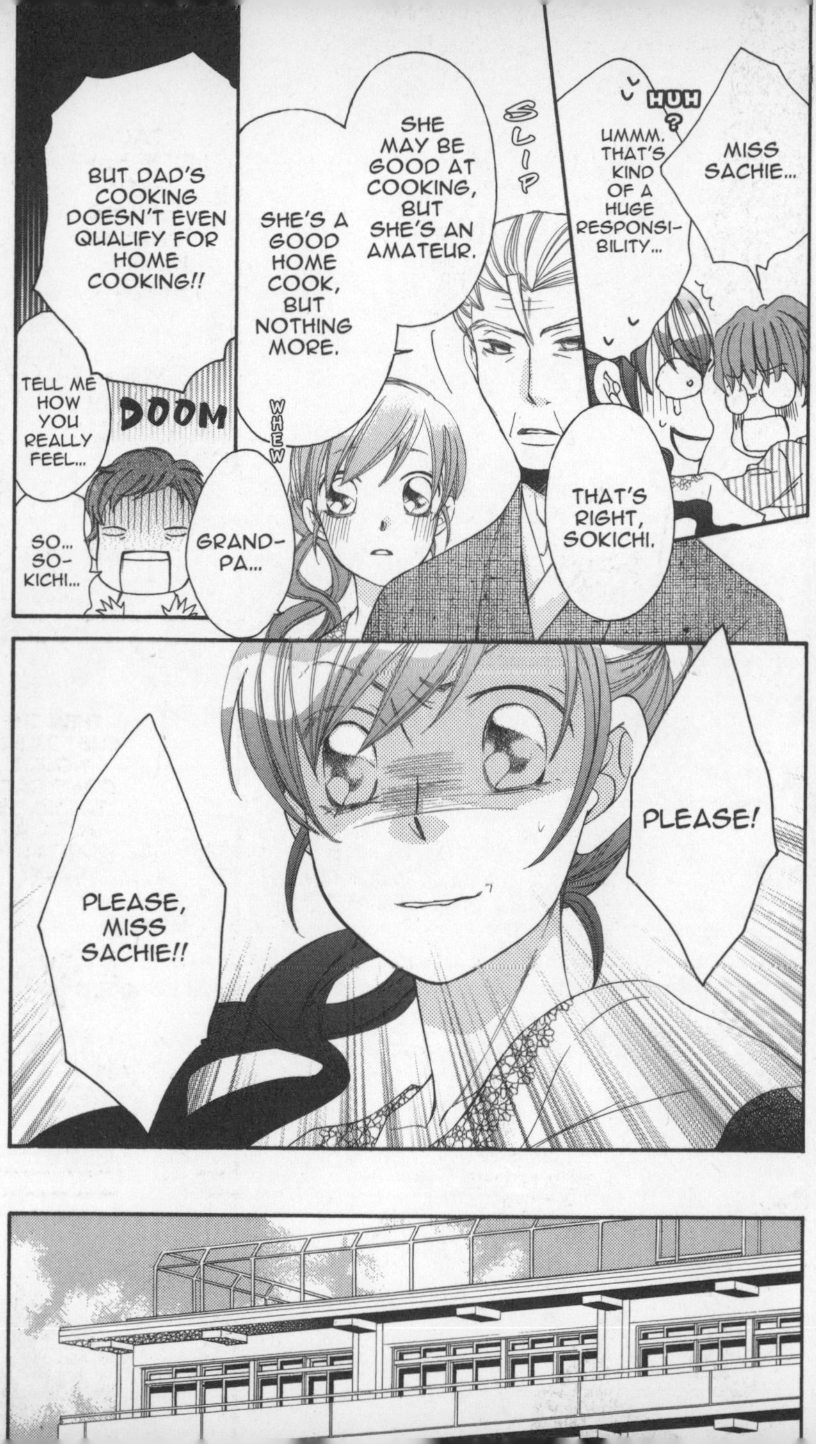
MISS SACHIE...
HUH?
UMMM. THAT'S KIND OF A HUGE RESPONSIBILITY...
THAT'S RIGHT, SOKICHI.
SLIP
SHE MAY BE GOOD AT COOKING, BUT SHE'S AN AMATEUR.
SHE'S A GOOD HOME COOK, BUT NOTHING MORE.
WHEW
GRANDPA...
BUT DAD'S COOKING DOESN'T EVEN QUALIFY FOR HOME COOKING!!
DOOM
TELL ME HOW YOU REALLY FEEL...
SO... SO-KICHI...
PLEASE!
PLEASE, MISS SACHIE!!

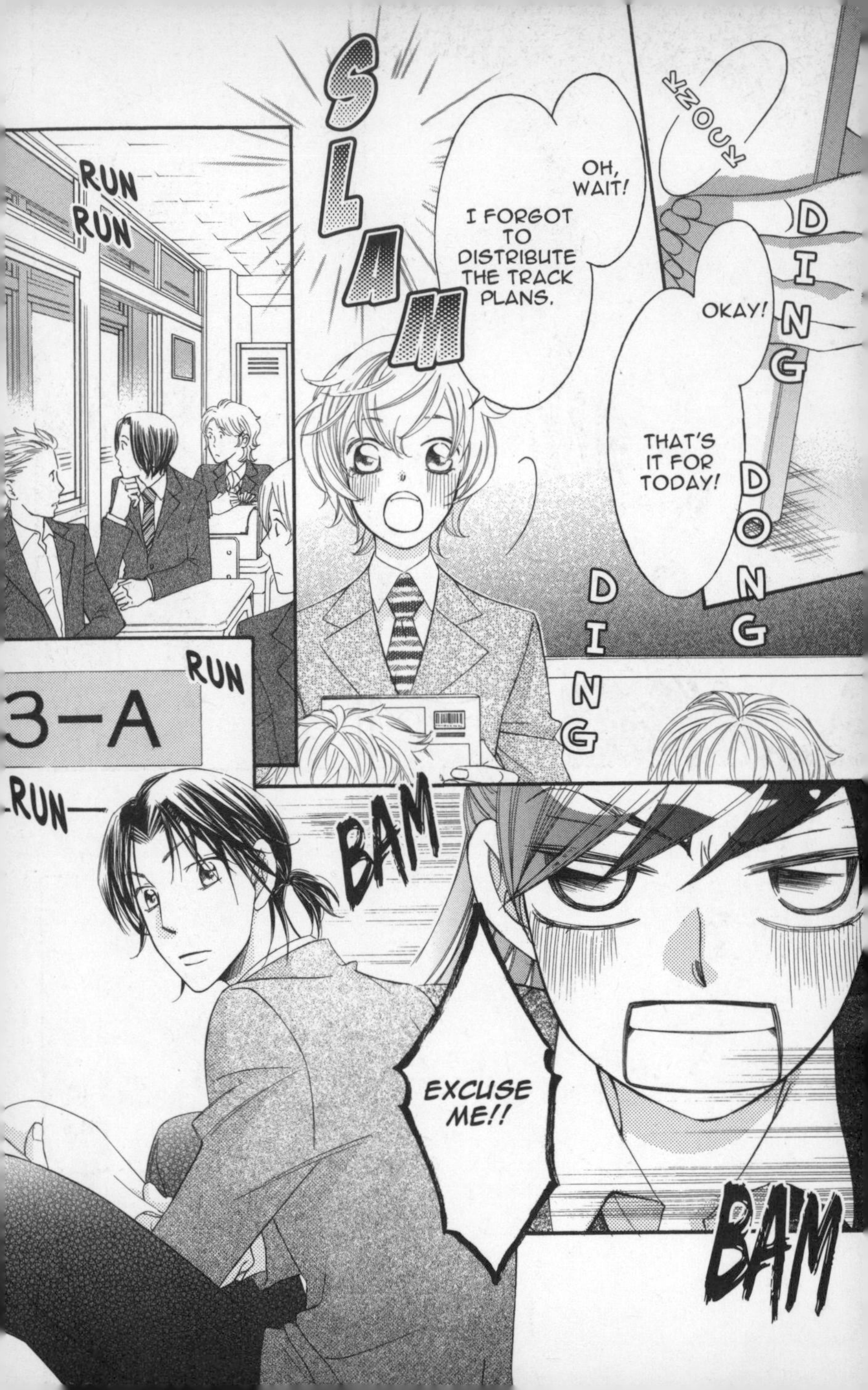
KNOCK
DING
OKAY!
THAT'S IT FOR TODAY!
DONG
DING
SLAM
OH, WAIT!
I FORGOT TO DISTRIBUTE THE TRACK PLANS.
RUN RUN
RUN
3-A
BAM
EXCUSE ME!!
BAM
RUN—

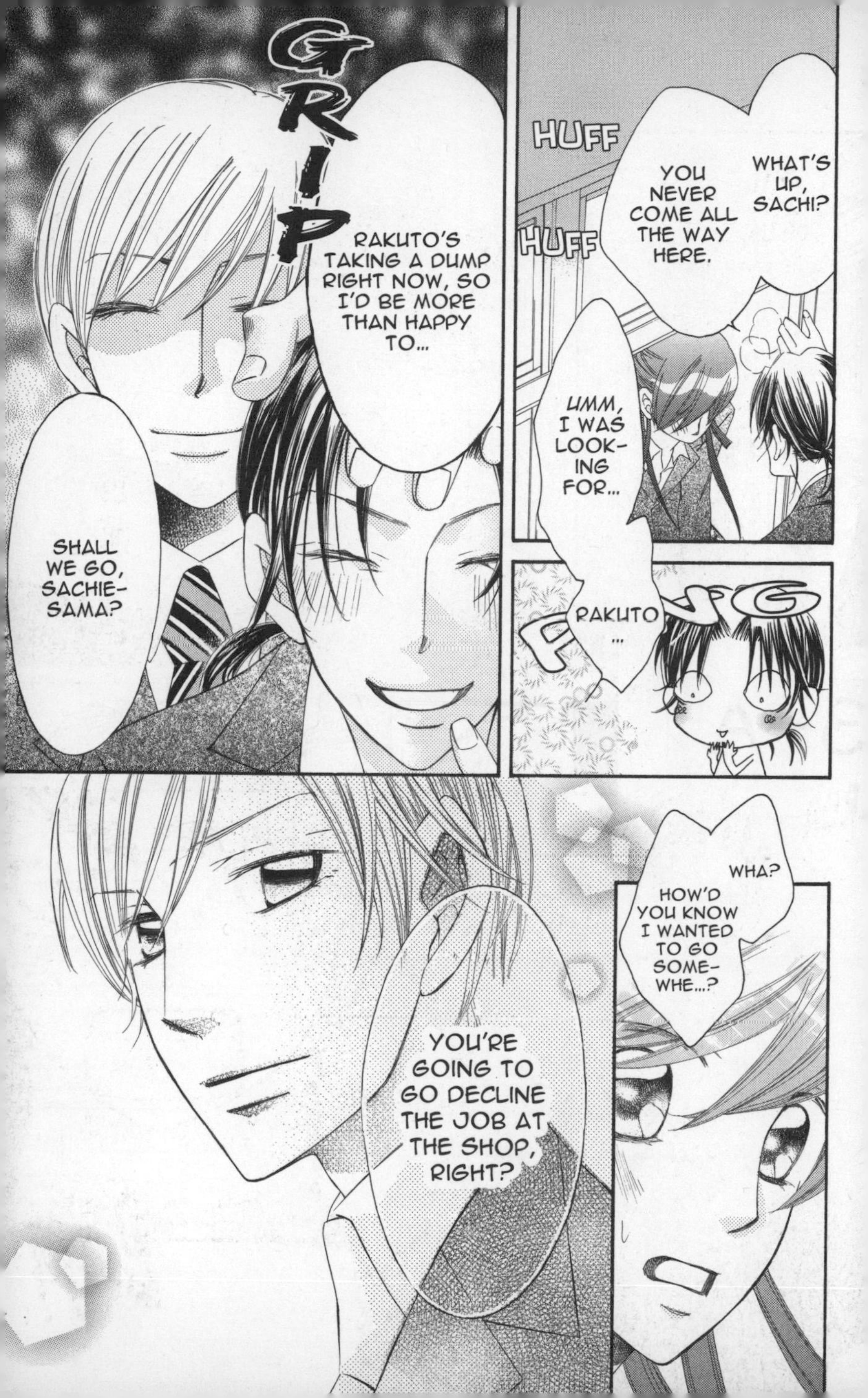
WHAT'S UP, SACHI?
YOU NEVER COME ALL THE WAY HERE.
HUFF
HUFF
UMM, I WAS LOOKING-ING FOR...
RAKUTO ...
GRIP
RAKUTO'S TAKING A DUMP RIGHT NOW, SO I'D BE MORE THAN HAPPY TO...
SHALL WE GO, SACHIE-SAMA?
WHA?
HOW'D YOU KNOW I WANTED TO GO SOME-WHE...?
YOU'RE GOING TO GO DECLINE THE JOB AT THE SHOP, RIGHT?

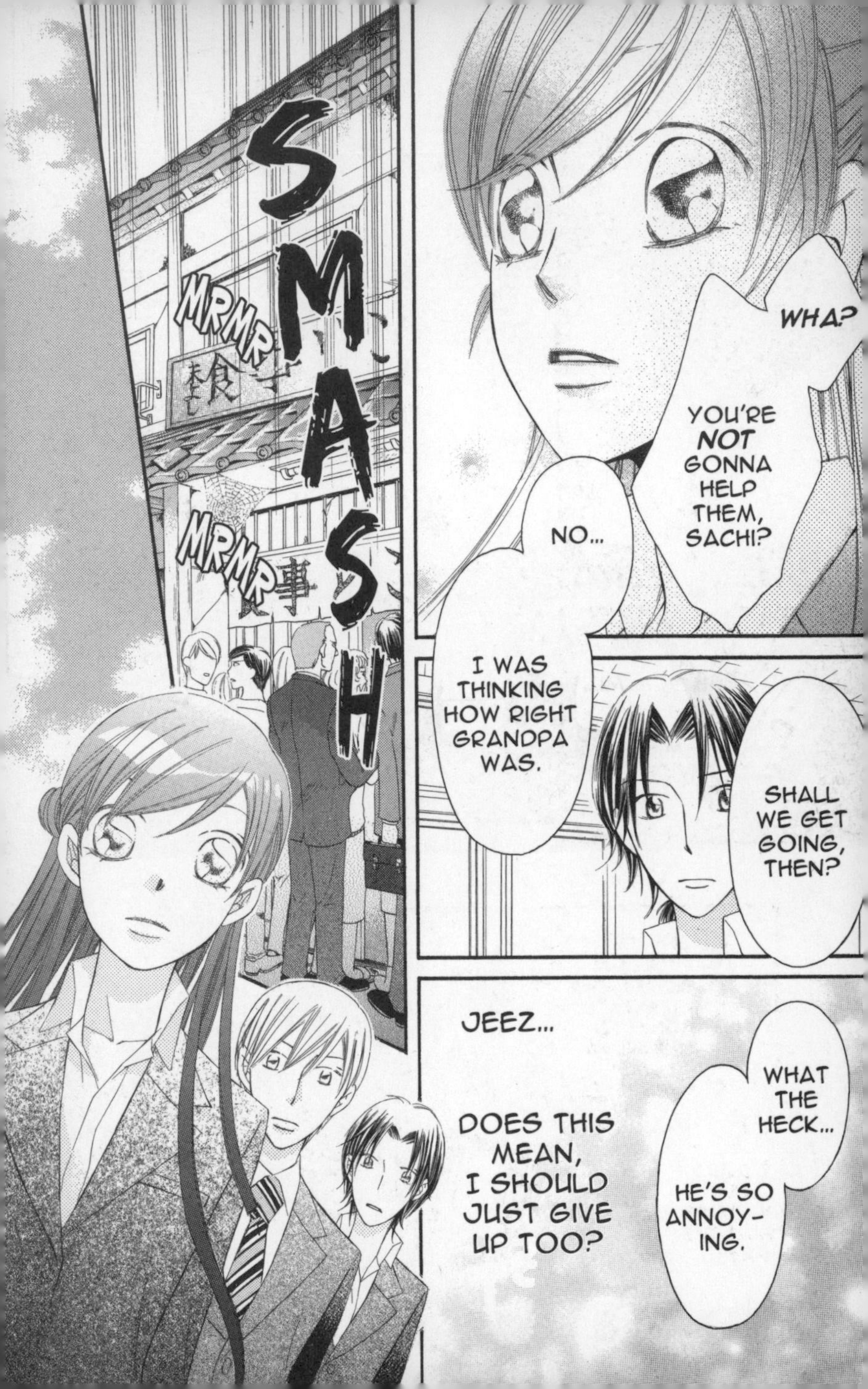
WHA?
YOU'RE **NOT** GONNA HELP THEM, SACHI?
NO...
I WAS THINKING HOW RIGHT GRANDPA WAS.
SHALL WE GET GOING, THEN?
WHAT THE HECK...
HE'S SO ANNOY-ING.
JEEZ...
DOES THIS MEAN, I SHOULD JUST GIVE UP TOO?
SMASH
MRMR
MRMR

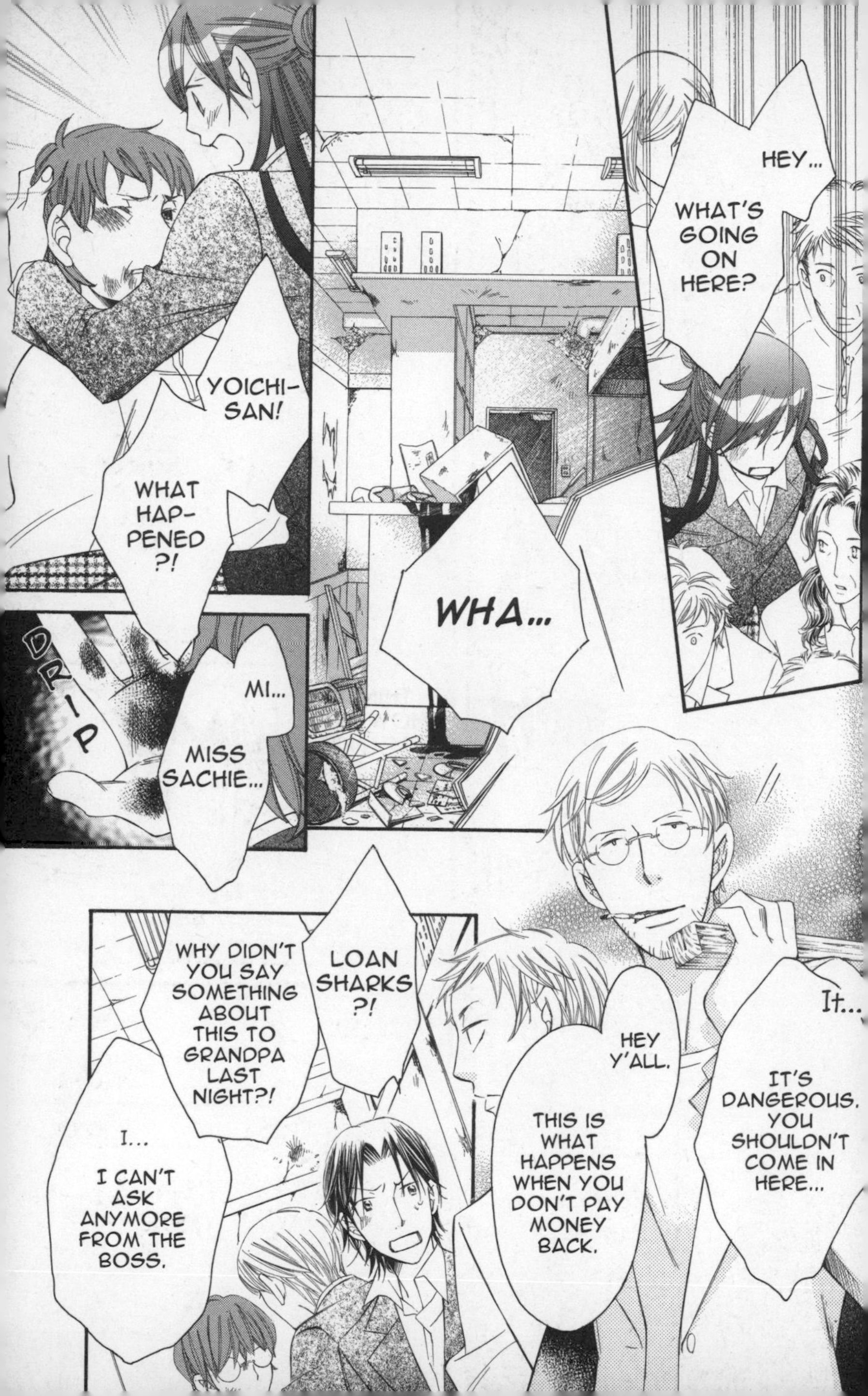
HEY...
WHAT'S GOING ON HERE?
WHA...
YOICHI-SAN!
WHAT HAPPENED?!
DRIP
MI...
MISS SACHIE...
It...
IT'S DANGEROUS. YOU SHOULDN'T COME IN HERE...
HEY Y'ALL.
THIS IS WHAT HAPPENS WHEN YOU DON'T PAY MONEY BACK.
LOAN SHARKS?!
WHY DIDN'T YOU SAY SOMETHING ABOUT THIS TO GRANDPA LAST NIGHT?!
I...
I CAN'T ASK ANYMORE FROM THE BOSS.

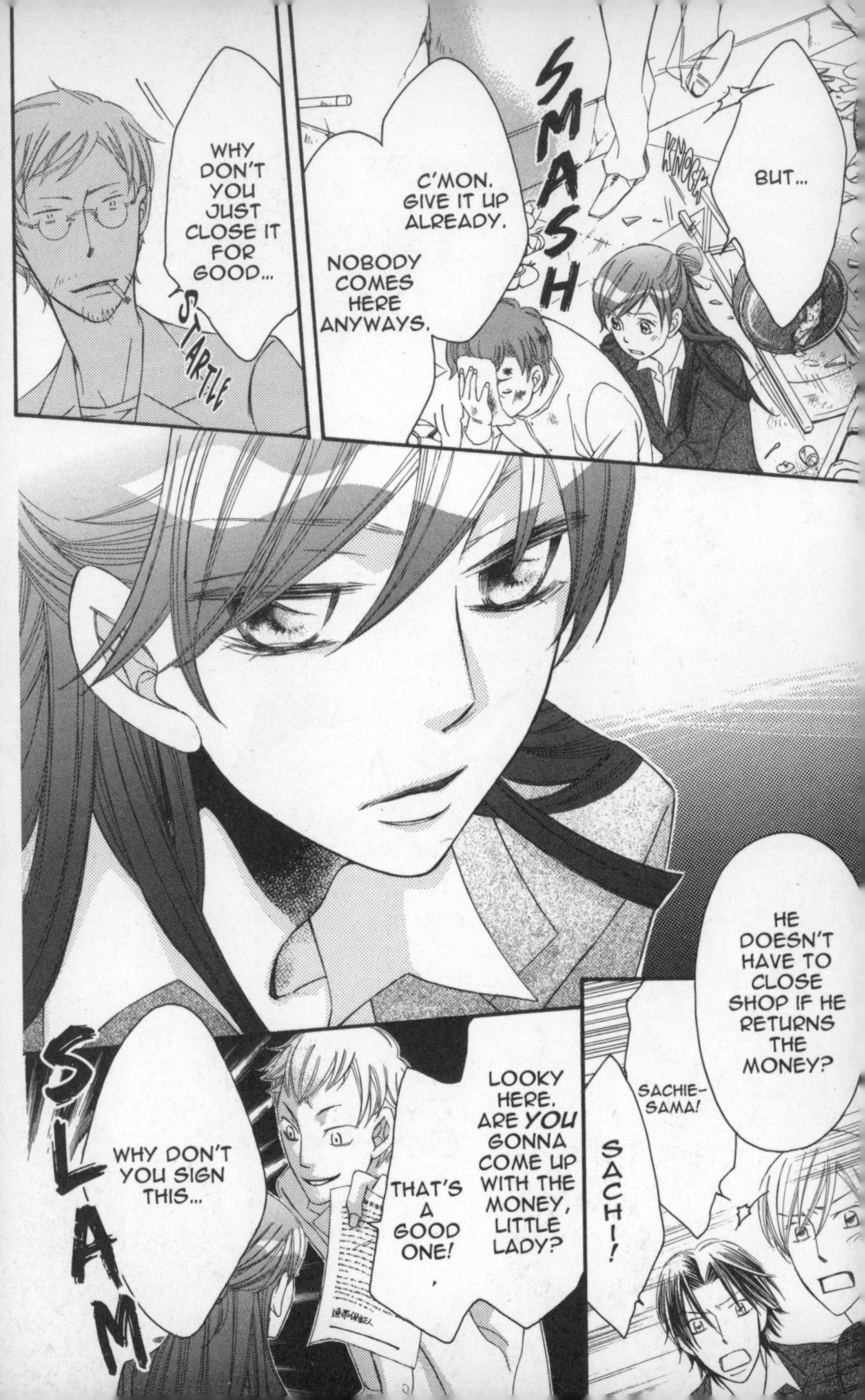
BUT...
SMASH
KNOCK
C'MON. GIVE IT UP ALREADY.
NOBODY COMES HERE ANYWAYS.
WHY DON'T YOU JUST CLOSE IT FOR GOOD...
STARTLE
HE DOESN'T HAVE TO CLOSE SHOP IF HE RETURNS THE MONEY?
SACHIE-SAMA!
SACHI!
LOOKY HERE. ARE *YOU* GONNA COME UP WITH THE MONEY, LITTLE LADY?
THAT'S A GOOD ONE!
WHY DON'T YOU SIGN THIS...
SLAM

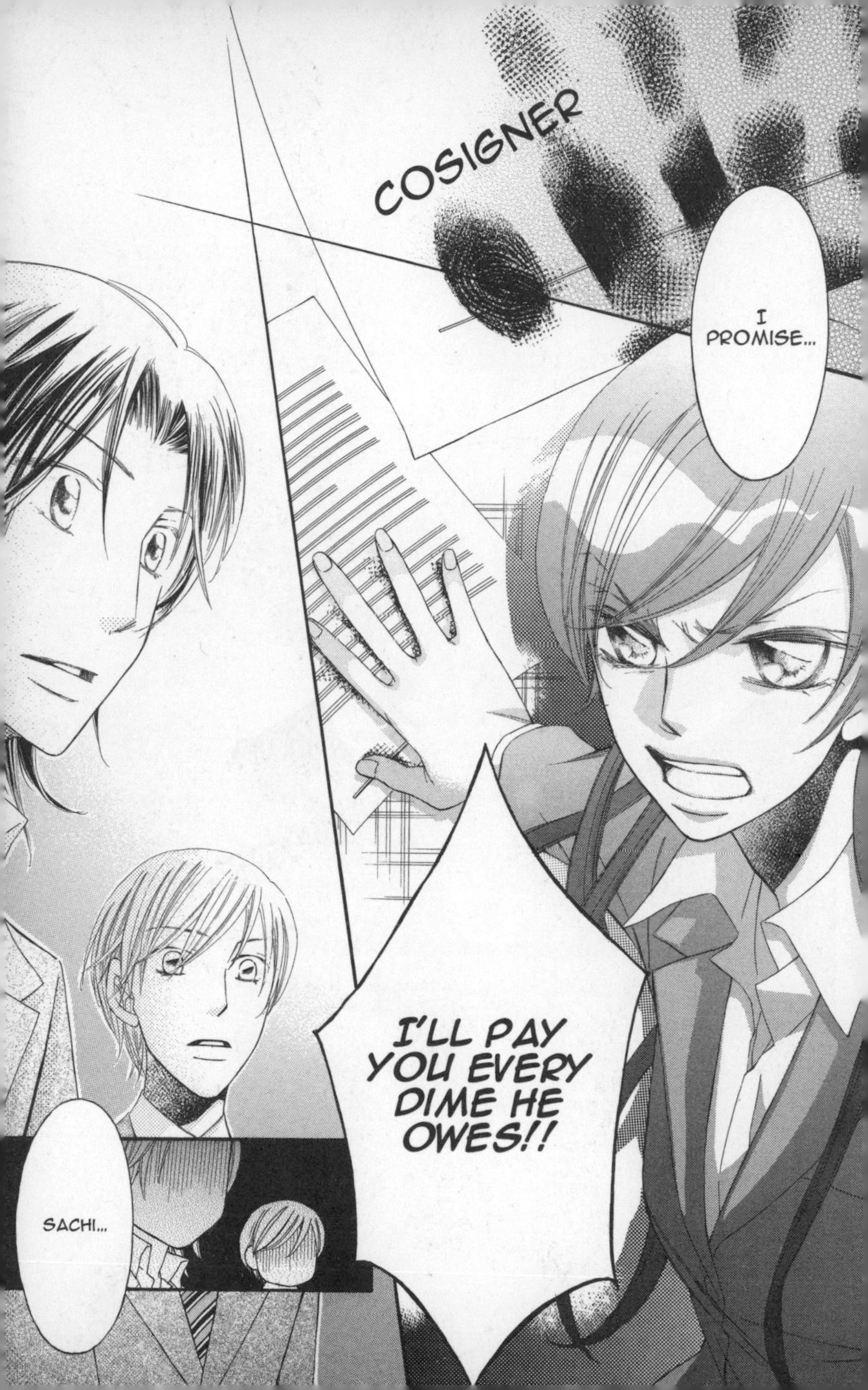
I PROMISE...
COSIGNER
I'LL PAY YOU EVERY DIME HE OWES!!
SACHI...

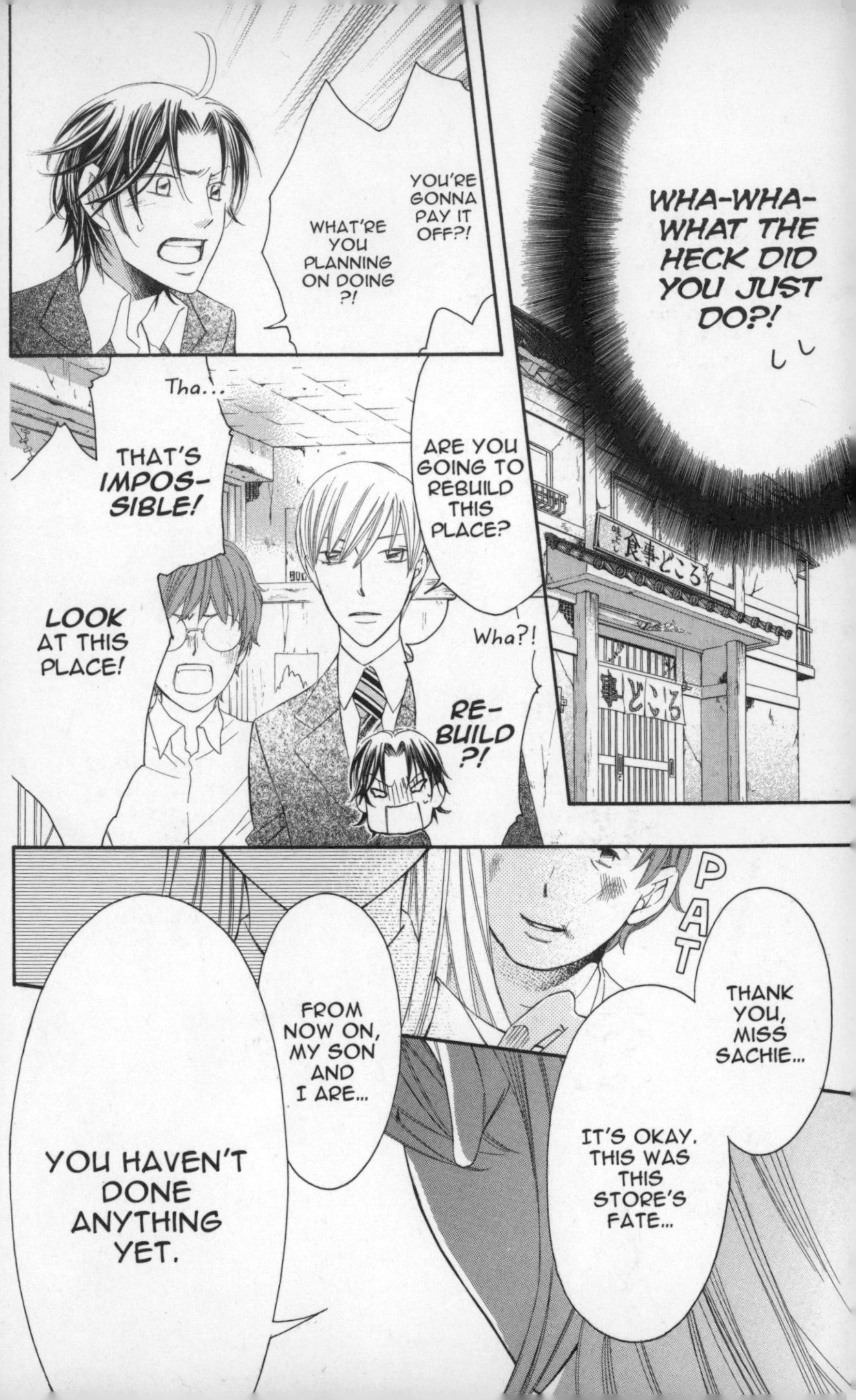
WHA-WHA-WHAT THE HECK DID YOU JUST DO?!
食事どころ
YOU'RE GONNA PAY IT OFF?!
WHAT'RE YOU PLANNING ON DOING ?!
ARE YOU GOING TO REBUILD THIS PLACE?
Wha?!
RE-BUILD ?!
Tha...
THAT'S IMPOS-SIBLE!
LOOK AT THIS PLACE!
PAT
THANK YOU, MISS SACHIE...
IT'S OKAY. THIS WAS THIS STORE'S FATE...
FROM NOW ON, MY SON AND I ARE...
YOU HAVEN'T DONE ANYTHING YET.

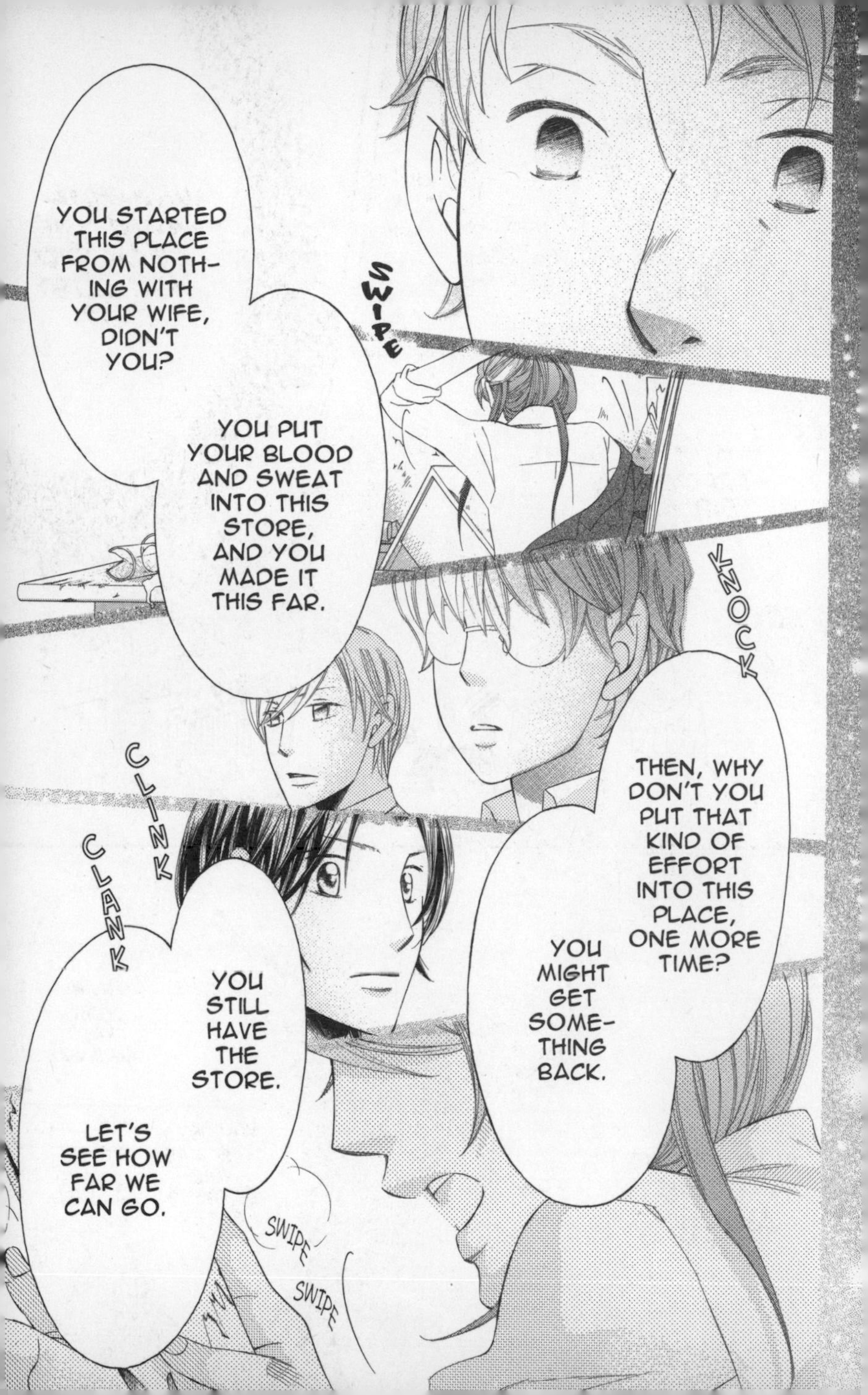
YOU STARTED THIS PLACE FROM NOTHING WITH YOUR WIFE, DIDN'T YOU?
YOU PUT YOUR BLOOD AND SWEAT INTO THIS STORE, AND YOU MADE IT THIS FAR.
SWIPE
KNOCK
CLINK
THEN, WHY DON'T YOU PUT THAT KIND OF EFFORT INTO THIS PLACE, ONE MORE TIME?
YOU MIGHT GET SOMETHING BACK.
CLANK
YOU STILL HAVE THE STORE.
LET'S SEE HOW FAR WE CAN GO.
SWIPE
SWIPE

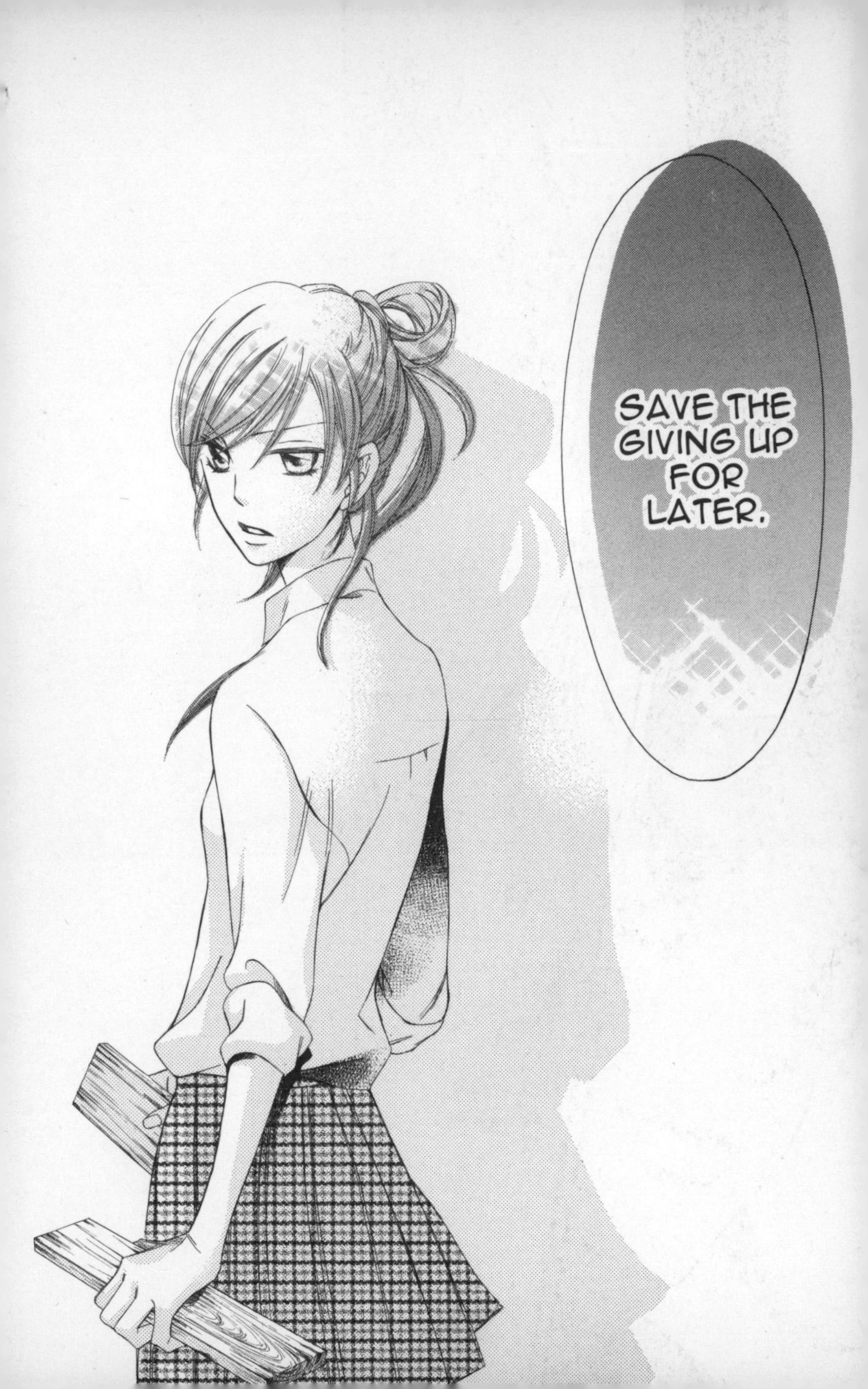
SAVE THE GIVING UP FOR LATER.

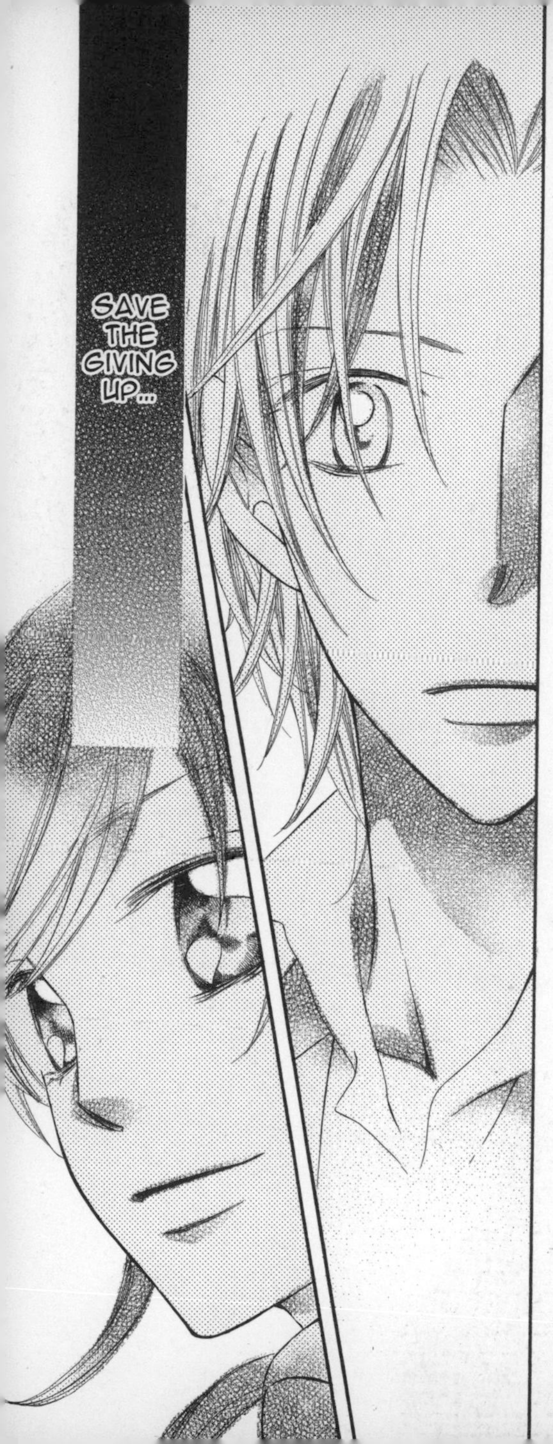
SAVE THE GIVING UP...

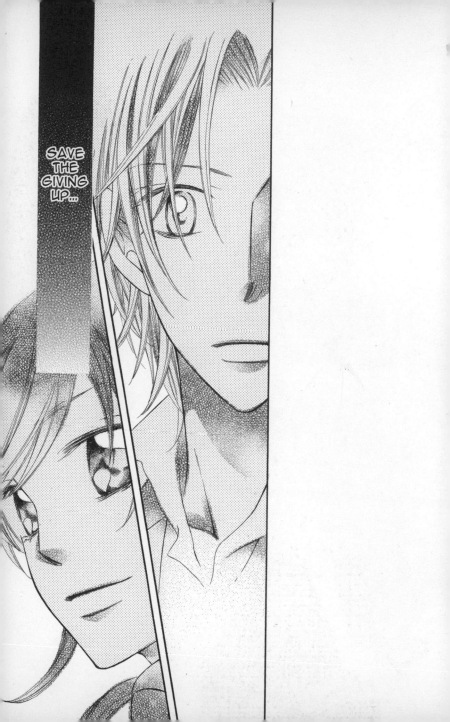

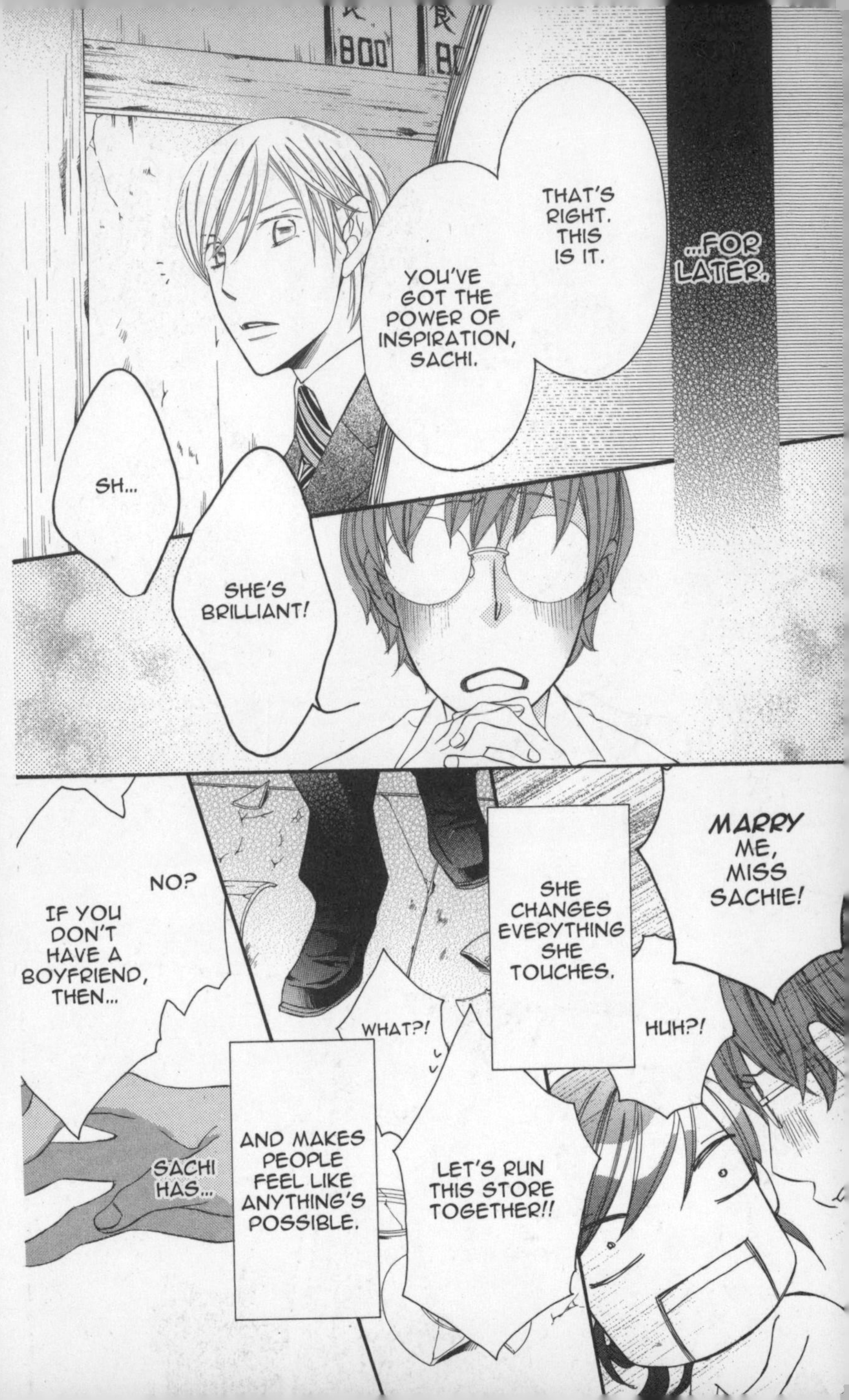
...FOR LATER.
THAT'S RIGHT. THIS IS IT.
YOU'VE GOT THE POWER OF INSPIRATION, SACHI.
SH...
SHE'S BRILLIANT!
MARRY ME, MISS SACHIE!
HUH?!
SHE CHANGES EVERYTHING SHE TOUCHES.
LET'S RUN THIS STORE TOGETHER!!
WHAT?!
AND MAKES PEOPLE FEEL LIKE ANYTHING'S POSSIBLE.
NO?
IF YOU DON'T HAVE A BOYFRIEND, THEN...
SACHI HAS...

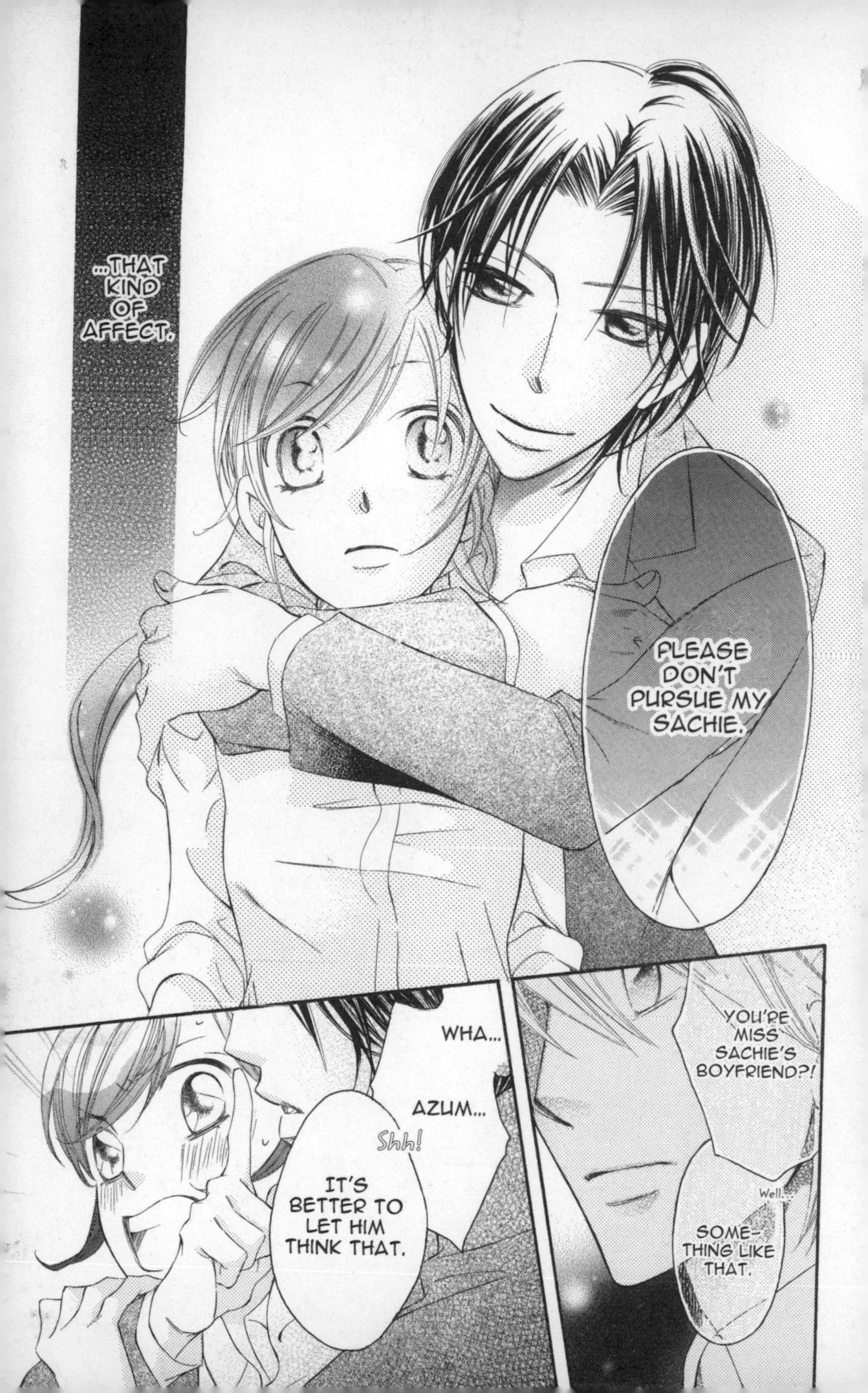
...THAT KIND OF AFFECT.
PLEASE DON'T PURSUE MY SACHIE.
YOU'RE MISS SACHIE'S BOYFRIEND?!
Well...
SOME-THING LIKE THAT.
WHA...
AZUM...
Shh!
IT'S BETTER TO LET HIM THINK THAT.

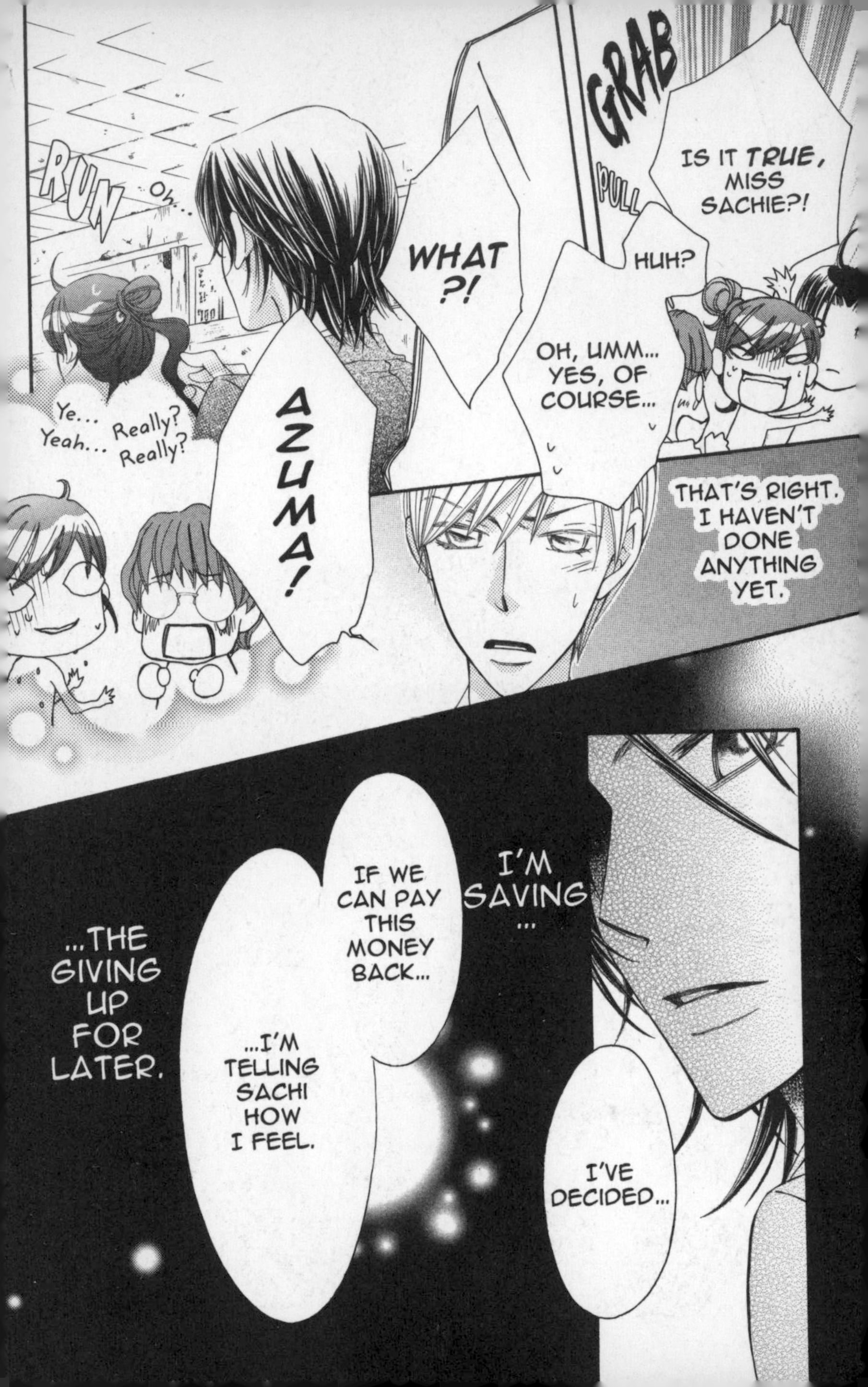
GRAB
IS IT TRUE, MISS SACHIE?!
PULL
HUH?
WHAT?!
OH, UMM... YES, OF COURSE...
THAT'S RIGHT. I HAVEN'T DONE ANYTHING YET.
RUN
Oh...
AZUMA!
Ye... Really?
Yeah... Really?
I'VE DECIDED...
I'M SAVING...
IF WE CAN PAY THIS MONEY BACK...
...I'M TELLING SACHI HOW I FEEL.
...THE GIVING UP FOR LATER.

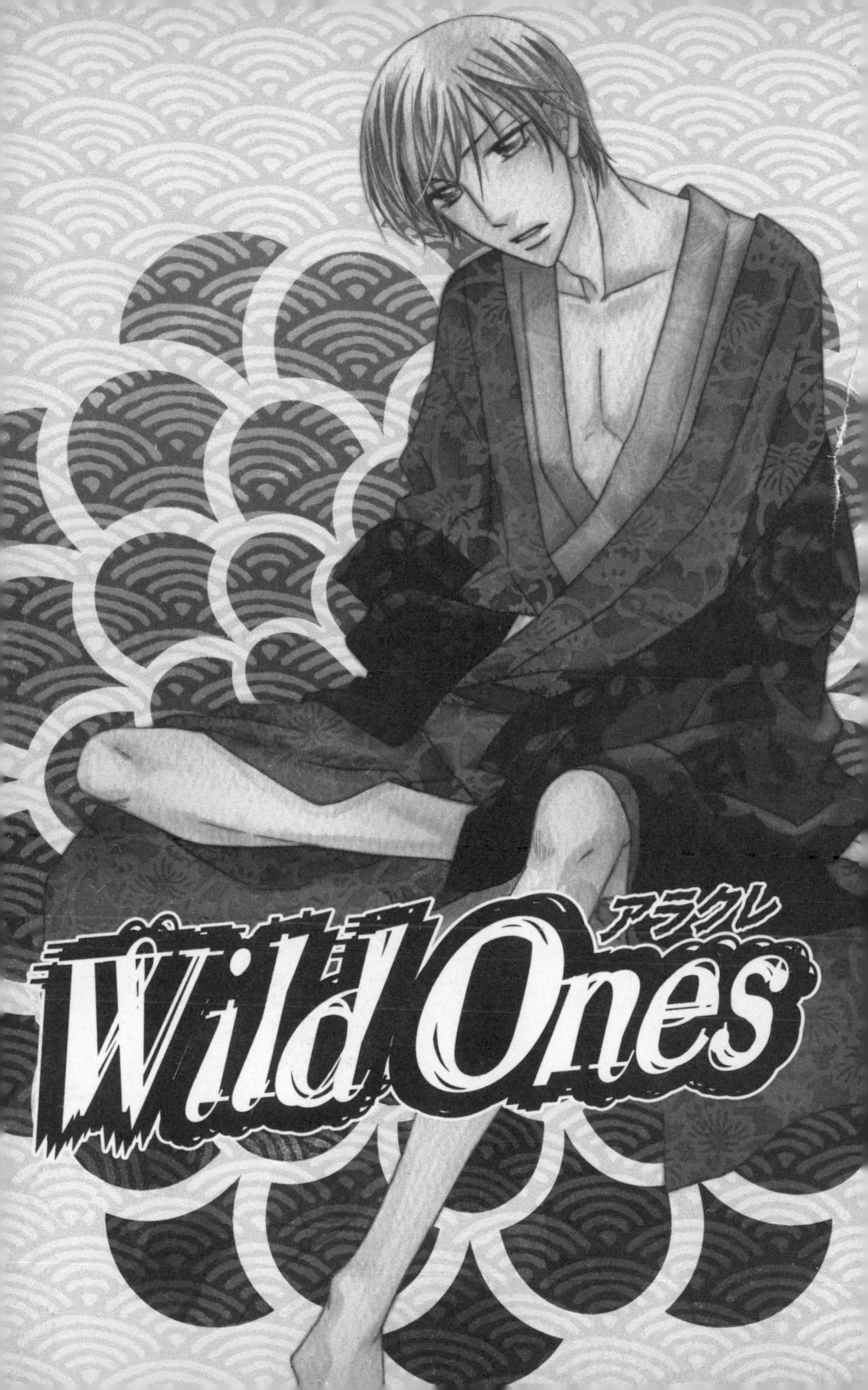

アラクレ
Wild Ones

COSTUME GALLERY

(Theme: Tracksuits)

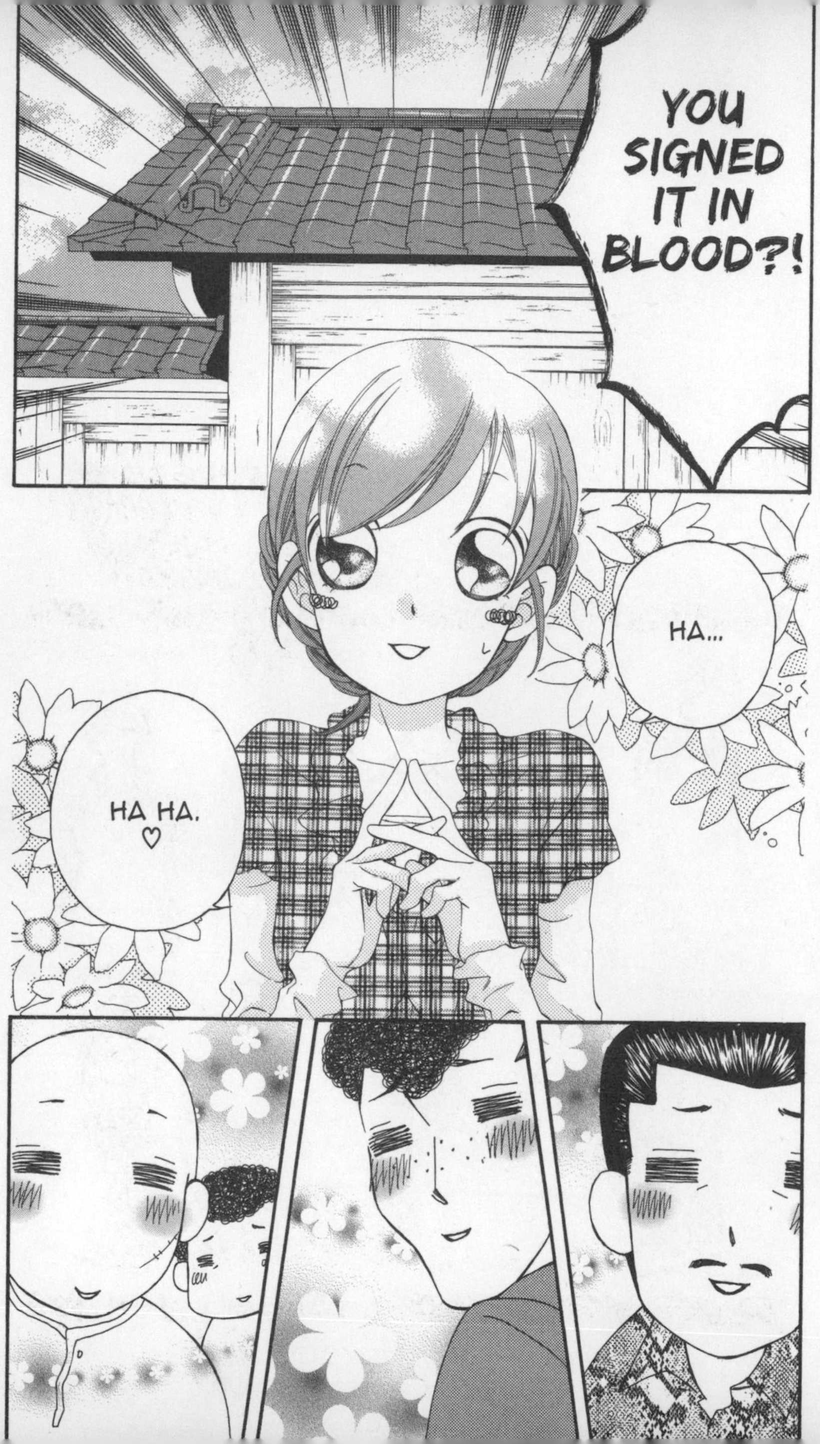
YOU SIGNED IT IN BLOOD?!
HA...
HA HA. ♡

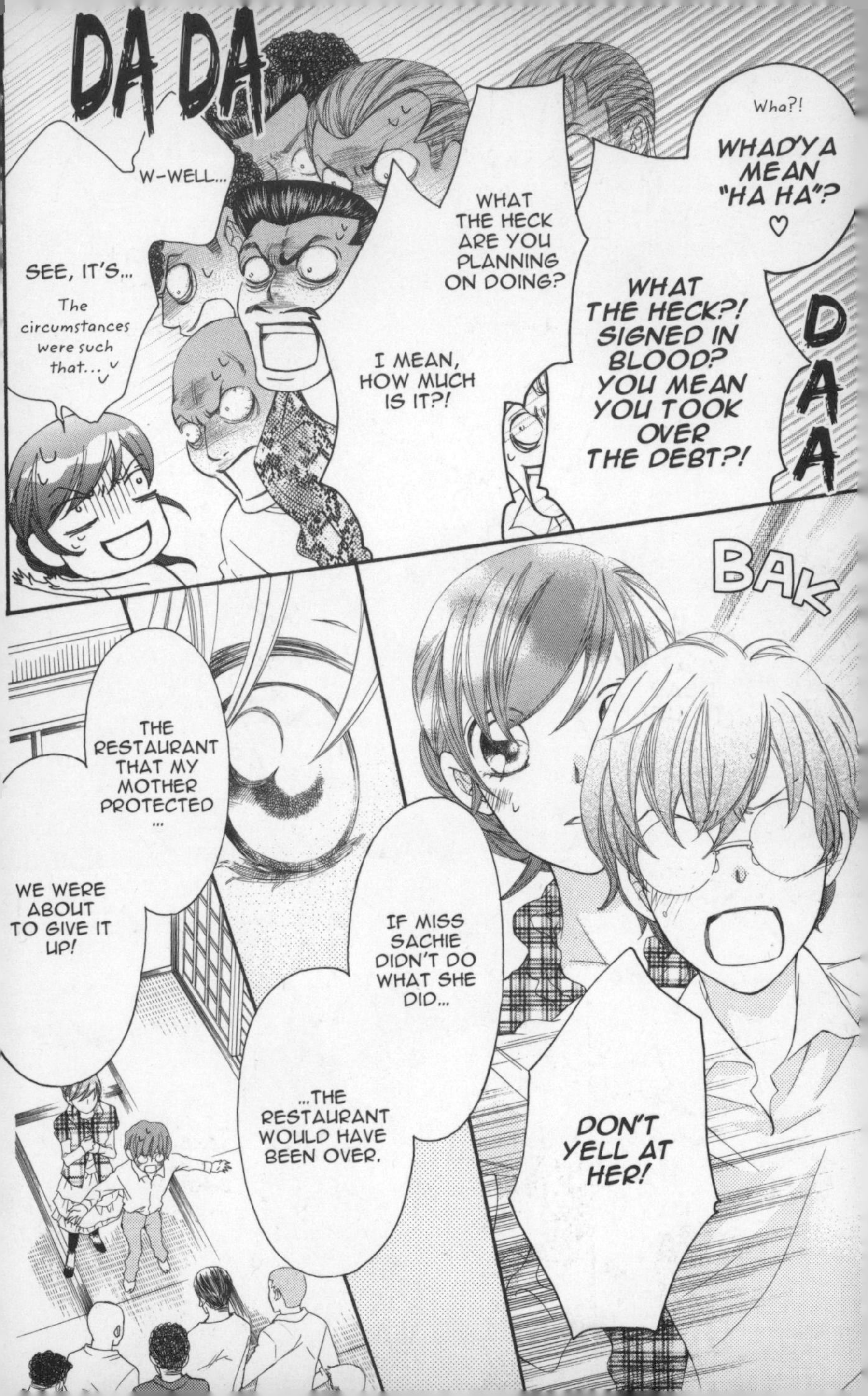

Wha?!
WHAD'YA MEAN "HA HA"? ♡
DA DA
WHAT THE HECK?! SIGNED IN BLOOD? YOU MEAN YOU TOOK OVER THE DEBT?!
WHAT THE HECK ARE YOU PLANNING ON DOING?
I MEAN, HOW MUCH IS IT?!
DA DA
W-WELL...
SEE, IT'S...
The circumstances were such that...
BAK
DON'T YELL AT HER!
IF MISS SACHIE DIDN'T DO WHAT SHE DID...
...THE RESTAURANT WOULD HAVE BEEN OVER.
THE RESTAURANT THAT MY MOTHER PROTECTED...
WE WERE ABOUT TO GIVE IT UP!

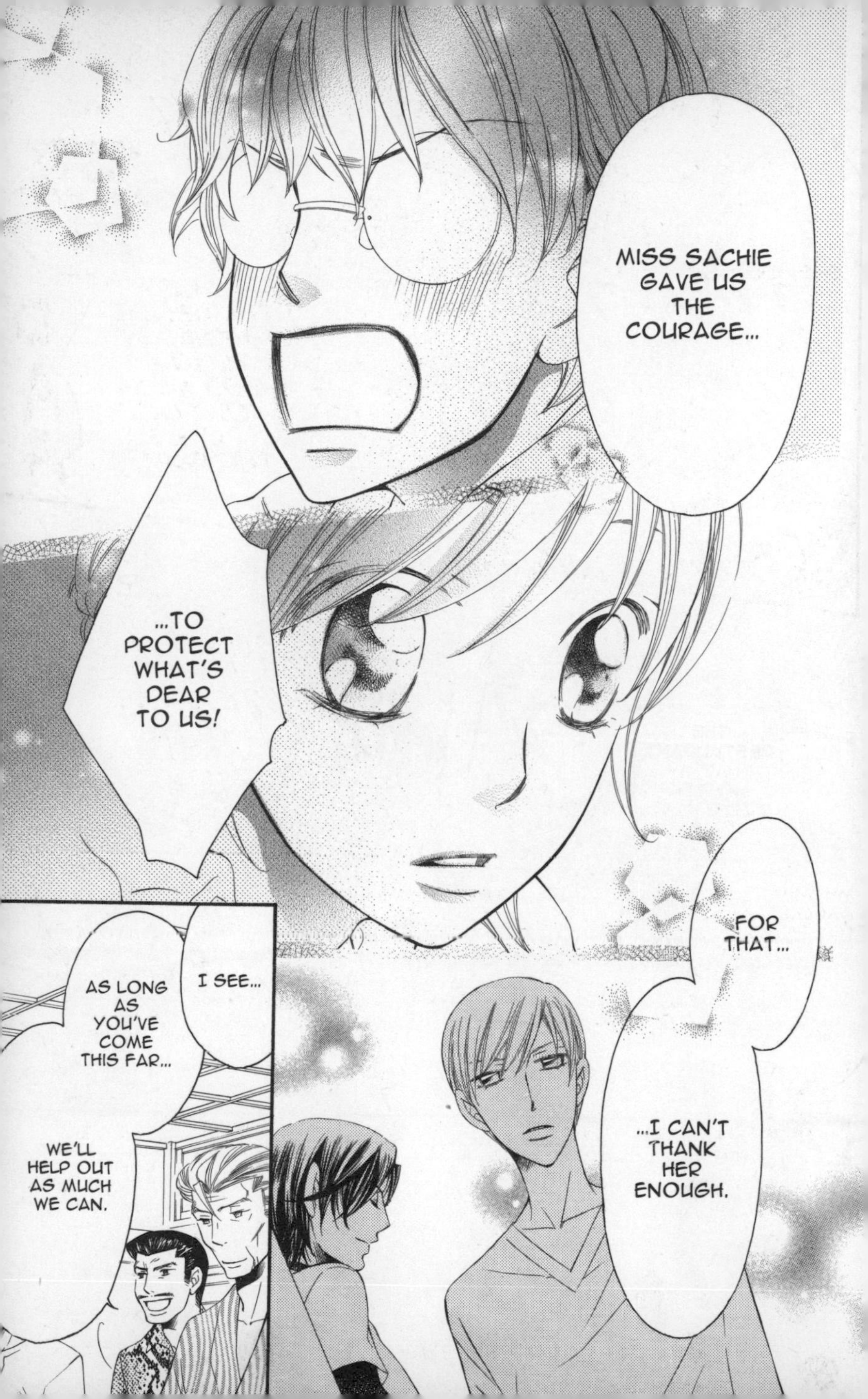
MISS SACHIE GAVE US THE COURAGE...
...TO PROTECT WHAT'S DEAR TO US!
FOR THAT...
...I CAN'T THANK HER ENOUGH.
I SEE...
AS LONG AS YOU'VE COME THIS FAR...
WE'LL HELP OUT AS MUCH WE CAN.

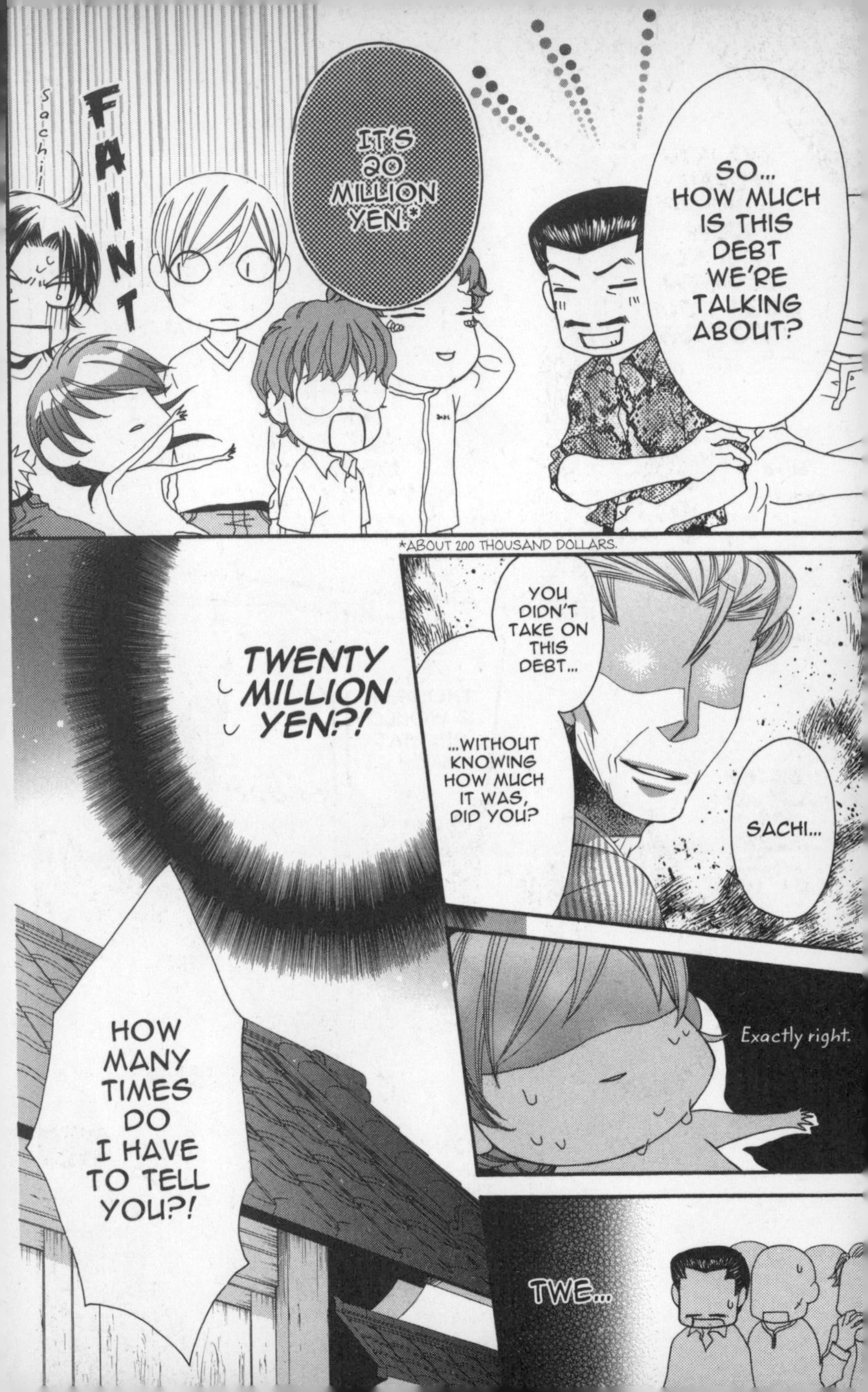
SO... HOW MUCH IS THIS DEBT WE'RE TALKING ABOUT?
IT'S 20 MILLION YEN.*
FAINT
Sachi!
*ABOUT 200 THOUSAND DOLLARS.
YOU DIDN'T TAKE ON THIS DEBT...
...WITHOUT KNOWING HOW MUCH IT WAS, DID YOU?
SACHI...
TWENTY MILLION YEN?!
Exactly right.
TWE...
HOW MANY TIMES DO I HAVE TO TELL YOU?!

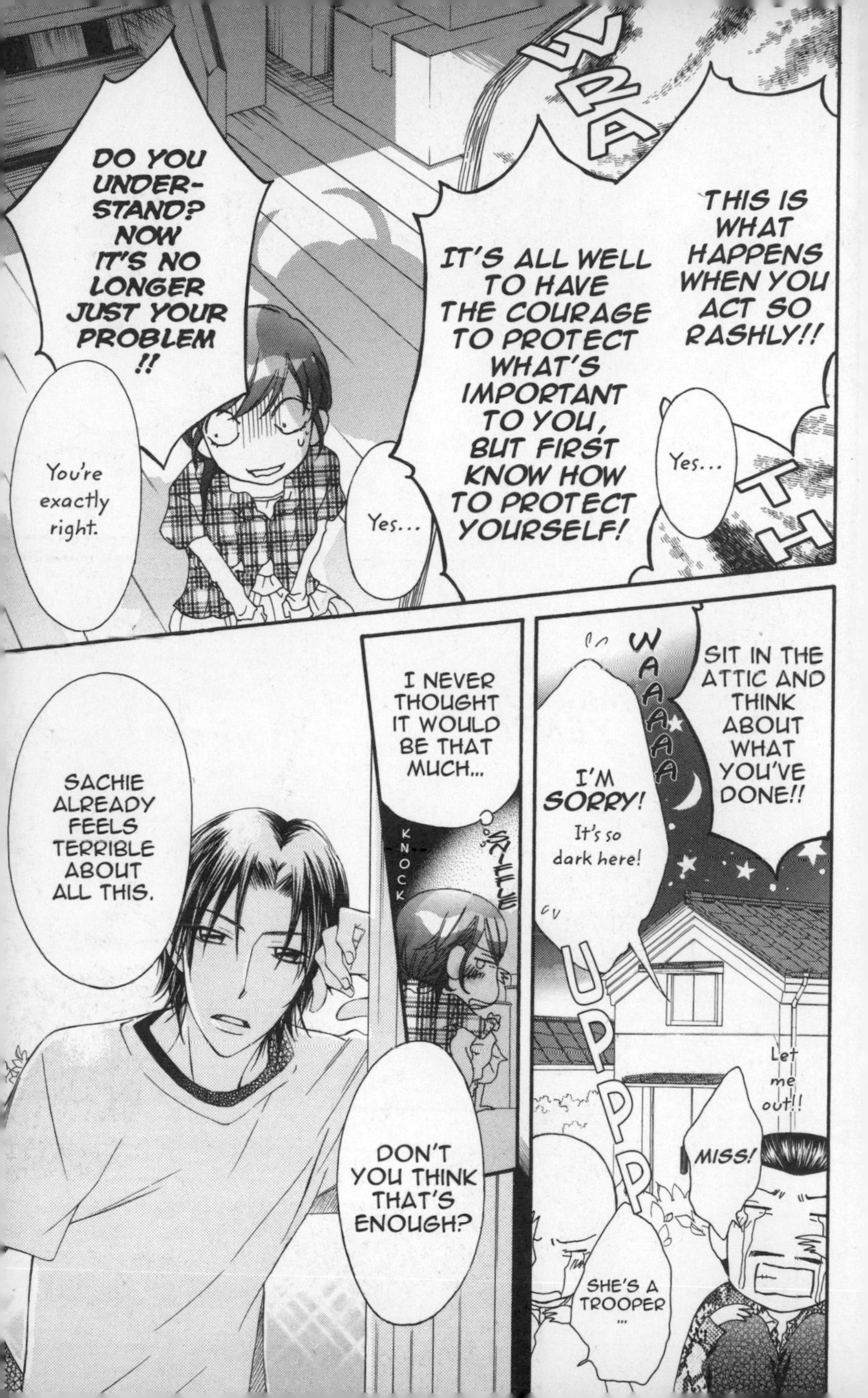
THIS IS WHAT HAPPENS WHEN YOU ACT SO RASHLY!!
Yes...
IT'S ALL WELL TO HAVE THE COURAGE TO PROTECT WHAT'S IMPORTANT TO YOU, BUT FIRST KNOW HOW TO PROTECT YOURSELF!
Yes...
DO YOU UNDER-STAND? NOW IT'S NO LONGER JUST YOUR PROBLEM !!
You're exactly right.
SIT IN THE ATTIC AND THINK ABOUT WHAT YOU'VE DONE!!
WAAAAAA
I'M SORRY! It's so dark here!
Let me out!!
MISS!
SHE'S A TROOPER ...
I NEVER THOUGHT IT WOULD BE THAT MUCH...
SNIFFLE
KNOCK
DON'T YOU THINK THAT'S ENOUGH?
SACHIE ALREADY FEELS TERRIBLE ABOUT ALL THIS.

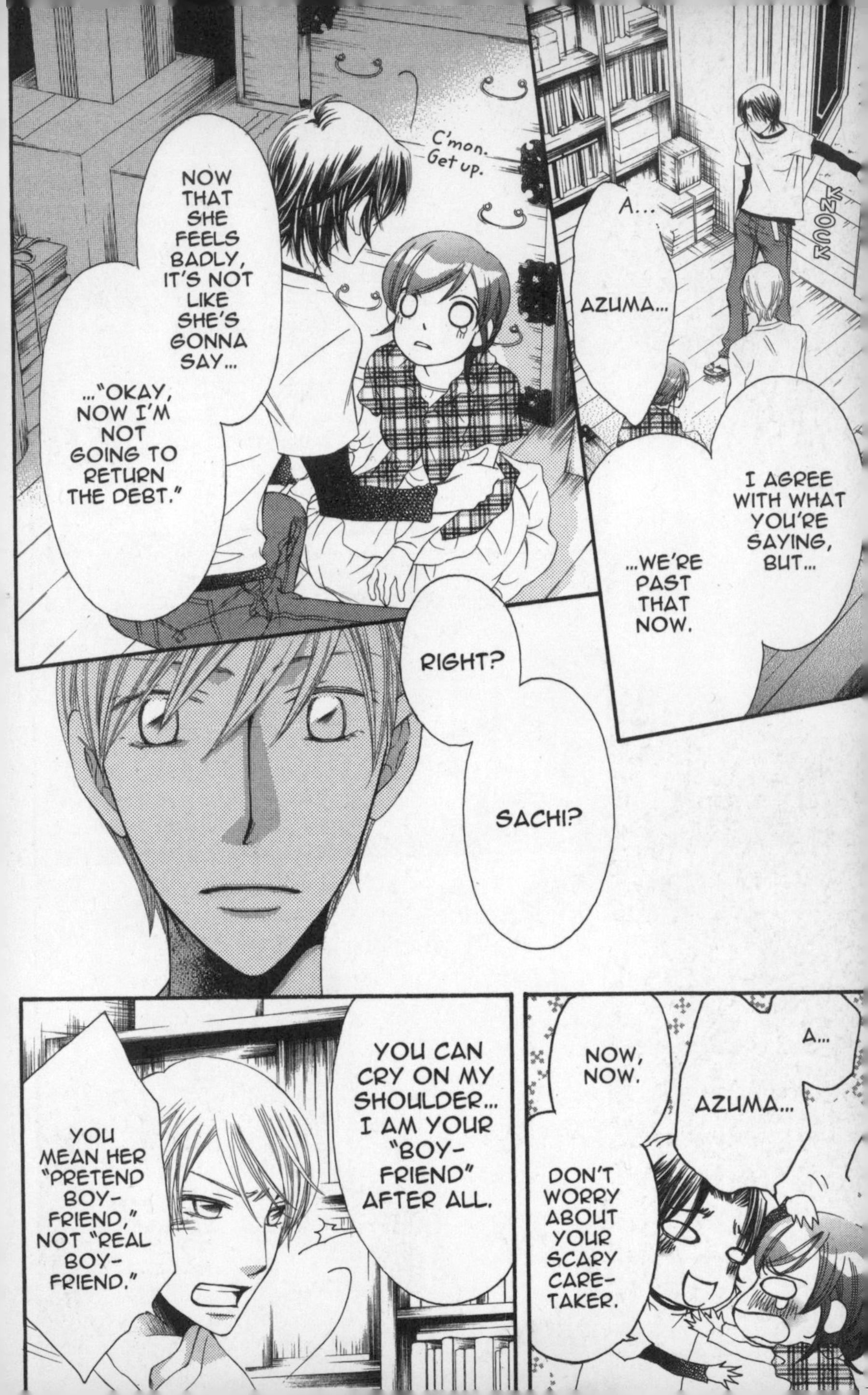
KNOCK
A...
AZUMA...
I AGREE WITH WHAT YOU'RE SAYING, BUT...
...WE'RE PAST THAT NOW.
C'mon. Get up.
NOW THAT SHE FEELS BADLY, IT'S NOT LIKE SHE'S GONNA SAY...
..."OKAY, NOW I'M NOT GOING TO RETURN THE DEBT."
RIGHT?
SACHI?
A...
AZUMA...
NOW, NOW.
DON'T WORRY ABOUT YOUR SCARY CARE-TAKER.
YOU CAN CRY ON MY SHOULDER... I AM YOUR "BOY-FRIEND" AFTER ALL.
YOU MEAN HER "PRETEND BOY-FRIEND," NOT "REAL BOY-FRIEND."

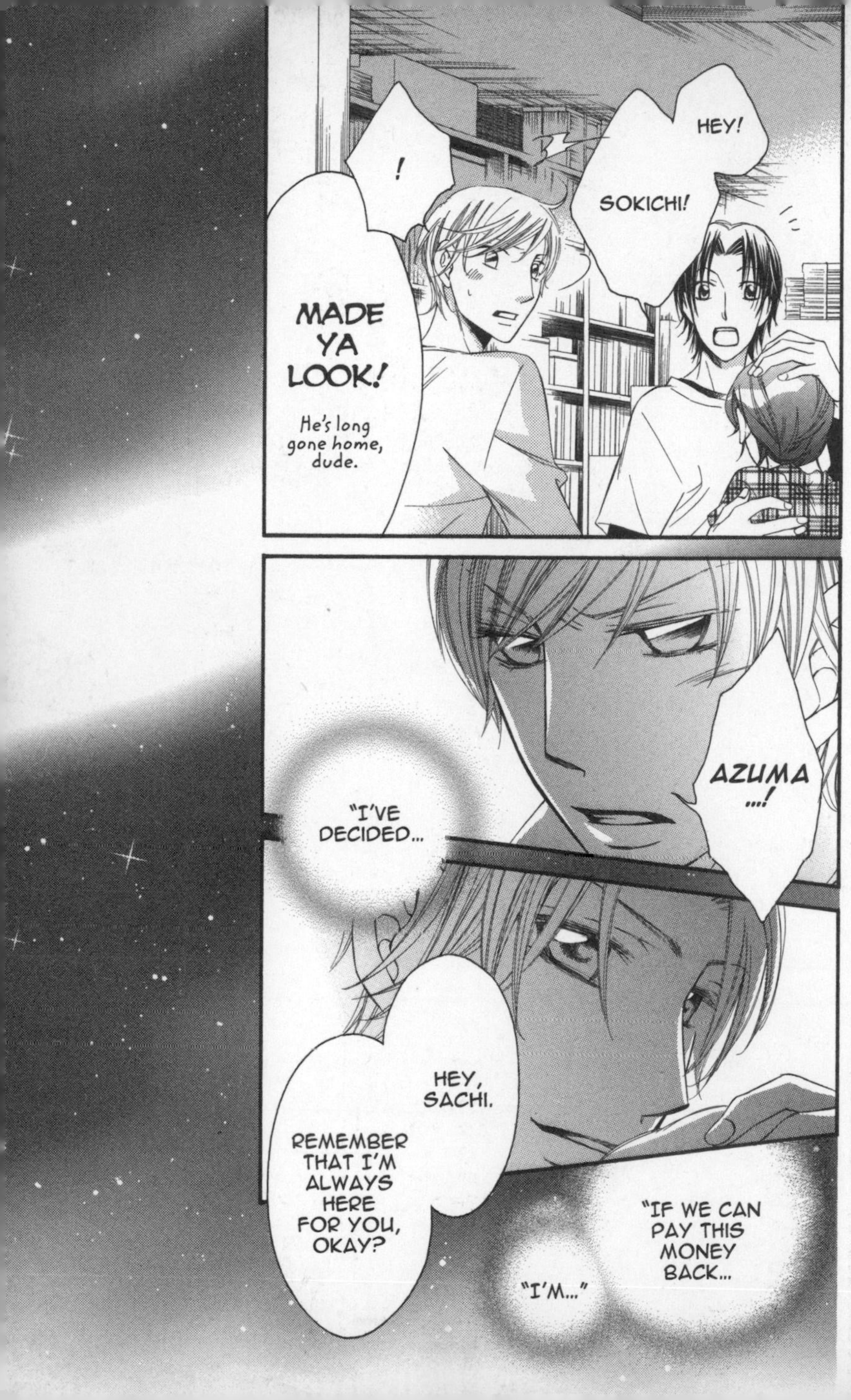
HEY!
SOKICHI!
!
MADE YA LOOK!
He's long gone home, dude.
AZUMA ...!
"I'VE DECIDED...
HEY, SACHI.
REMEMBER THAT I'M ALWAYS HERE FOR YOU, OKAY?
"IF WE CAN PAY THIS MONEY BACK...
"I'M..."

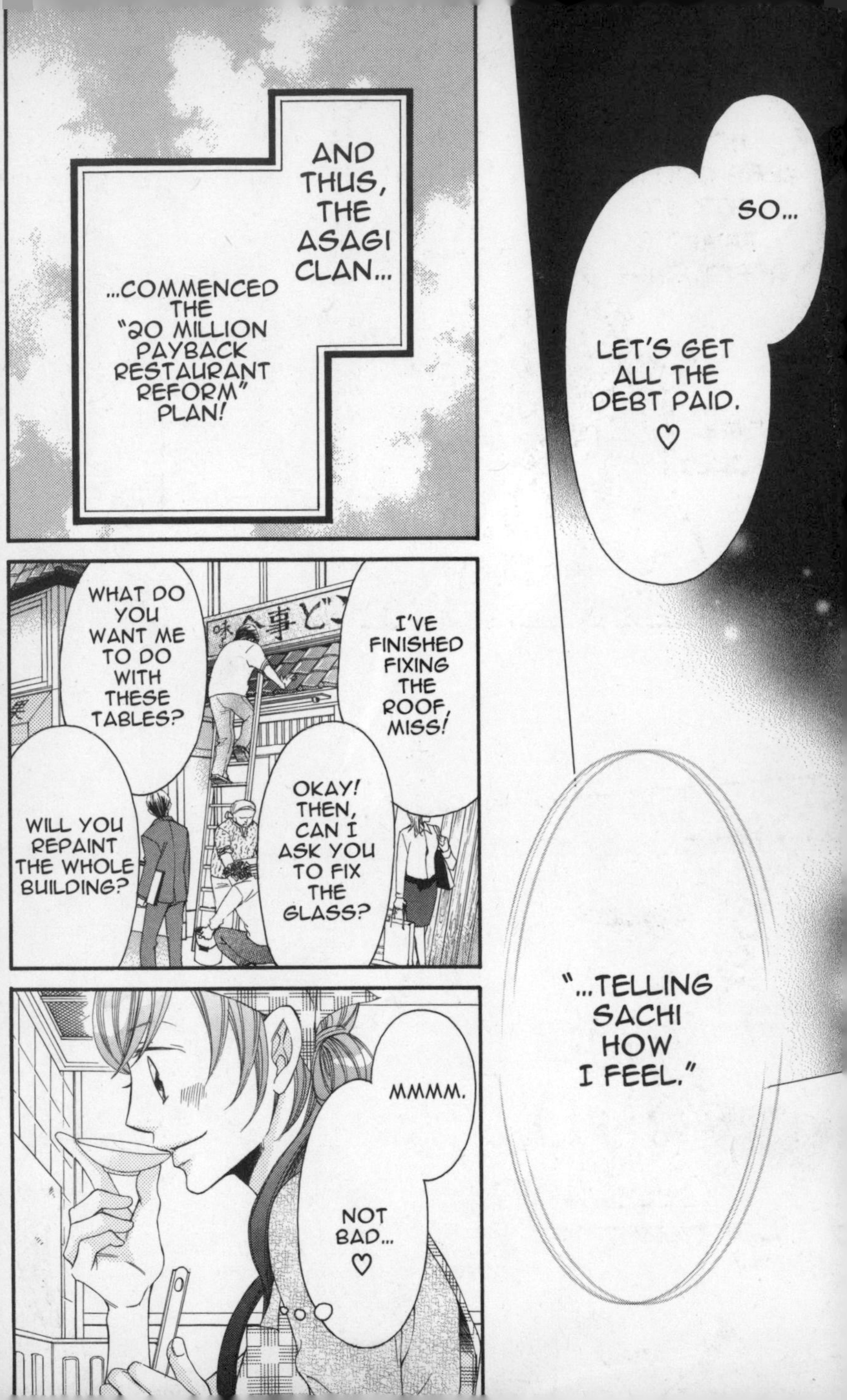
SO...
LET'S GET ALL THE DEBT PAID. ♡
"...TELLING SACHI HOW I FEEL."
AND THUS, THE ASAGI CLAN...
...COMMENCED THE "20 MILLION PAYBACK RESTAURANT REFORM" PLAN!
I'VE FINISHED FIXING THE ROOF, MISS!
WHAT DO YOU WANT ME TO DO WITH THESE TABLES?
OKAY! THEN, CAN I ASK YOU TO FIX THE GLASS?
WILL YOU REPAINT THE WHOLE BUILDING?
MMMM.
NOT BAD... ♡

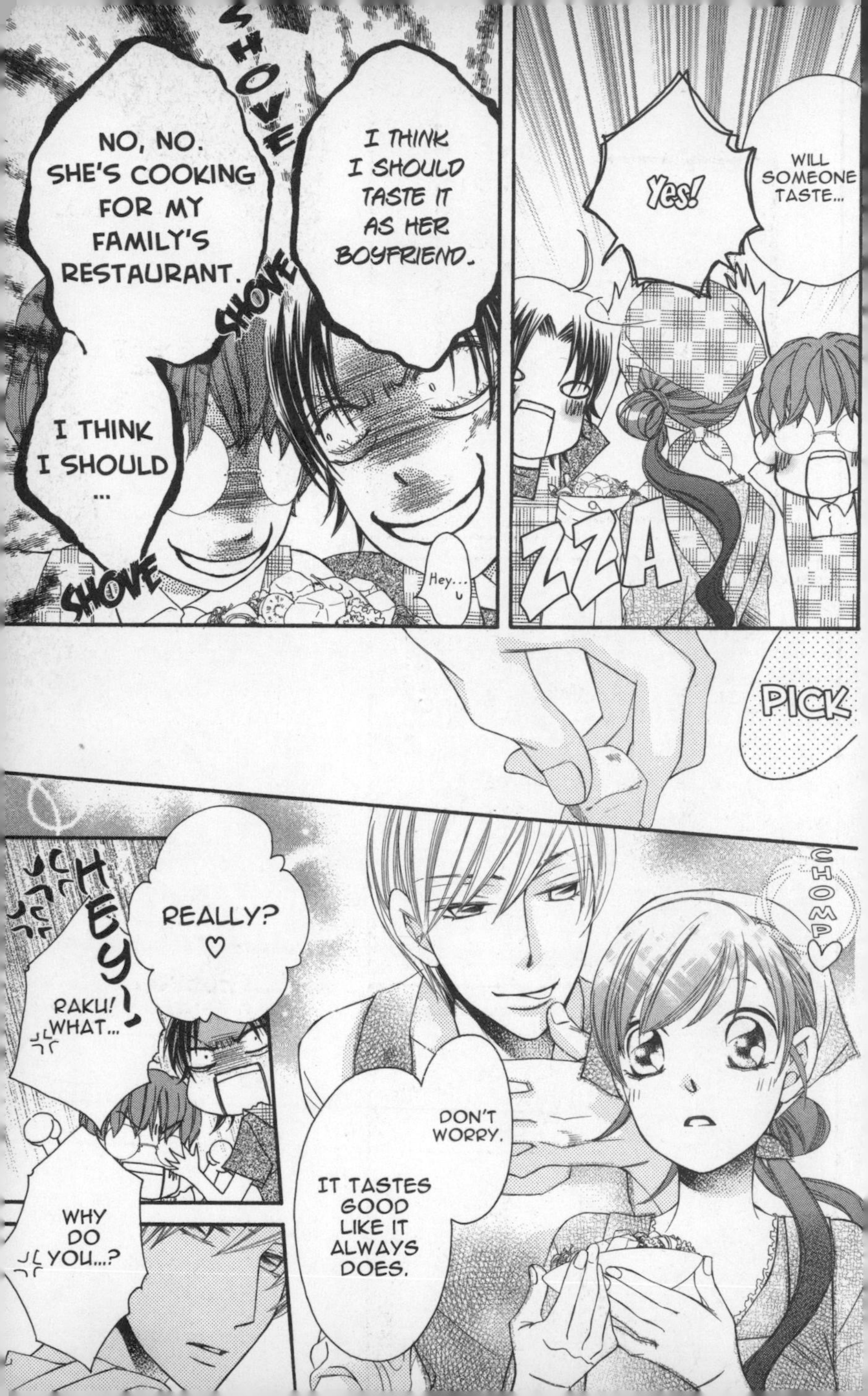
WILL SOMEONE TASTE...
Yes!
ZZA
I THINK I SHOULD TASTE IT AS HER BOYFRIEND.
SHOVE
NO, NO. SHE'S COOKING FOR MY FAMILY'S RESTAURANT.
SHOVE
I THINK I SHOULD ...
SHOVE
Hey...
PICK
CHOMP
REALLY? ♡
HEY!
RAKU! WHAT...
DON'T WORRY.
IT TASTES GOOD LIKE IT ALWAYS DOES.
WHY DO YOU...?

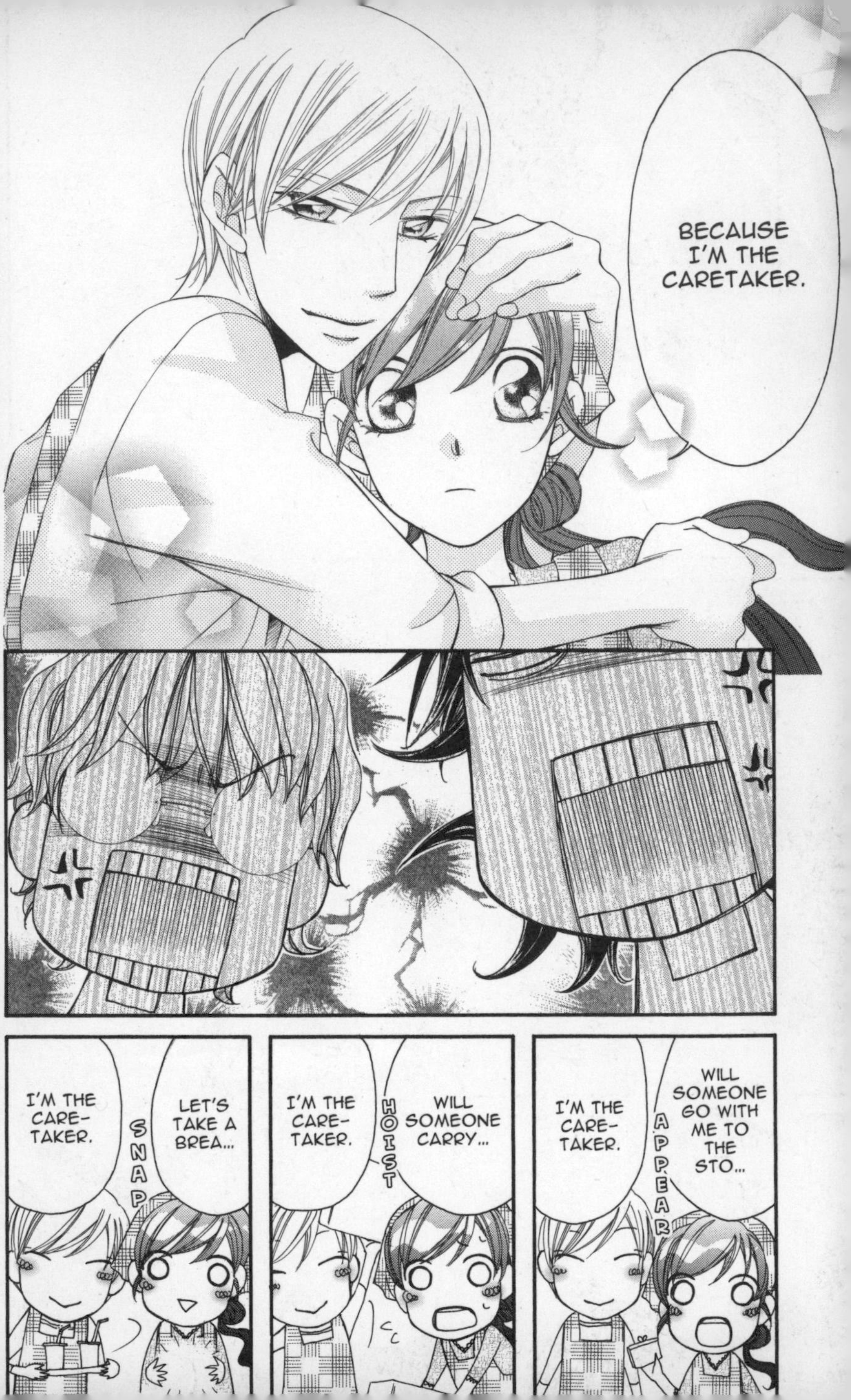
BECAUSE I'M THE CARETAKER.
WILL SOMEONE GO WITH ME TO THE STO...
APPEAR
I'M THE CARE-TAKER.
WILL SOMEONE CARRY...
HOIST
I'M THE CARE-TAKER.
LET'S TAKE A BREA...
SNAP
I'M THE CARE-TAKER.

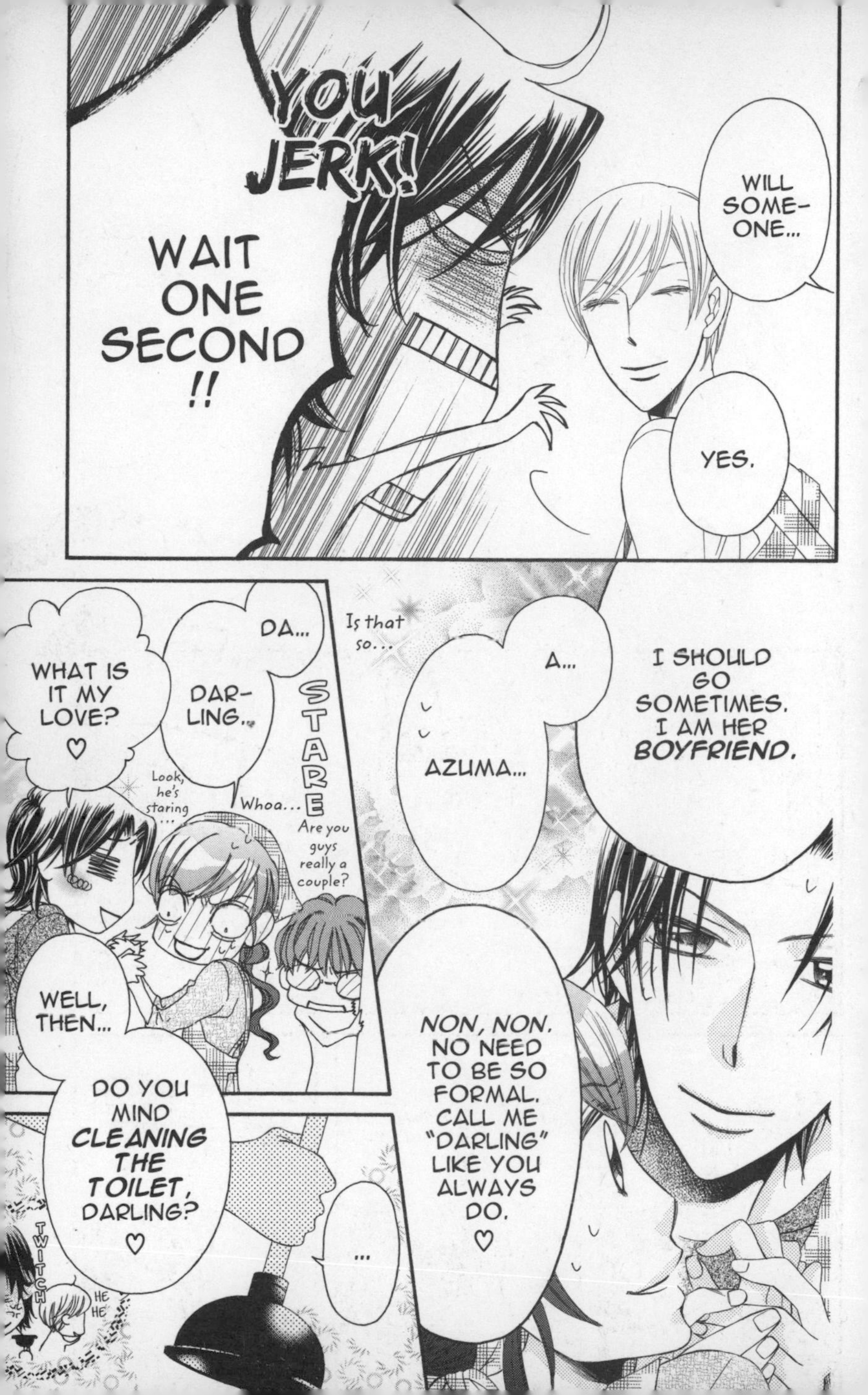
WILL SOME-ONE...
YES.
YOU JERK!
WAIT ONE SECOND !!
I SHOULD GO SOMETIMES. I AM HER BOYFRIEND.
A... AZUMA...
Is that so...
NON, NON. NO NEED TO BE SO FORMAL. CALL ME "DARLING" LIKE YOU ALWAYS DO. ♡
...
DA... DAR-LING..
STARE
Whoa...
Are you guys really a couple?
Look, he's staring...
WHAT IS IT MY LOVE? ♡
WELL, THEN...
DO YOU MIND CLEANING THE TOILET, DARLING? ♡
TWITCH
HE HE

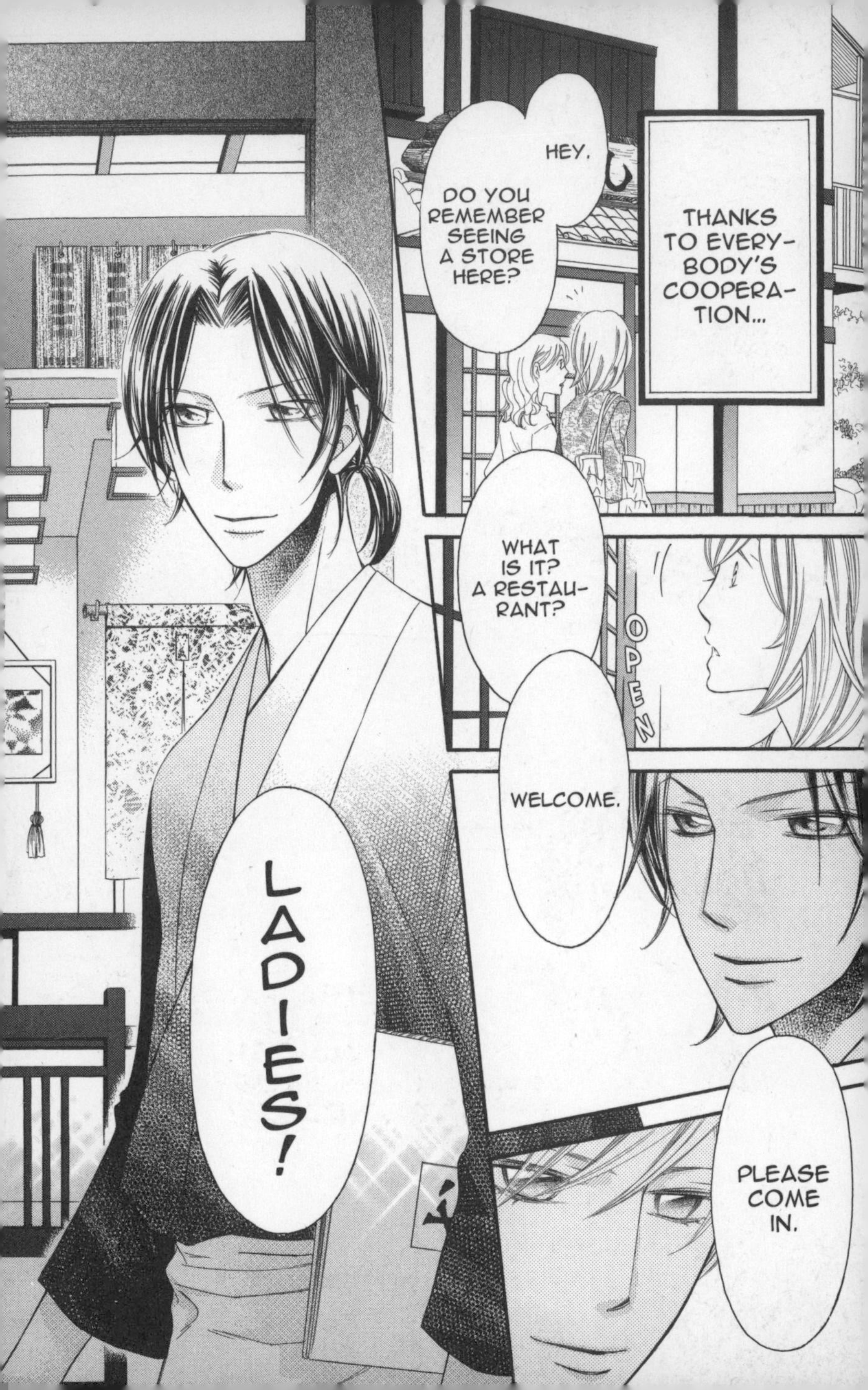
THANKS TO EVERYBODY'S COOPERATION...
HEY.
DO YOU REMEMBER SEEING A STORE HERE?
OPEN
WHAT IS IT? A RESTAURANT?
WELCOME.
PLEASE COME IN.
LADIES!

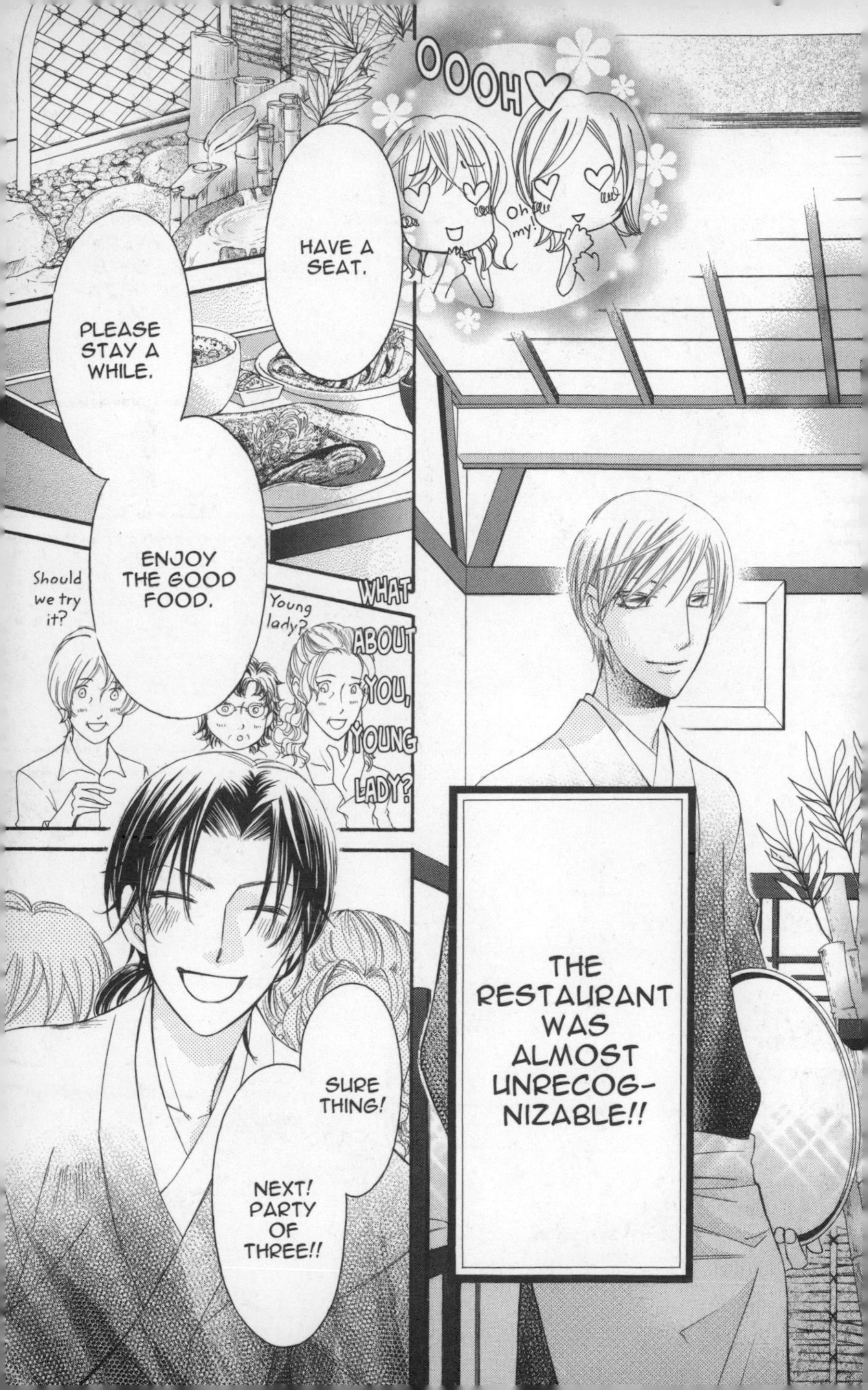
OOOH
Oh my!
THE RESTAURANT WAS ALMOST UNRECOG-NIZABLE!!
HAVE A SEAT.
PLEASE STAY A WHILE.
ENJOY THE GOOD FOOD.
WHAT ABOUT YOU, YOUNG LADY?
Young lady?
Should we try it?
SURE THING!
NEXT! PARTY OF THREE!!

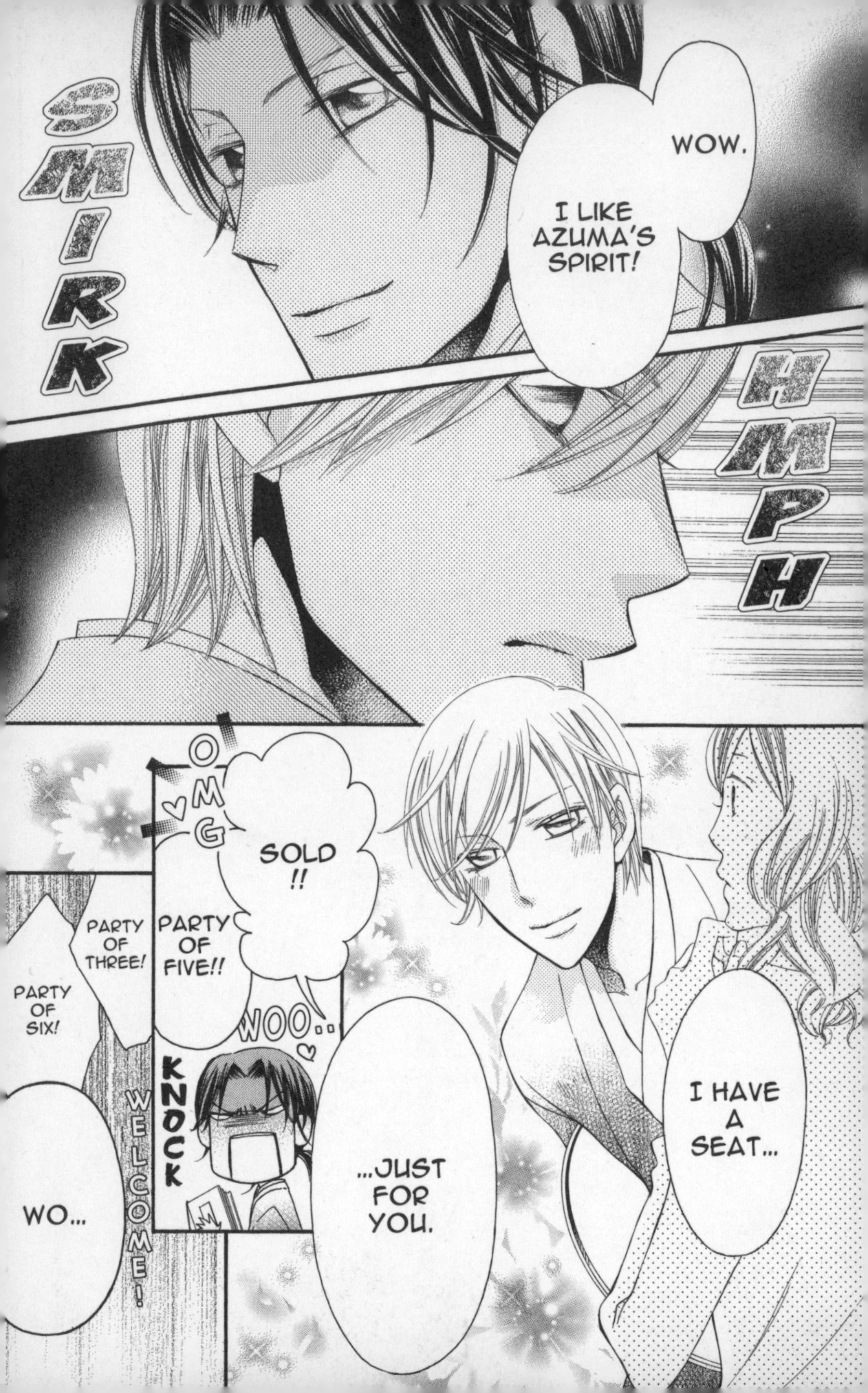
WOW.
I LIKE AZUMA'S SPIRIT!
SMIRK
HMPH
I HAVE A SEAT...
...JUST FOR YOU.
OMG
SOLD !!
PARTY OF FIVE!!
WOO..
KNOCK
PARTY OF THREE!
PARTY OF SIX!
WO...
WELCOME!

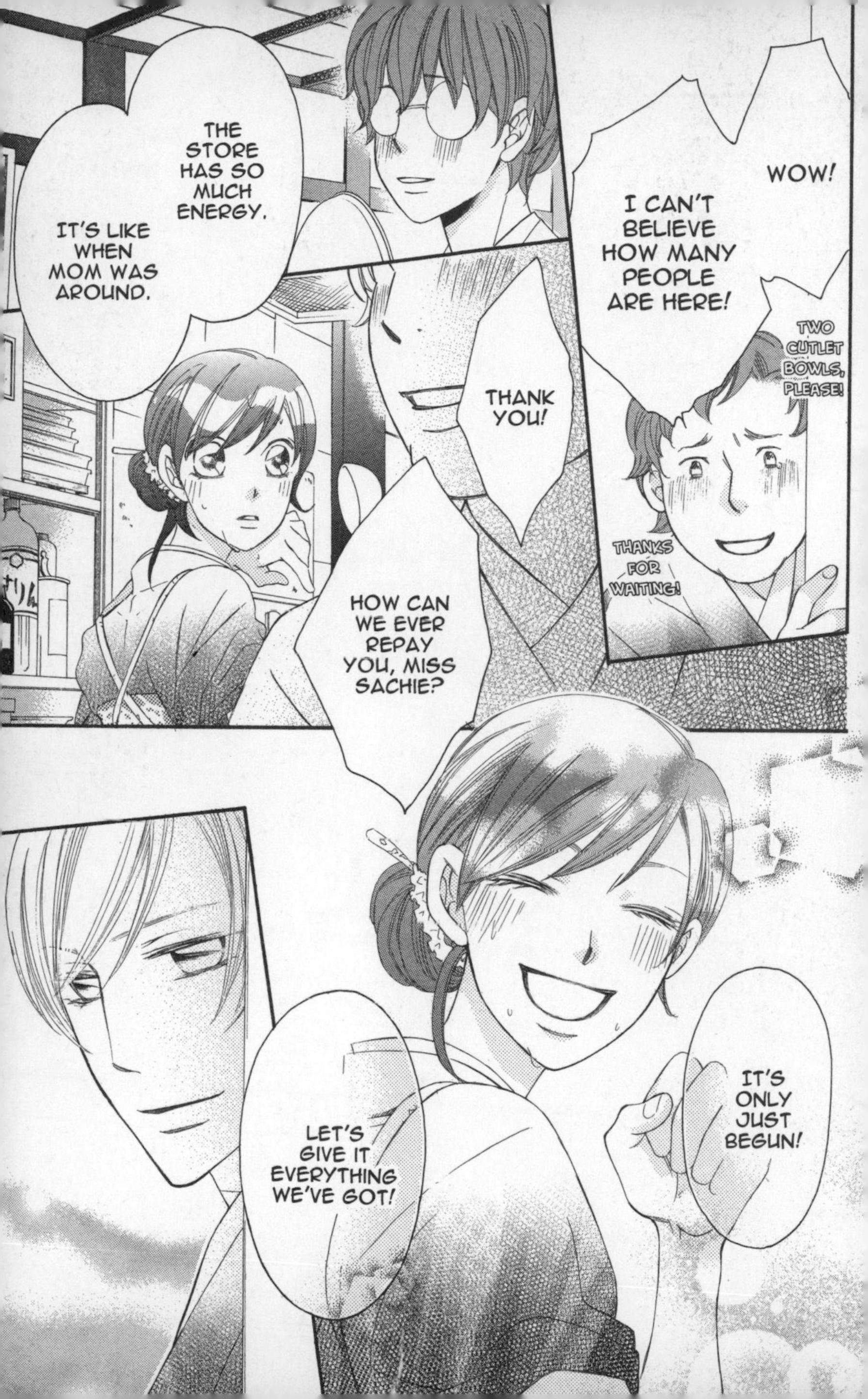
WOW!
I CAN'T BELIEVE HOW MANY PEOPLE ARE HERE!
TWO CUTLET BOWLS, PLEASE!
THANKS FOR WAITING!
THE STORE HAS SO MUCH ENERGY.
IT'S LIKE WHEN MOM WAS AROUND.
THANK YOU!
HOW CAN WE EVER REPAY YOU, MISS SACHIE?
IT'S ONLY JUST BEGUN!
LET'S GIVE IT EVERYTHING WE'VE GOT!

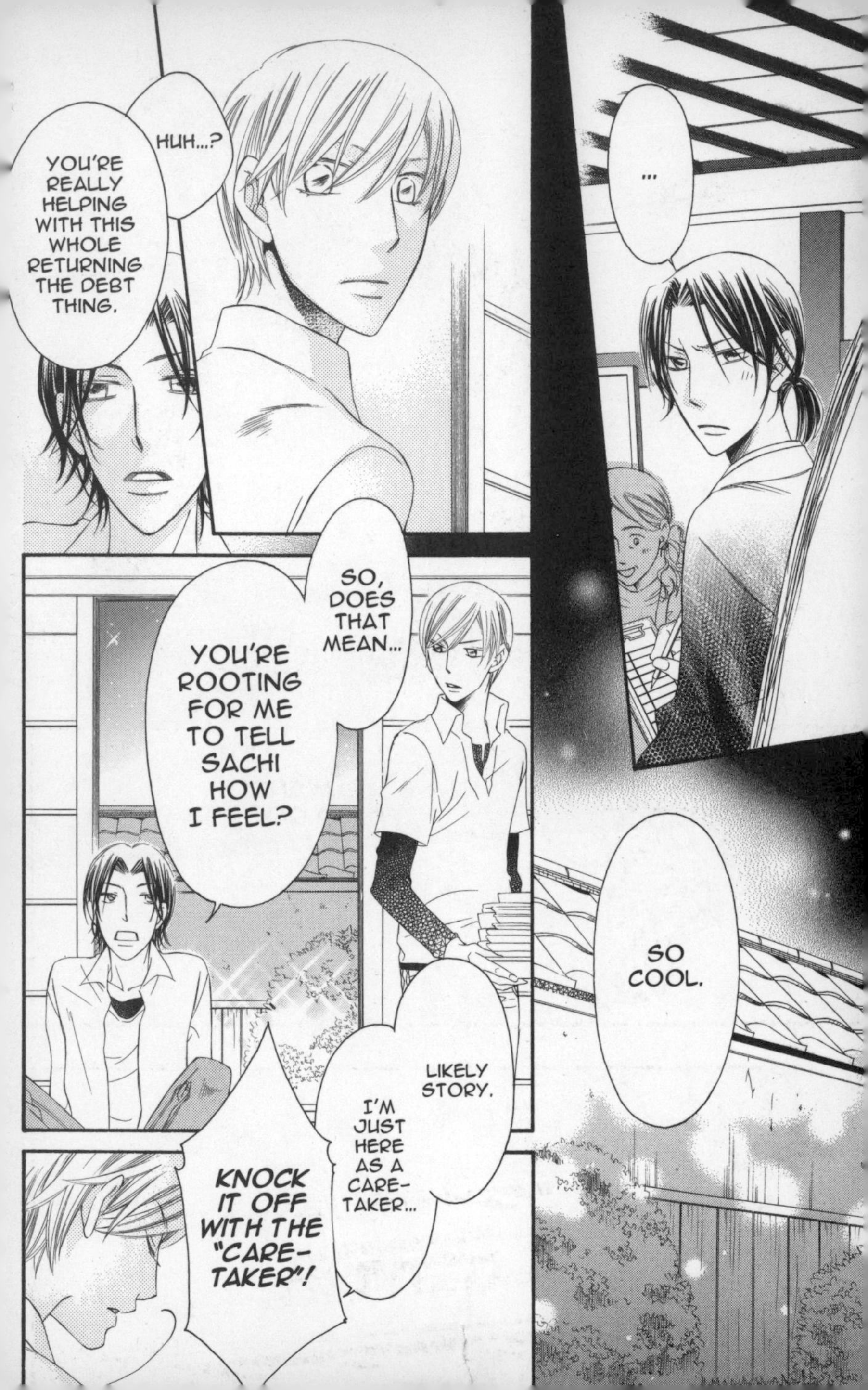
...
SO COOL.
HUH...?
YOU'RE REALLY HELPING WITH THIS WHOLE RETURNING THE DEBT THING.
SO, DOES THAT MEAN...
YOU'RE ROOTING FOR ME TO TELL SACHI HOW I FEEL?
LIKELY STORY.
I'M JUST HERE AS A CARE-TAKER...
KNOCK IT OFF WITH THE "CARE-TAKER"!

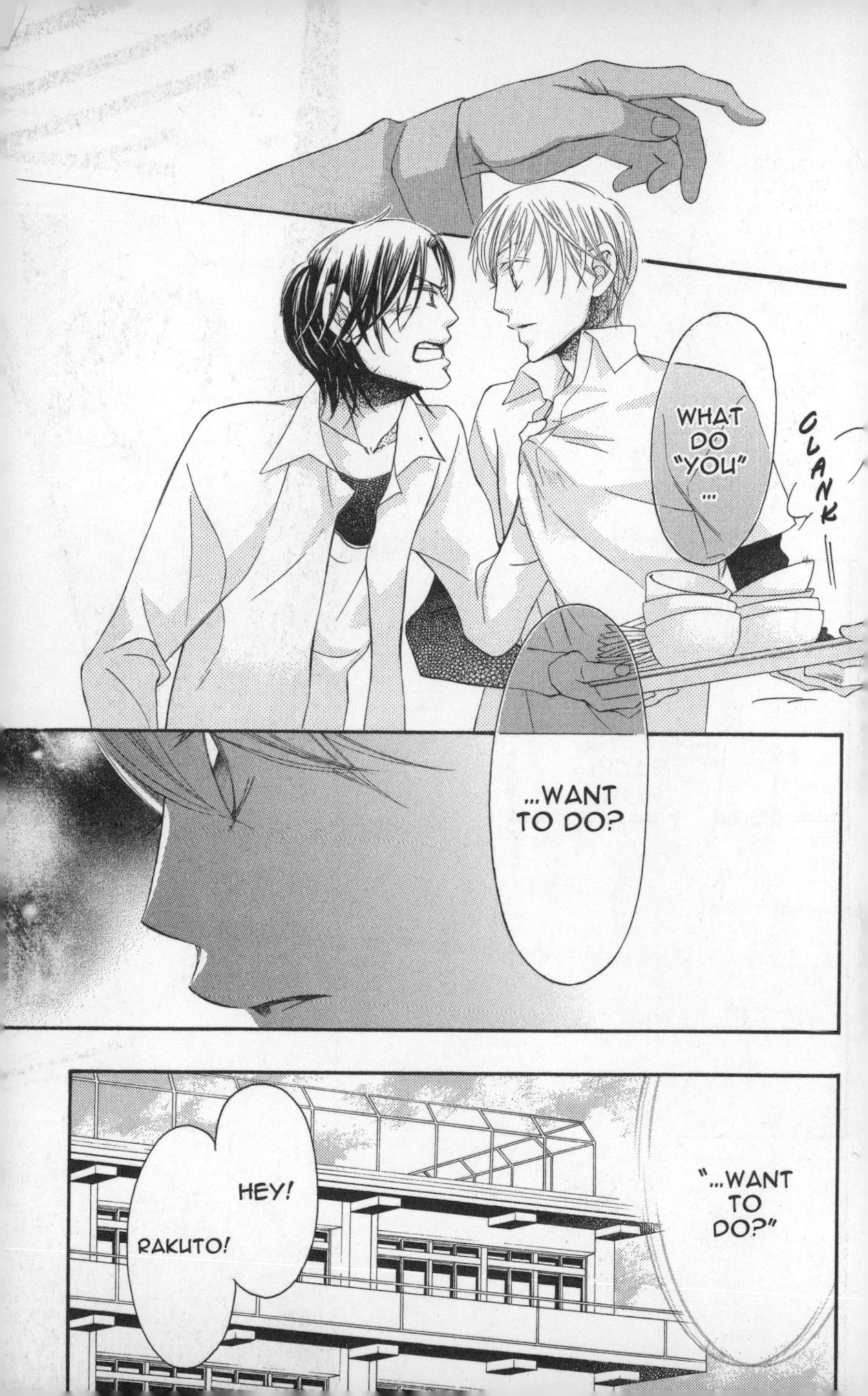
CLANK
WHAT DO "YOU" ...
...WANT TO DO?
"...WANT TO DO?"
HEY!
RAKUTO!

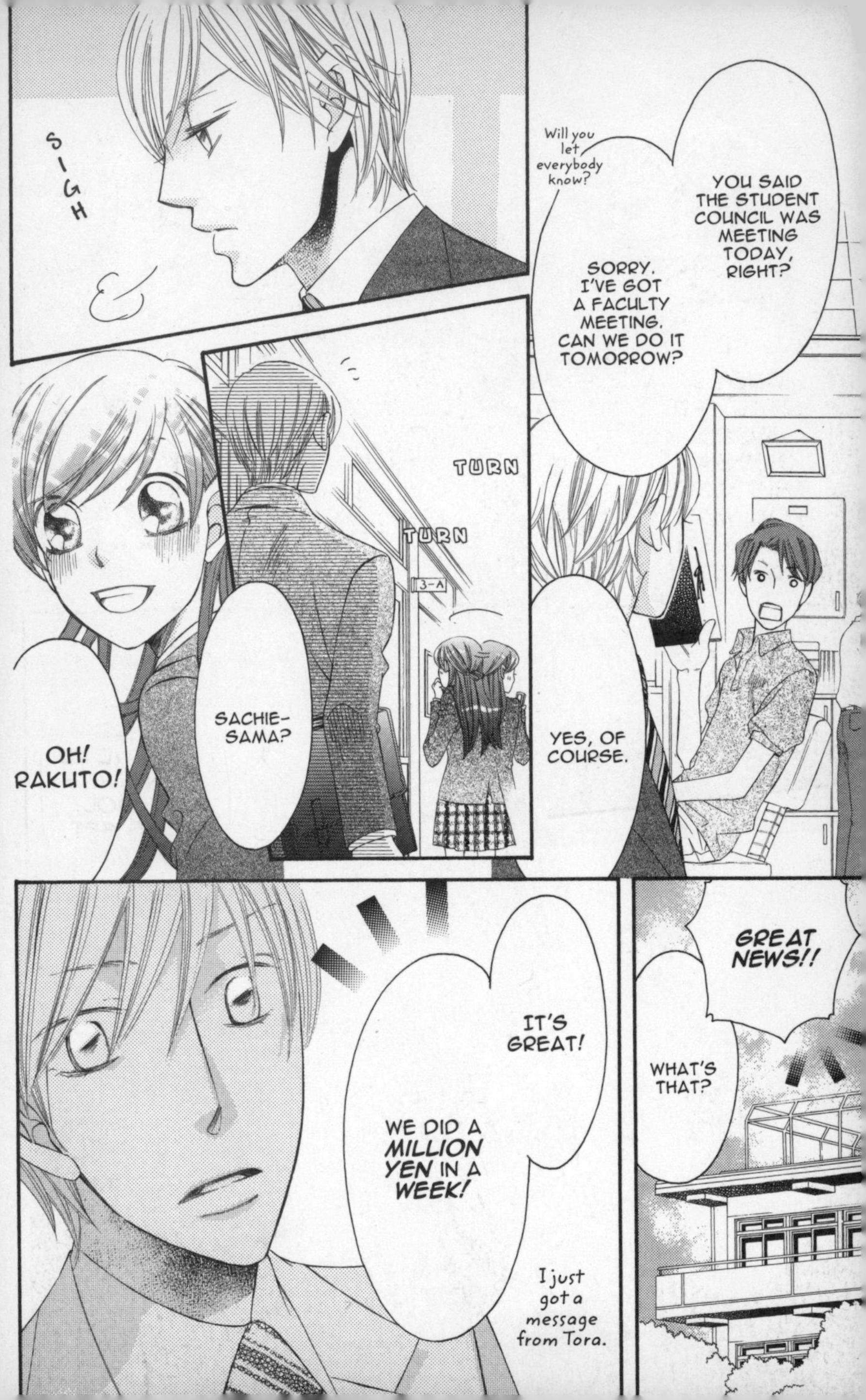
YOU SAID THE STUDENT COUNCIL WAS MEETING TODAY, RIGHT?
Will you let everybody know?
SORRY. I'VE GOT A FACULTY MEETING. CAN WE DO IT TOMORROW?
YES, OF COURSE.
SIGH
TURN
TURN
3-A
SACHIE-SAMA?
OH! RAKUTO!
GREAT NEWS!!
WHAT'S THAT?
I just got a message from Tora.
IT'S GREAT!
WE DID A MILLION YEN IN A WEEK!

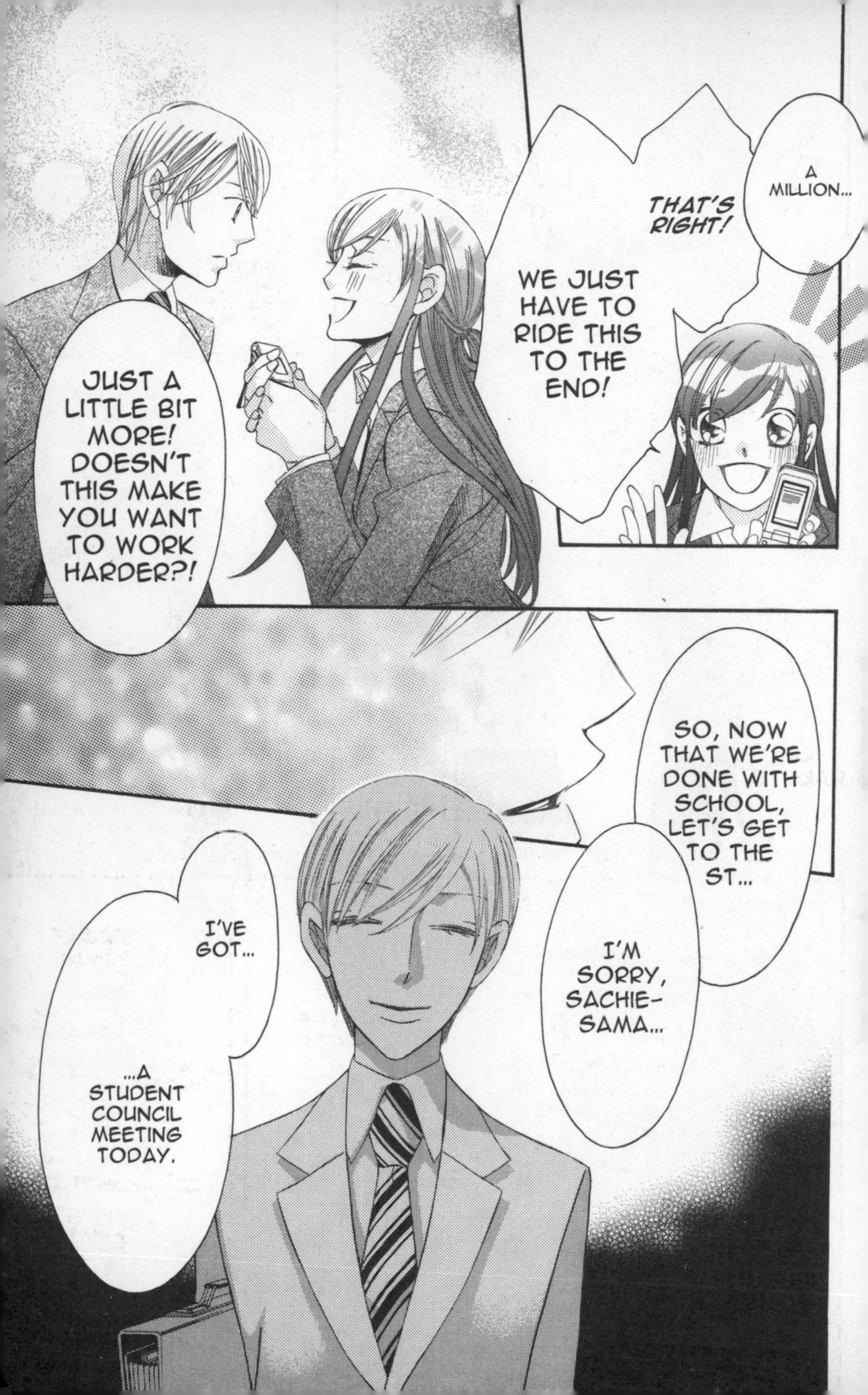
A MILLION...
THAT'S RIGHT!
WE JUST HAVE TO RIDE THIS TO THE END!
JUST A LITTLE BIT MORE! DOESN'T THIS MAKE YOU WANT TO WORK HARDER?!
SO, NOW THAT WE'RE DONE WITH SCHOOL, LET'S GET TO THE ST...
I'M SORRY, SACHIE-SAMA...
I'VE GOT...
...A STUDENT COUNCIL MEETING TODAY.

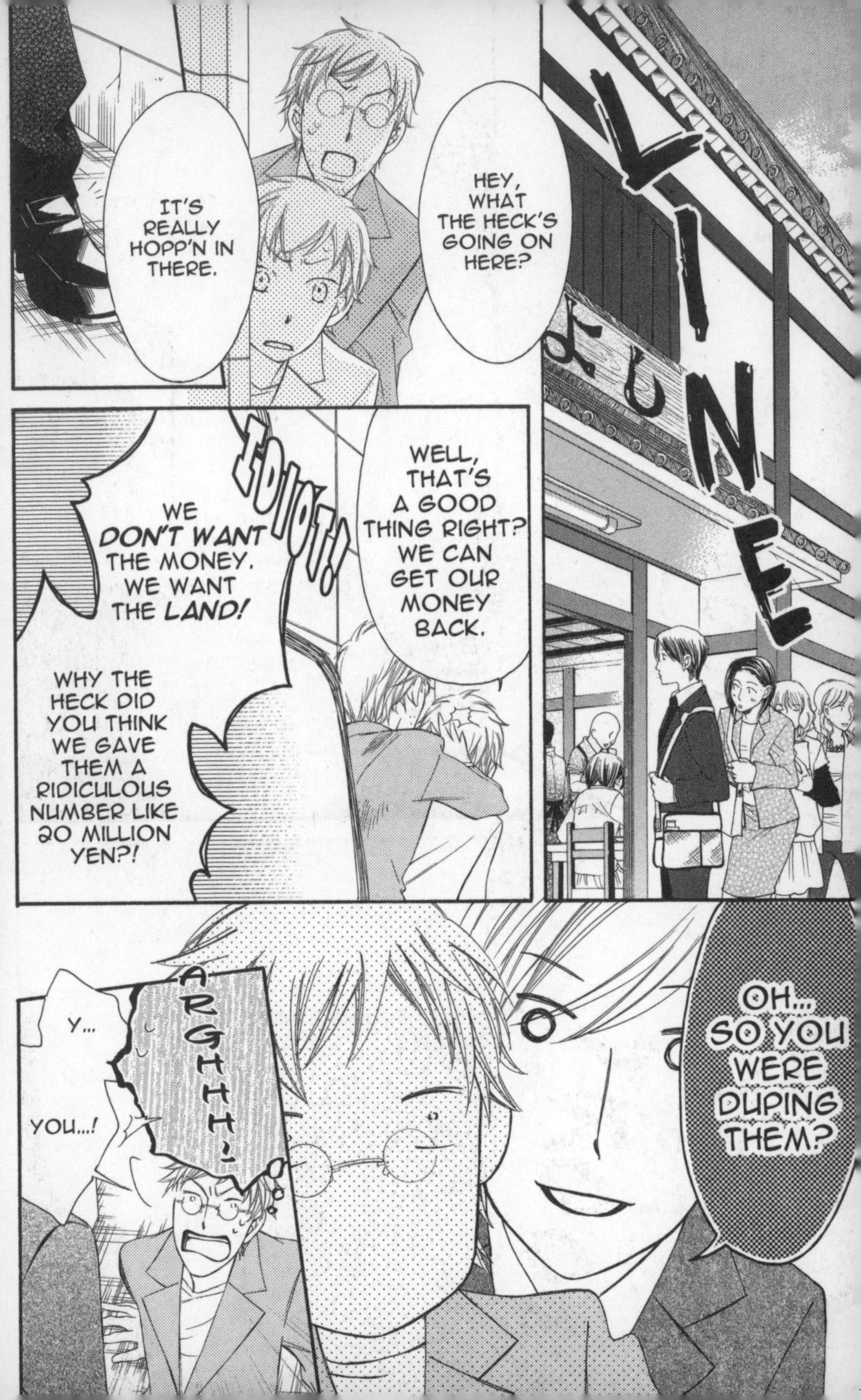
HEY, WHAT THE HECK'S GOING ON HERE?
IT'S REALLY HOPP'N IN THERE.
WELL, THAT'S A GOOD THING RIGHT? WE CAN GET OUR MONEY BACK.
IDIOT!!
WE *DON'T WANT* THE MONEY. WE WANT THE *LAND!*
WHY THE HECK DID YOU THINK WE GAVE THEM A RIDICULOUS NUMBER LIKE 20 MILLION YEN?!
OH... SO YOU WERE DUPING THEM?
ARGHHH!
Y...
YOU...!

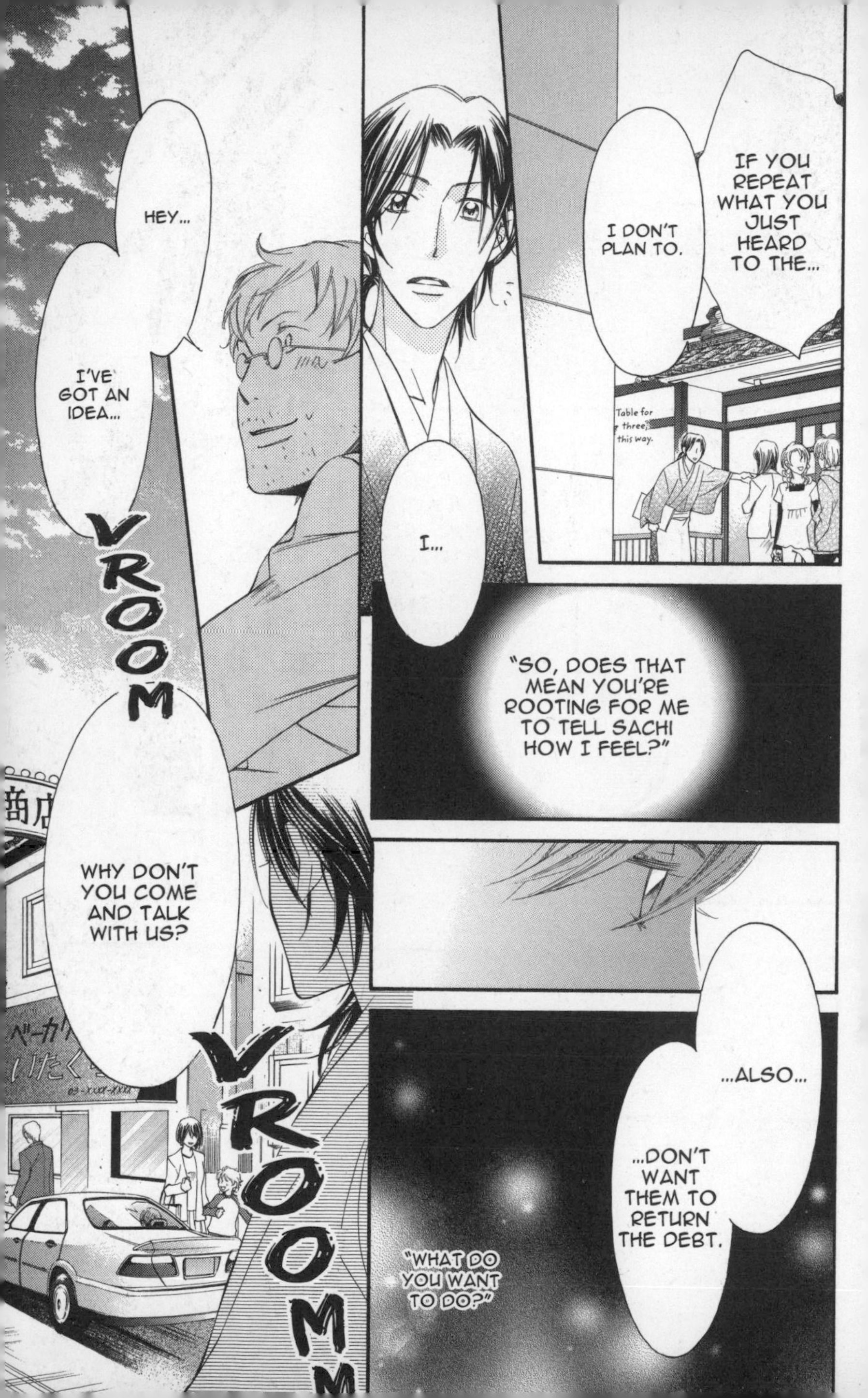
IF YOU REPEAT WHAT YOU JUST HEARD TO THE...
I DON'T PLAN TO.
Table for three, this way.
I...
"SO, DOES THAT MEAN YOU'RE ROOTING FOR ME TO TELL SACHI HOW I FEEL?"
...ALSO...
...DON'T WANT THEM TO RETURN THE DEBT.
"WHAT DO YOU WANT TO DO?"
HEY...
I'VE GOT AN IDEA...
VROOM
WHY DON'T YOU COME AND TALK WITH US?
VROOMM

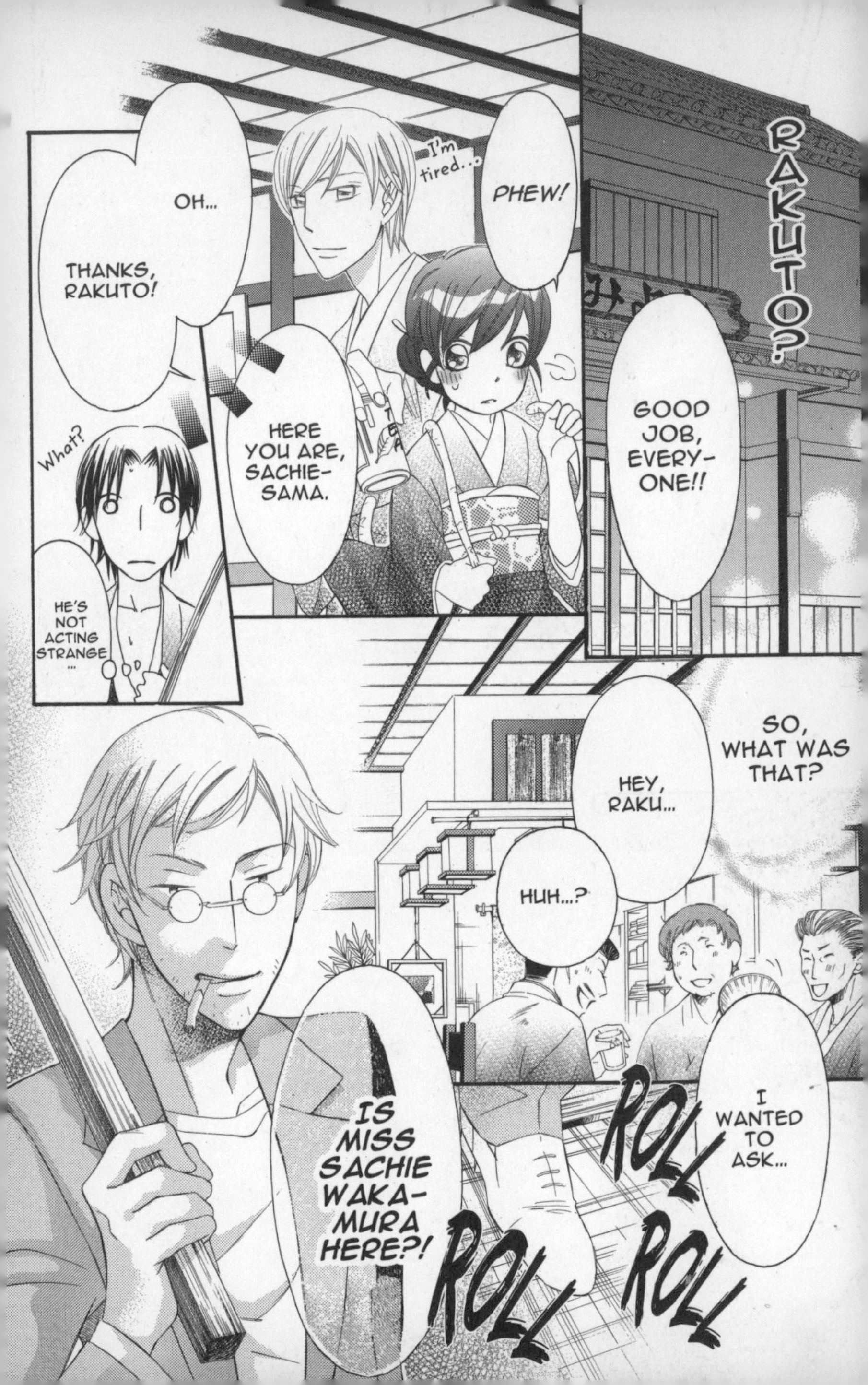
RAKUTO?
GOOD JOB, EVERY-ONE!!
PHEW!
I'm tired...
HERE YOU ARE, SACHIE-SAMA.
OH...
THANKS, RAKUTO!
What?
HE'S NOT ACTING STRANGE...
SO, WHAT WAS THAT?
HEY, RAKU...
HUH...?
I WANTED TO ASK...
IS MISS SACHIE WAKAMURA HERE?!
ROLL
ROLL
ROLL
ROLL

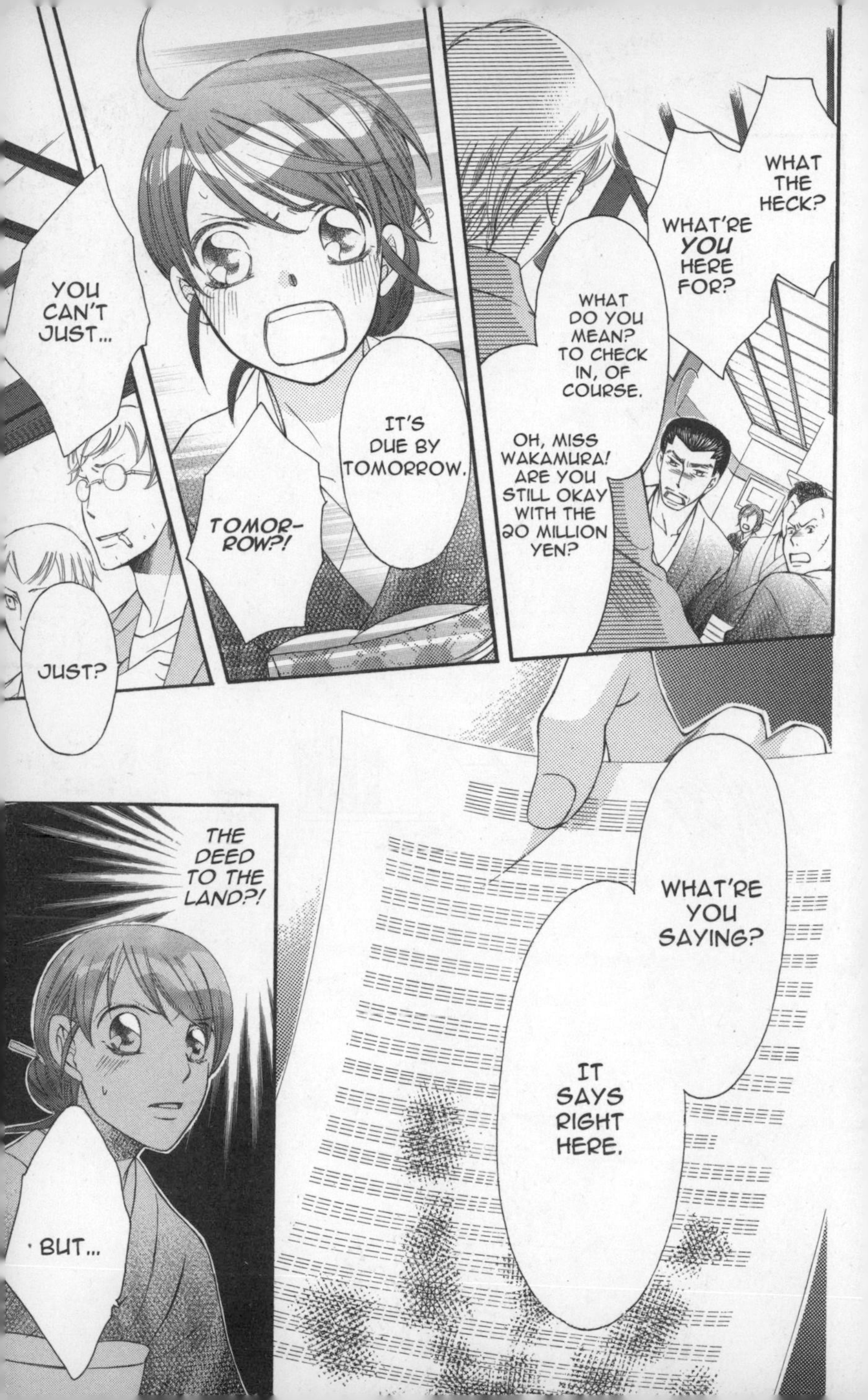
WHAT THE HECK?
WHAT'RE *YOU* HERE FOR?
WHAT DO YOU MEAN? TO CHECK IN, OF COURSE.
OH, MISS WAKAMURA! ARE YOU STILL OKAY WITH THE 20 MILLION YEN?
IT'S DUE BY TOMORROW.
TOMORROW?!
YOU CAN'T JUST...
JUST?
WHAT'RE YOU SAYING?
IT SAYS RIGHT HERE.
THE DEED TO THE LAND?!
BUT...

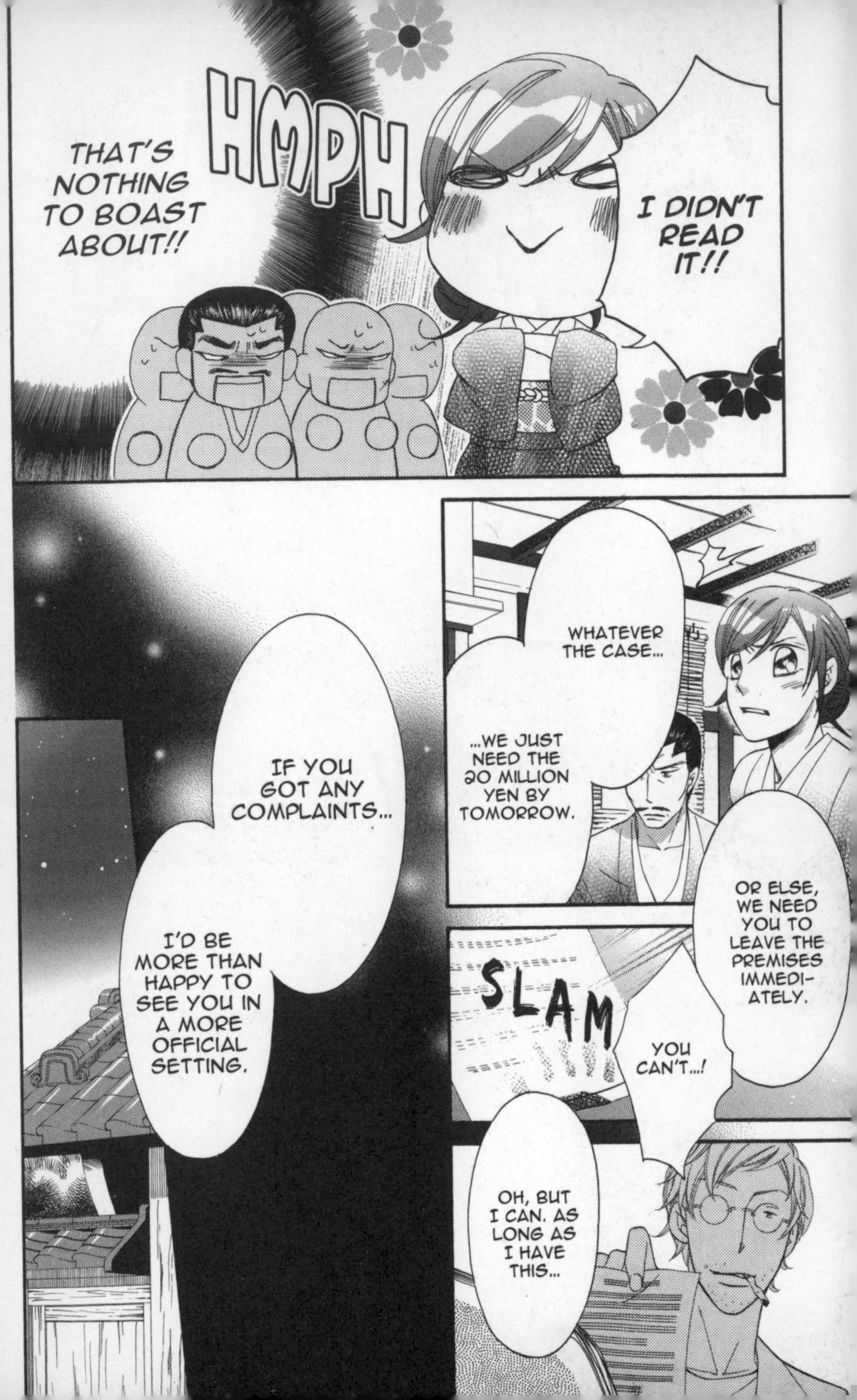
I DIDN'T READ IT!!
HMPH
THAT'S NOTHING TO BOAST ABOUT!!
WHATEVER THE CASE...
...WE JUST NEED THE 20 MILLION YEN BY TOMORROW.
OR ELSE, WE NEED YOU TO LEAVE THE PREMISES IMMEDI-ATELY.
SLAM
YOU CAN'T...!
OH, BUT I CAN. AS LONG AS I HAVE THIS...
IF YOU GOT ANY COMPLAINTS...
I'D BE MORE THAN HAPPY TO SEE YOU IN A MORE OFFICIAL SETTING.

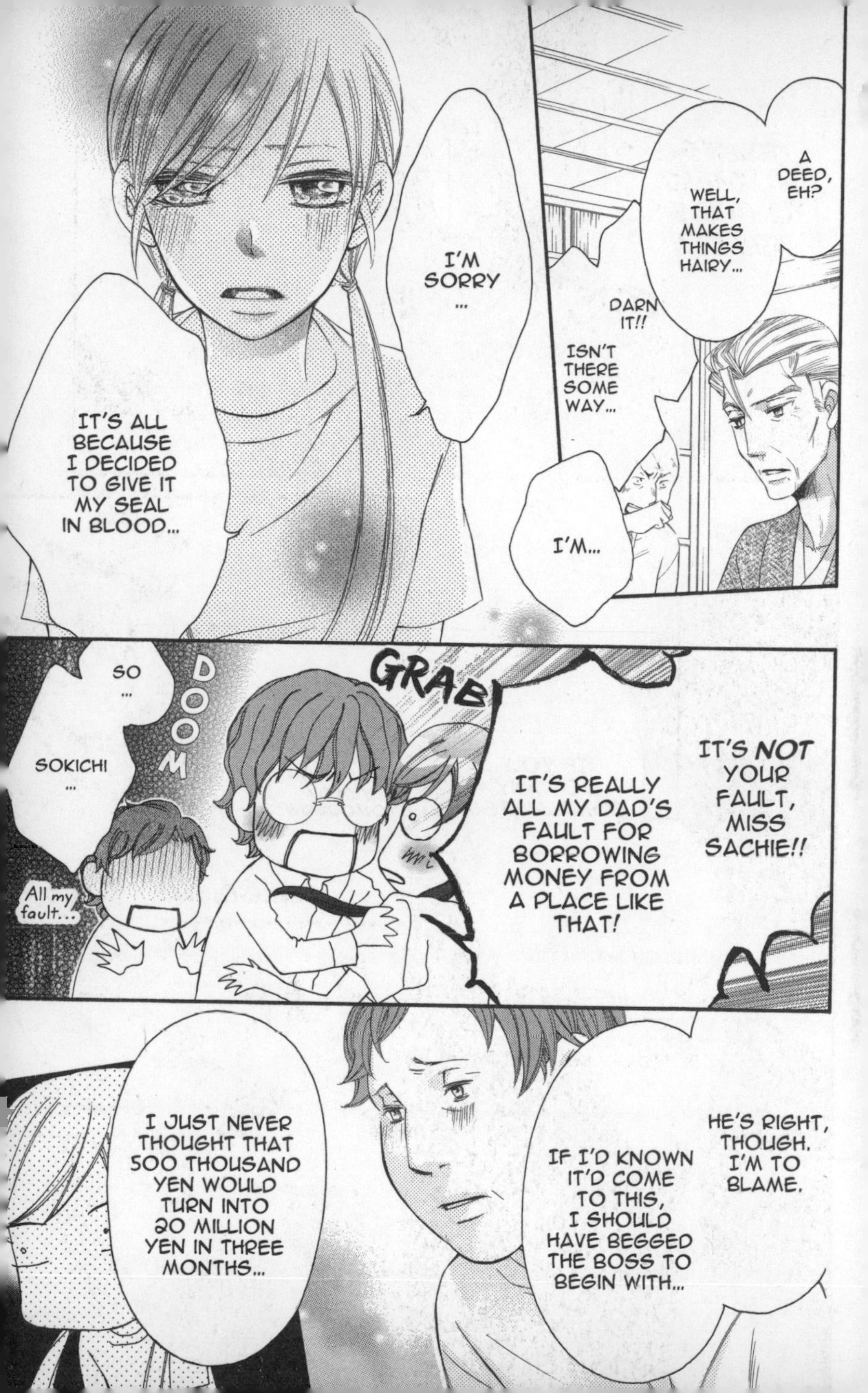
A DEED, EH?
WELL, THAT MAKES THINGS HAIRY...
DARN IT!!
ISN'T THERE SOME WAY...
I'M...
I'M SORRY...
IT'S ALL BECAUSE I DECIDED TO GIVE IT MY SEAL IN BLOOD...
IT'S NOT YOUR FAULT, MISS SACHIE!!
IT'S REALLY ALL MY DAD'S FAULT FOR BORROWING MONEY FROM A PLACE LIKE THAT!
GRAB
DOOOM
SO... SOKICHI...
All my fault...
HE'S RIGHT, THOUGH. I'M TO BLAME.
IF I'D KNOWN IT'D COME TO THIS, I SHOULD HAVE BEGGED THE BOSS TO BEGIN WITH...
I JUST NEVER THOUGHT THAT 500 THOUSAND YEN WOULD TURN INTO 20 MILLION YEN IN THREE MONTHS...

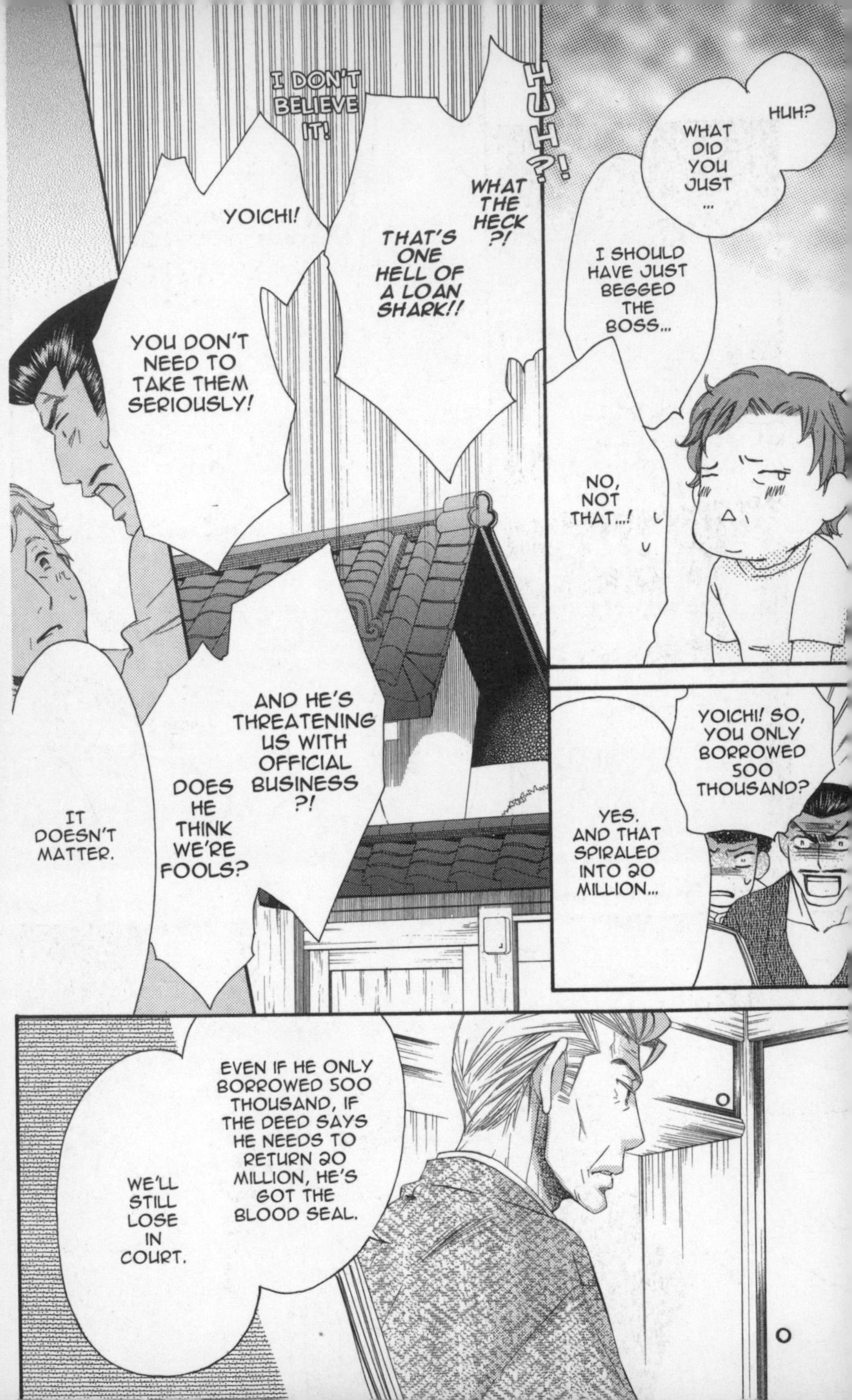
HUH?
WHAT DID YOU JUST ...
I SHOULD HAVE JUST BEGGED THE BOSS...
NO, NOT THAT...!
YOICHI! SO, YOU ONLY BORROWED 500 THOUSAND?
YES. AND THAT SPIRALED INTO 20 MILLION...
HUH?!
WHAT THE HECK?!
THAT'S ONE HELL OF A LOAN SHARK!!
I DON'T BELIEVE IT!
YOICHI!
YOU DON'T NEED TO TAKE THEM SERIOUSLY!
AND HE'S THREATENING US WITH OFFICIAL BUSINESS?!
DOES HE THINK WE'RE FOOLS?
IT DOESN'T MATTER.
EVEN IF HE ONLY BORROWED 500 THOUSAND, IF THE DEED SAYS HE NEEDS TO RETURN 20 MILLION, HE'S GOT THE BLOOD SEAL.
WE'LL STILL LOSE IN COURT.

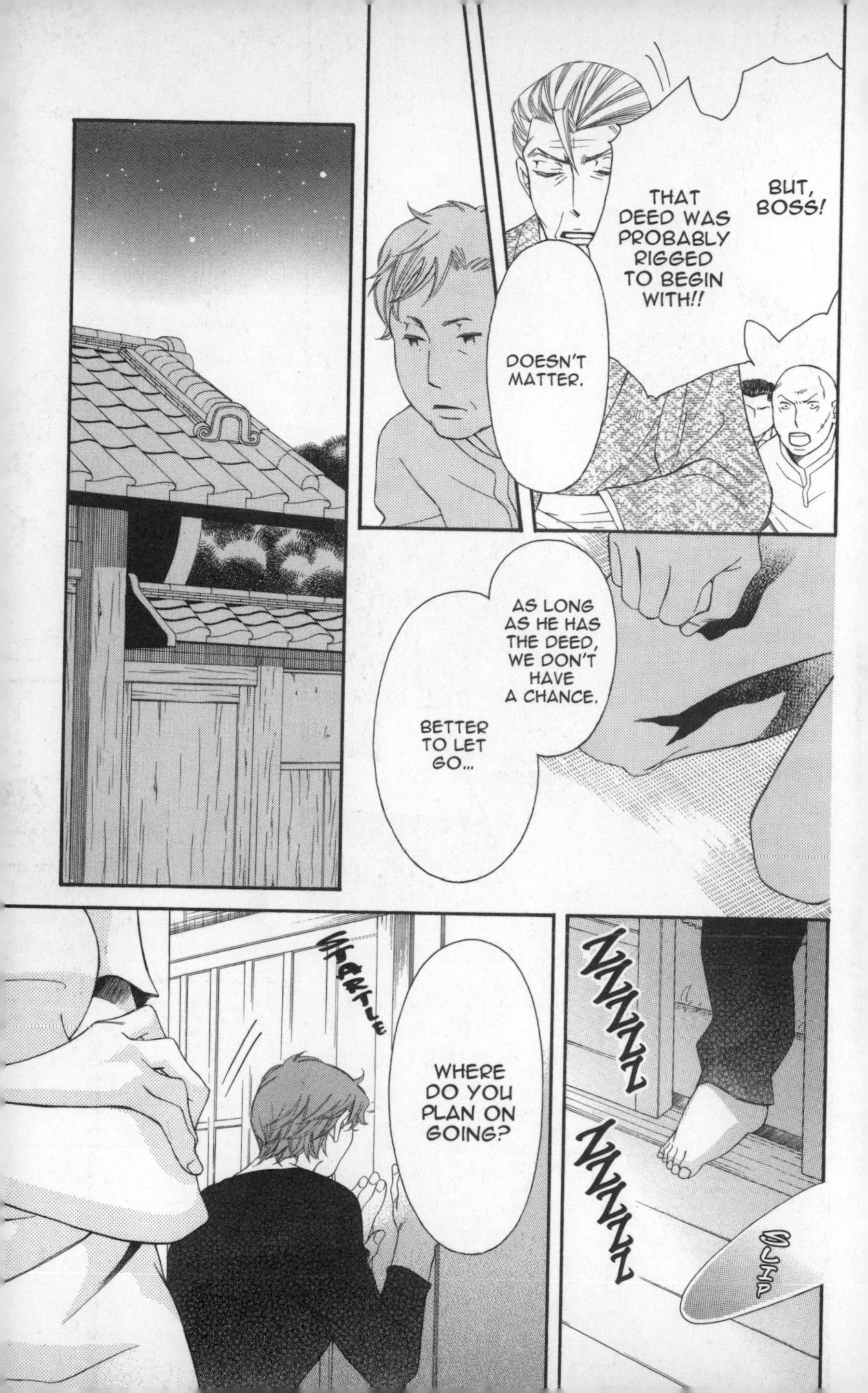
BUT, BOSS!
THAT DEED WAS PROBABLY RIGGED TO BEGIN WITH!!
DOESN'T MATTER.
AS LONG AS HE HAS THE DEED, WE DON'T HAVE A CHANCE.
BETTER TO LET GO...
ZZZZZ
ZZZZZ
SLIP
STARTLE
WHERE DO YOU PLAN ON GOING?

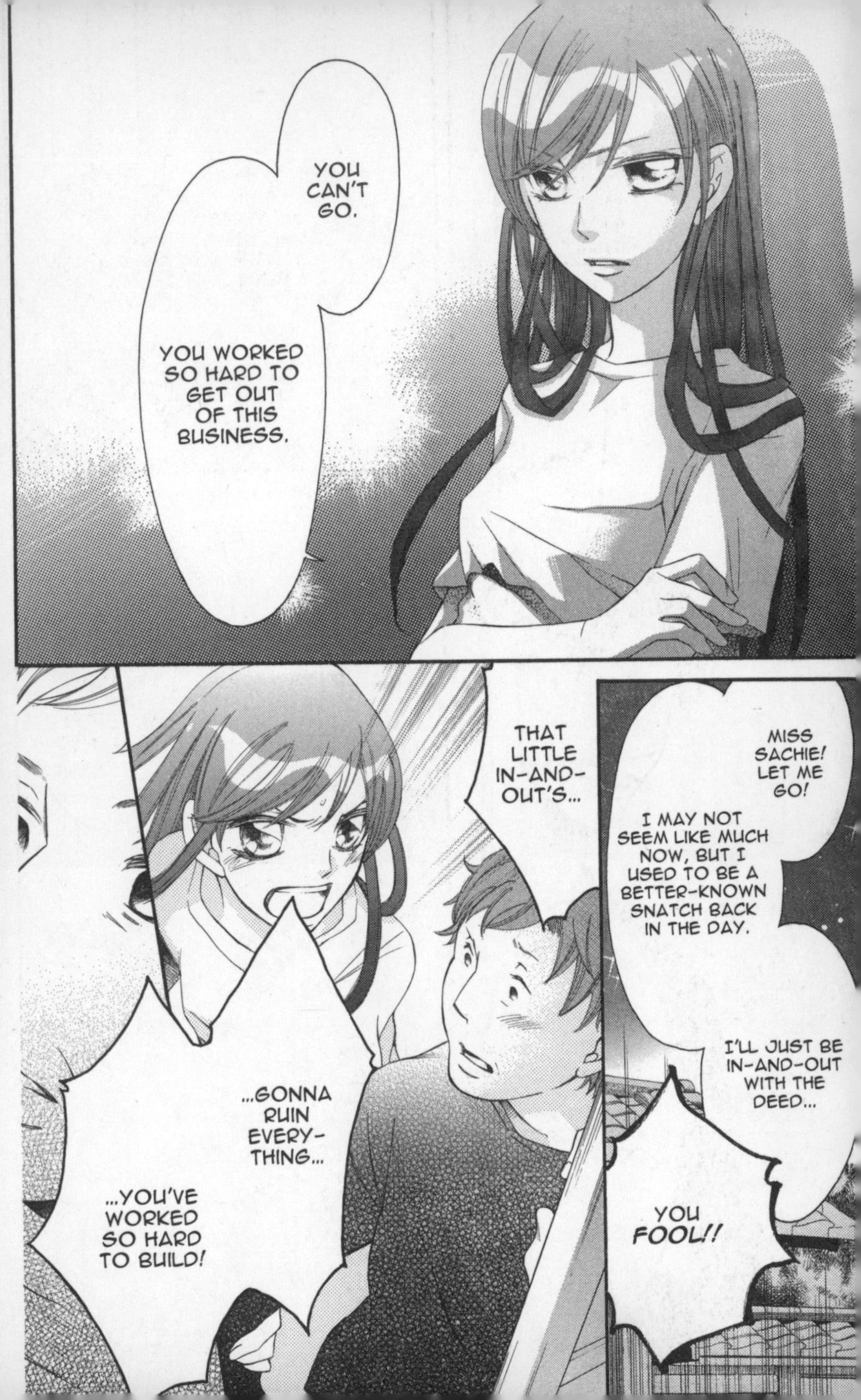
YOU CAN'T GO.
YOU WORKED SO HARD TO GET OUT OF THIS BUSINESS.
MISS SACHIE! LET ME GO!
I MAY NOT SEEM LIKE MUCH NOW, BUT I USED TO BE A BETTER-KNOWN SNATCH BACK IN THE DAY.
I'LL JUST BE IN-AND-OUT WITH THE DEED...
YOU *FOOL!!*
THAT LITTLE IN-AND-OUT'S...
...GONNA RUIN EVERY-THING...
...YOU'VE WORKED SO HARD TO BUILD!

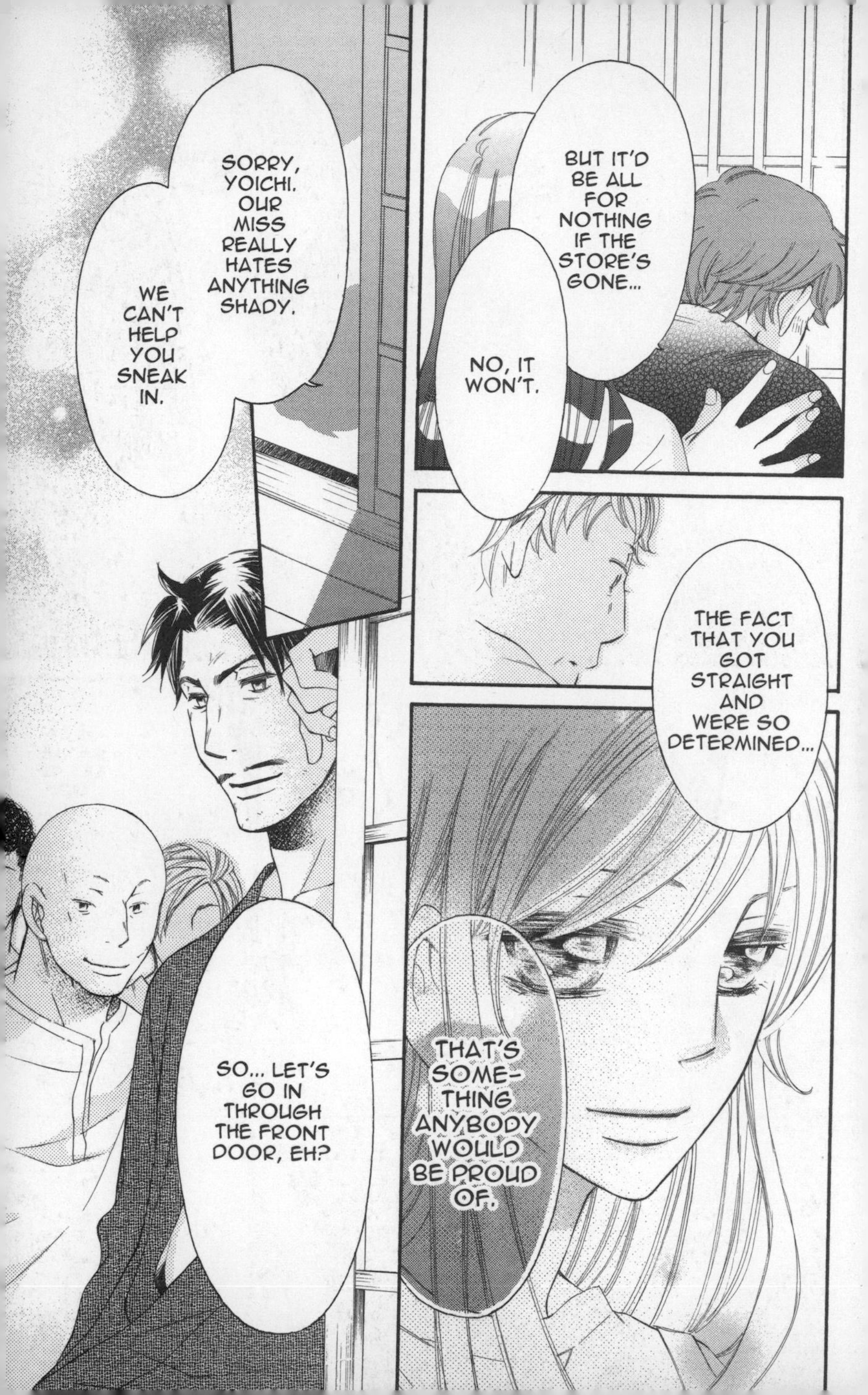
BUT IT'D BE ALL FOR NOTHING IF THE STORE'S GONE...
NO, IT WON'T.
THE FACT THAT YOU GOT STRAIGHT AND WERE SO DETERMINED...
THAT'S SOME-THING ANYBODY WOULD BE PROUD OF.
SORRY, YOICHI. OUR MISS REALLY HATES ANYTHING SHADY.
WE CAN'T HELP YOU SNEAK IN.
SO... LET'S GO IN THROUGH THE FRONT DOOR, EH?

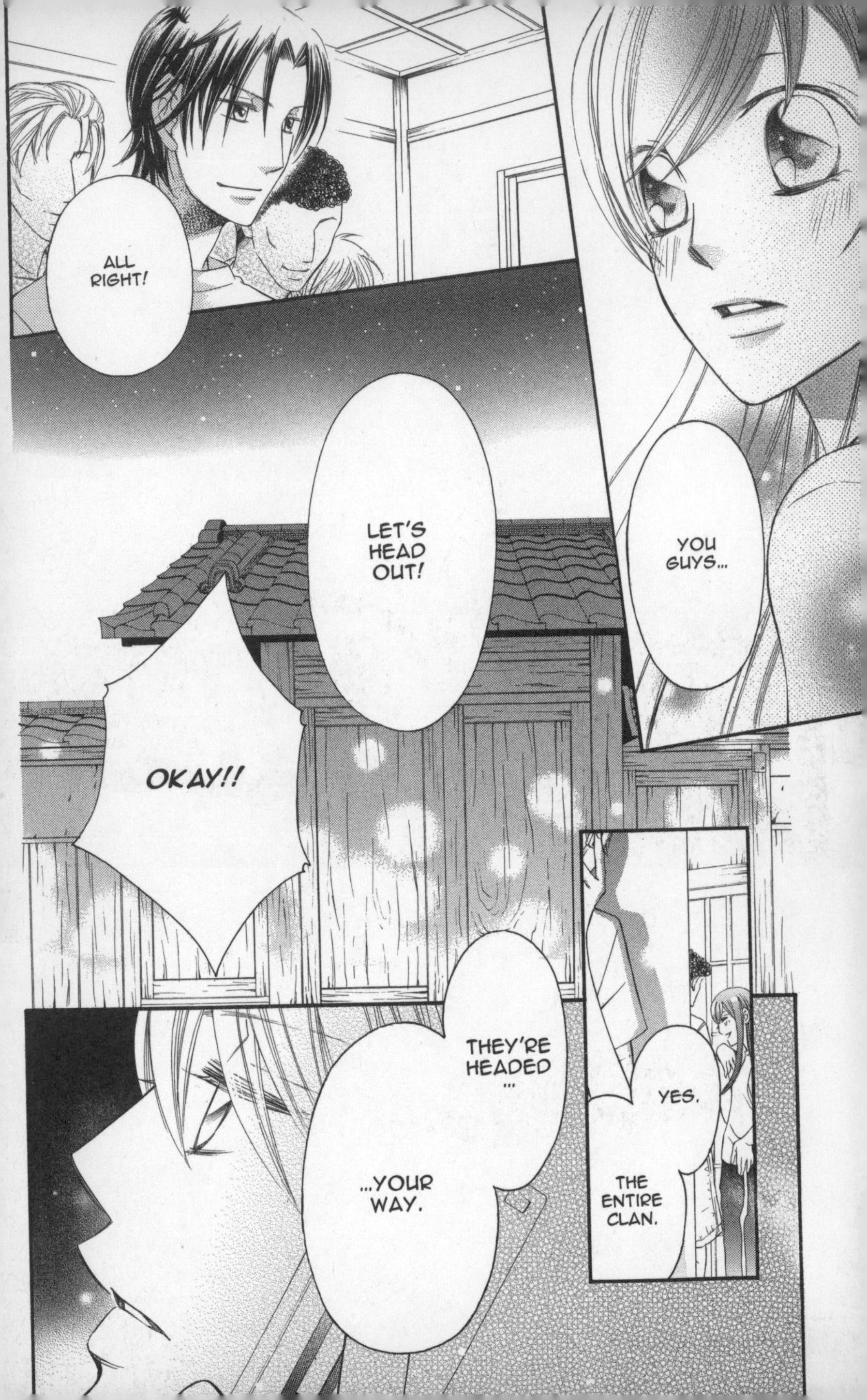
YOU GUYS...
ALL RIGHT!
LET'S HEAD OUT!
OKAY!!
YES.
THE ENTIRE CLAN.
THEY'RE HEADED ...
...YOUR WAY.

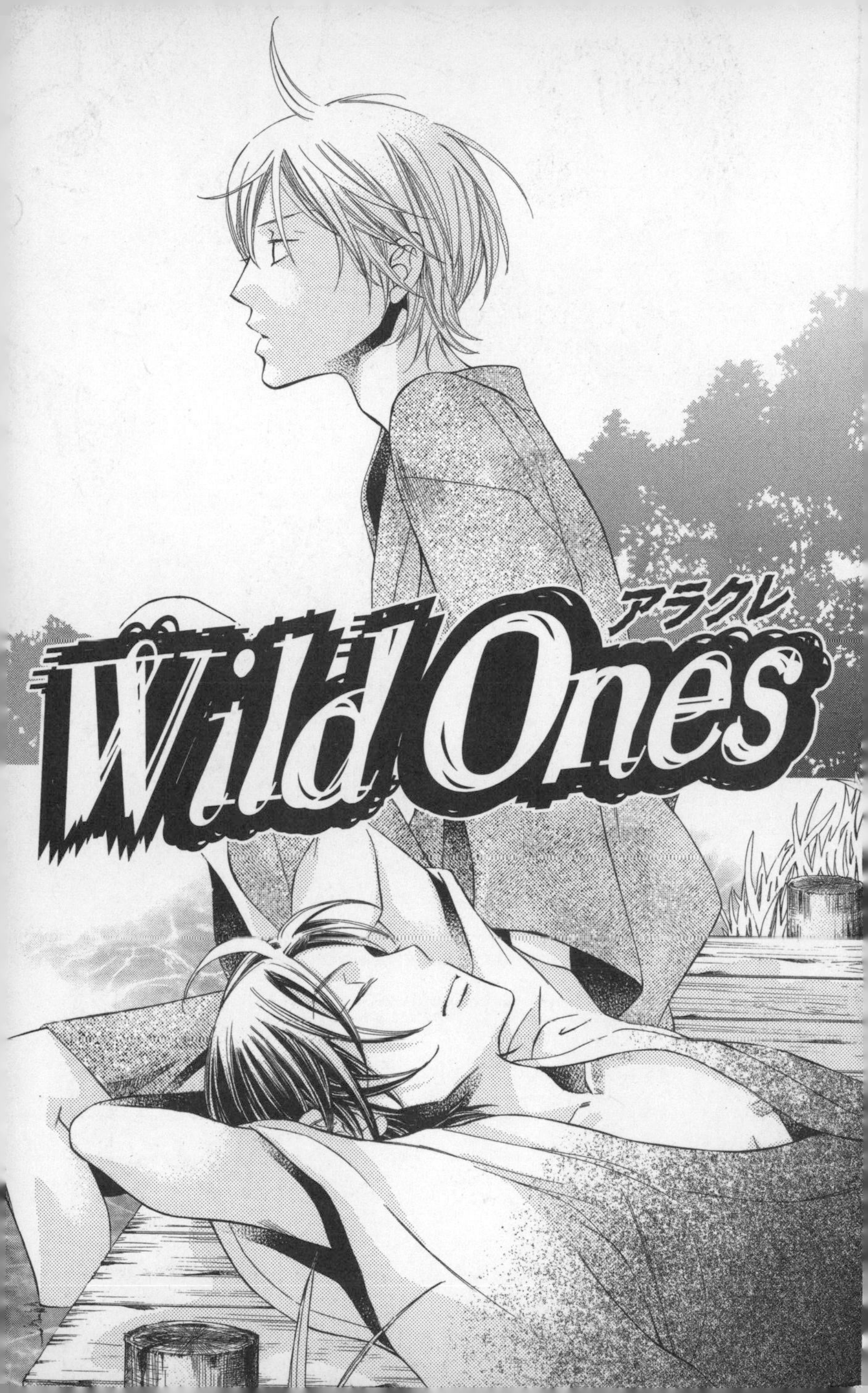
Wild Ones
アラクレ

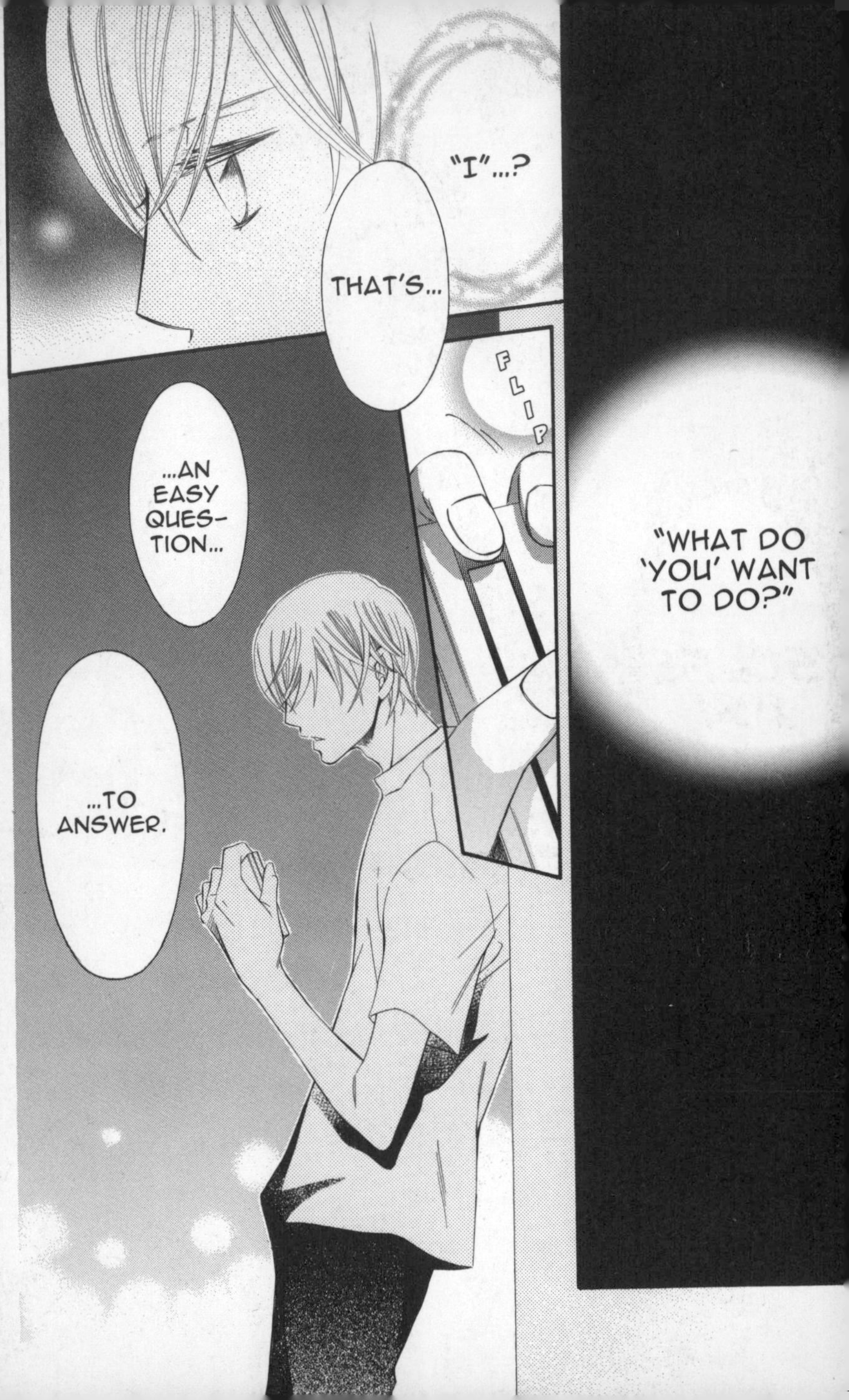
"WHAT DO 'YOU' WANT TO DO?"
"I"...?
THAT'S...
FLIP
...AN EASY QUES-TION...
...TO ANSWER.

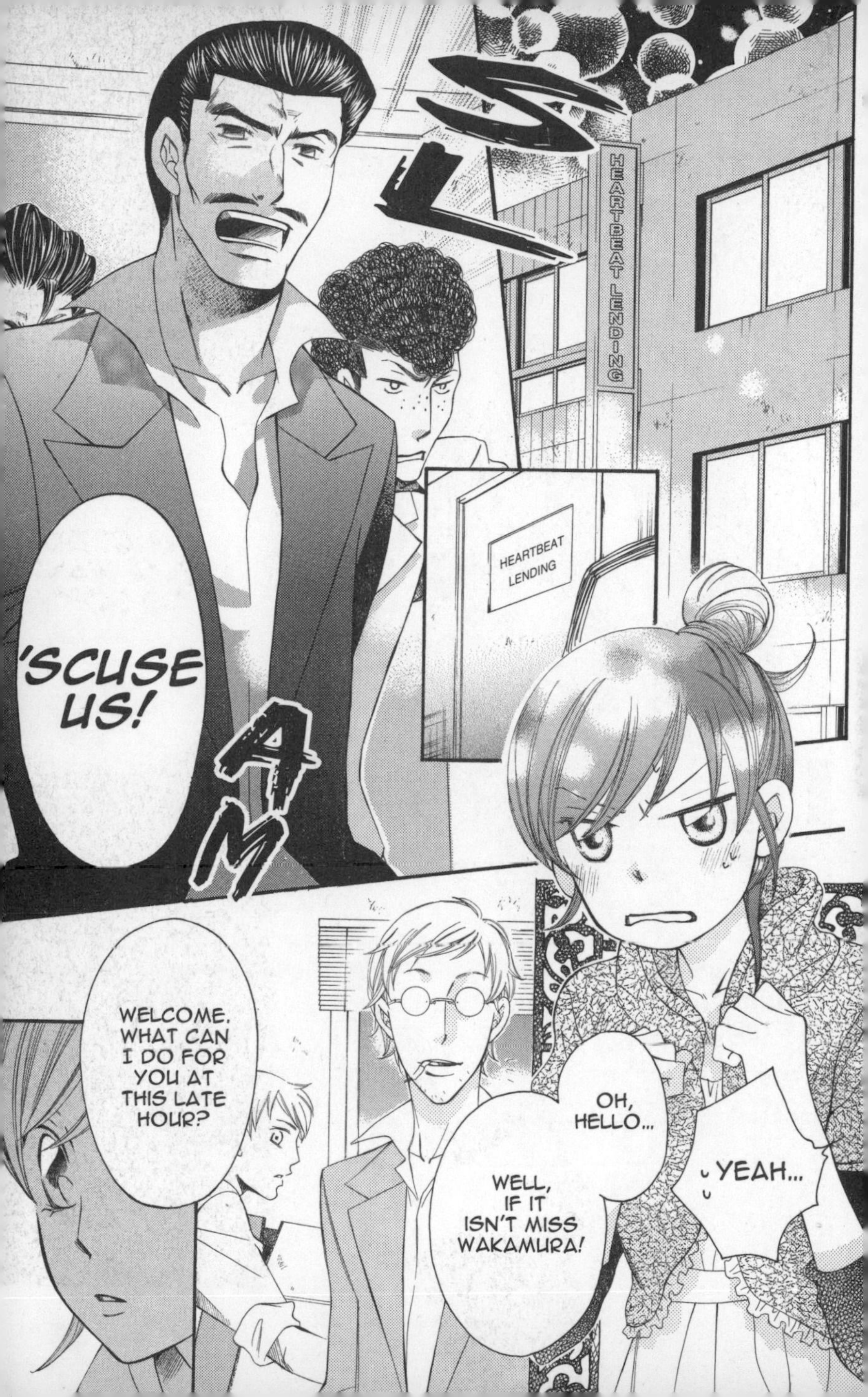
HEARTBEAT LENDING
Z
HEARTBEAT LENDING
'SCUSE US!
AM
OH, HELLO...
YEAH...
WELL, IF IT ISN'T MISS WAKAMURA!
WELCOME. WHAT CAN I DO FOR YOU AT THIS LATE HOUR?

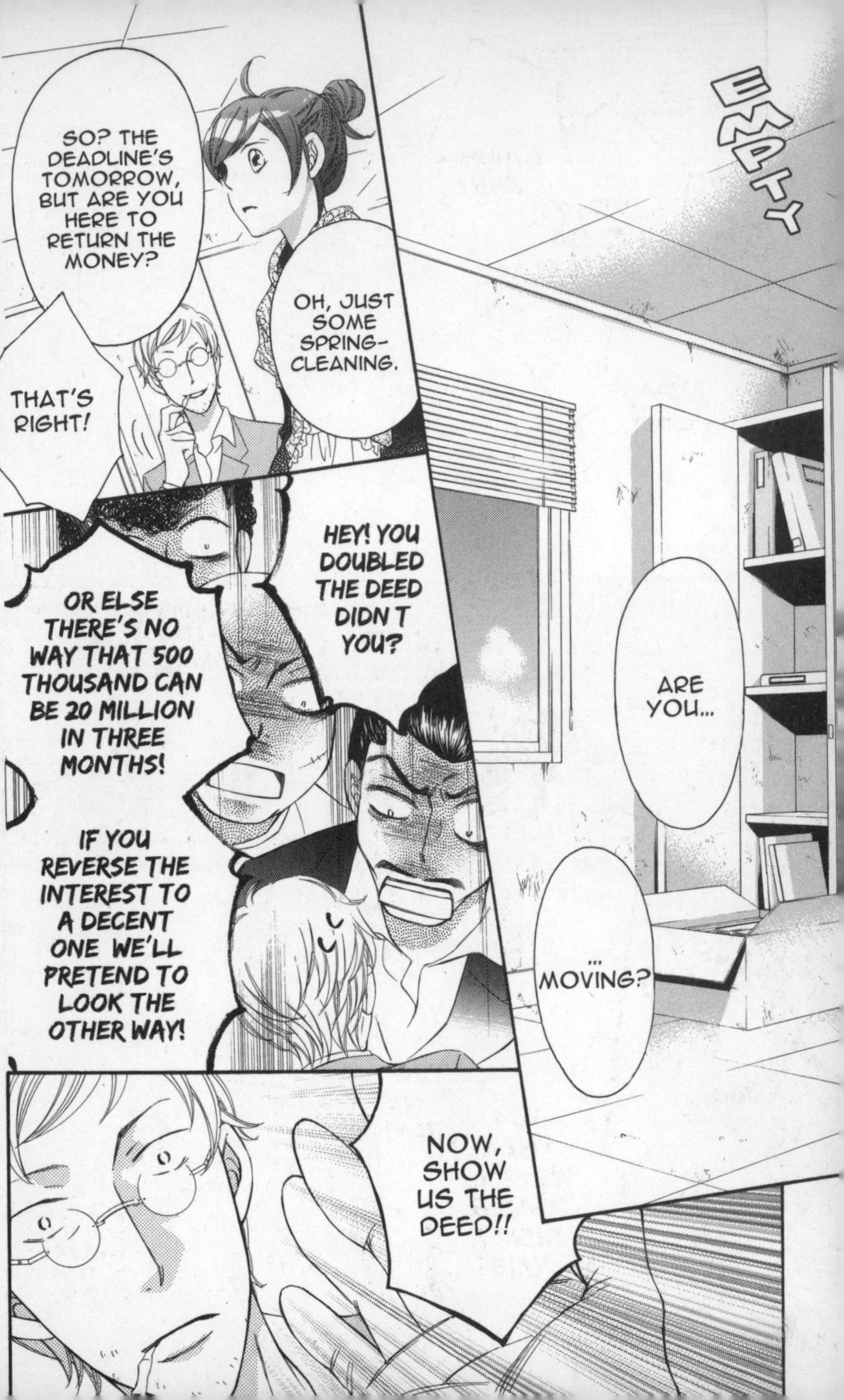
EMPTY
ARE YOU...
... MOVING?
OH, JUST SOME SPRING-CLEANING.
SO? THE DEADLINE'S TOMORROW, BUT ARE YOU HERE TO RETURN THE MONEY?
THAT'S RIGHT!
HEY! YOU DOUBLED THE DEED DIDN T YOU?
OR ELSE THERE'S NO WAY THAT 500 THOUSAND CAN BE 20 MILLION IN THREE MONTHS!
IF YOU REVERSE THE INTEREST TO A DECENT ONE WE'LL PRETEND TO LOOK THE OTHER WAY!
NOW, SHOW US THE DEED!!

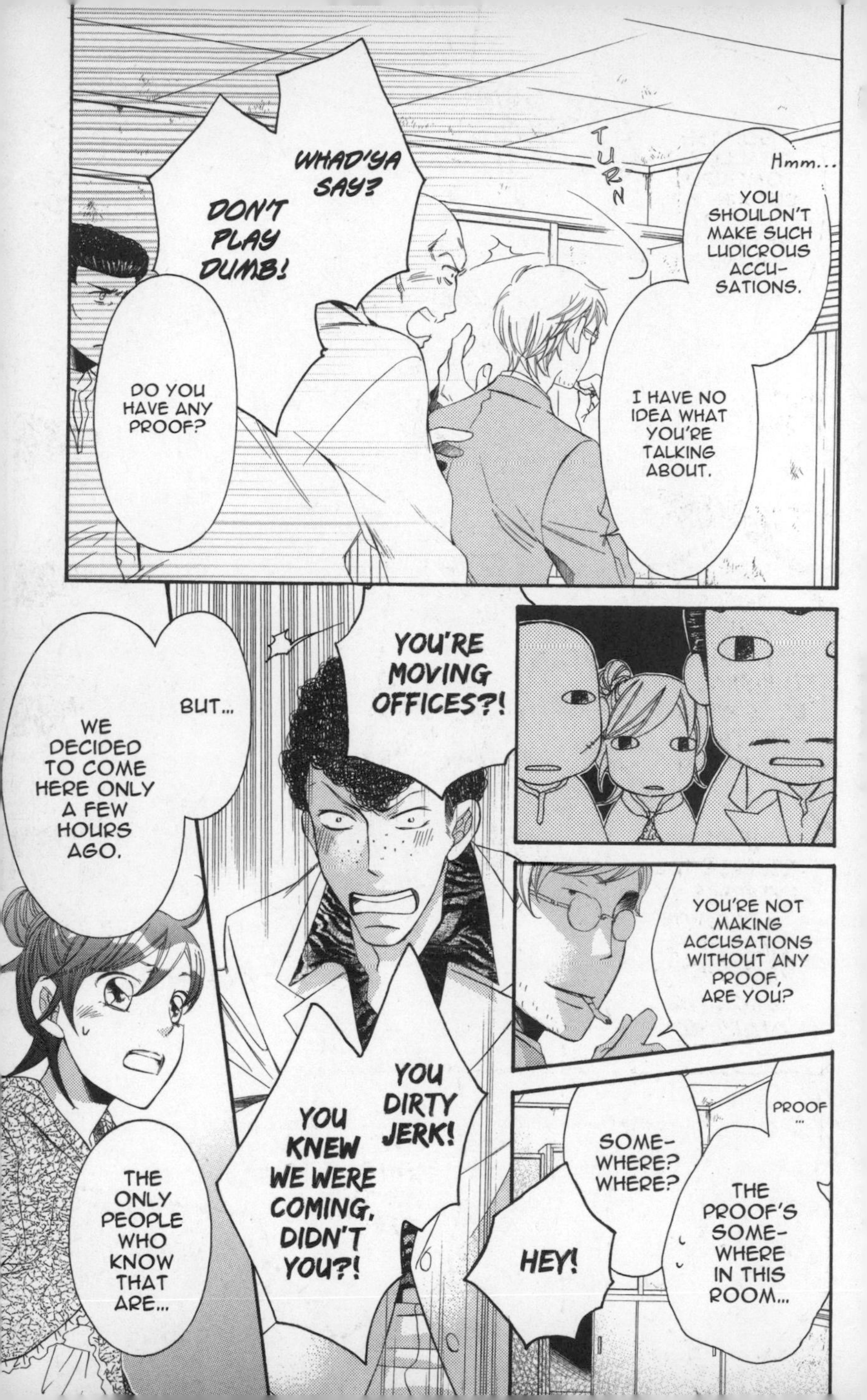
Hmm...
YOU SHOULDN'T MAKE SUCH LUDICROUS ACCU-SATIONS.
TURN
WHAD'YA SAY?
DON'T PLAY DUMB!
I HAVE NO IDEA WHAT YOU'RE TALKING ABOUT.
DO YOU HAVE ANY PROOF?
YOU'RE NOT MAKING ACCUSATIONS WITHOUT ANY PROOF, ARE YOU?
PROOF ...
THE PROOF'S SOME-WHERE IN THIS ROOM...
SOME-WHERE? WHERE?
HEY!
YOU'RE MOVING OFFICES?!
BUT...
WE DECIDED TO COME HERE ONLY A FEW HOURS AGO.
YOU DIRTY JERK!
YOU KNEW WE WERE COMING, DIDN'T YOU?!
THE ONLY PEOPLE WHO KNOW THAT ARE...

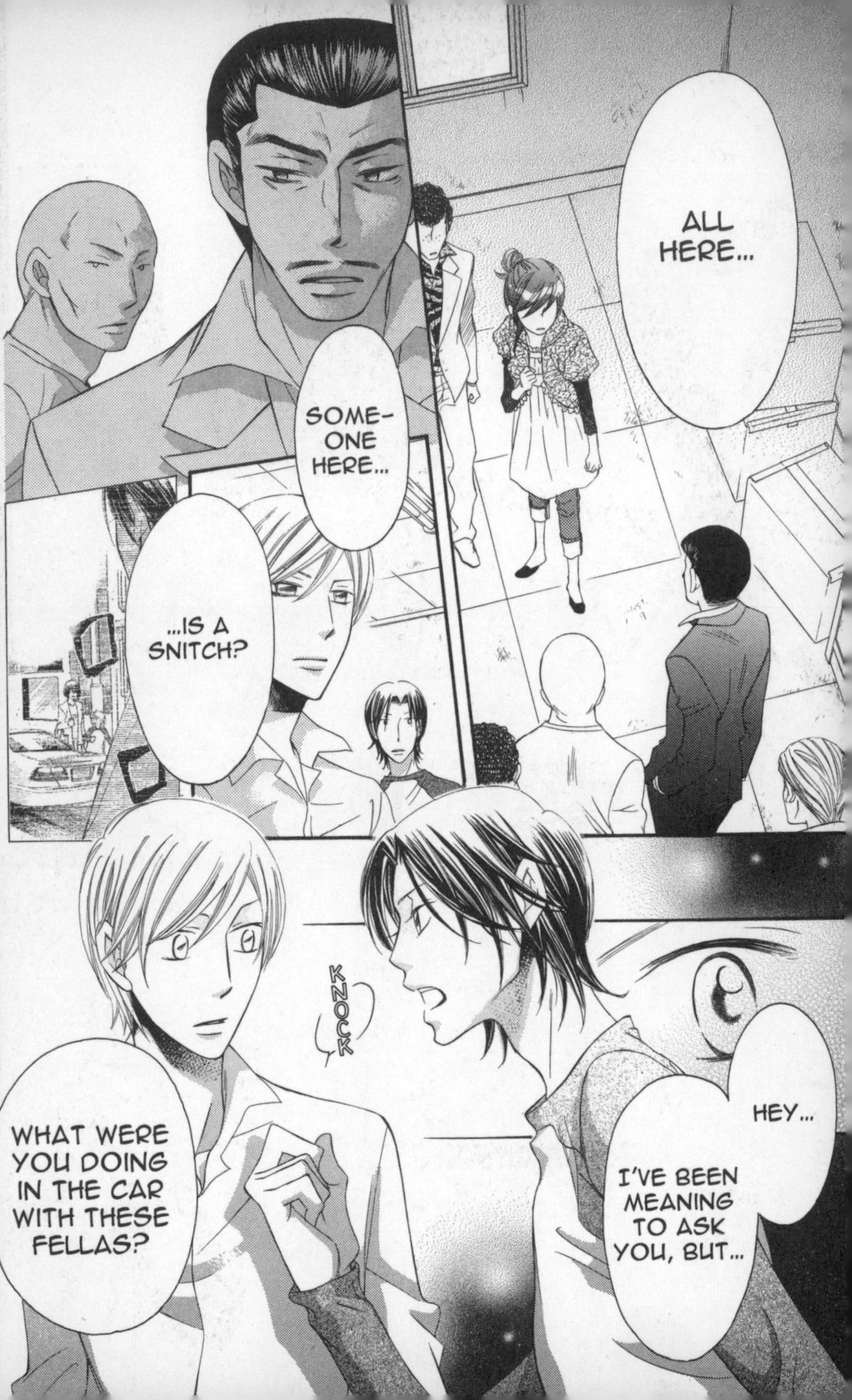
ALL HERE...
SOME-ONE HERE...
...IS A SNITCH?
HEY...
I'VE BEEN MEANING TO ASK YOU, BUT...
KNOCK
WHAT WERE YOU DOING IN THE CAR WITH THESE FELLAS?

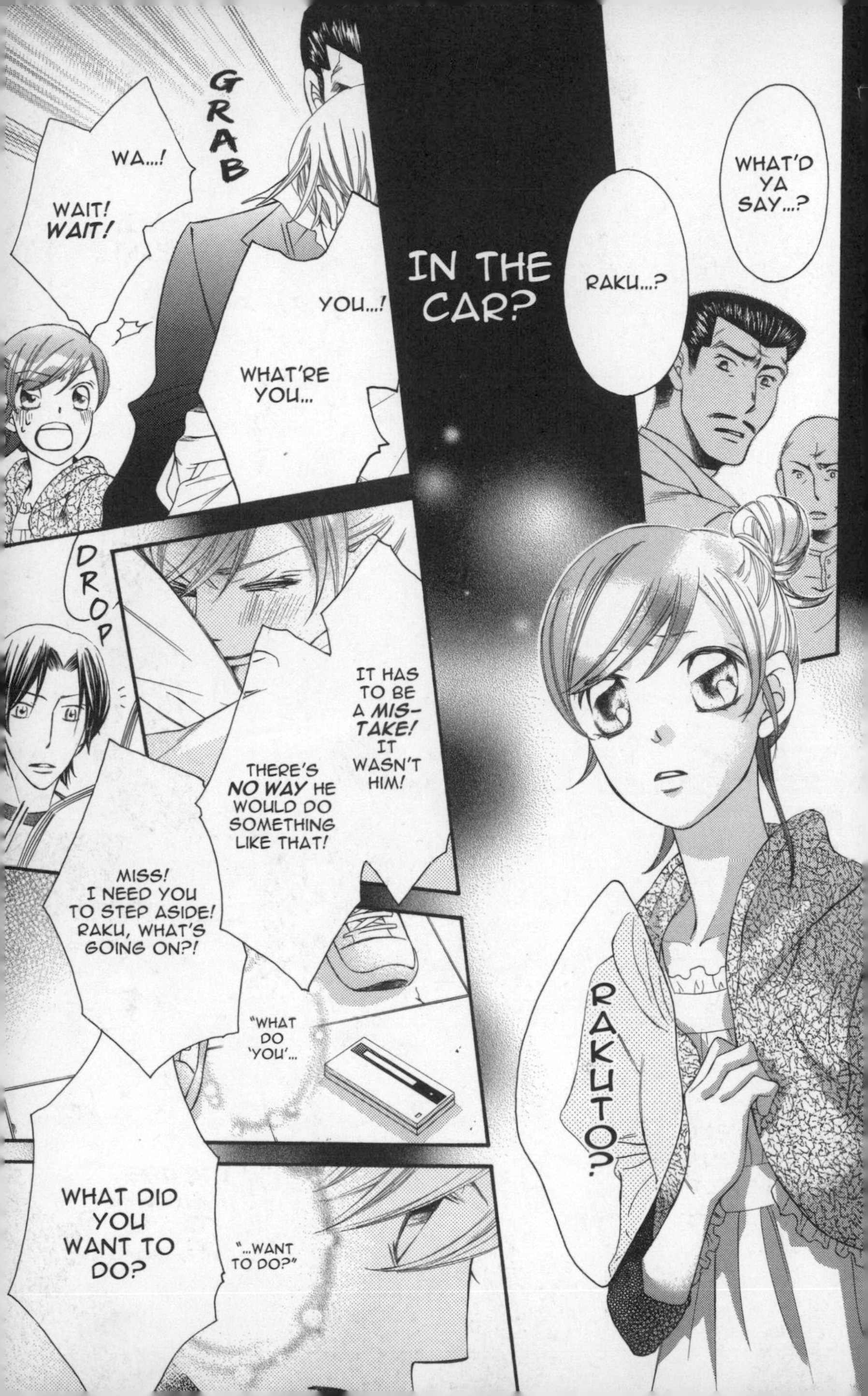
WHAT'D YA SAY...?
RAKU...?
IN THE CAR?
RAKUTO?
GRAB
WA...!
WAIT! *WAIT!*
YOU...!
WHAT'RE YOU...
DROP
IT HAS TO BE A *MIS-TAKE!* IT WASN'T HIM!
THERE'S ***NO WAY*** HE WOULD DO SOMETHING LIKE THAT!
MISS! I NEED YOU TO STEP ASIDE! RAKU, WHAT'S GOING ON?!
"WHAT DO 'YOU'...
"...WANT TO DO?"
WHAT DID YOU WANT TO DO?

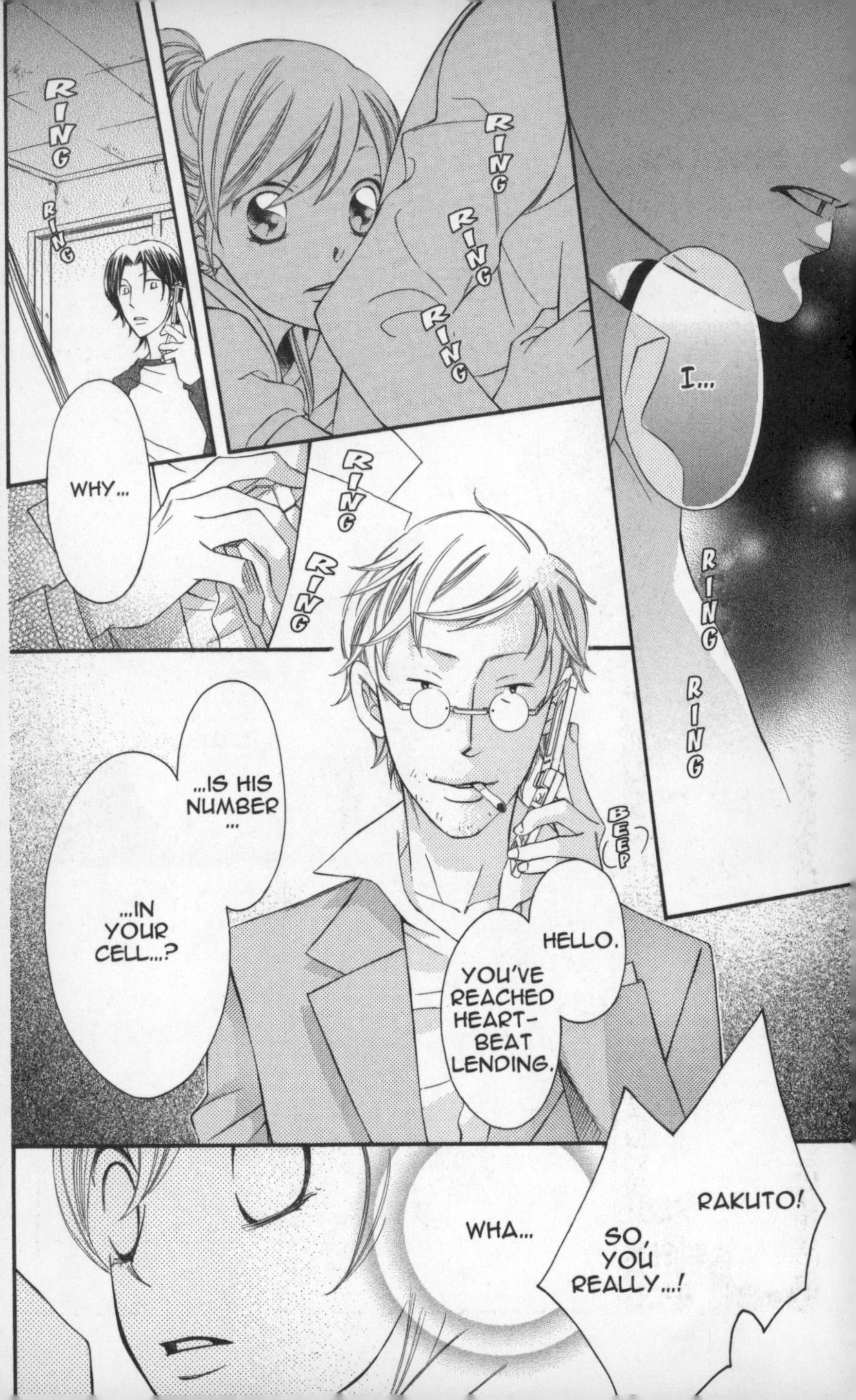
I...
RING
RING
RING
RING
RING
RING
RING
RING
RING
WHY...
BEEP
HELLO.
YOU'VE REACHED HEART-BEAT LENDING.
...IS HIS NUMBER ...
...IN YOUR CELL...?
RAKUTO!
SO, YOU REALLY...!
WHA...

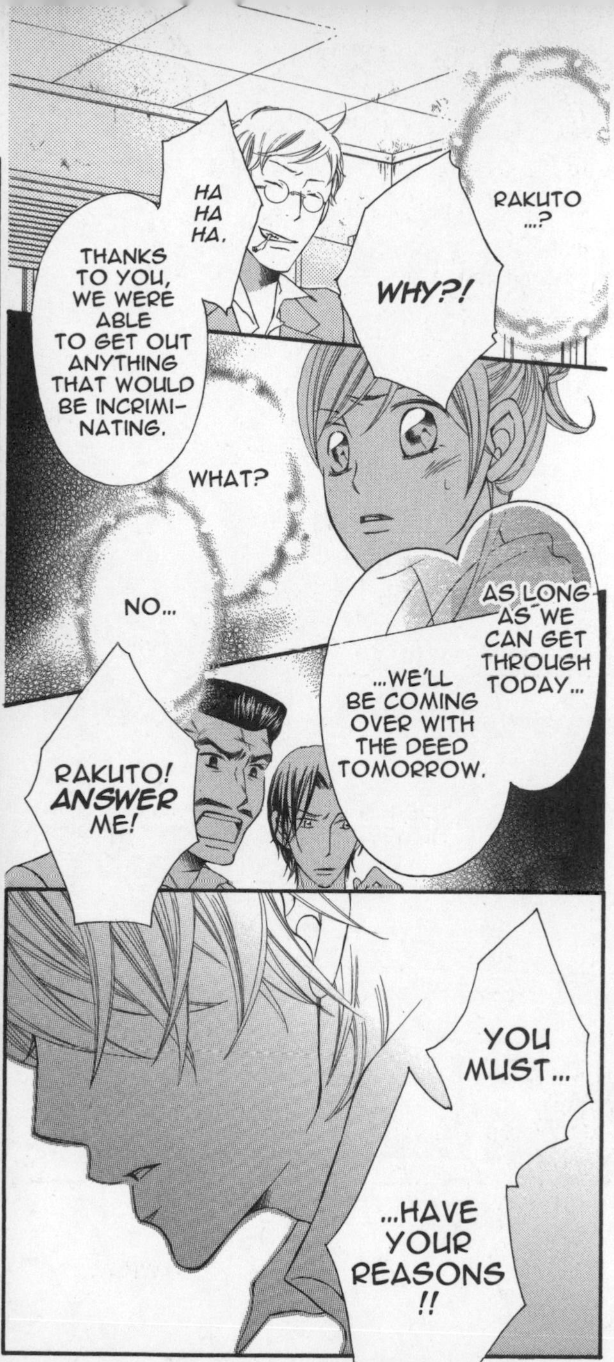
RAKUTO ...?
WHY?!
HA HA HA.
THANKS TO YOU, WE WERE ABLE TO GET OUT ANYTHING THAT WOULD BE INCRIMI-NATING.
AS LONG AS WE CAN GET THROUGH TODAY...
...WE'LL BE COMING OVER WITH THE DEED TOMORROW.
WHAT?
NO...
RAKUTO! ANSWER ME!
YOU MUST...
...HAVE YOUR REASONS !!

I JUST FOUND THE STORYBOARDS I DID FOR BOKUHANE, AND THOUGHT, "WOW" BUT I WONDER WHAT PEOPLE DO WITH THESE.

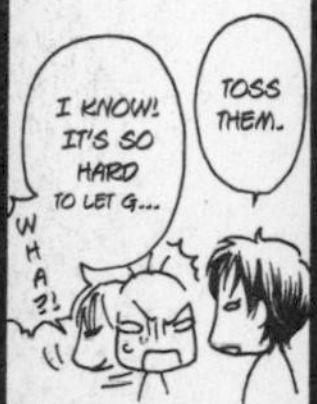
TOSS THEM.
I KNOW! IT'S SO HARD TO LET G...
WHA?!

SIMPLE

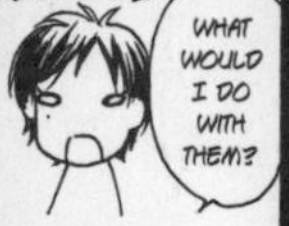
WHAT WOULD I DO WITH THEM?

(MISS AYA KANNO)

I GUESS SHE'S RIGHT... I SHOULD TOSS THEM...

Okay!!

I THINK I WILL WHEN I MOVE!!

(T HAS LEARNED NOTHING...)

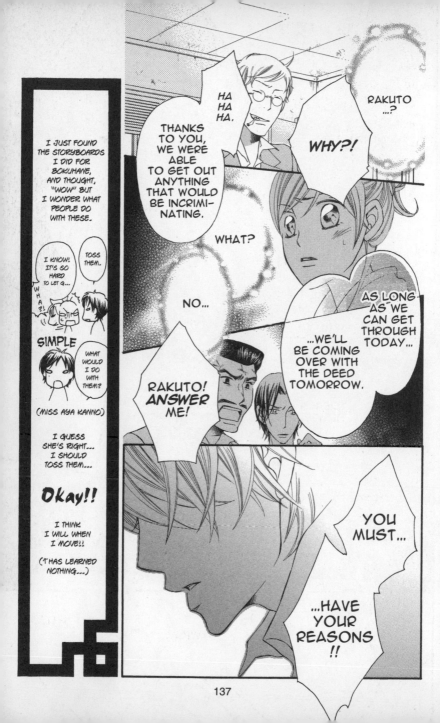

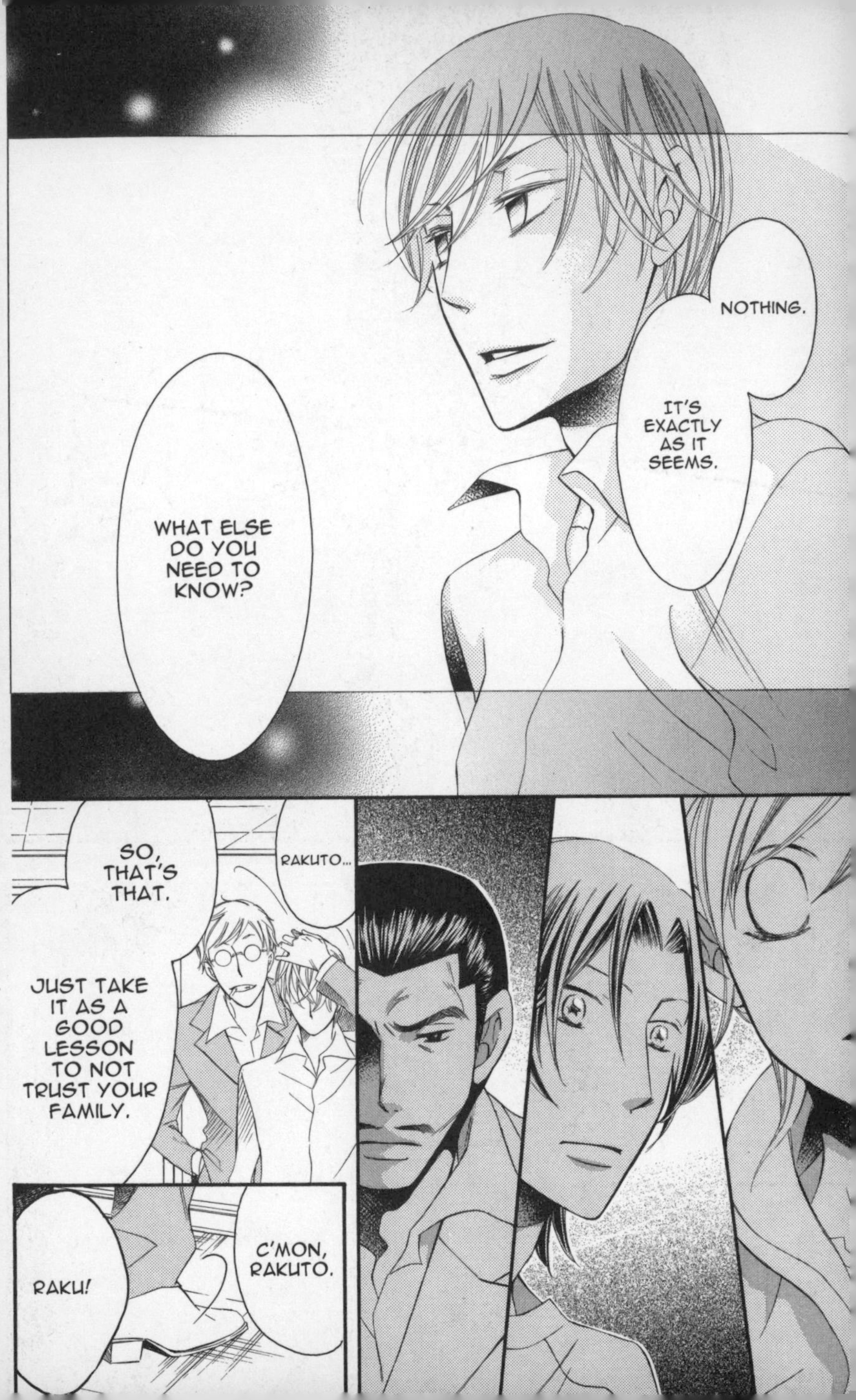
NOTHING.
IT'S EXACTLY AS IT SEEMS.
WHAT ELSE DO YOU NEED TO KNOW?
RAKUTO...
SO, THAT'S THAT.
JUST TAKE IT AS A GOOD LESSON TO NOT TRUST YOUR FAMILY.
C'MON, RAKUTO.
RAKU!

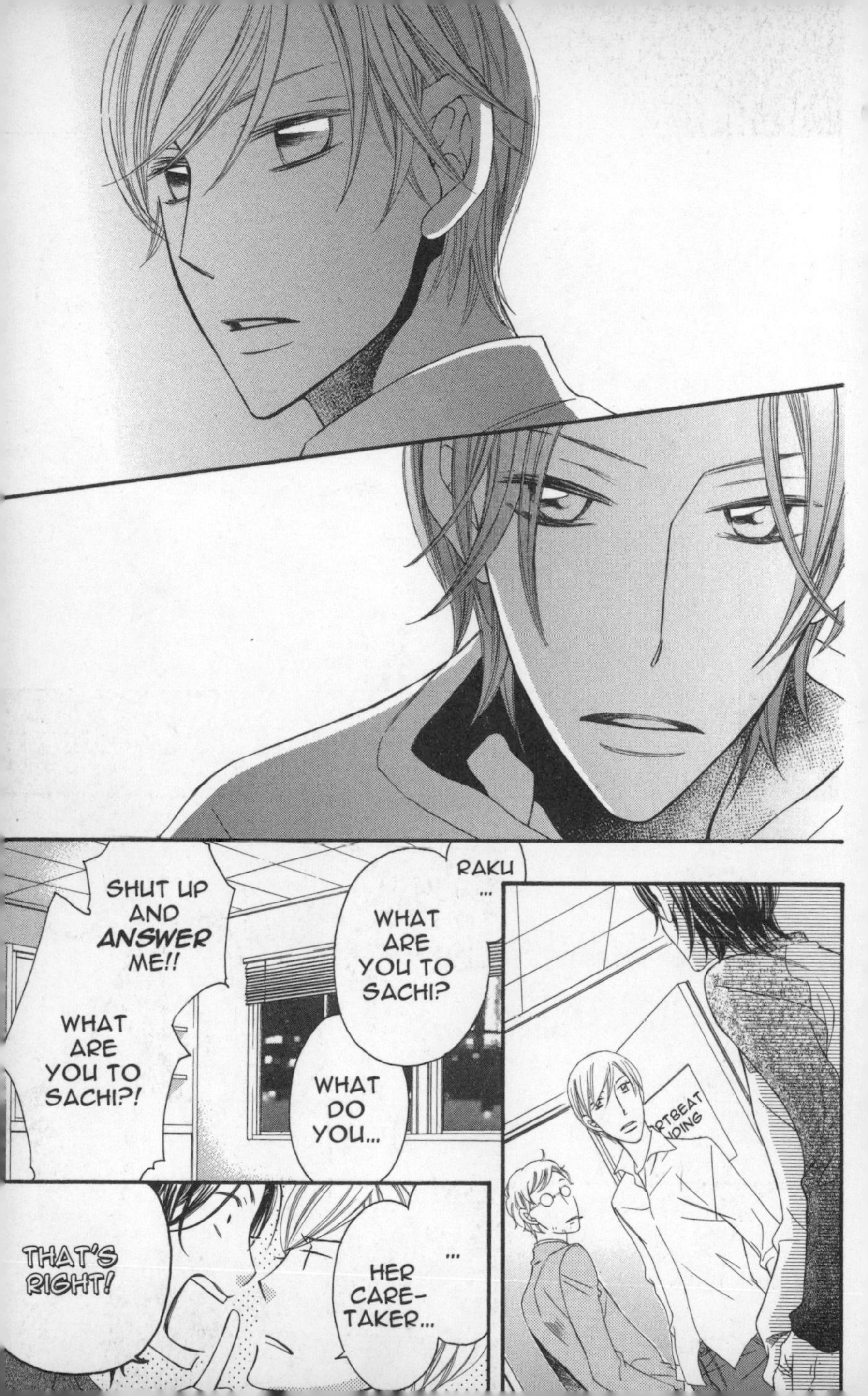
RAKU ... WHAT ARE YOU TO SACHI?
WHAT DO YOU...
SHUT UP AND ANSWER ME!!
WHAT ARE YOU TO SACHI?!
... HER CARE-TAKER...
THAT'S RIGHT!

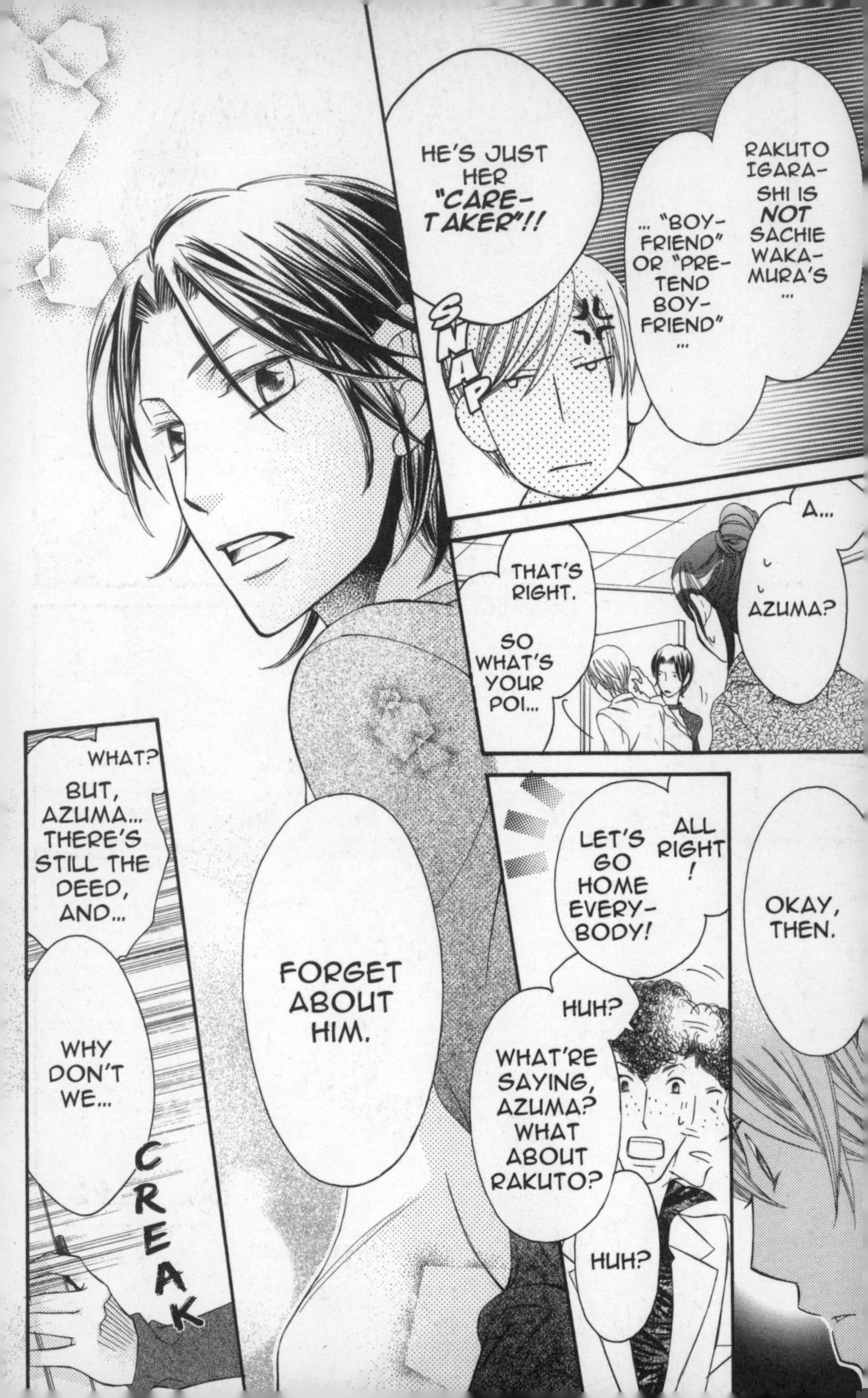
RAKUTO IGARASHI IS NOT SACHIE WAKAMURA'S ...
... "BOY-FRIEND" OR "PRETEND BOY-FRIEND" ...
HE'S JUST HER "CARE-TAKER"!!
SNAP
A... AZUMA?
THAT'S RIGHT. SO WHAT'S YOUR POI...
OKAY, THEN.
ALL RIGHT!
LET'S GO HOME EVERY-BODY!
HUH?
WHAT'RE SAYING, AZUMA? WHAT ABOUT RAKUTO?
HUH?
FORGET ABOUT HIM.
WHAT?
BUT, AZUMA... THERE'S STILL THE DEED, AND...
WHY DON'T WE...
CREAK

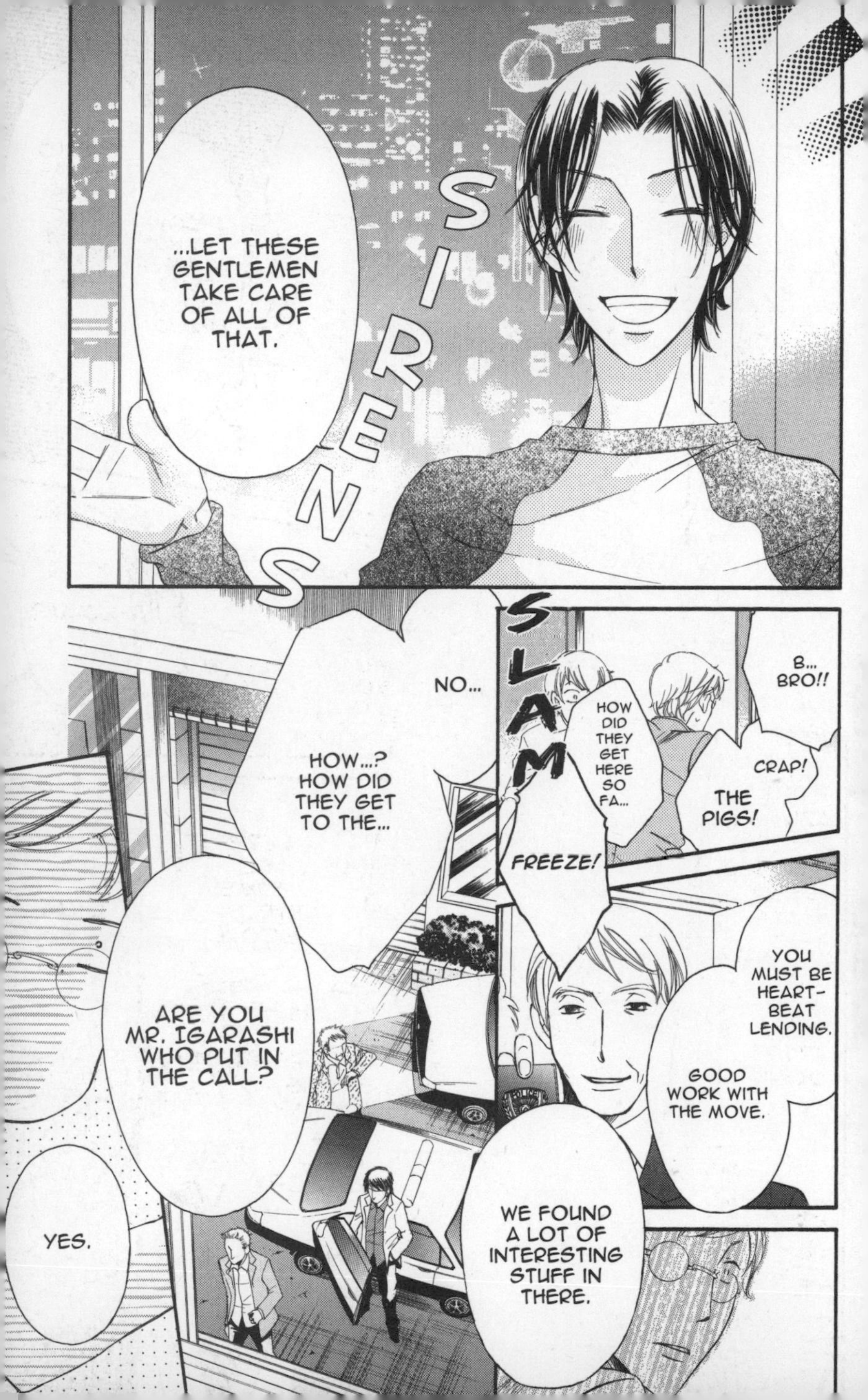
...LET THESE GENTLEMEN TAKE CARE OF ALL OF THAT.
SIRENS
B... BRO!!
SLAM
HOW DID THEY GET HERE SO FA...
CRAP!
THE PIGS!
FREEZE!
YOU MUST BE HEART-BEAT LENDING.
GOOD WORK WITH THE MOVE.
WE FOUND A LOT OF INTERESTING STUFF IN THERE.
NO...
HOW...? HOW DID THEY GET TO THE...
ARE YOU MR. IGARASHI WHO PUT IN THE CALL?
YES.

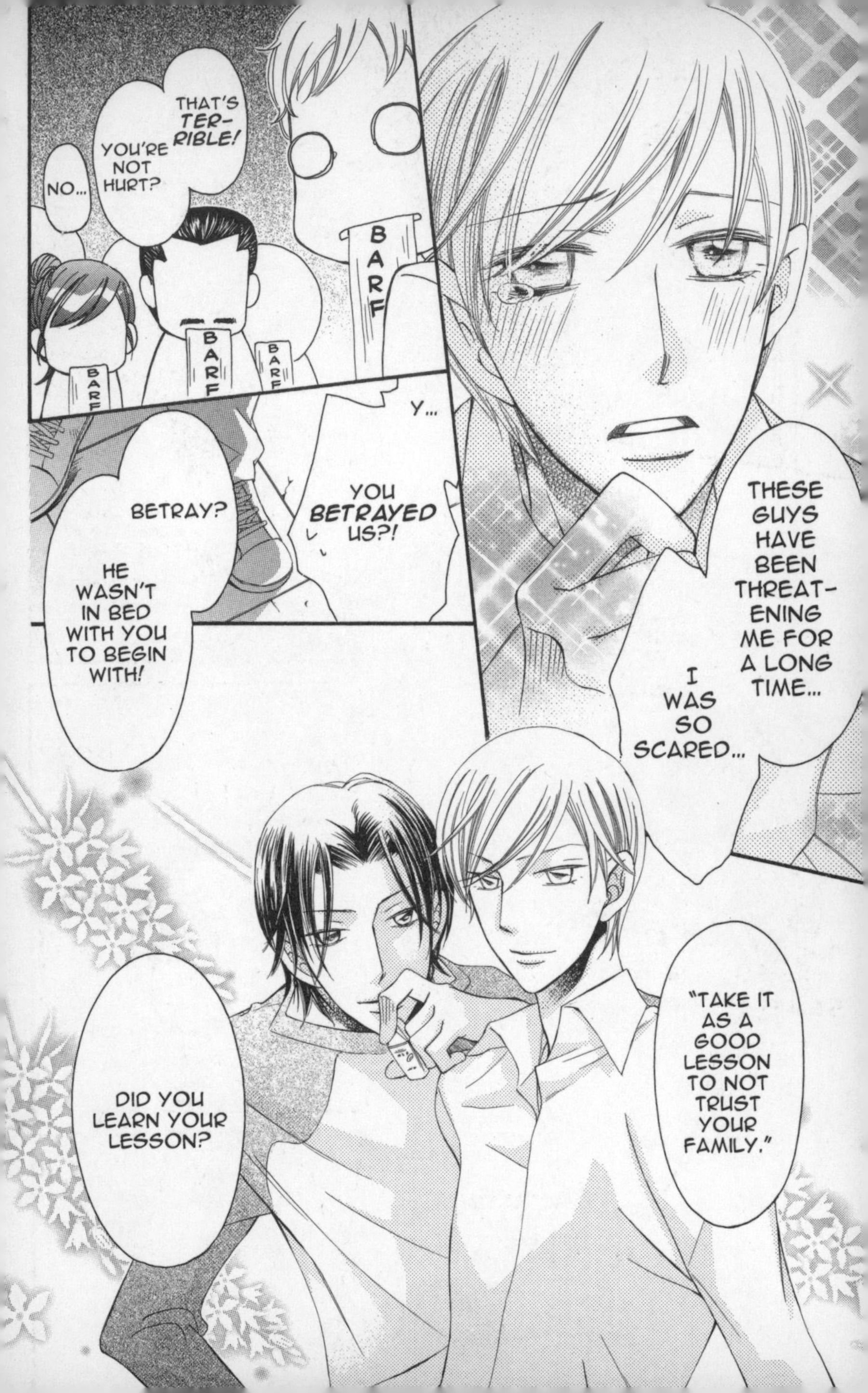
THESE GUYS HAVE BEEN THREATENING ME FOR A LONG TIME...
I WAS SO SCARED...
THAT'S TERRIBLE!
YOU'RE NOT HURT?
NO...
BARF
BARF
BARF
BARF
Y...
YOU BETRAYED US?!
BETRAY?
HE WASN'T IN BED WITH YOU TO BEGIN WITH!
"TAKE IT AS A GOOD LESSON TO NOT TRUST YOUR FAMILY."
DID YOU LEARN YOUR LESSON?

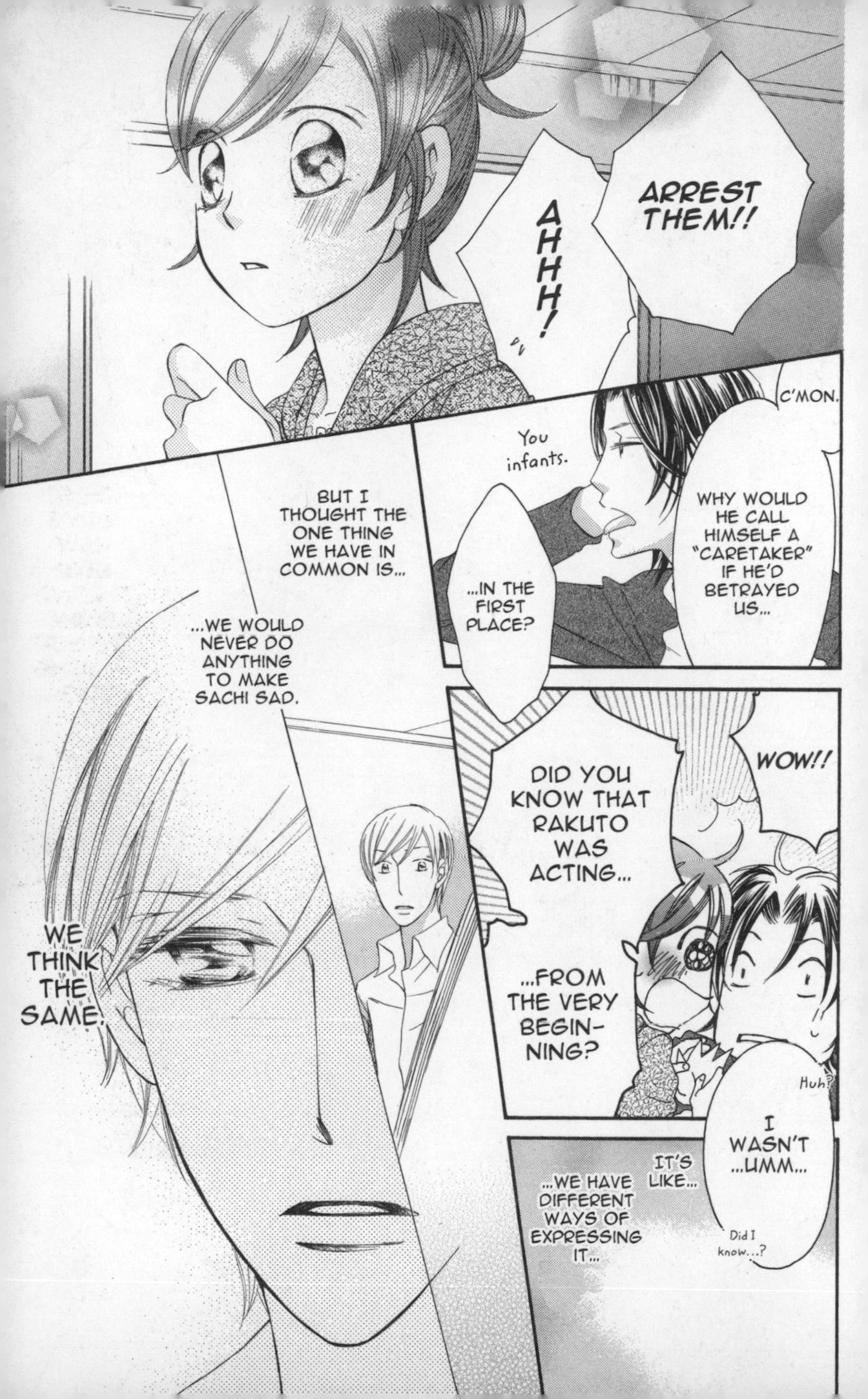
ARREST THEM!!
AHHH!
C'MON.
WHY WOULD HE CALL HIMSELF A "CARETAKER" IF HE'D BETRAYED US...
...IN THE FIRST PLACE?
You infants.
WOW!!
DID YOU KNOW THAT RAKUTO WAS ACTING...
...FROM THE VERY BEGINNING?
Huh?
I WASN'T ...UMM...
Did I know...?
IT'S LIKE...
...WE HAVE DIFFERENT WAYS OF EXPRESSING IT...
BUT I THOUGHT THE ONE THING WE HAVE IN COMMON IS...
...WE WOULD NEVER DO ANYTHING TO MAKE SACHI SAD.
WE THINK THE SAME.

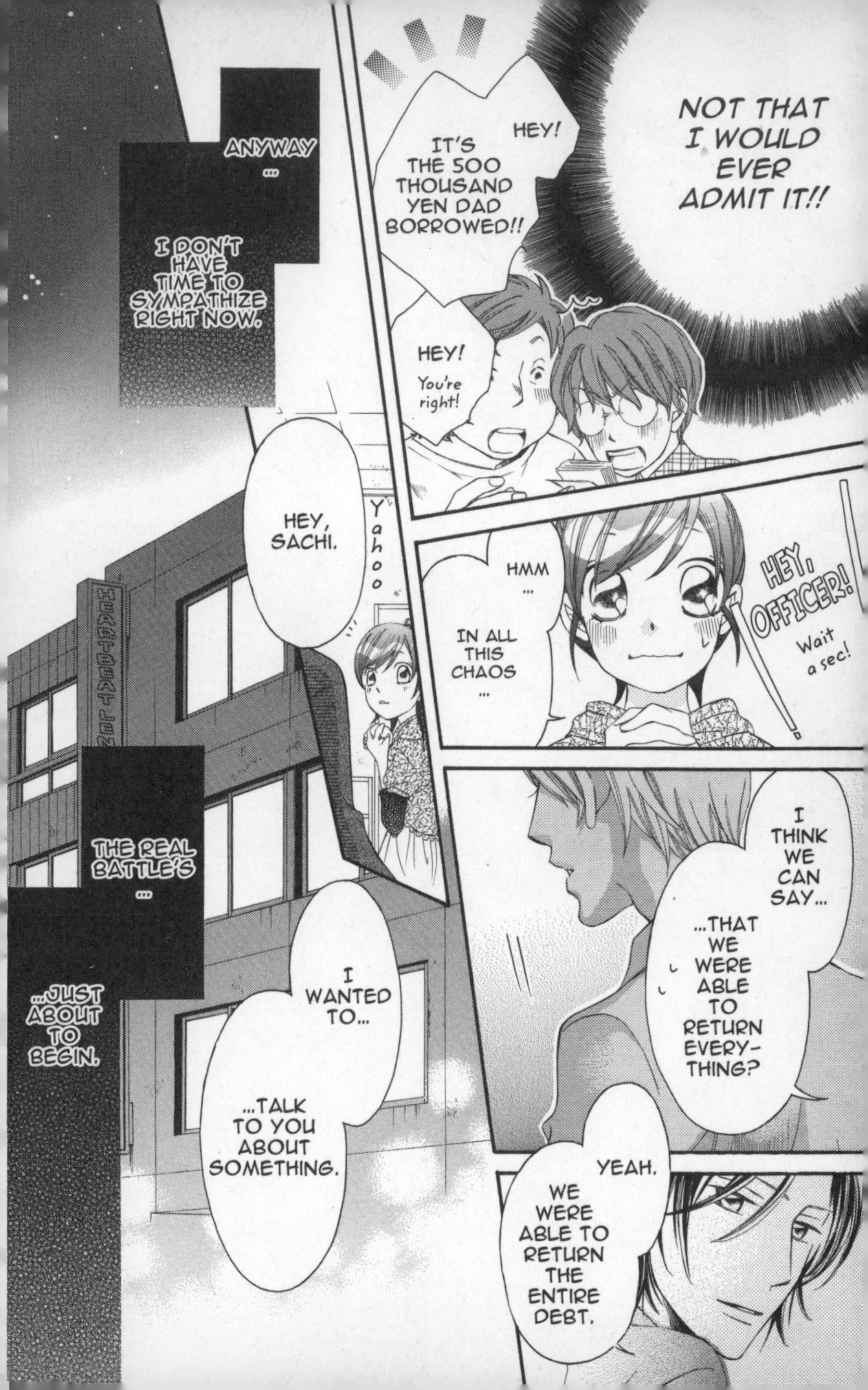

NOT THAT I WOULD EVER ADMIT IT!!
HEY! IT'S THE 500 THOUSAND YEN DAD BORROWED!!
HEY! You're right!
HEY, OFFICER! Wait a sec!
HMM... IN ALL THIS CHAOS...
I THINK WE CAN SAY... ...THAT WE WERE ABLE TO RETURN EVERYTHING?
YEAH. WE WERE ABLE TO RETURN THE ENTIRE DEBT.
ANYWAY...
I DON'T HAVE TIME TO SYMPATHIZE RIGHT NOW.
HEY, SACHI.
Yahoo
I WANTED TO...
...TALK TO YOU ABOUT SOMETHING.
THE REAL BATTLE'S...
...JUST ABOUT TO BEGIN.

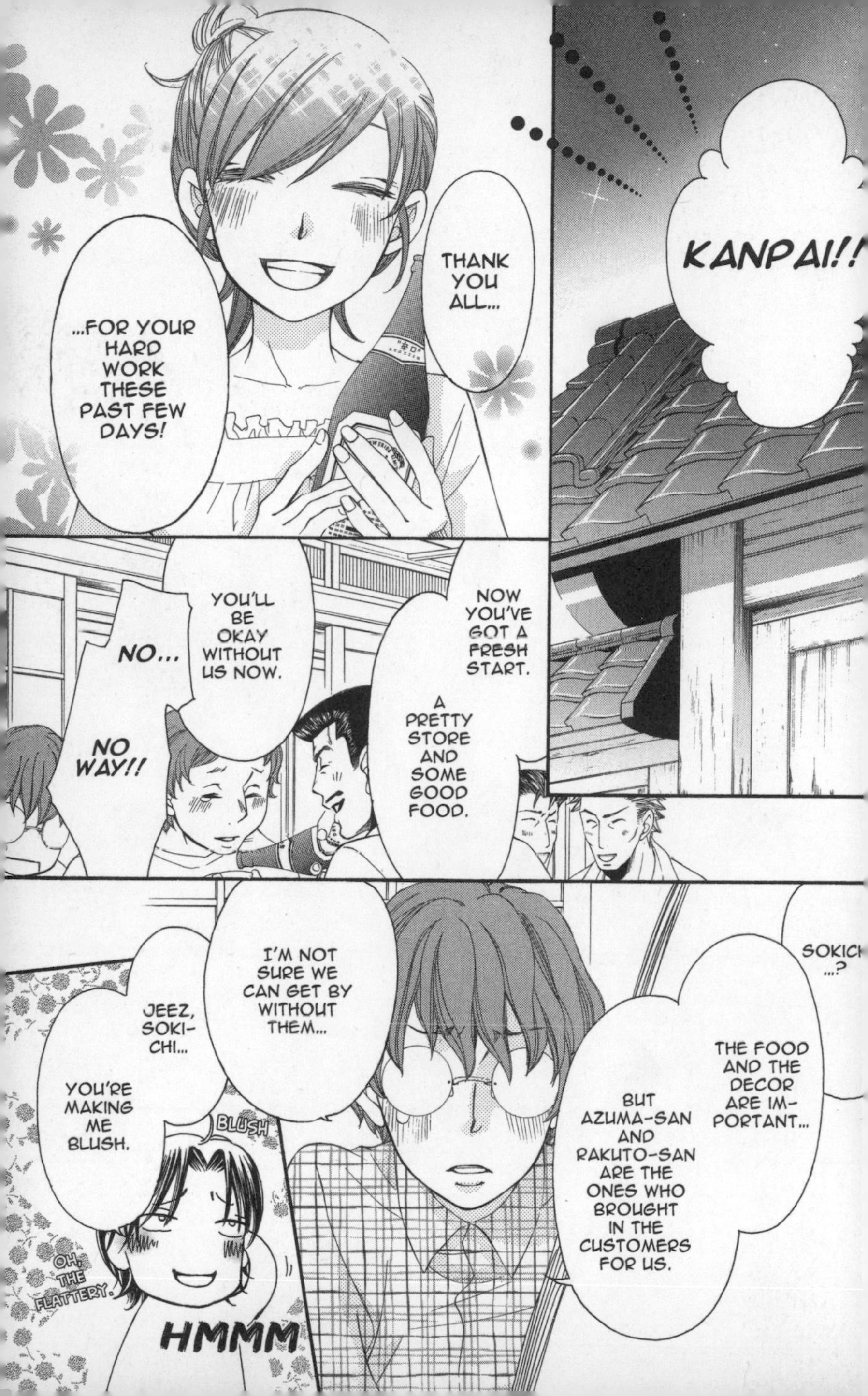
KANPAI!!
THANK YOU ALL...
...FOR YOUR HARD WORK THESE PAST FEW DAYS!
NOW YOU'VE GOT A FRESH START.
A PRETTY STORE AND SOME GOOD FOOD.
YOU'LL BE OKAY WITHOUT US NOW.
NO...
NO WAY!!
SOKICH ...?
THE FOOD AND THE DECOR ARE IM- PORTANT...
BUT AZUMA-SAN AND RAKUTO-SAN ARE THE ONES WHO BROUGHT IN THE CUSTOMERS FOR US.
I'M NOT SURE WE CAN GET BY WITHOUT THEM...
JEEZ, SOKI- CHI...
YOU'RE MAKING ME BLUSH.
BLUSH
OH, THE FLATTERY.
HMMM

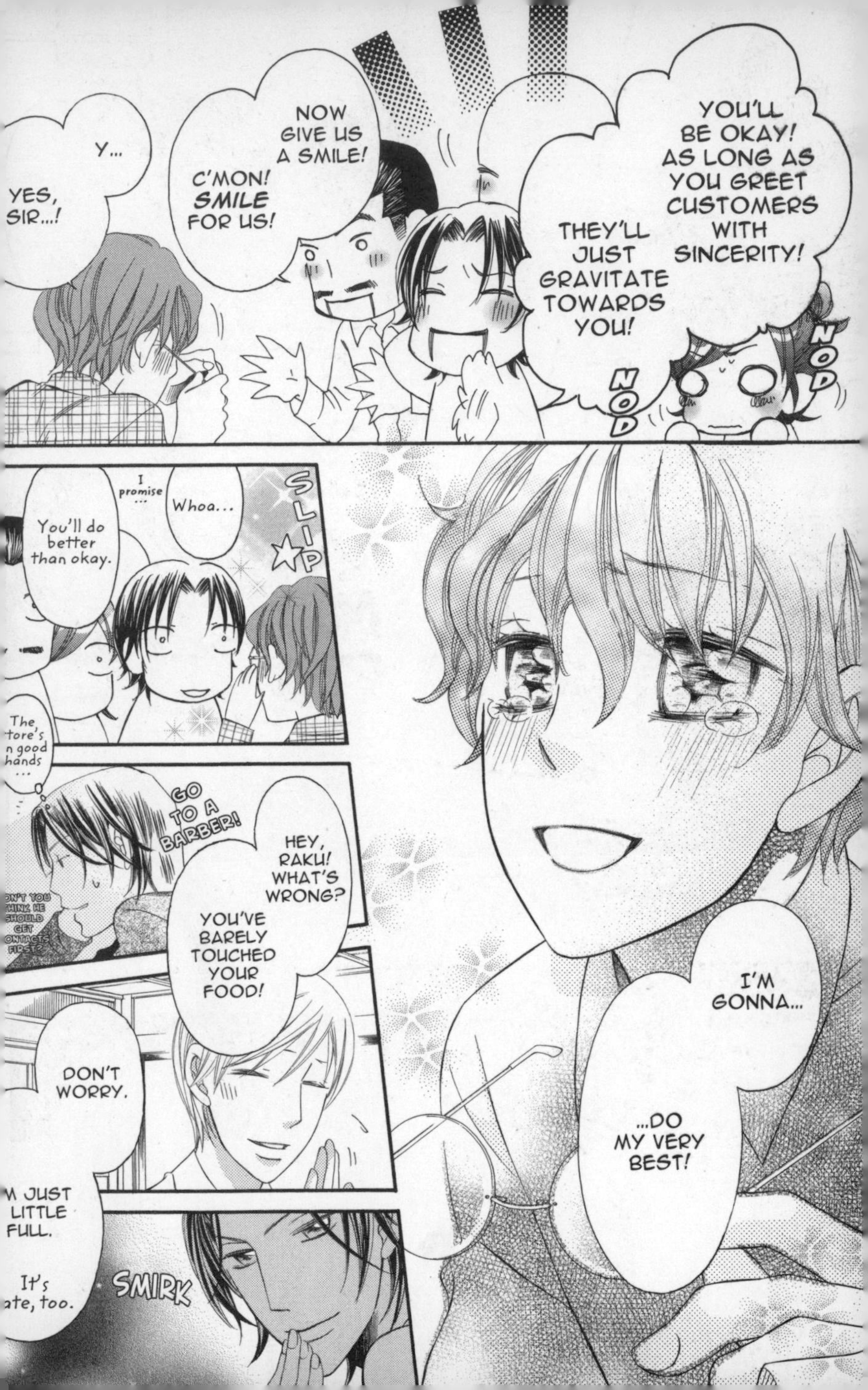
YOU'LL BE OKAY! AS LONG AS YOU GREET CUSTOMERS WITH SINCERITY!
THEY'LL JUST GRAVITATE TOWARDS YOU!
NOD
NOD
NOW GIVE US A SMILE!
C'MON! SMILE FOR US!
Y...
YES, SIR...!
I'M GONNA...
...DO MY VERY BEST!
SLIP
Whoa...
I promise...
You'll do better than okay.
The, tore's n good hands ...
GO TO A BARBER!
N'T YOU THINK HE SHOULD GET ONTACTS FIRST?
HEY, RAKU! WHAT'S WRONG?
YOU'VE BARELY TOUCHED YOUR FOOD!
DON'T WORRY.
M JUST LITTLE FULL.
SMIRK
It's ate, too.

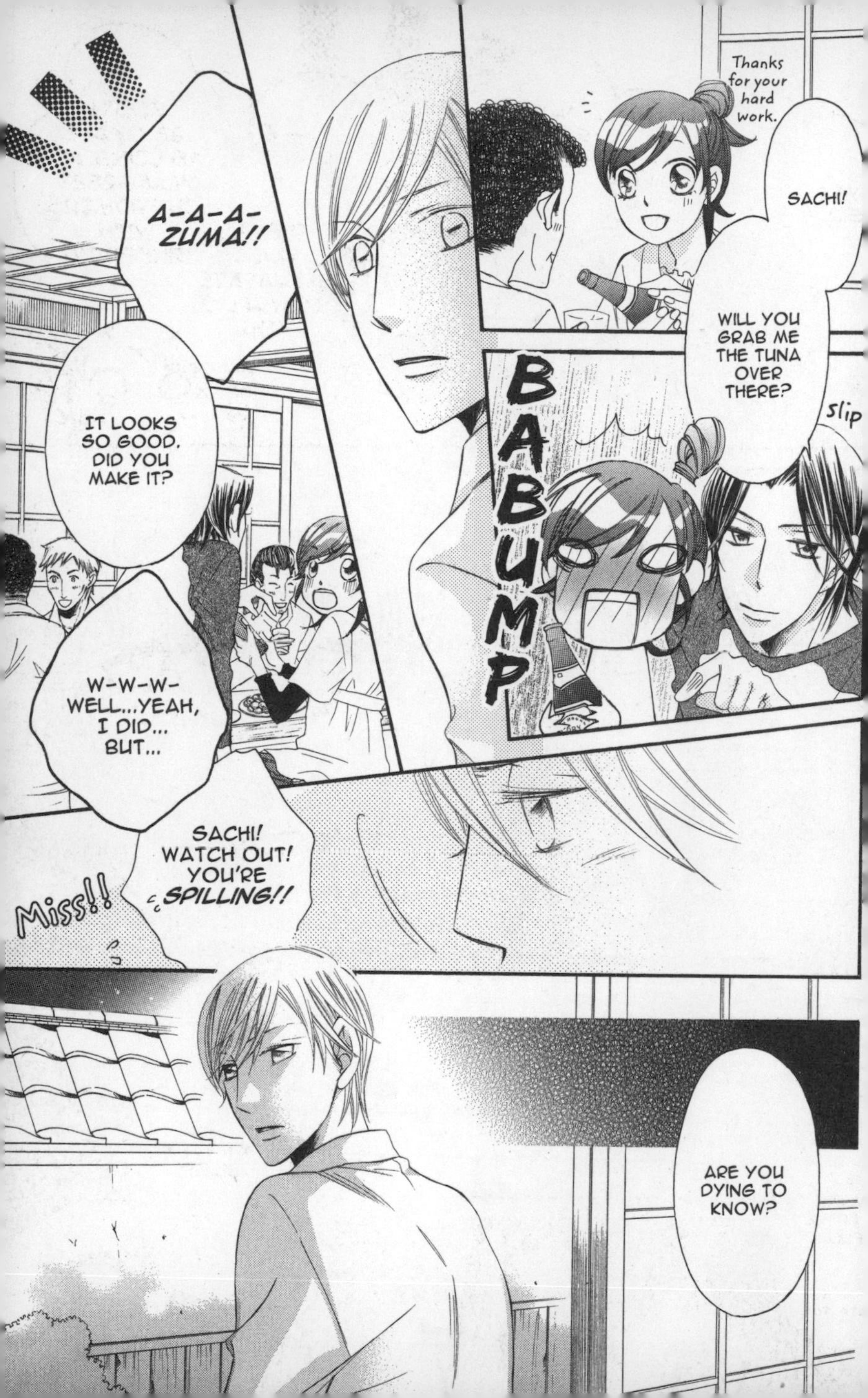
Thanks for your hard work.
SACHI!
WILL YOU GRAB ME THE TUNA OVER THERE?
slip
BABUMP
A-A-A-ZUMA!!
IT LOOKS SO GOOD. DID YOU MAKE IT?
W-W-W-WELL...YEAH, I DID... BUT...
SACHI! WATCH OUT! YOU'RE SPILLING!!
Miss!!
ARE YOU DYING TO KNOW?

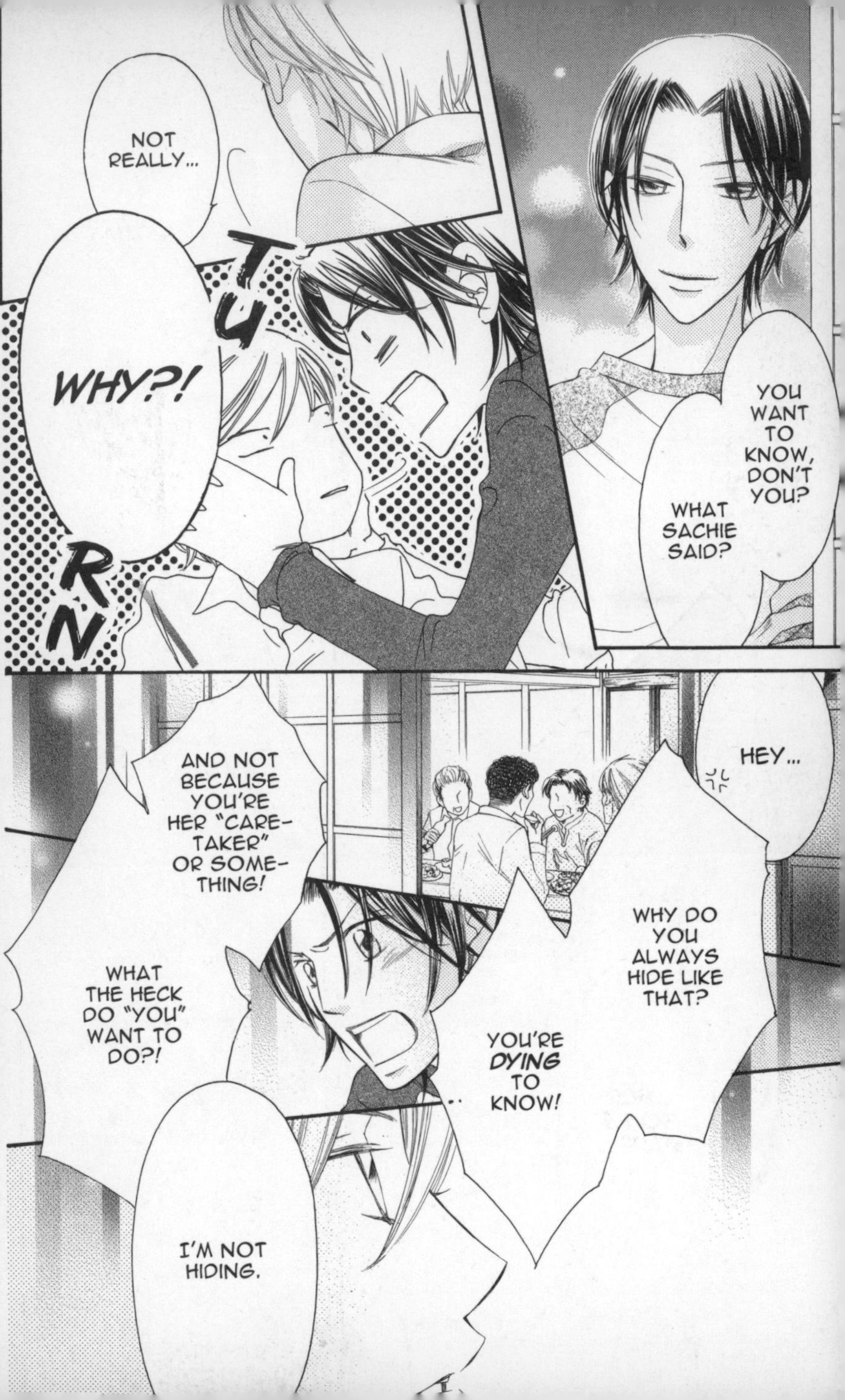
YOU WANT TO KNOW, DON'T YOU?
WHAT SACHIE SAID?
NOT REALLY...
WHY?!
TURN
HEY...
WHY DO YOU ALWAYS HIDE LIKE THAT?
YOU'RE *DYING* TO KNOW!
AND NOT BECAUSE YOU'RE HER "CARE-TAKER" OR SOME-THING!
WHAT THE HECK DO "YOU" WANT TO DO?!
I'M NOT HIDING.

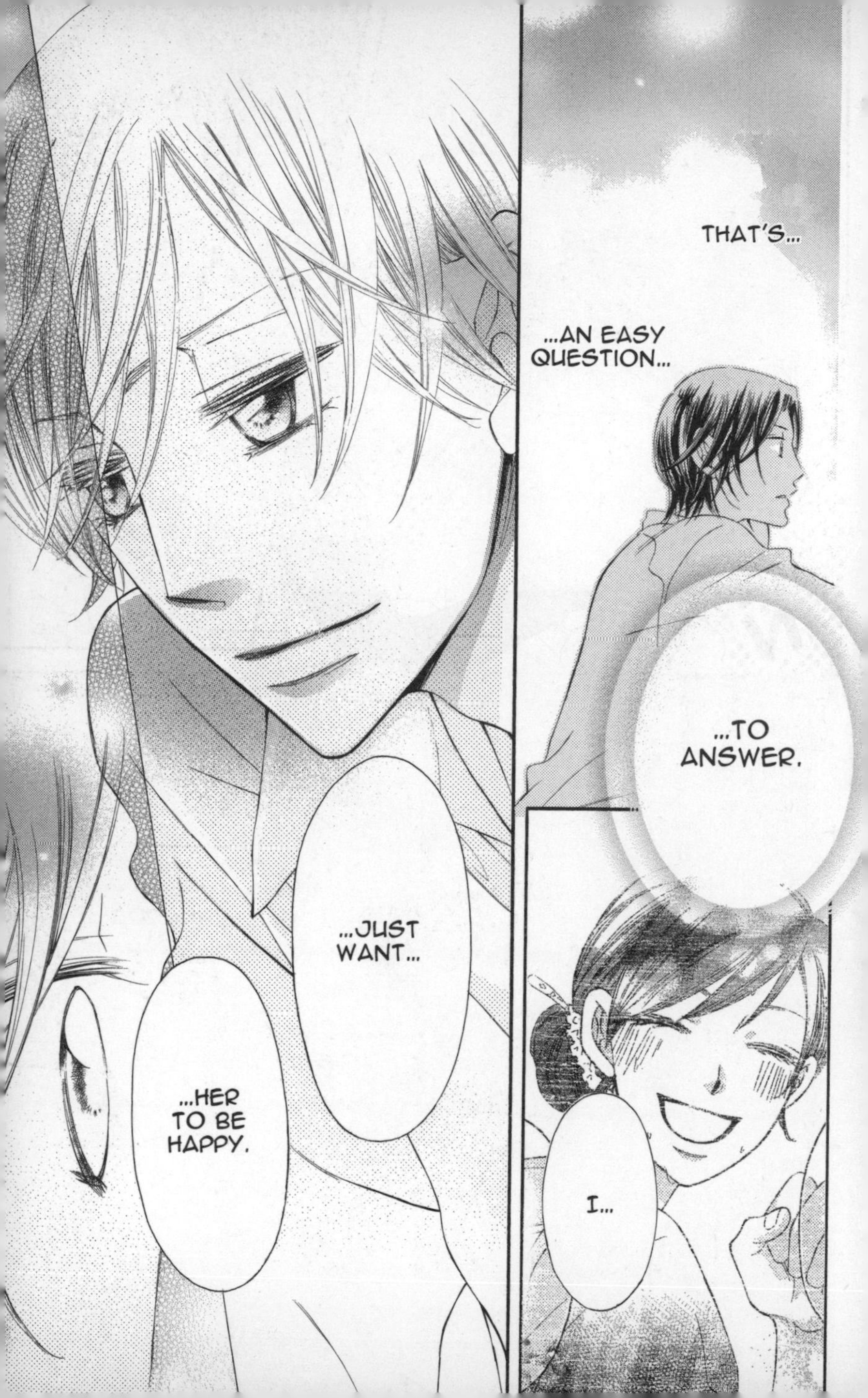
THAT'S...
...AN EASY QUESTION...
...TO ANSWER.
I...
...JUST WANT...
...HER TO BE HAPPY.

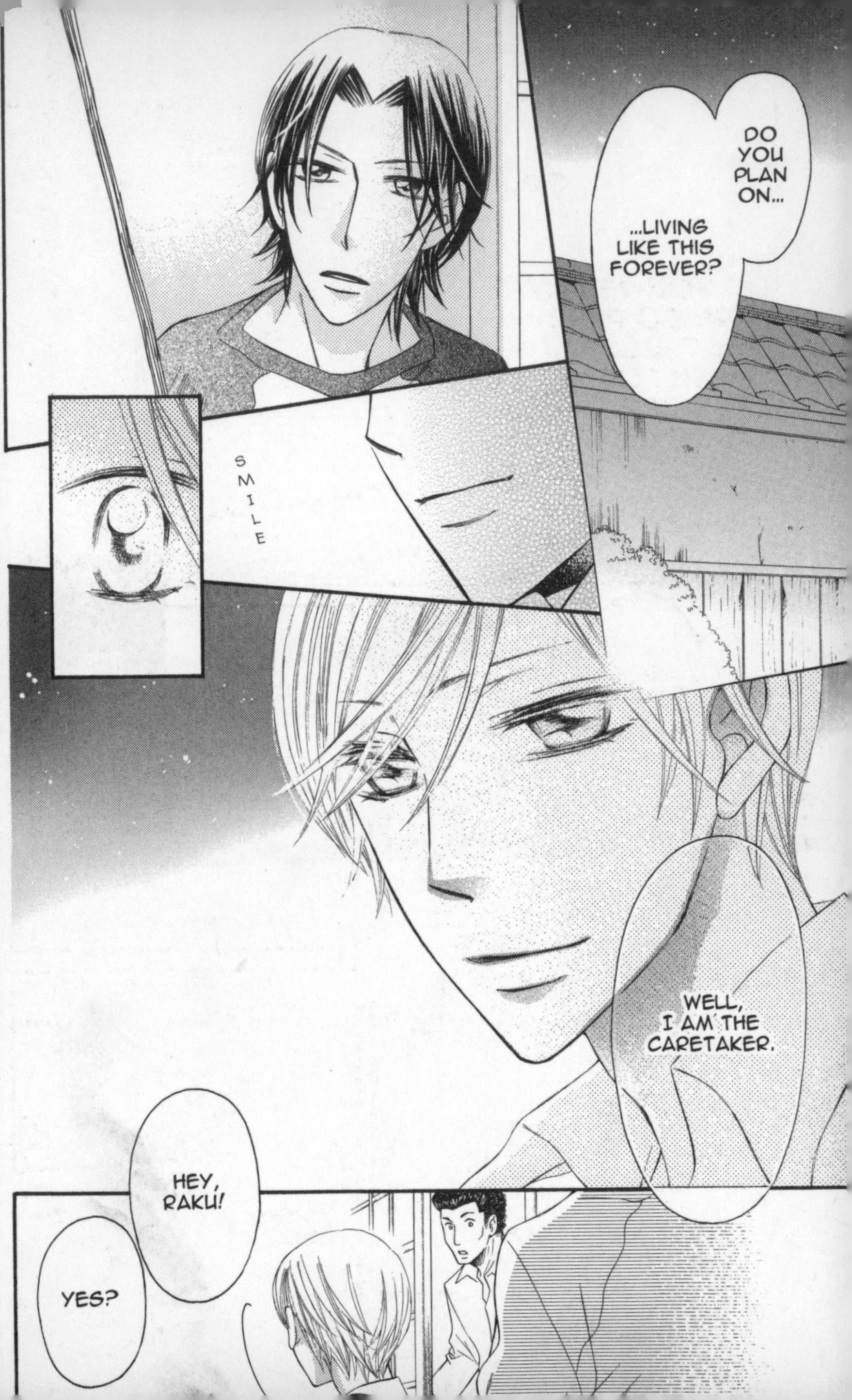
DO YOU PLAN ON...
...LIVING LIKE THIS FOREVER?
SMILE
WELL, I AM THE CARETAKER.
HEY, RAKU!
YES?

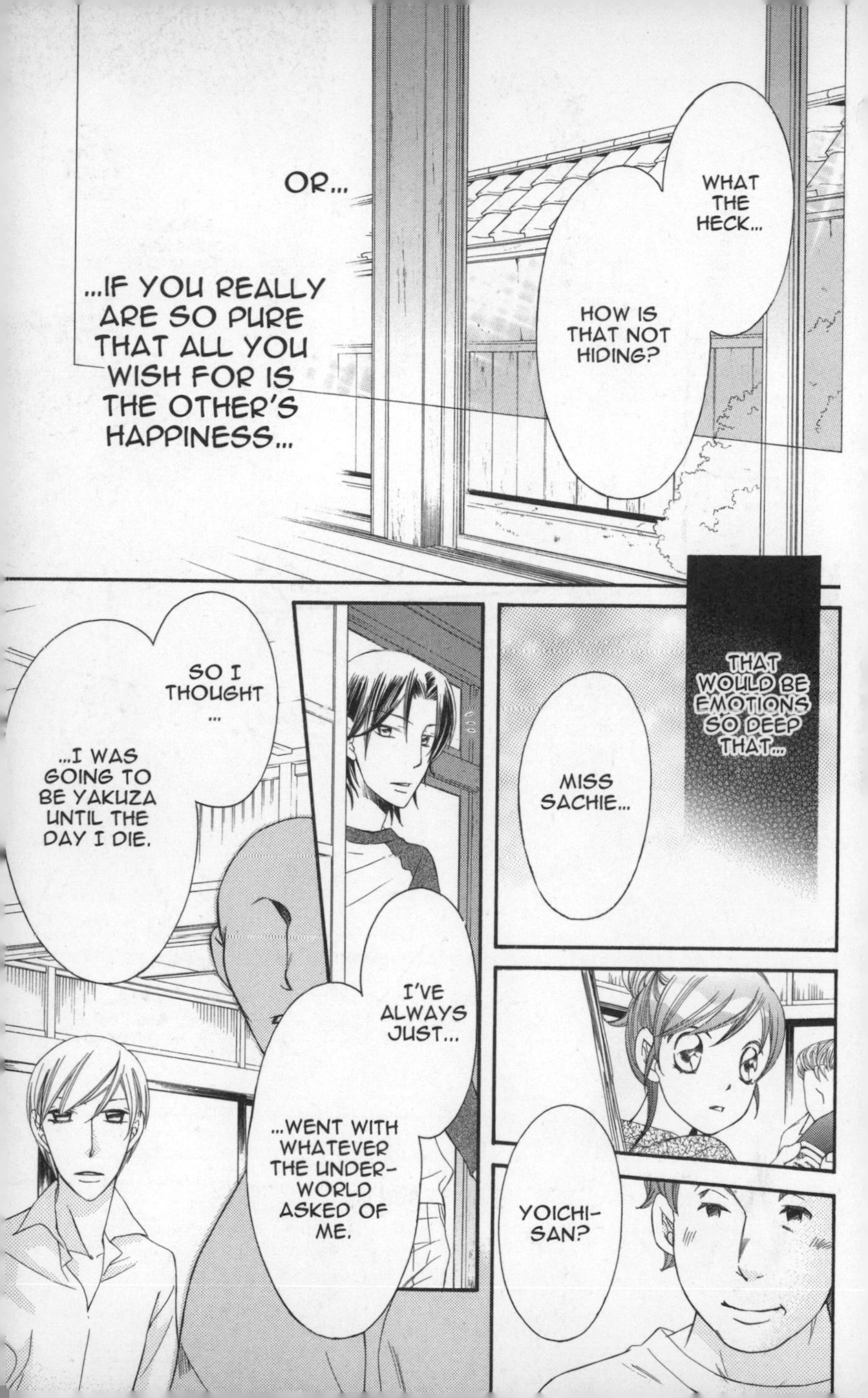
WHAT THE HECK...
HOW IS THAT NOT HIDING?
OR...
THAT WOULD BE EMOTIONS SO DEEP THAT...
...IF YOU REALLY ARE SO PURE THAT ALL YOU WISH FOR IS THE OTHER'S HAPPINESS...
MISS SACHIE...
YOICHI-SAN?
I'VE ALWAYS JUST...
...WENT WITH WHATEVER THE UNDER-WORLD ASKED OF ME.
SO I THOUGHT ...
...I WAS GOING TO BE YAKUZA UNTIL THE DAY I DIE.

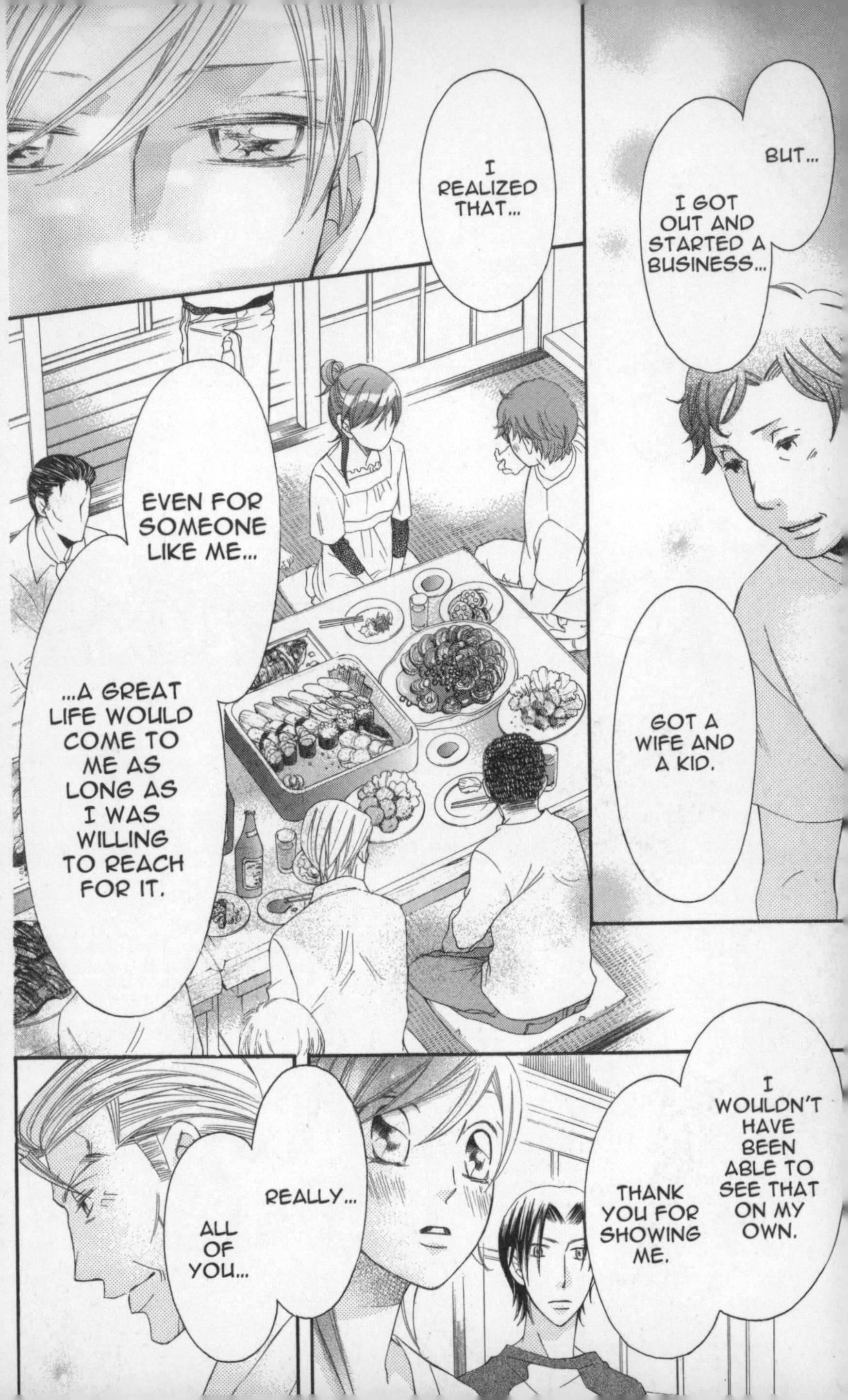
BUT...
I GOT OUT AND STARTED A BUSINESS...
GOT A WIFE AND A KID.
I REALIZED THAT...
EVEN FOR SOMEONE LIKE ME...
...A GREAT LIFE WOULD COME TO ME AS LONG AS I WAS WILLING TO REACH FOR IT.
I WOULDN'T HAVE BEEN ABLE TO SEE THAT ON MY OWN.
THANK YOU FOR SHOWING ME.
REALLY...
ALL OF YOU...

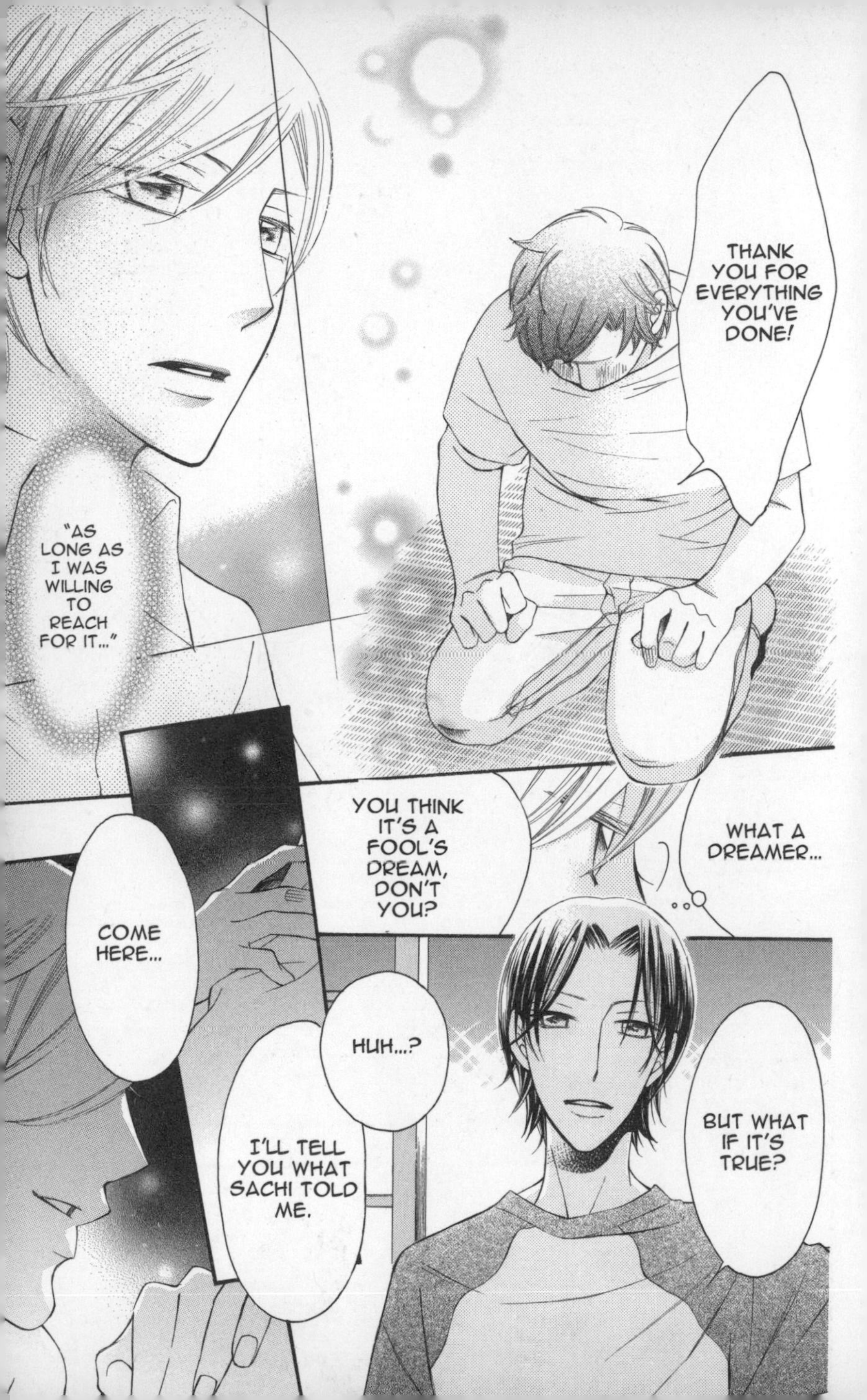
THANK YOU FOR EVERYTHING YOU'VE DONE!
"AS LONG AS I WAS WILLING TO REACH FOR IT..."
WHAT A DREAMER...
YOU THINK IT'S A FOOL'S DREAM, DON'T YOU?
BUT WHAT IF IT'S TRUE?
HUH...?
I'LL TELL YOU WHAT SACHI TOLD ME.
COME HERE...

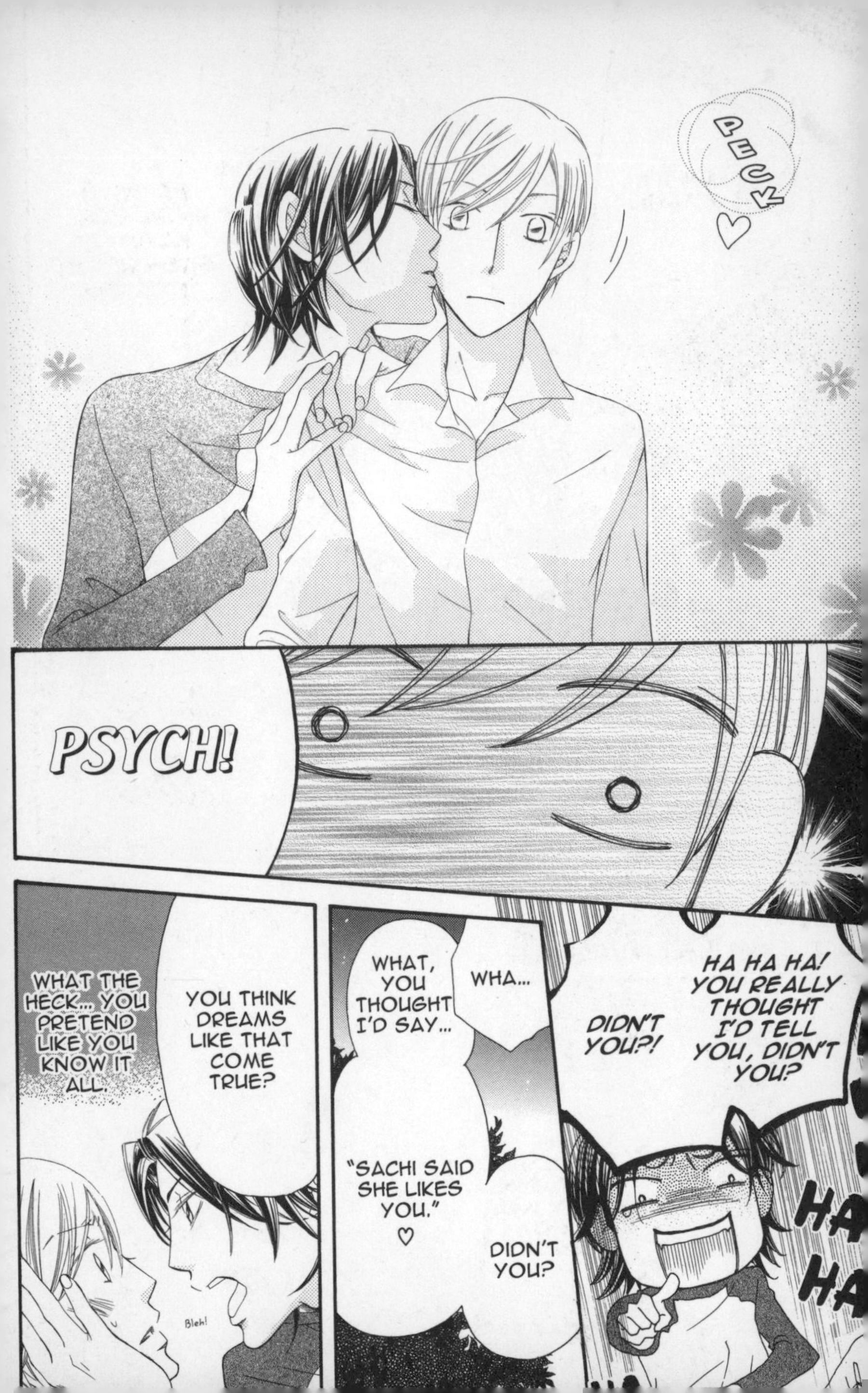
PECK ♡
PSYCH!
HA HA HA! YOU REALLY THOUGHT I'D TELL YOU, DIDN'T YOU?
DIDN'T YOU?!
HA HA
WHA...
WHAT, YOU THOUGHT I'D SAY...
"SACHI SAID SHE LIKES YOU." ♡
DIDN'T YOU?
YOU THINK DREAMS LIKE THAT COME TRUE?
WHAT THE HECK... YOU PRETEND LIKE YOU KNOW IT ALL.
Bleh!

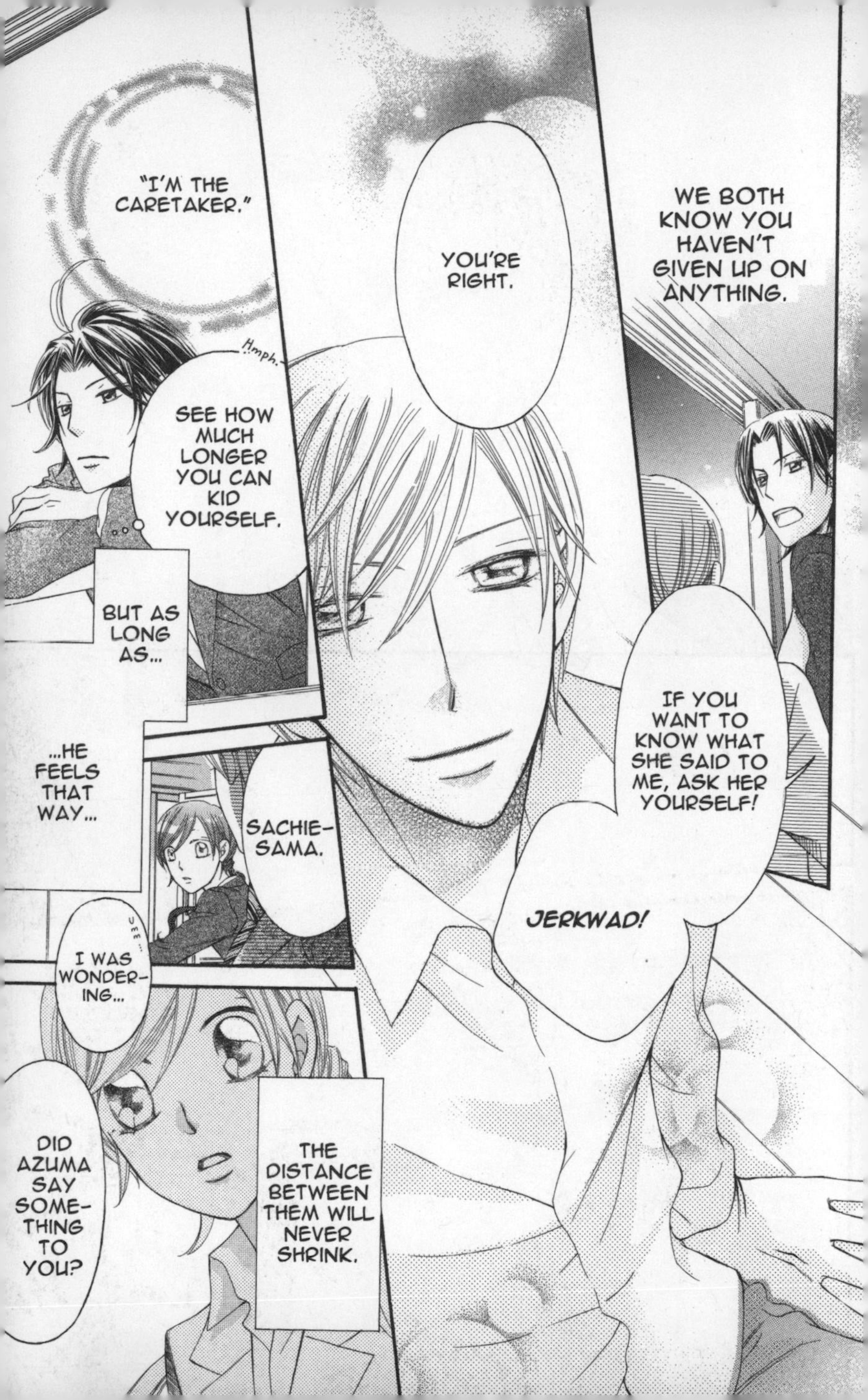
WE BOTH KNOW YOU HAVEN'T GIVEN UP ON ANYTHING.
IF YOU WANT TO KNOW WHAT SHE SAID TO ME, ASK HER YOURSELF!
JERKWAD!
YOU'RE RIGHT.
"I'M THE CARETAKER."
Hmph.
SEE HOW MUCH LONGER YOU CAN KID YOURSELF.
BUT AS LONG AS...
SACHIE-SAMA.
...HE FEELS THAT WAY...
I WAS WONDERING...
THE DISTANCE BETWEEN THEM WILL NEVER SHRINK.
DID AZUMA SAY SOMETHING TO YOU?

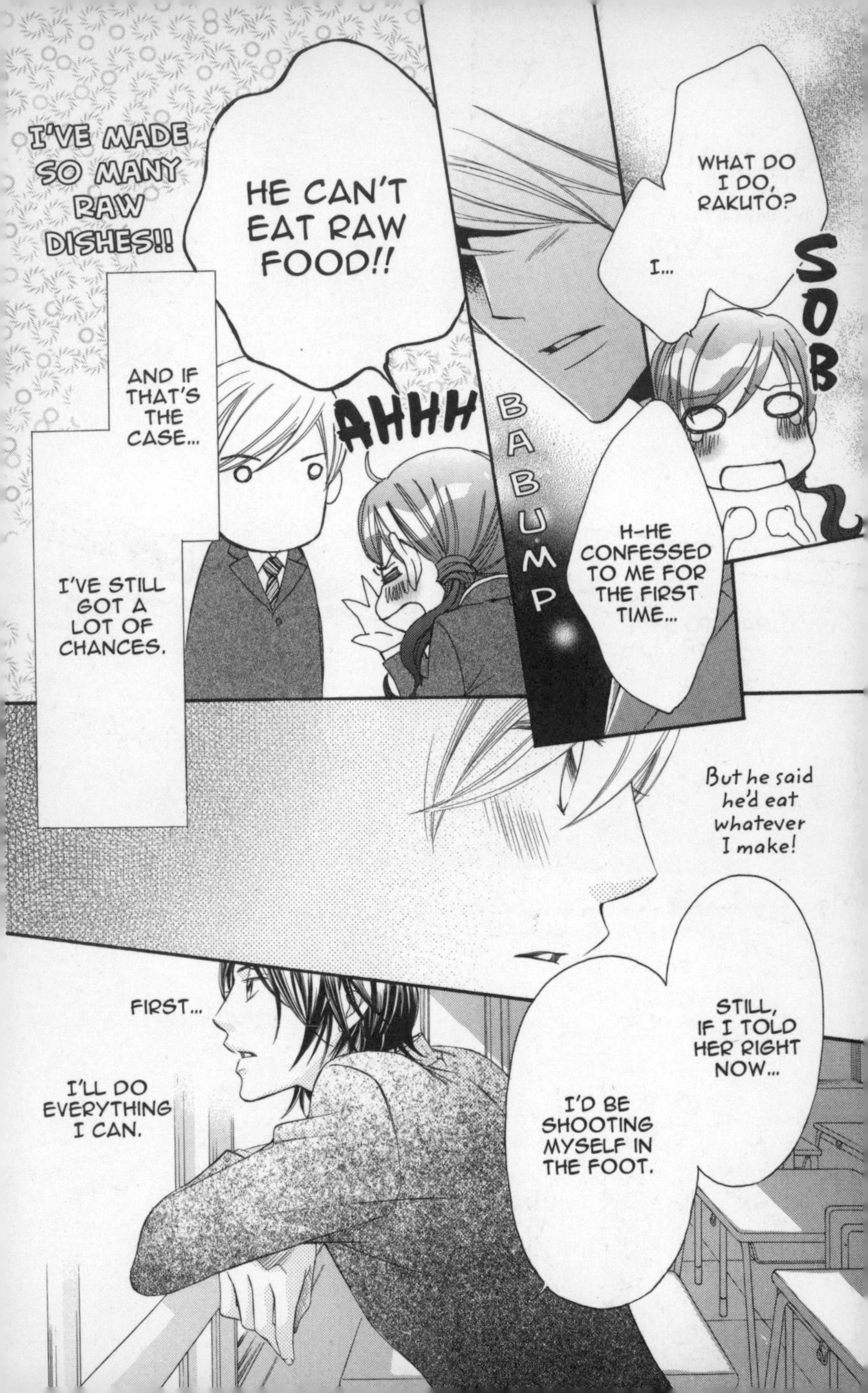
WHAT DO I DO, RAKUTO?
I...
SOB
H-HE CONFESSED TO ME FOR THE FIRST TIME...
BABUMP
HE CAN'T EAT RAW FOOD!!
I'VE MADE SO MANY RAW DISHES!!
AHHH
AND IF THAT'S THE CASE...
I'VE STILL GOT A LOT OF CHANCES.
But he said he'd eat whatever I make!
STILL, IF I TOLD HER RIGHT NOW...
I'D BE SHOOTING MYSELF IN THE FOOT.
FIRST...
I'LL DO EVERYTHING I CAN.

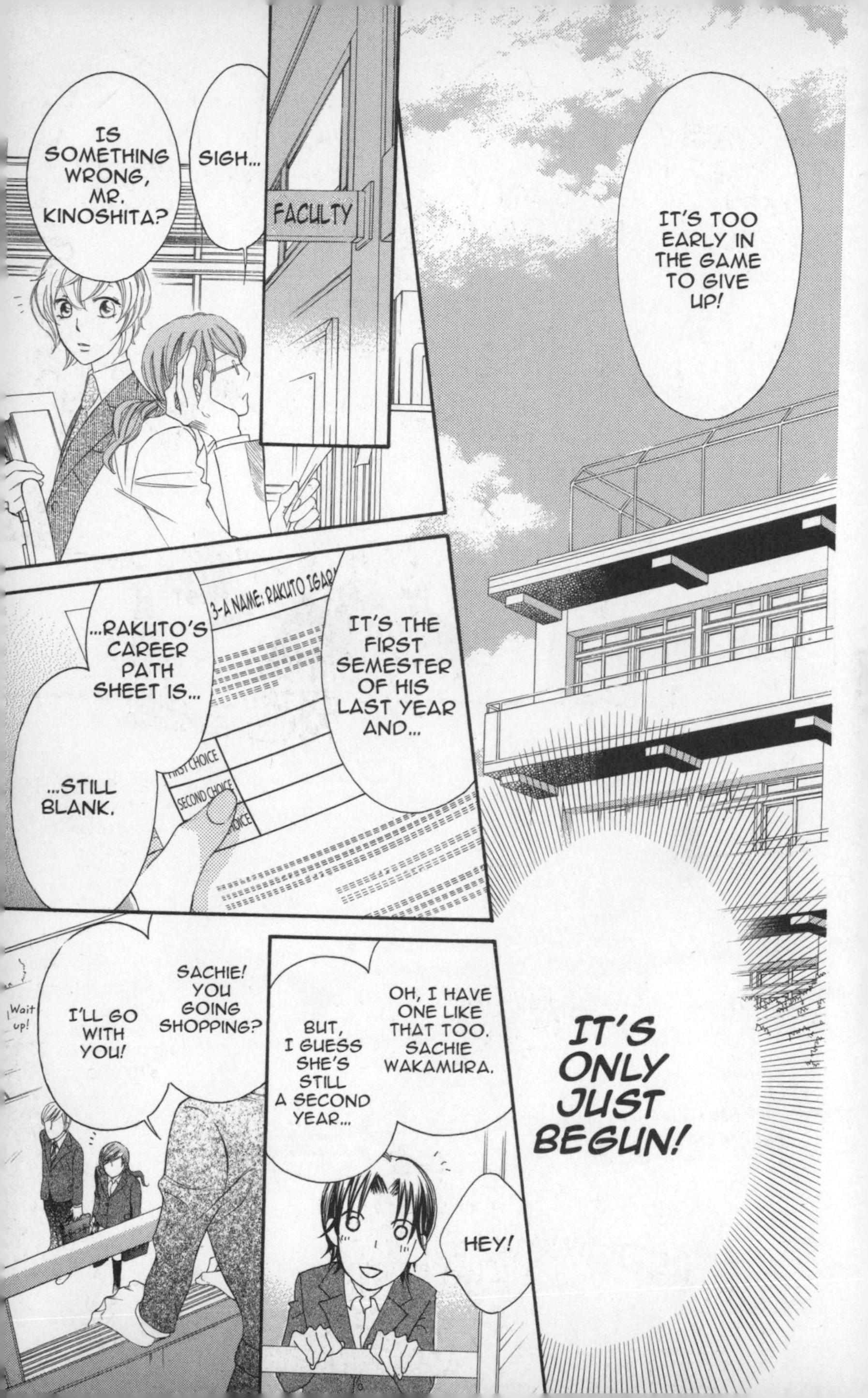
IT'S TOO EARLY IN THE GAME TO GIVE UP!
IT'S ONLY JUST BEGUN!
FACULTY
SIGH...
IS SOMETHING WRONG, MR. KINOSHITA?
IT'S THE FIRST SEMESTER OF HIS LAST YEAR AND...
...RAKUTO'S CAREER PATH SHEET IS...
FIRST CHOICE
SECOND CHOICE
...STILL BLANK.
HEY!
OH, I HAVE ONE LIKE THAT TOO. SACHIE WAKAMURA.
BUT, I GUESS SHE'S STILL A SECOND YEAR...
SACHIE! YOU GOING SHOPPING?
I'LL GO WITH YOU!
Wait up!

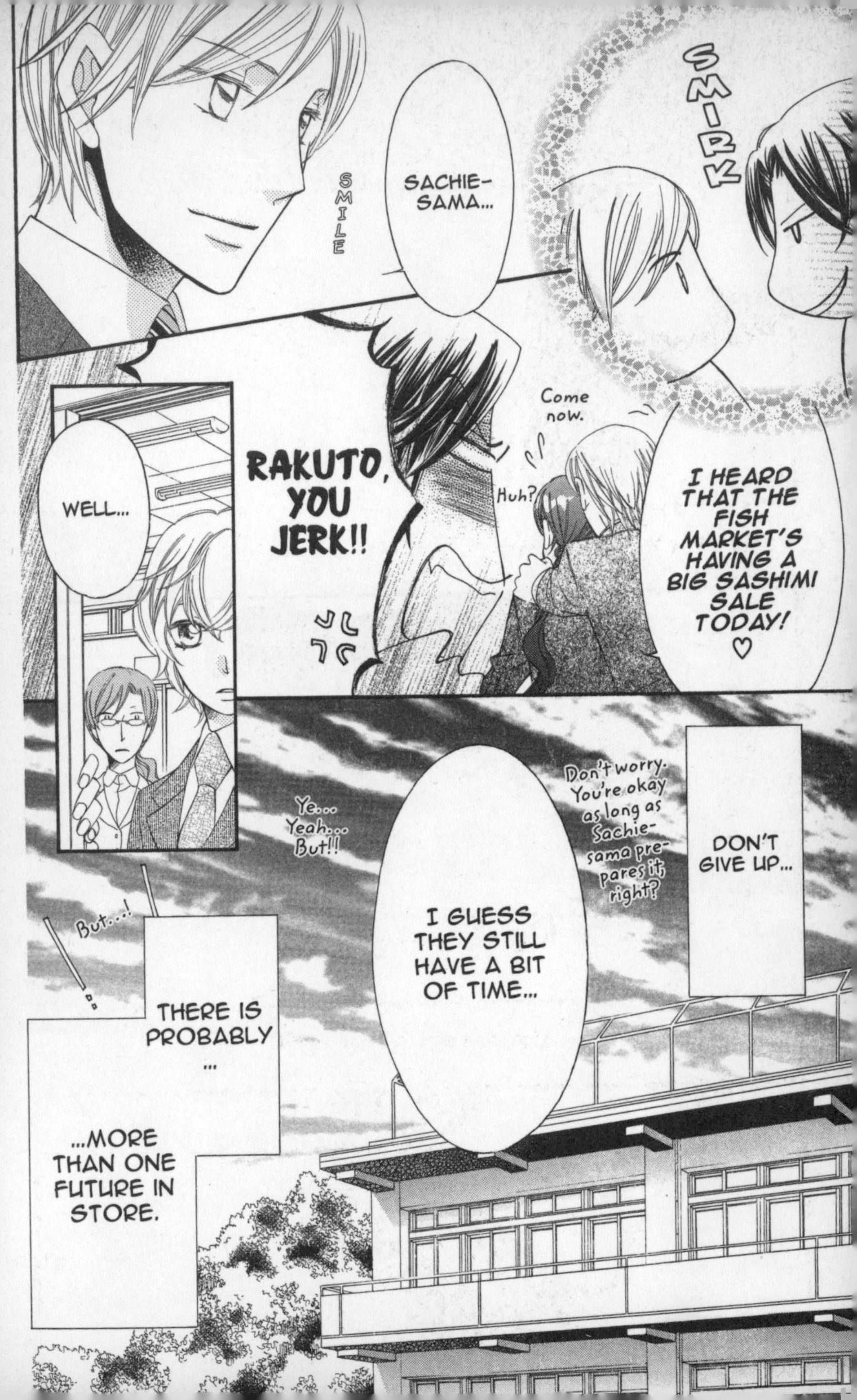
SMIRK
SACHIE-SAMA...
SMILE
I HEARD THAT THE FISH MARKET'S HAVING A BIG SASHIMI SALE TODAY! ♡
Come now.
Huh?
RAKUTO, YOU JERK!!
WELL...
DON'T GIVE UP...
Don't worry. You're okay as long as Sachie-sama prepares it, right?
I GUESS THEY STILL HAVE A BIT OF TIME...
Ye... Yeah... But!!
But...!
THERE IS PROBABLY ...
...MORE THAN ONE FUTURE IN STORE.

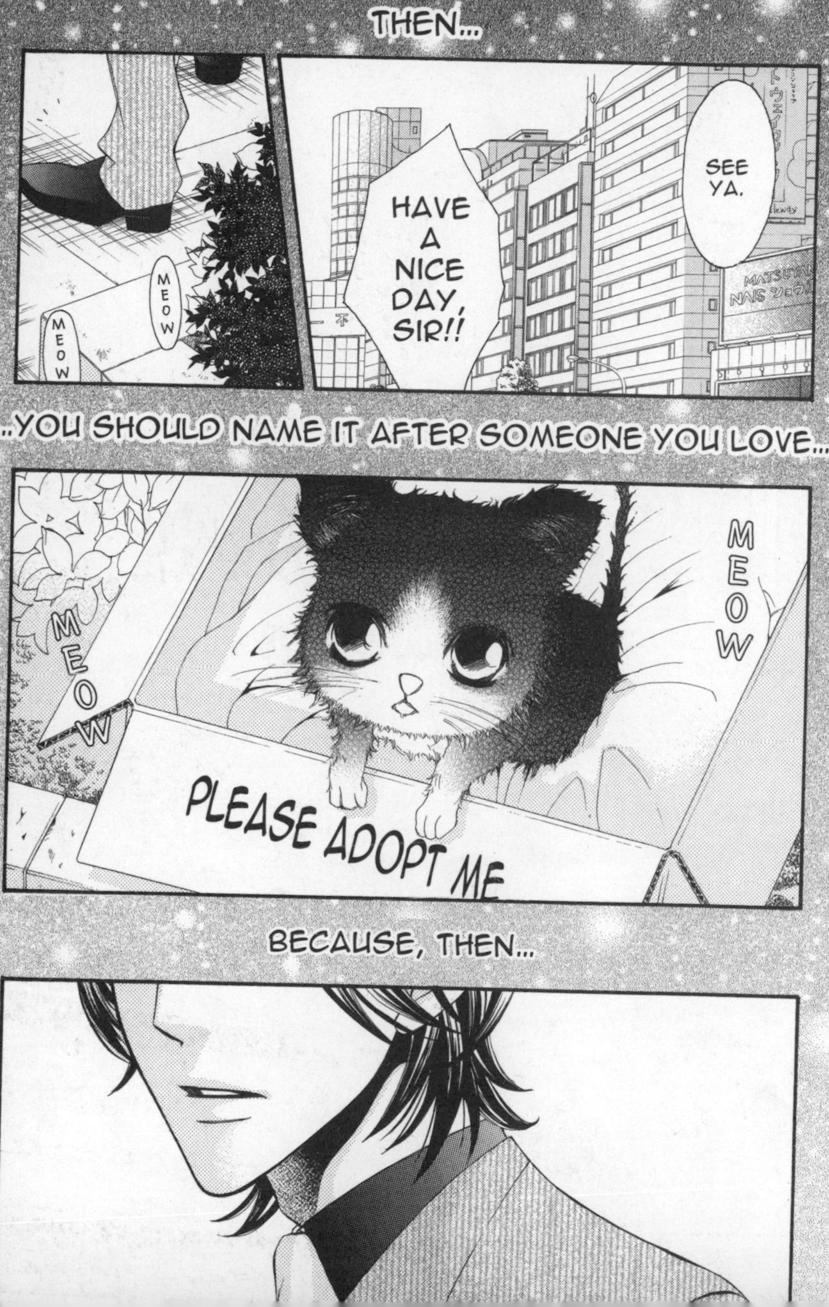
THEN...
SEE YA.
HAVE A NICE DAY, SIR!!
MEOW
MEOW
...YOU SHOULD NAME IT AFTER SOMEONE YOU LOVE...
MEOW
MEOW
PLEASE ADOPT ME
BECAUSE, THEN...

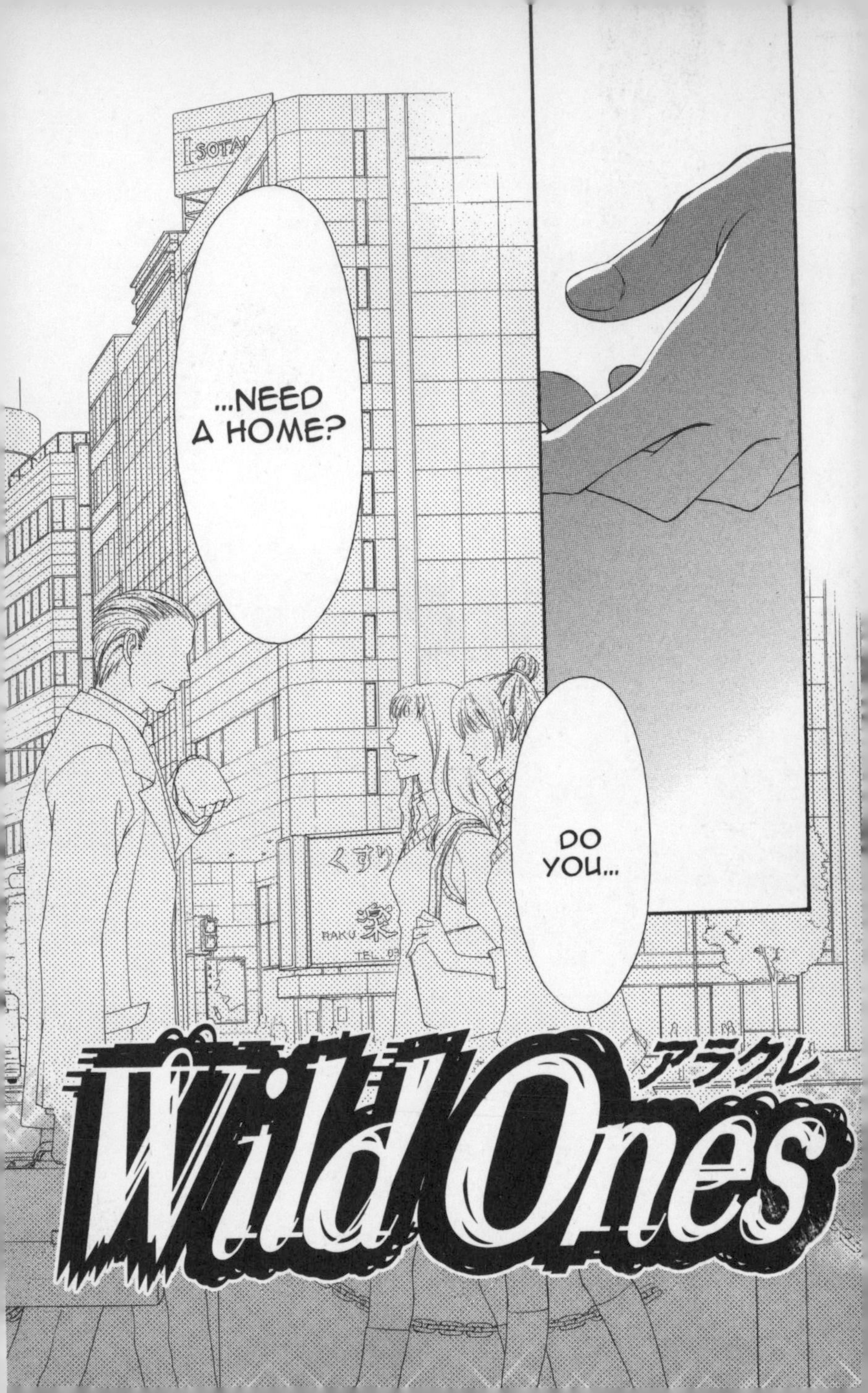
DO YOU...
...NEED A HOME?
くすり
Wild Ones
アラクレ

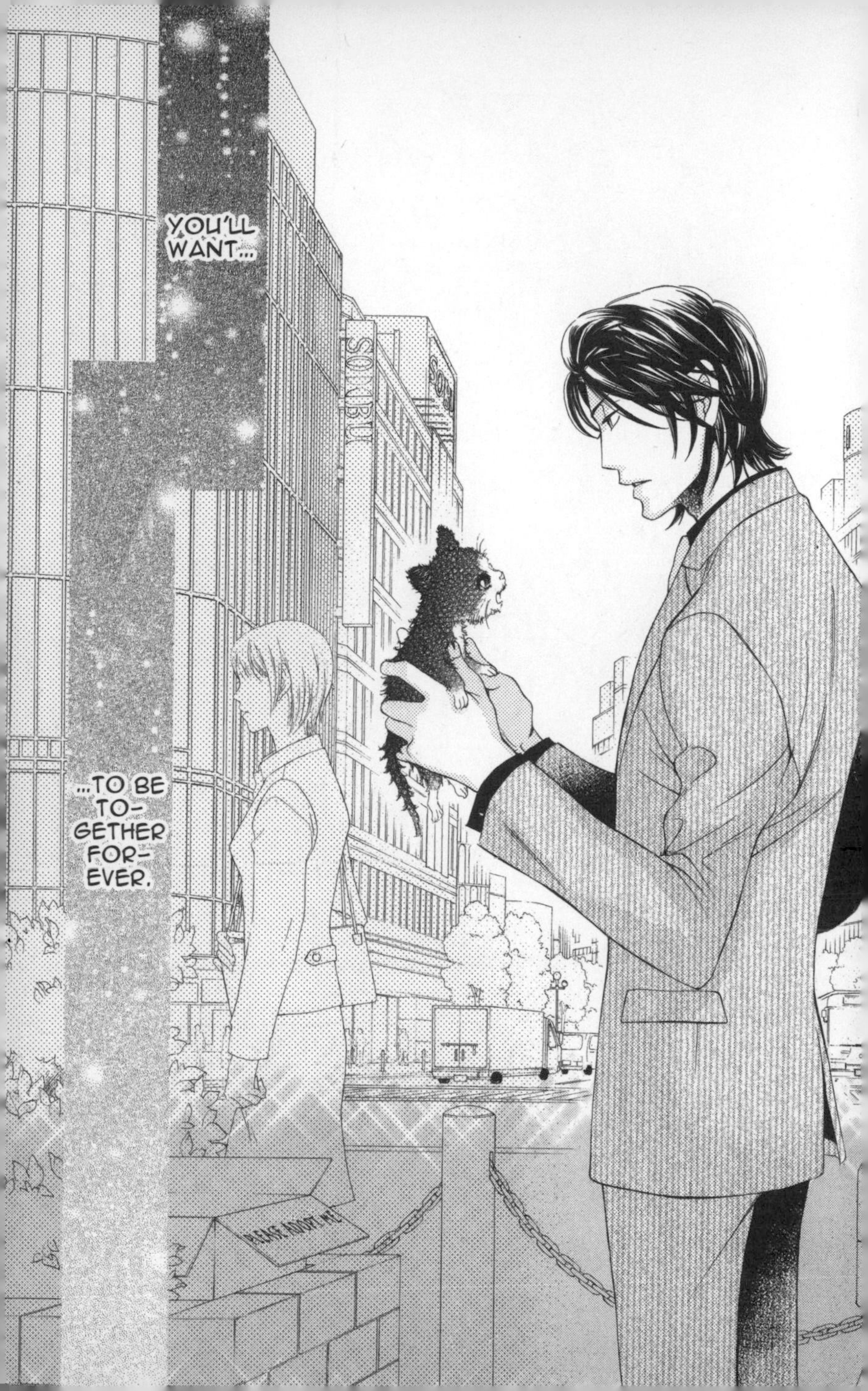
YOU'LL WANT...
...TO BE TO-GETHER FOR-EVER.
SOMBU
PLEASE ADOPT ME

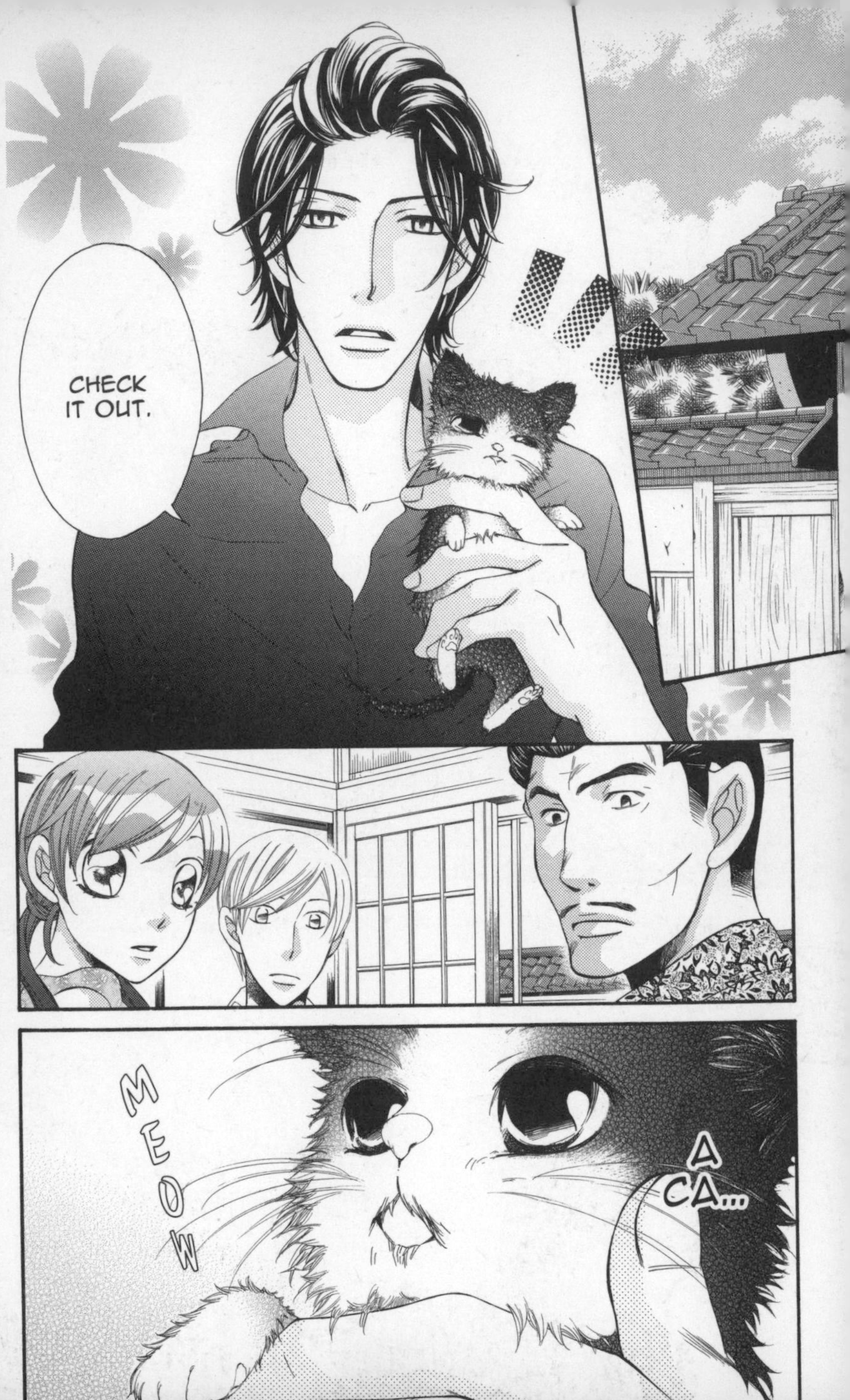
CHECK IT OUT.
A CA...
MEOW

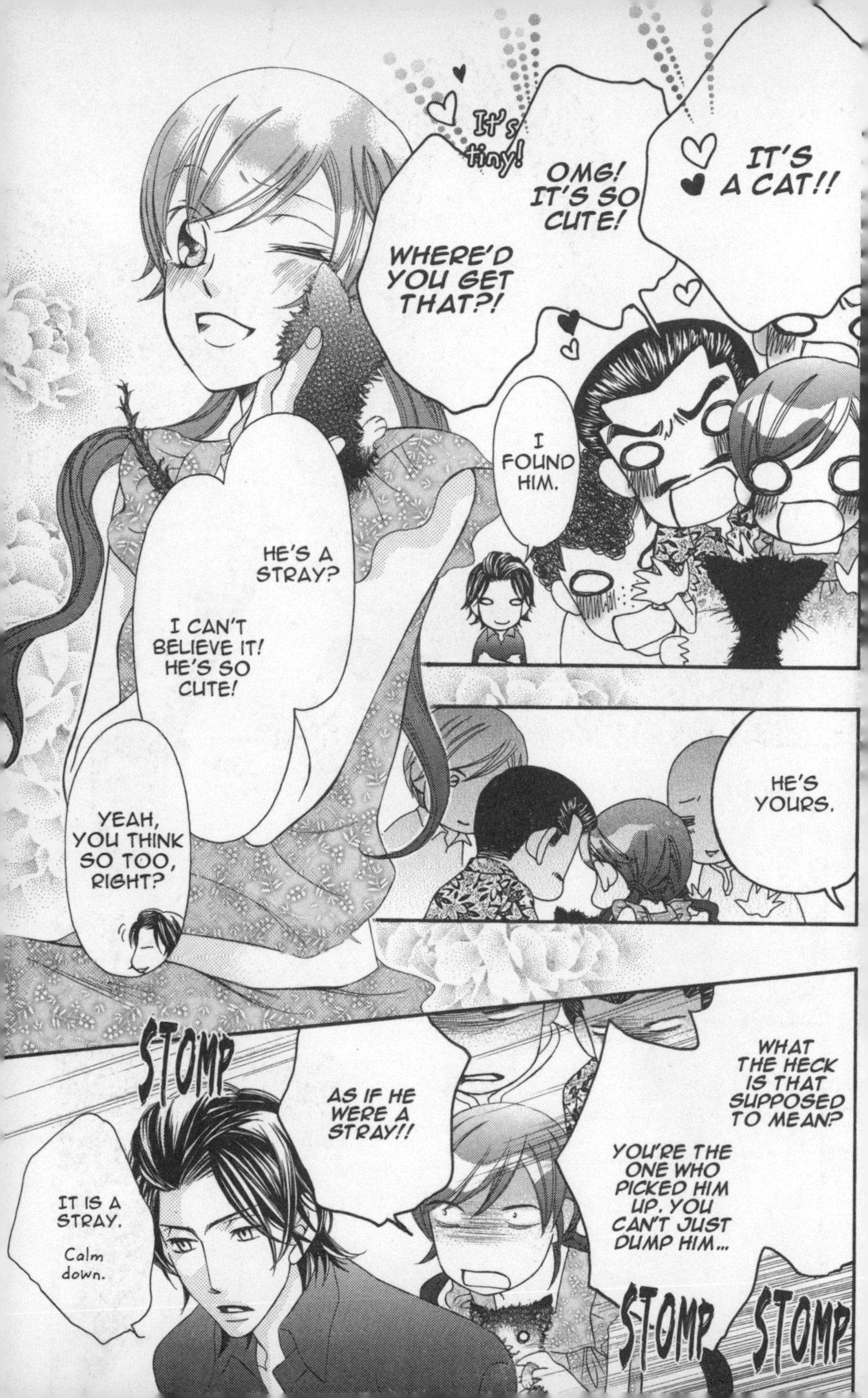

IT'S A CAT!!
OMG! IT'S SO CUTE!
It's tiny!
WHERE'D YOU GET THAT?!
I FOUND HIM.
HE'S YOURS.
HE'S A STRAY?
I CAN'T BELIEVE IT! HE'S SO CUTE!
YEAH, YOU THINK SO TOO, RIGHT?
WHAT THE HECK IS THAT SUPPOSED TO MEAN?
YOU'RE THE ONE WHO PICKED HIM UP. YOU CAN'T JUST DUMP HIM...
STOMP
STOMP
AS IF HE WERE A STRAY!!
STOMP
IT IS A STRAY.
Calm down.

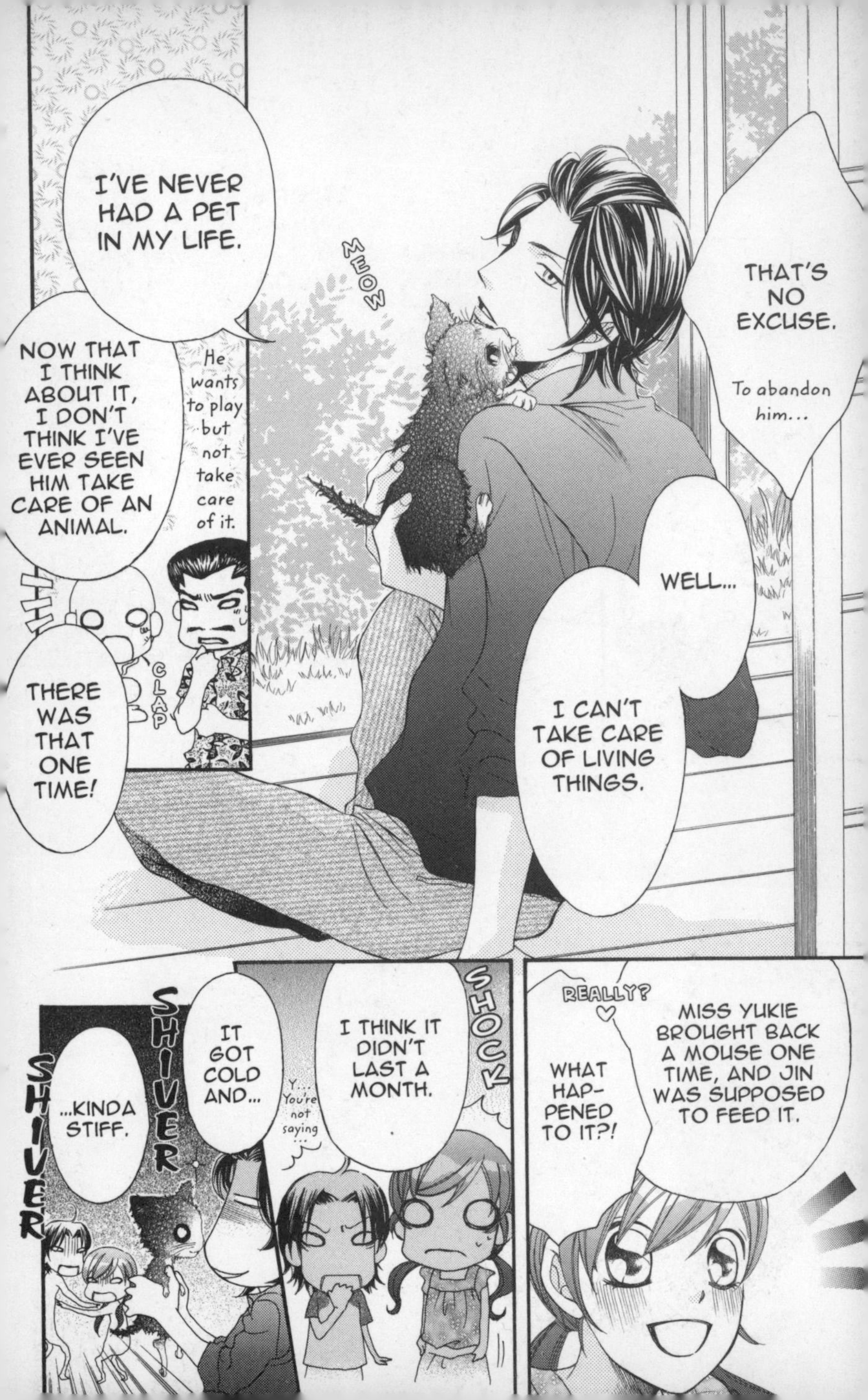
THAT'S NO EXCUSE.
To abandon him...
WELL...
I CAN'T TAKE CARE OF LIVING THINGS.
MEOW
I'VE NEVER HAD A PET IN MY LIFE.
NOW THAT I THINK ABOUT IT, I DON'T THINK I'VE EVER SEEN HIM TAKE CARE OF AN ANIMAL.
He wants to play but not take care of it.
THERE WAS THAT ONE TIME!
CLAP
MISS YUKIE BROUGHT BACK A MOUSE ONE TIME, AND JIN WAS SUPPOSED TO FEED IT.
REALLY? ♥
WHAT HAP-PENED TO IT?!
SHOCK
I THINK IT DIDN'T LAST A MONTH.
Y... You're not saying...
IT GOT COLD AND...
...KINDA STIFF.
SHIVER
SHIVER

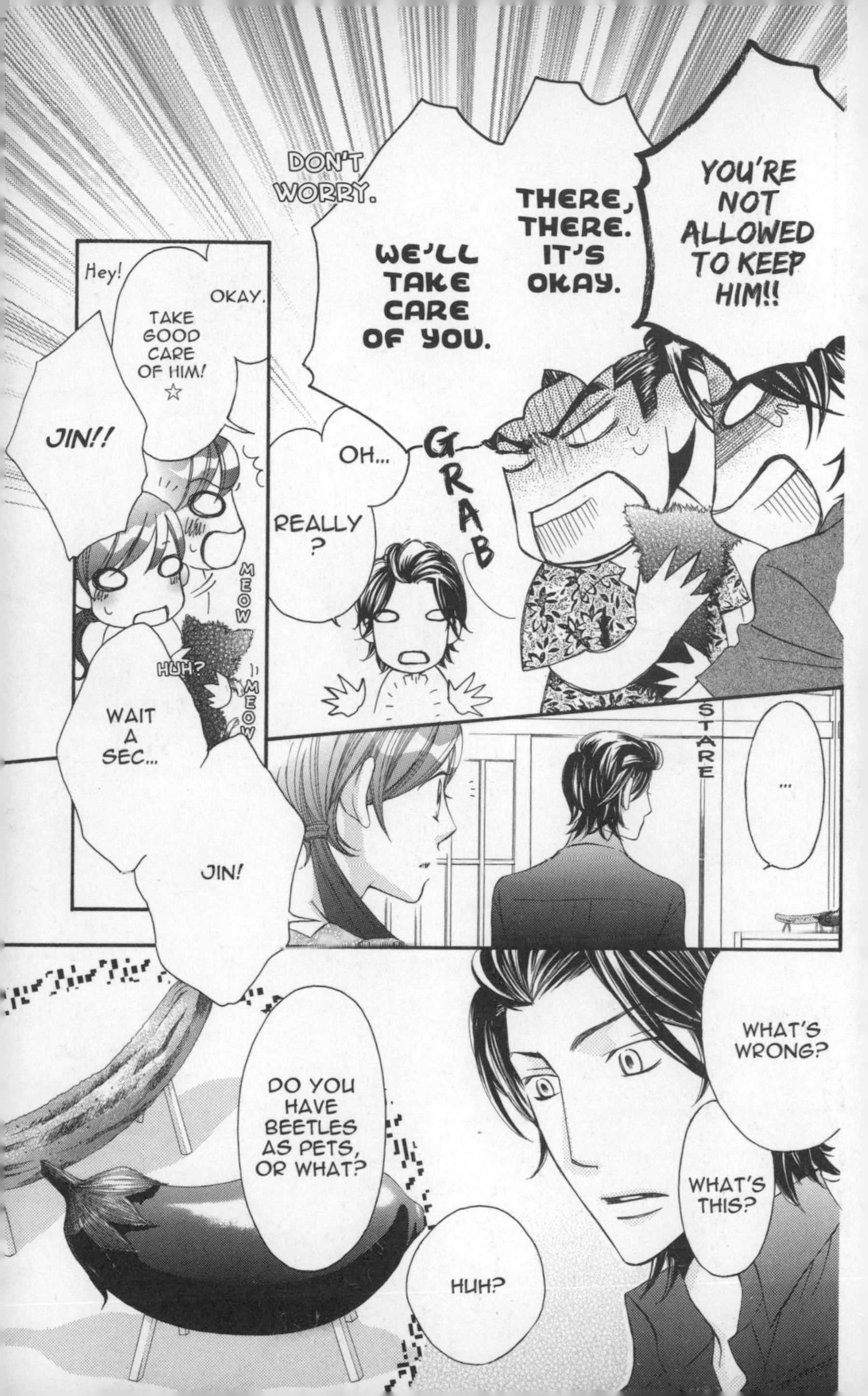
YOU'RE NOT ALLOWED TO KEEP HIM!!
THERE, THERE. IT'S OKAY.
WE'LL TAKE CARE OF YOU.
DON'T WORRY.
GRAB
OH... REALLY?
OKAY.
Hey!
TAKE GOOD CARE OF HIM! ☆
JIN!!
MEOW
HUH?
MEOW
WAIT A SEC...
STARE
...
JIN!
WHAT'S WRONG?
WHAT'S THIS?
DO YOU HAVE BEETLES AS PETS, OR WHAT?
HUH?

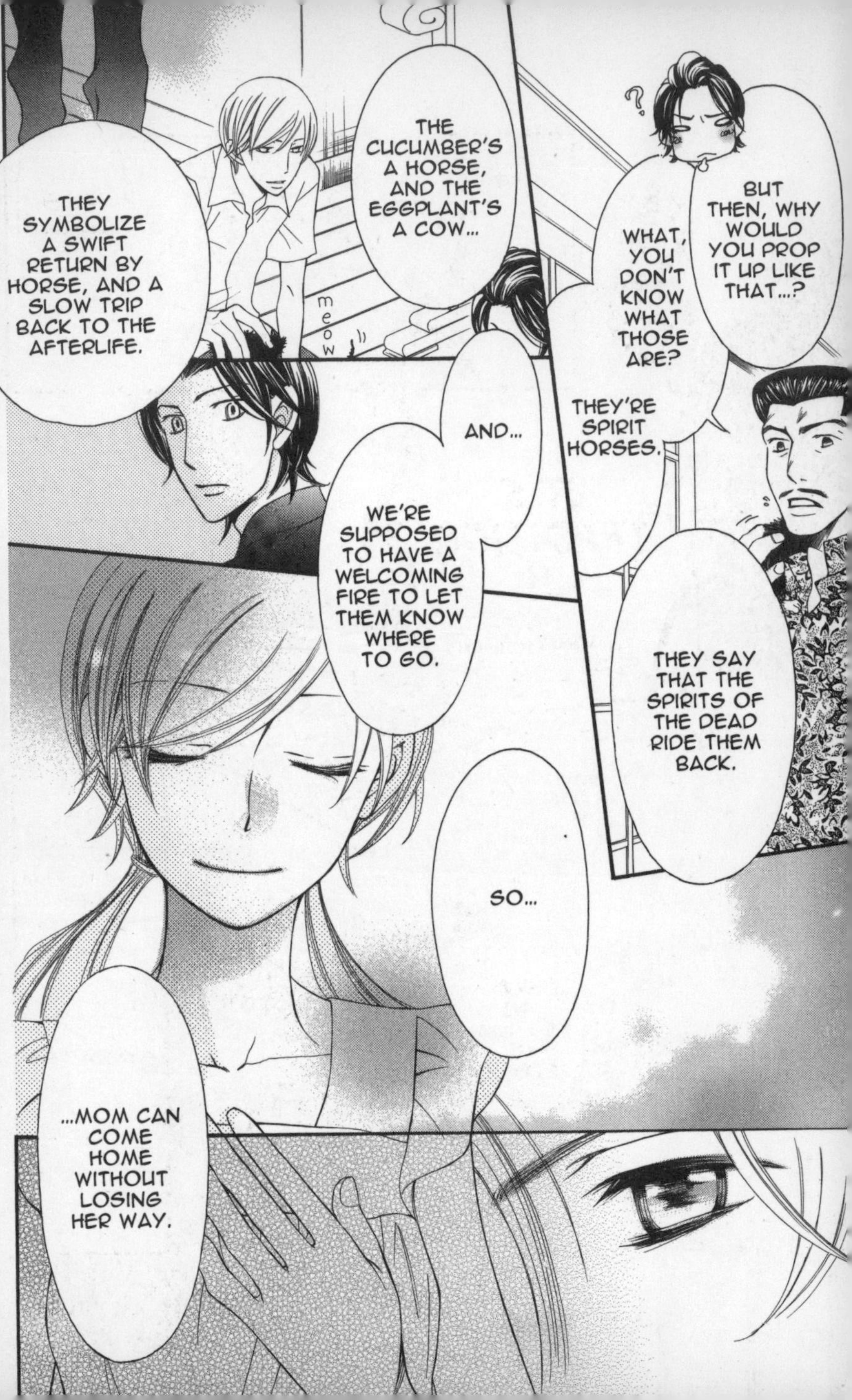
BUT THEN, WHY WOULD YOU PROP IT UP LIKE THAT...?
WHAT, YOU DON'T KNOW WHAT THOSE ARE?
THEY'RE SPIRIT HORSES.
THEY SAY THAT THE SPIRITS OF THE DEAD RIDE THEM BACK.
THE CUCUMBER'S A HORSE, AND THE EGGPLANT'S A COW...
THEY SYMBOLIZE A SWIFT RETURN BY HORSE, AND A SLOW TRIP BACK TO THE AFTERLIFE.
meow
AND...
WE'RE SUPPOSED TO HAVE A WELCOMING FIRE TO LET THEM KNOW WHERE TO GO.
SO...
...MOM CAN COME HOME WITHOUT LOSING HER WAY.

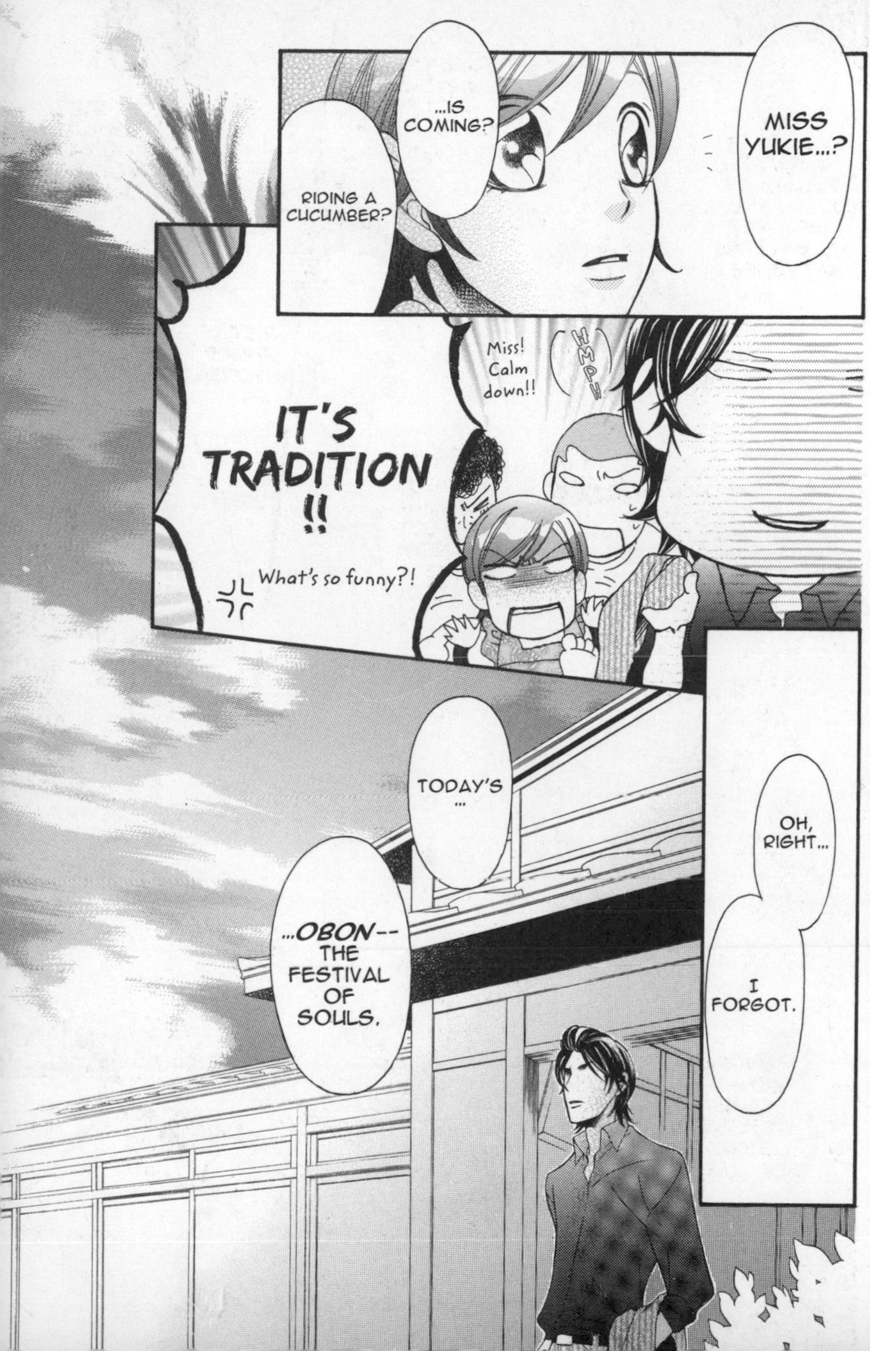
MISS YUKIE...?
...IS COMING?
RIDING A CUCUMBER?
HMPH
Miss! Calm down!!
IT'S TRADITION !!
What's so funny?!
OH, RIGHT...
I FORGOT.
TODAY'S ...
...OBON-- THE FESTIVAL OF SOULS.

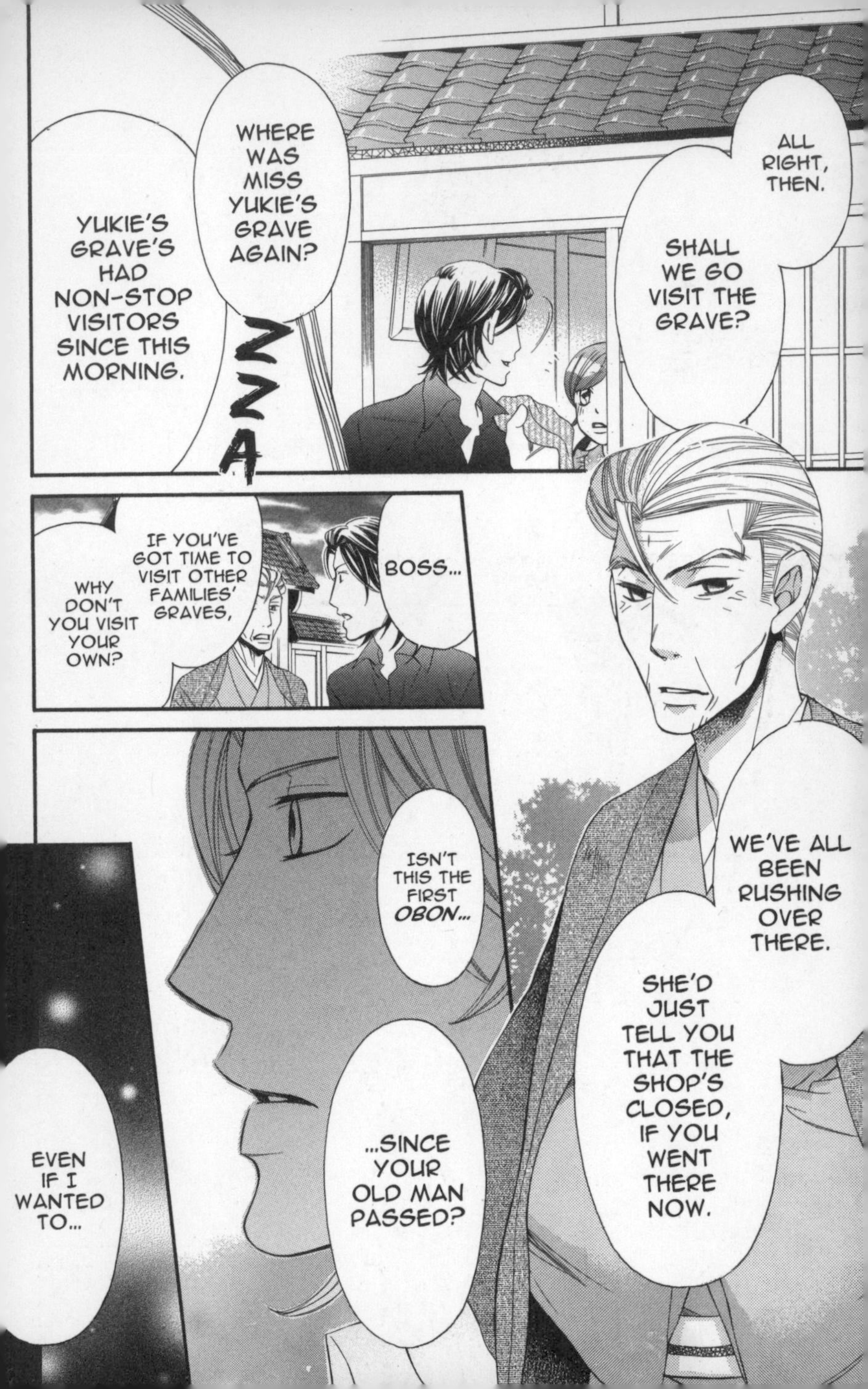
ALL RIGHT, THEN.
SHALL WE GO VISIT THE GRAVE?
WHERE WAS MISS YUKIE'S GRAVE AGAIN?
YUKIE'S GRAVE'S HAD NON-STOP VISITORS SINCE THIS MORNING.
ZZA
WE'VE ALL BEEN RUSHING OVER THERE.
SHE'D JUST TELL YOU THAT THE SHOP'S CLOSED, IF YOU WENT THERE NOW.
BOSS...
IF YOU'VE GOT TIME TO VISIT OTHER FAMILIES' GRAVES,
WHY DON'T YOU VISIT YOUR OWN?
ISN'T THIS THE FIRST *OBON*...
...SINCE YOUR OLD MAN PASSED?
EVEN IF I WANTED TO...

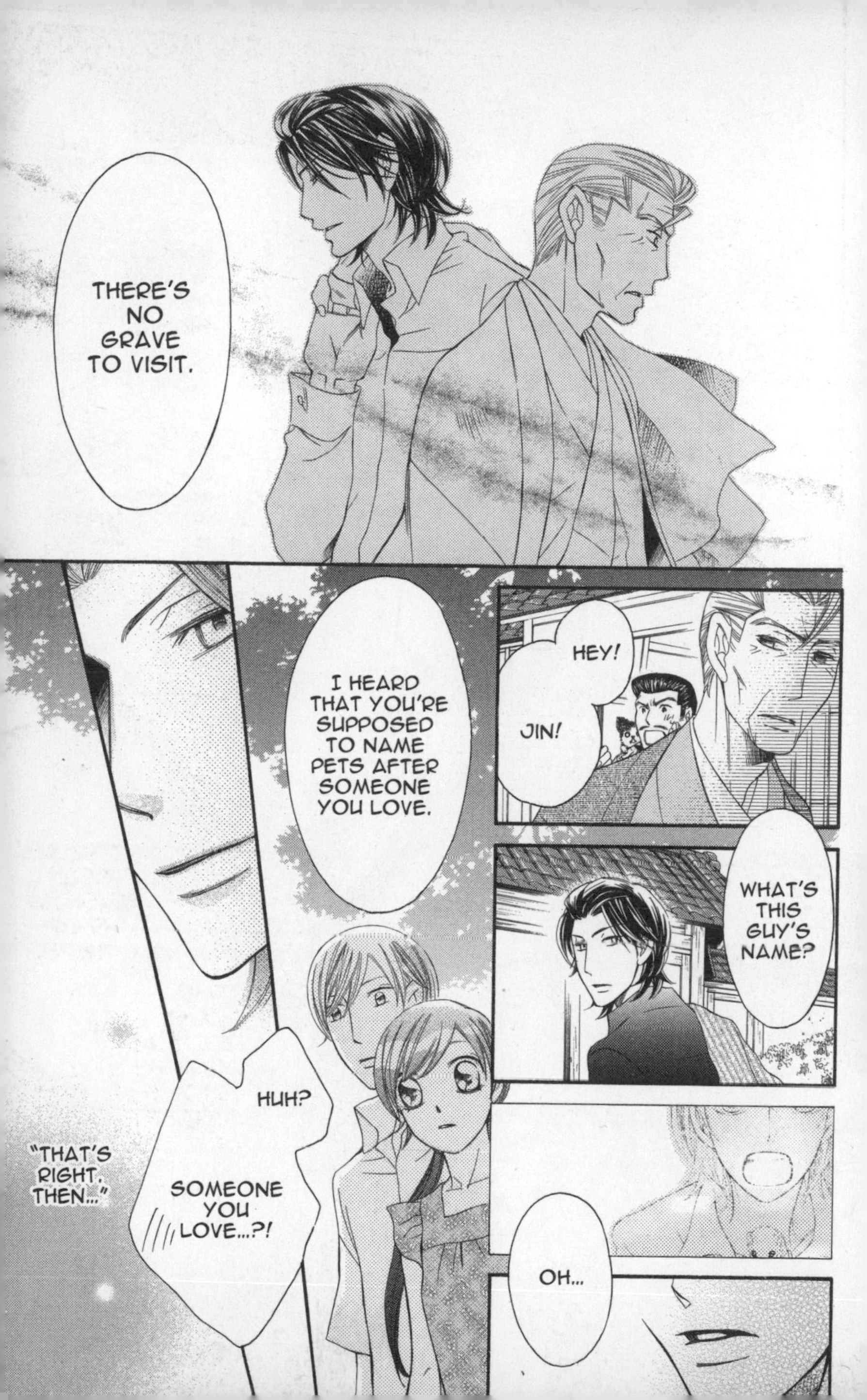
THERE'S NO GRAVE TO VISIT.
HEY!
JIN!
WHAT'S THIS GUY'S NAME?
OH...
I HEARD THAT YOU'RE SUPPOSED TO NAME PETS AFTER SOMEONE YOU LOVE.
HUH?
SOMEONE YOU LOVE...?!
"THAT'S RIGHT. THEN..."

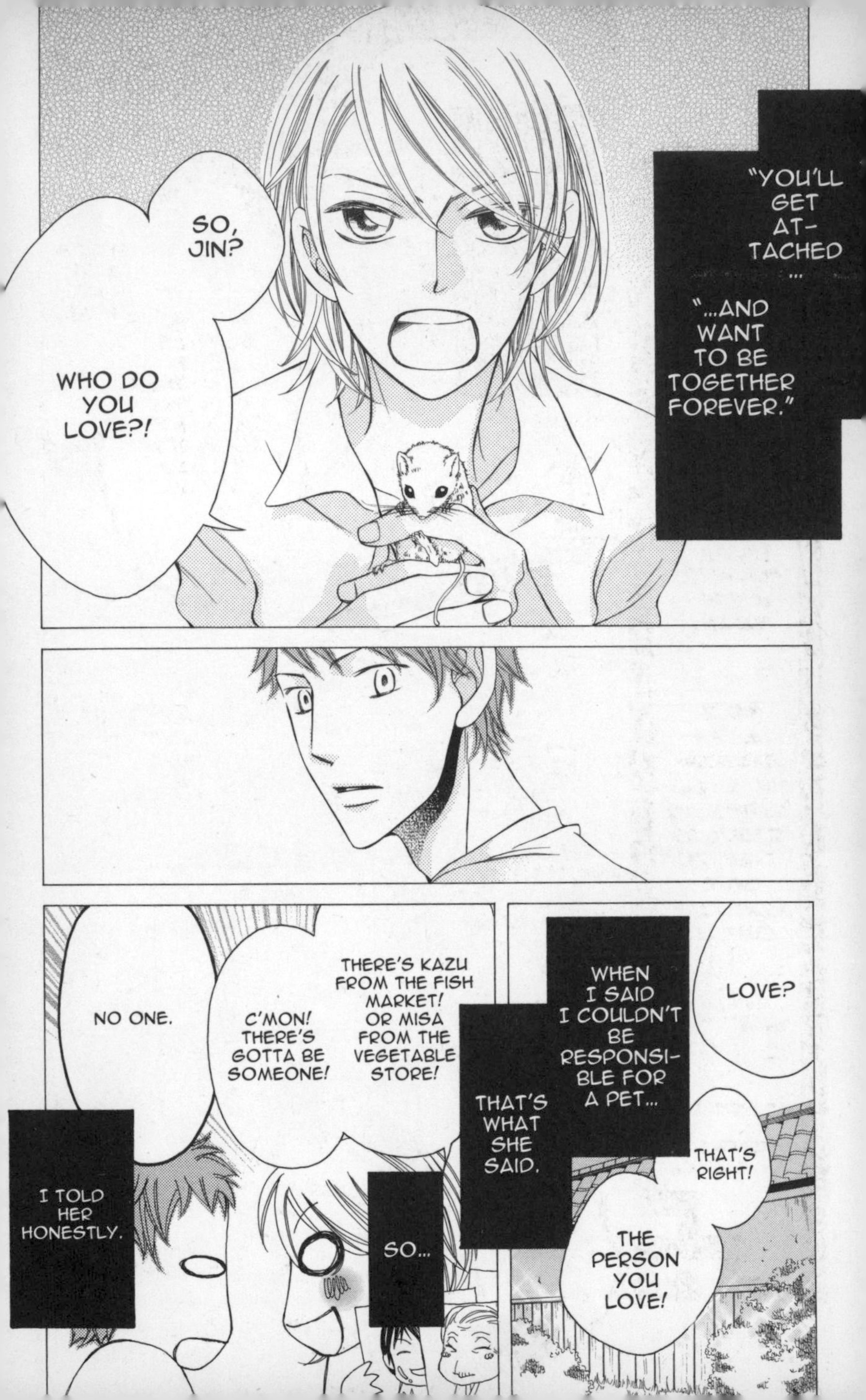
"YOU'LL GET AT-TACHED...
"...AND WANT TO BE TOGETHER FOREVER."
SO, JIN?
WHO DO YOU LOVE?!
LOVE?
WHEN I SAID I COULDN'T BE RESPONSI-BLE FOR A PET...
THAT'S RIGHT!
THE PERSON YOU LOVE!
THAT'S WHAT SHE SAID.
THERE'S KAZU FROM THE FISH MARKET! OR MISA FROM THE VEGETABLE STORE!
C'MON! THERE'S GOTTA BE SOMEONE!
NO ONE.
SO...
I TOLD HER HONESTLY.

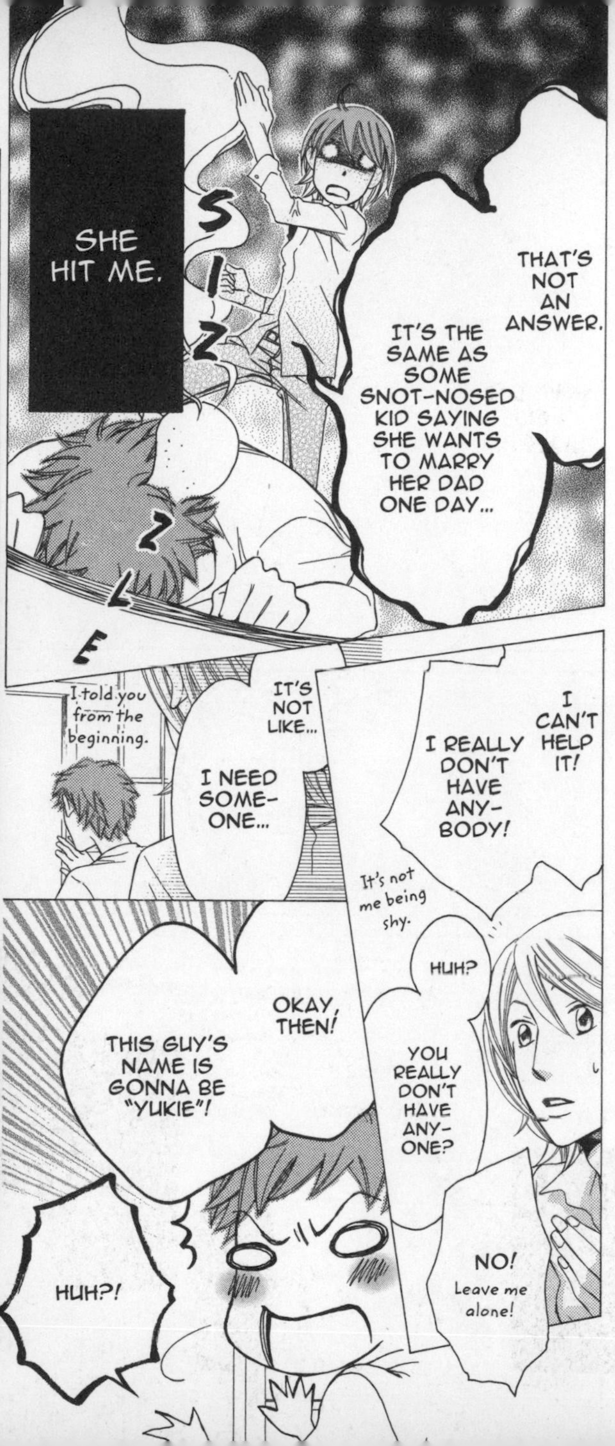
THAT'S NOT AN ANSWER.
IT'S THE SAME AS SOME SNOT-NOSED KID SAYING SHE WANTS TO MARRY HER DAD ONE DAY...
SIZZLE
SHE HIT ME.
I CAN'T HELP IT!
I REALLY DON'T HAVE ANYBODY!
IT'S NOT LIKE...
I NEED SOMEONE...
I told you from the beginning.
It's not me being shy.
HUH?
YOU REALLY DON'T HAVE ANYONE?
NO! Leave me alone!
OKAY, THEN!
THIS GUY'S NAME IS GONNA BE "YUKIE"!
HUH?!

THANX!!

- SHIMOSATO-SAN
- SHIBATA-SAN
- NAKAMURA-SAN
- HIRAOKA-SAN AND
- MO-CHAN!!

I CAN'T THANK YOU ENOUGH FOR WHAT YOU DO FOR ME.

AND TO ALL MY READERS—I'LL HUMBLY CONTINUE MY EFFORTS SO I ASK FOR YOUR CONTINUED SUPPORT!

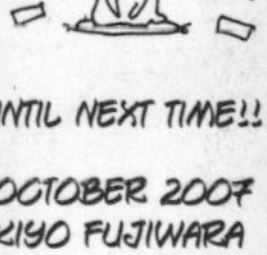

UNTIL NEXT TIME!!

OCTOBER 2007
KIYO FUJIWARA

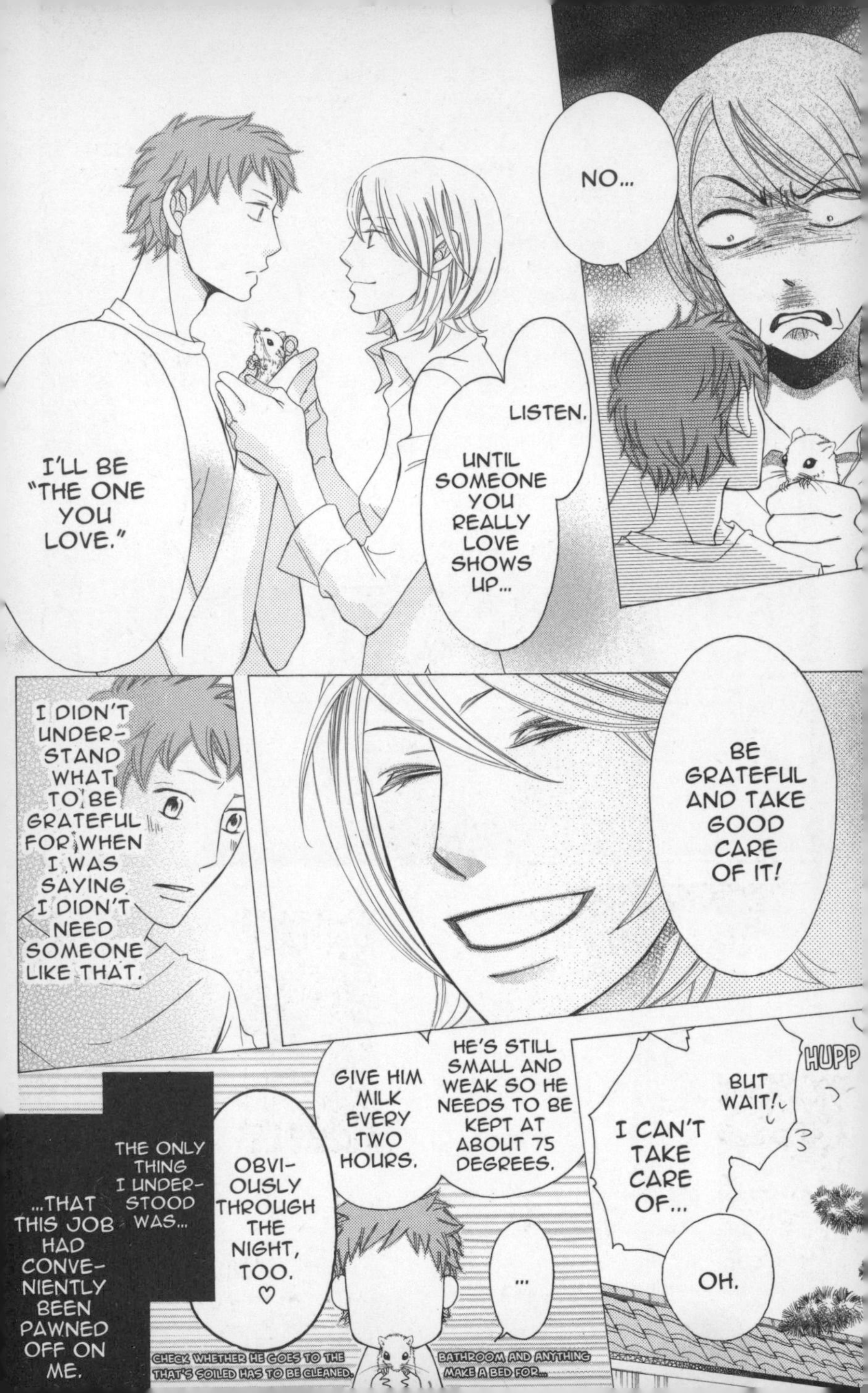
NO...
LISTEN.
UNTIL SOMEONE YOU REALLY LOVE SHOWS UP...
I'LL BE "THE ONE YOU LOVE."
BE GRATEFUL AND TAKE GOOD CARE OF IT!
I DIDN'T UNDER-STAND WHAT TO BE GRATEFUL FOR WHEN I WAS SAYING I DIDN'T NEED SOMEONE LIKE THAT.
HUPP
BUT WAIT!
I CAN'T TAKE CARE OF...
OH.
HE'S STILL SMALL AND WEAK SO HE NEEDS TO BE KEPT AT ABOUT 75 DEGREES.
GIVE HIM MILK EVERY TWO HOURS.
OBVI-OUSLY THROUGH THE NIGHT, TOO. ♡
...
CHECK WHETHER HE GOES TO THE BATHROOM AND ANYTHING THAT'S SOILED HAS TO BE CLEANED. MAKE A BED FOR...
THE ONLY THING I UNDER-STOOD WAS...
...THAT THIS JOB HAD CONVE-NIENTLY BEEN PAWNED OFF ON ME.

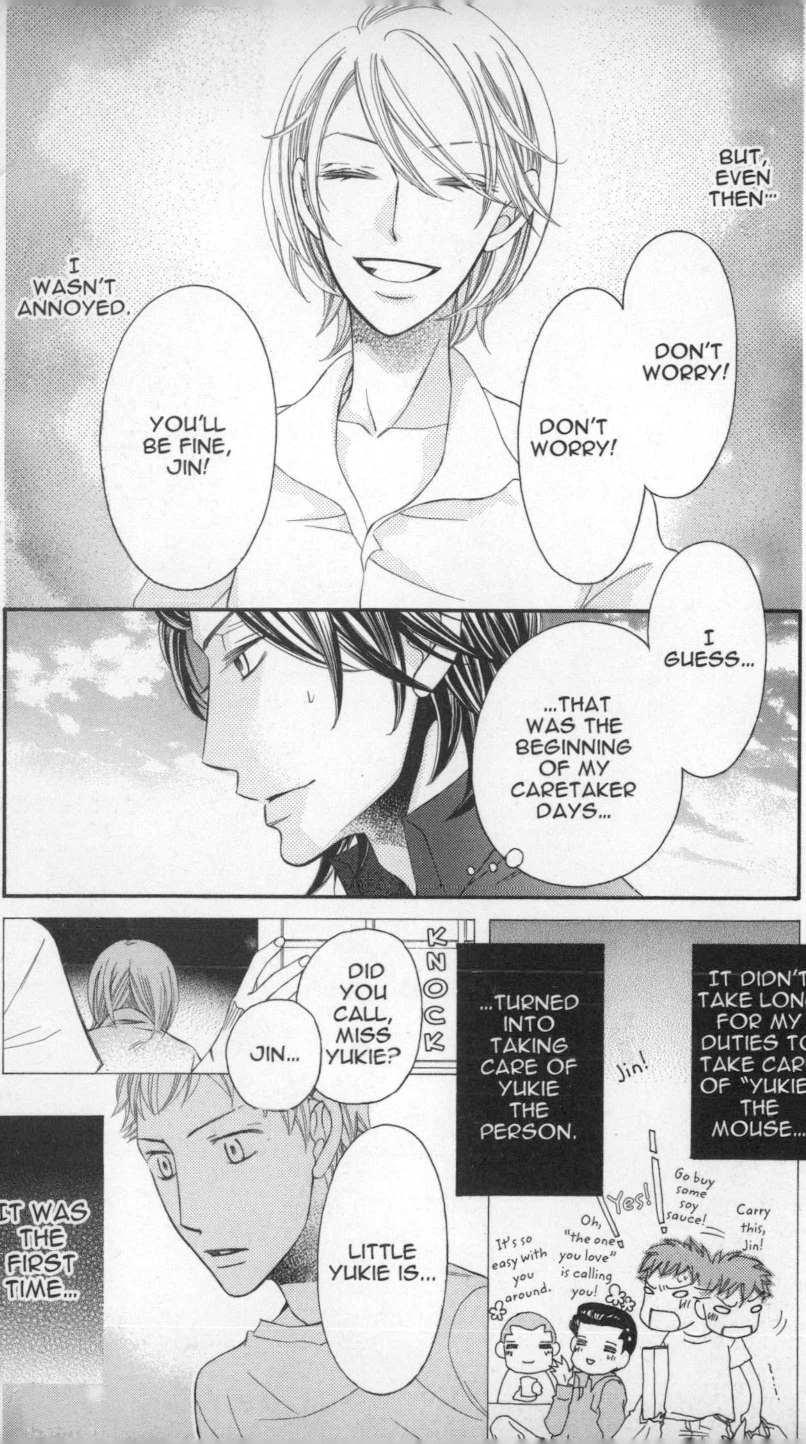
BUT, EVEN THEN...
DON'T WORRY!
DON'T WORRY!
YOU'LL BE FINE, JIN!
I WASN'T ANNOYED.
I GUESS...
...THAT WAS THE BEGINNING OF MY CARETAKER DAYS...
IT DIDN'T TAKE LONG FOR MY DUTIES TO TAKE CARE OF "YUKIE" THE MOUSE...
...TURNED INTO TAKING CARE OF YUKIE THE PERSON.
Jin!
Carry this, Jin!
Go buy some soy sauce!
Yes!
Oh, "the one you love" is calling you!
It's so easy with you around.
KNOCK
DID YOU CALL, MISS YUKIE?
JIN...
LITTLE YUKIE IS...
IT WAS THE FIRST TIME...

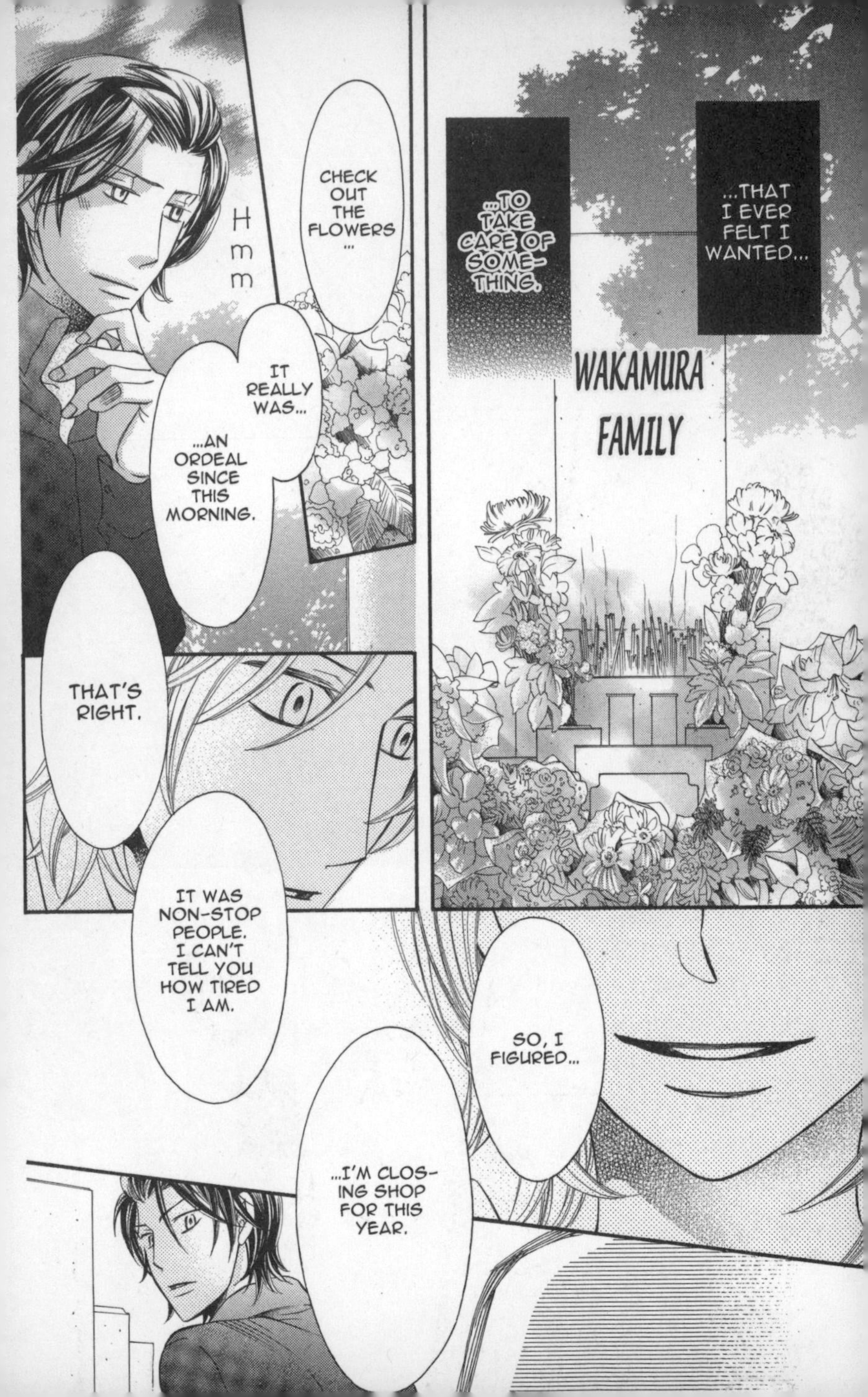
...THAT I EVER FELT I WANTED...
...TO TAKE CARE OF SOME-THING.
WAKAMURA FAMILY
CHECK OUT THE FLOWERS ...
Hmm
IT REALLY WAS...
...AN ORDEAL SINCE THIS MORNING.
THAT'S RIGHT.
IT WAS NON-STOP PEOPLE. I CAN'T TELL YOU HOW TIRED I AM.
SO, I FIGURED...
...I'M CLOSING SHOP FOR THIS YEAR.

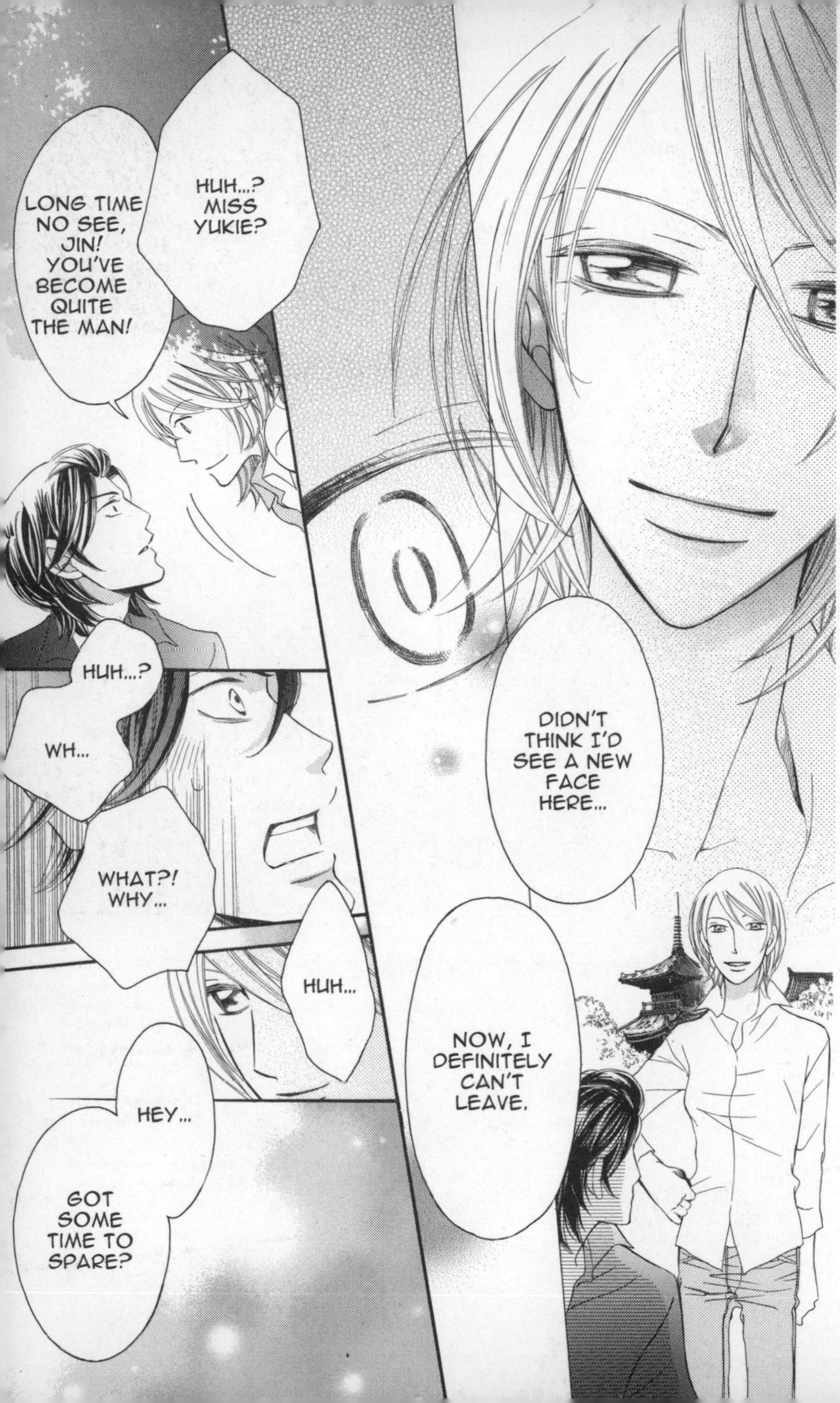

DIDN'T THINK I'D SEE A NEW FACE HERE...
NOW, I DEFINITELY CAN'T LEAVE.
HUH...? MISS YUKIE?
LONG TIME NO SEE, JIN! YOU'VE BECOME QUITE THE MAN!
HUH...?
WH...
WHAT?! WHY...
HUH...
HEY...
GOT SOME TIME TO SPARE?

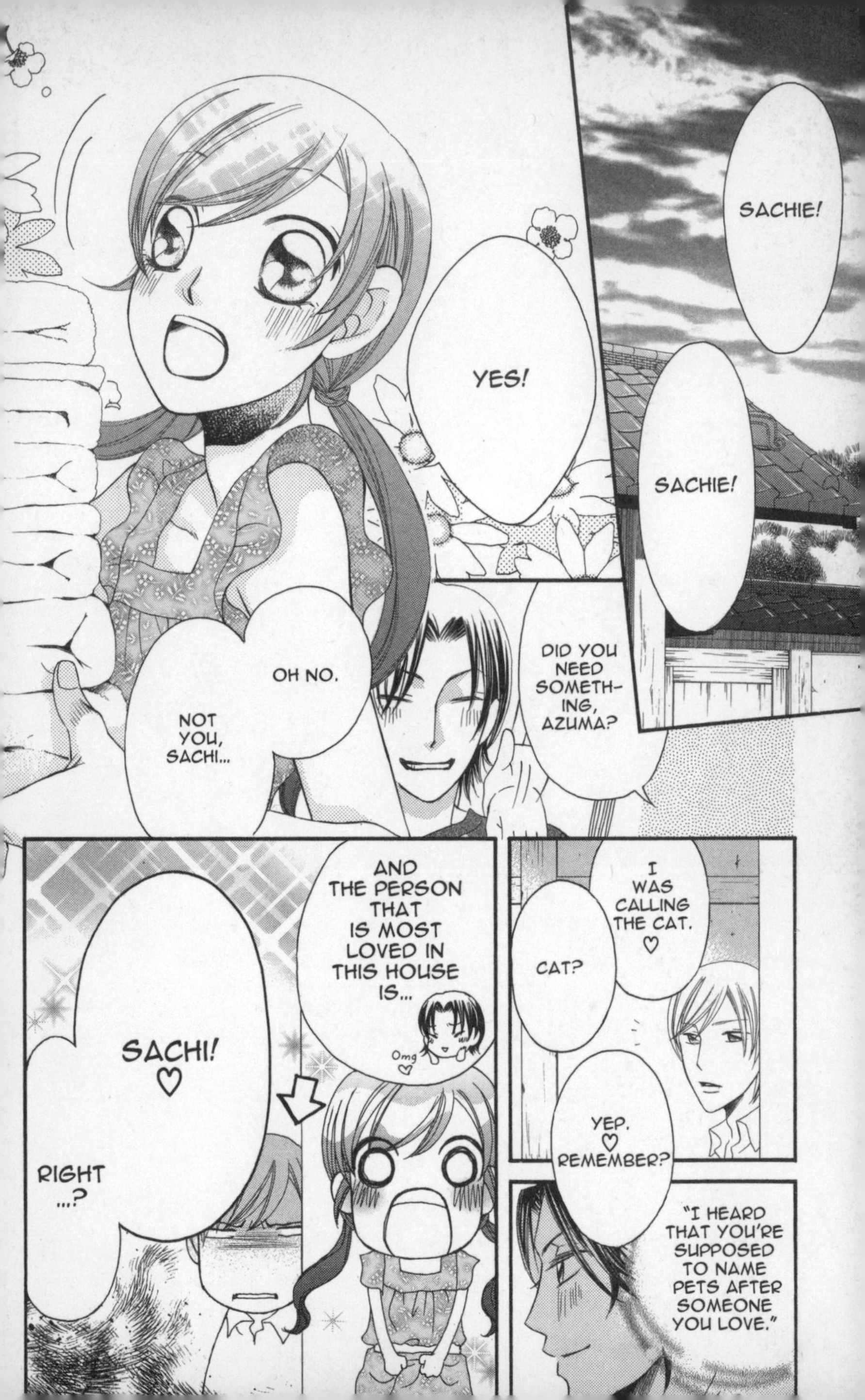
SACHIE!
SACHIE!
YES!
DID YOU NEED SOMETH-ING, AZUMA?
OH NO.
NOT YOU, SACHI...
I WAS CALLING THE CAT. ♡
CAT?
YEP. ♡ REMEMBER?
"I HEARD THAT YOU'RE SUPPOSED TO NAME PETS AFTER SOMEONE YOU LOVE."
AND THE PERSON THAT IS MOST LOVED IN THIS HOUSE IS...
Omg ♡
SACHI! ♡
RIGHT ...?

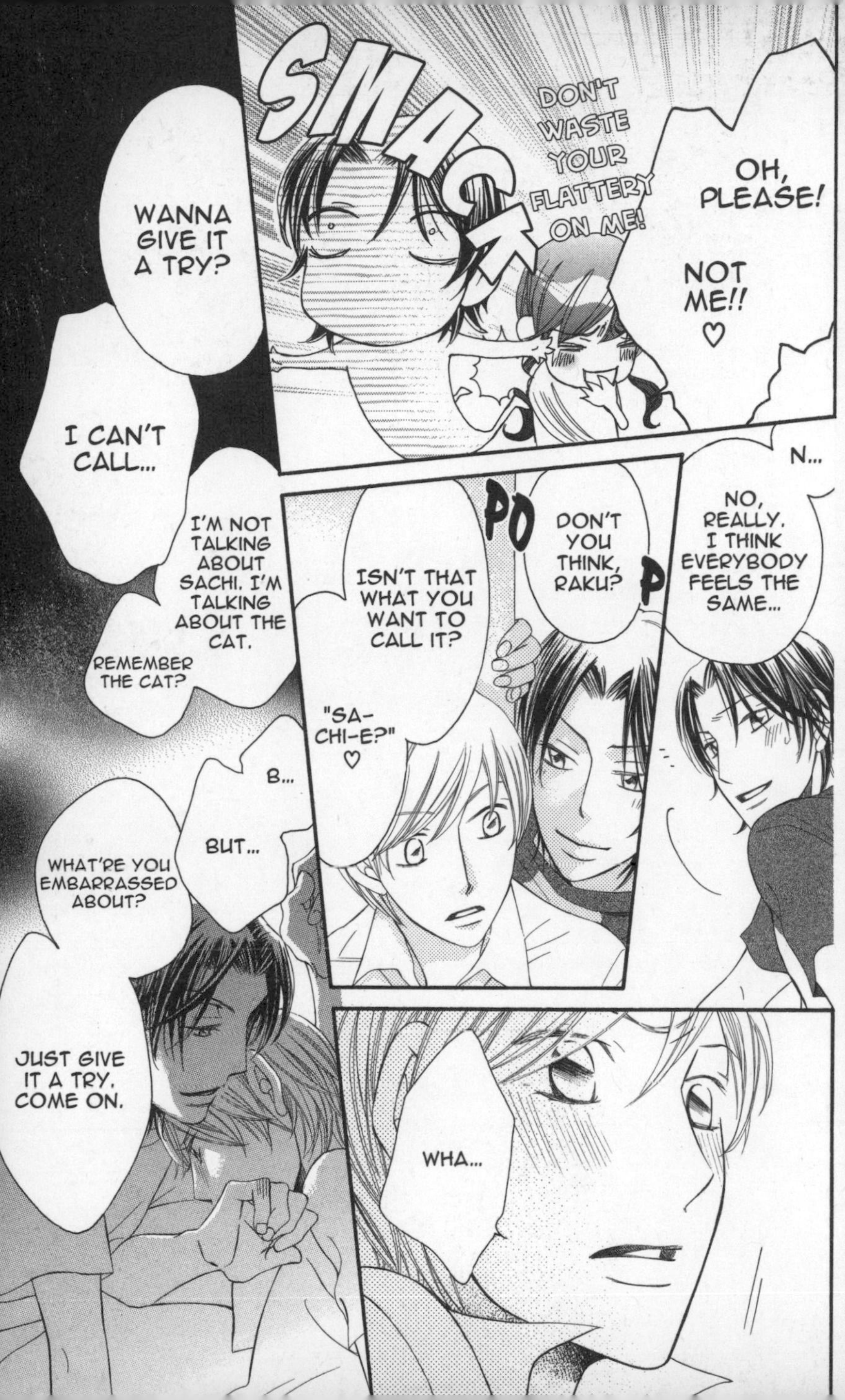
OH, PLEASE!
NOT ME!! ♡
DON'T WASTE YOUR FLATTERY ON ME!
SMACK
WANNA GIVE IT A TRY?
N...
NO, REALLY. I THINK EVERYBODY FEELS THE SAME...
DON'T YOU THINK, RAKU?
POP
ISN'T THAT WHAT YOU WANT TO CALL IT?
"SA-CHI-E?" ♡
I CAN'T CALL...
I'M NOT TALKING ABOUT SACHI. I'M TALKING ABOUT THE CAT.
REMEMBER THE CAT?
B...
BUT...
WHAT'RE YOU EMBARRASSED ABOUT?
WHA...
JUST GIVE IT A TRY. COME ON.

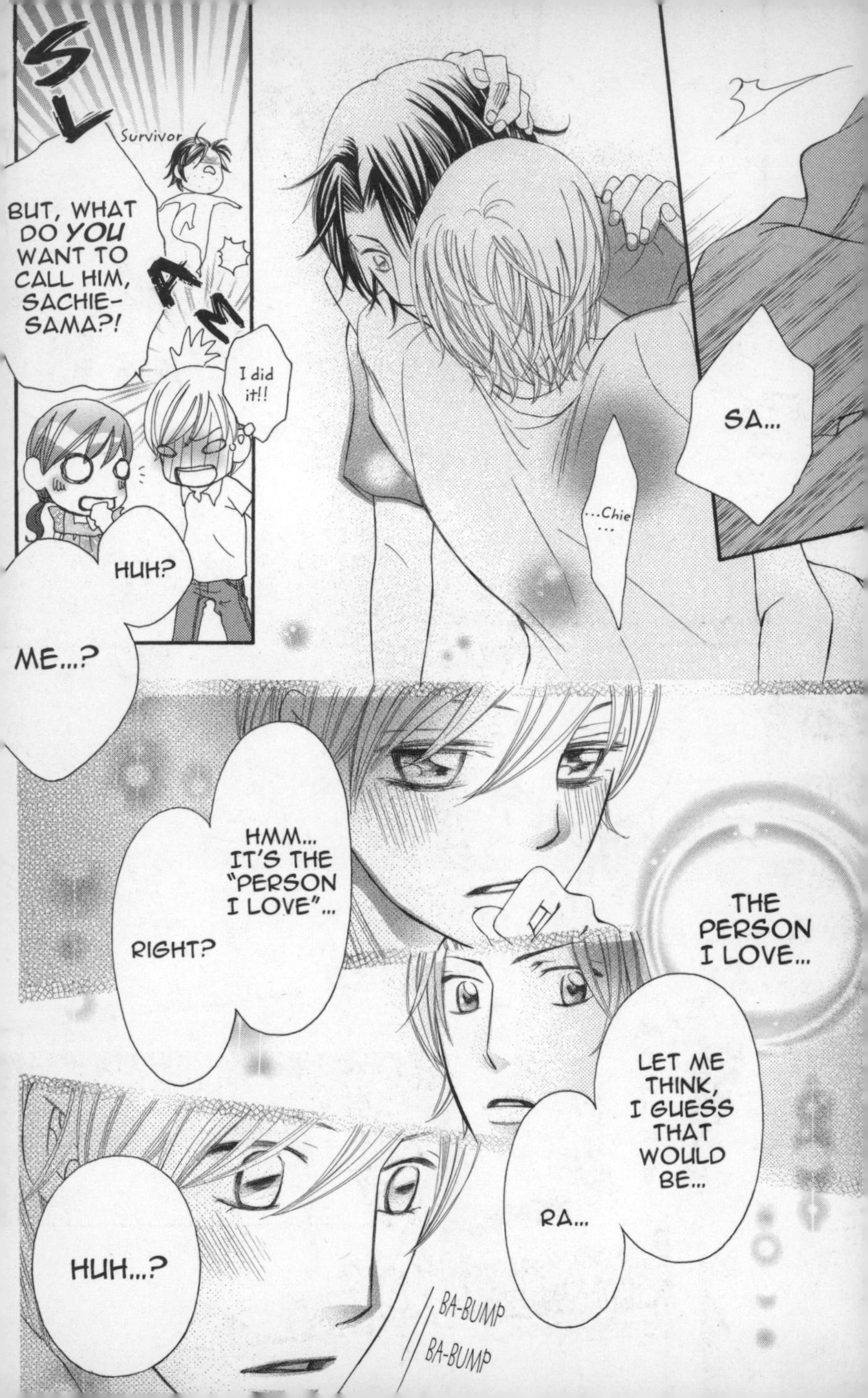
SA...
...Chie...
SLAM
Survivor
BUT, WHAT DO YOU WANT TO CALL HIM, SACHIE-SAMA?!
I did it!!
HUH? ME...?
HMM... IT'S THE "PERSON I LOVE"... RIGHT?
THE PERSON I LOVE...
LET ME THINK, I GUESS THAT WOULD BE... RA...
HUH...?
BA-BUMP
BA-BUMP

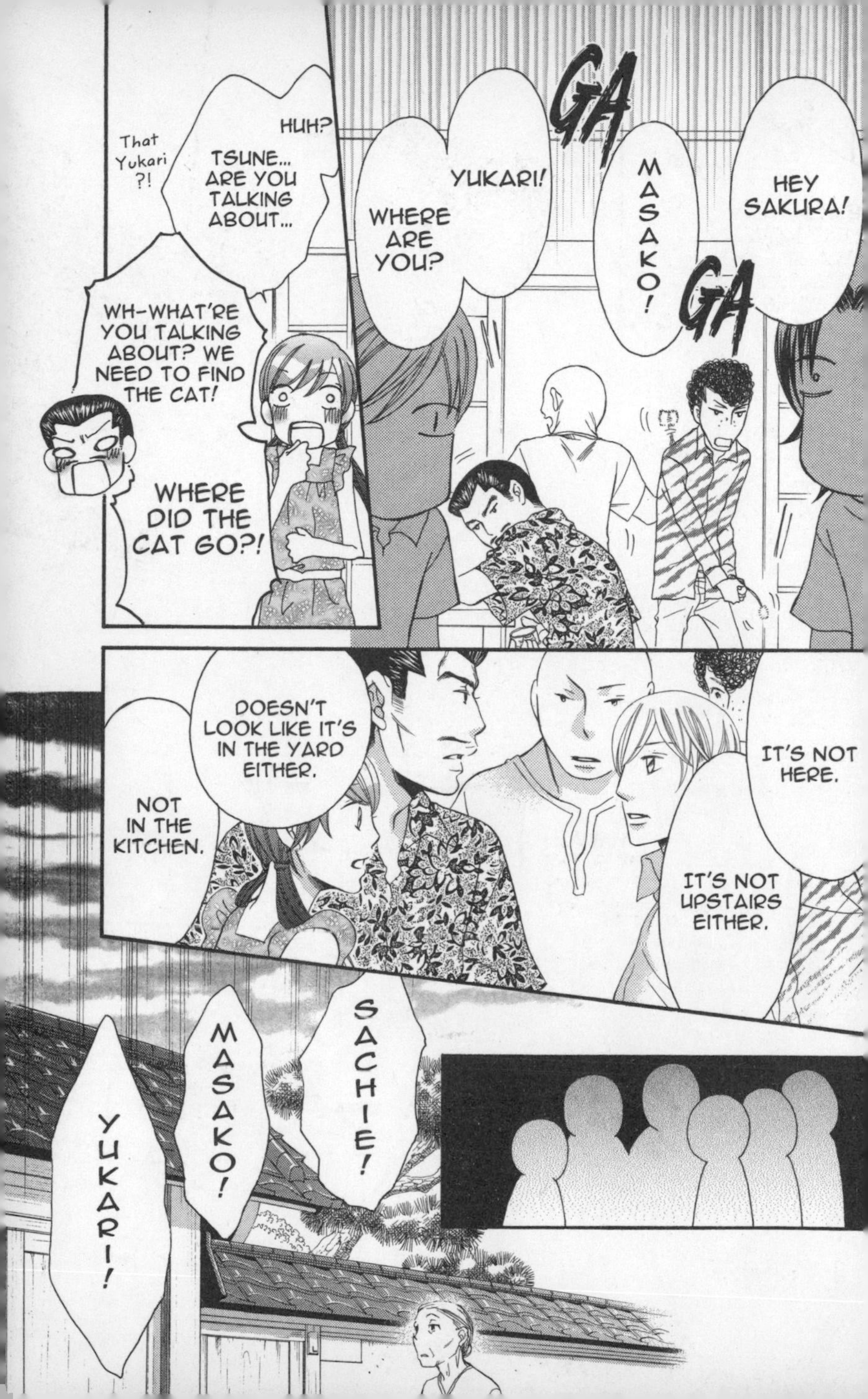
HEY SAKURA!
GA
MASAKO!
GA
YUKARI!
WHERE ARE YOU?
HUH?
TSUNE... ARE YOU TALKING ABOUT...
That Yukari ?!
WH-WHAT'RE YOU TALKING ABOUT? WE NEED TO FIND THE CAT!
WHERE DID THE CAT GO?!
IT'S NOT HERE.
IT'S NOT UPSTAIRS EITHER.
DOESN'T LOOK LIKE IT'S IN THE YARD EITHER.
NOT IN THE KITCHEN.
SACHIE!
MASAKO!
YUKARI!

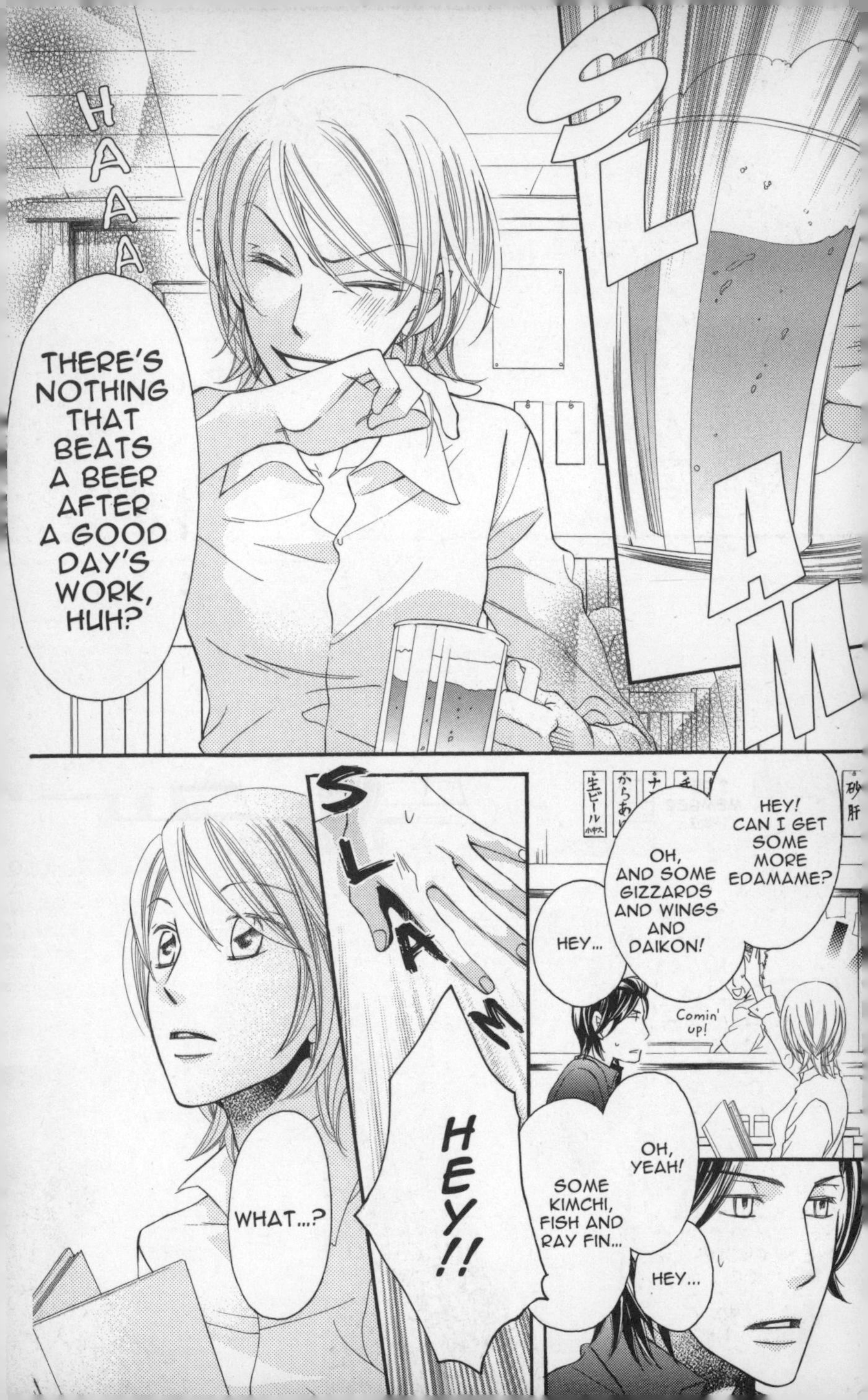
SLAM
HAAAA
THERE'S NOTHING THAT BEATS A BEER AFTER A GOOD DAY'S WORK, HUH?
生ビール
からあげ
砂肝
HEY! CAN I GET SOME MORE EDAMAME?
OH, AND SOME GIZZARDS AND WINGS AND DAIKON!
HEY...
Comin' up!
OH, YEAH!
SOME KIMCHI, FISH AND RAY FIN...
HEY...
SLAM
HEY!!
WHAT...?

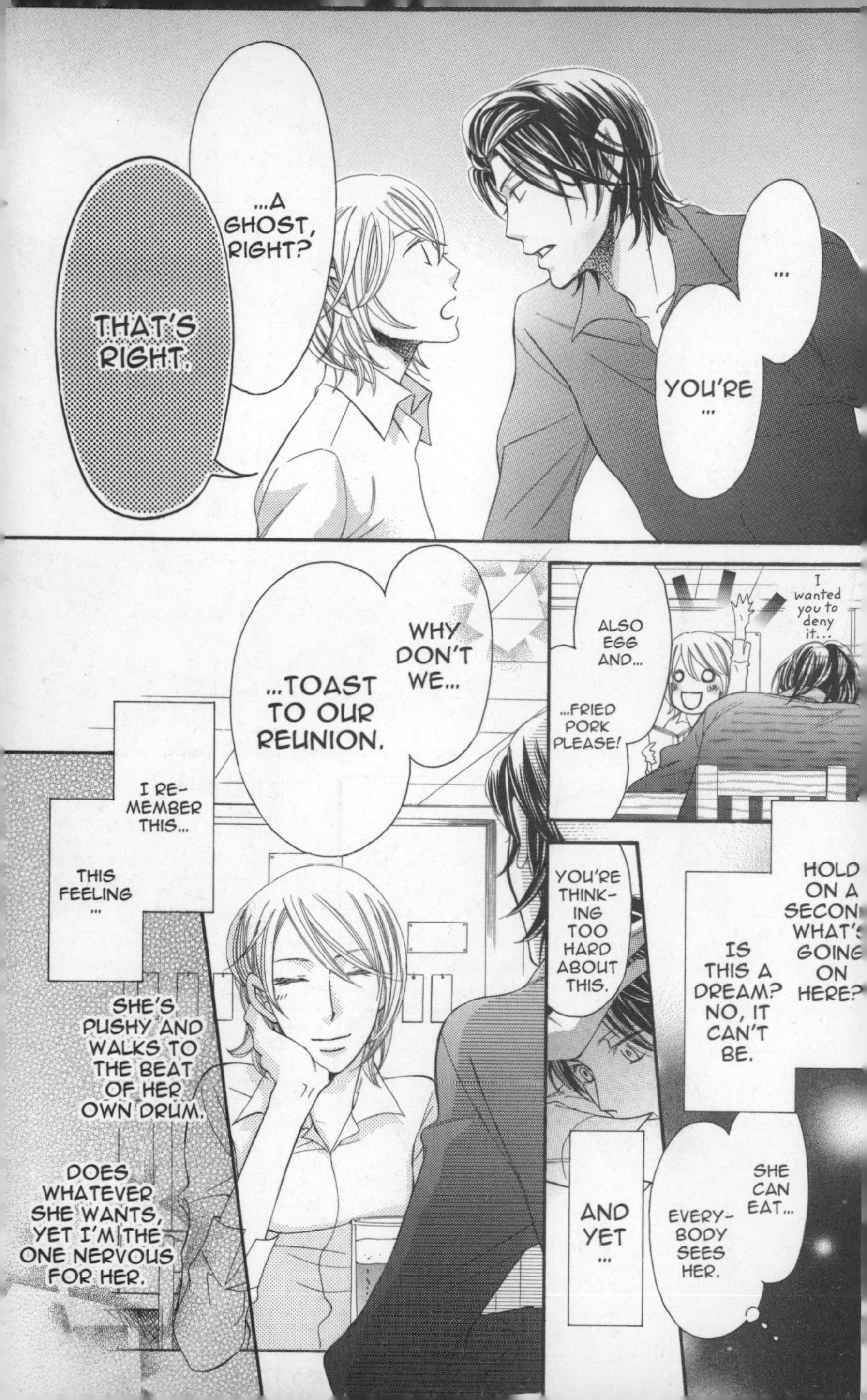
...
YOU'RE ...
...A GHOST, RIGHT?
THAT'S RIGHT.
I wanted you to deny it...
ALSO EGG AND...
...FRIED PORK PLEASE!
HOLD ON A SECON WHAT'S GOING ON HERE?
IS THIS A DREAM? NO, IT CAN'T BE.
YOU'RE THINKING-ING TOO HARD ABOUT THIS.
SHE CAN EAT...
EVERY-BODY SEES HER.
AND YET ...
WHY DON'T WE...
...TOAST TO OUR REUNION.
I RE-MEMBER THIS...
THIS FEELING ...
SHE'S PUSHY AND WALKS TO THE BEAT OF HER OWN DRUM.
DOES WHATEVER SHE WANTS, YET I'M THE ONE NERVOUS FOR HER.

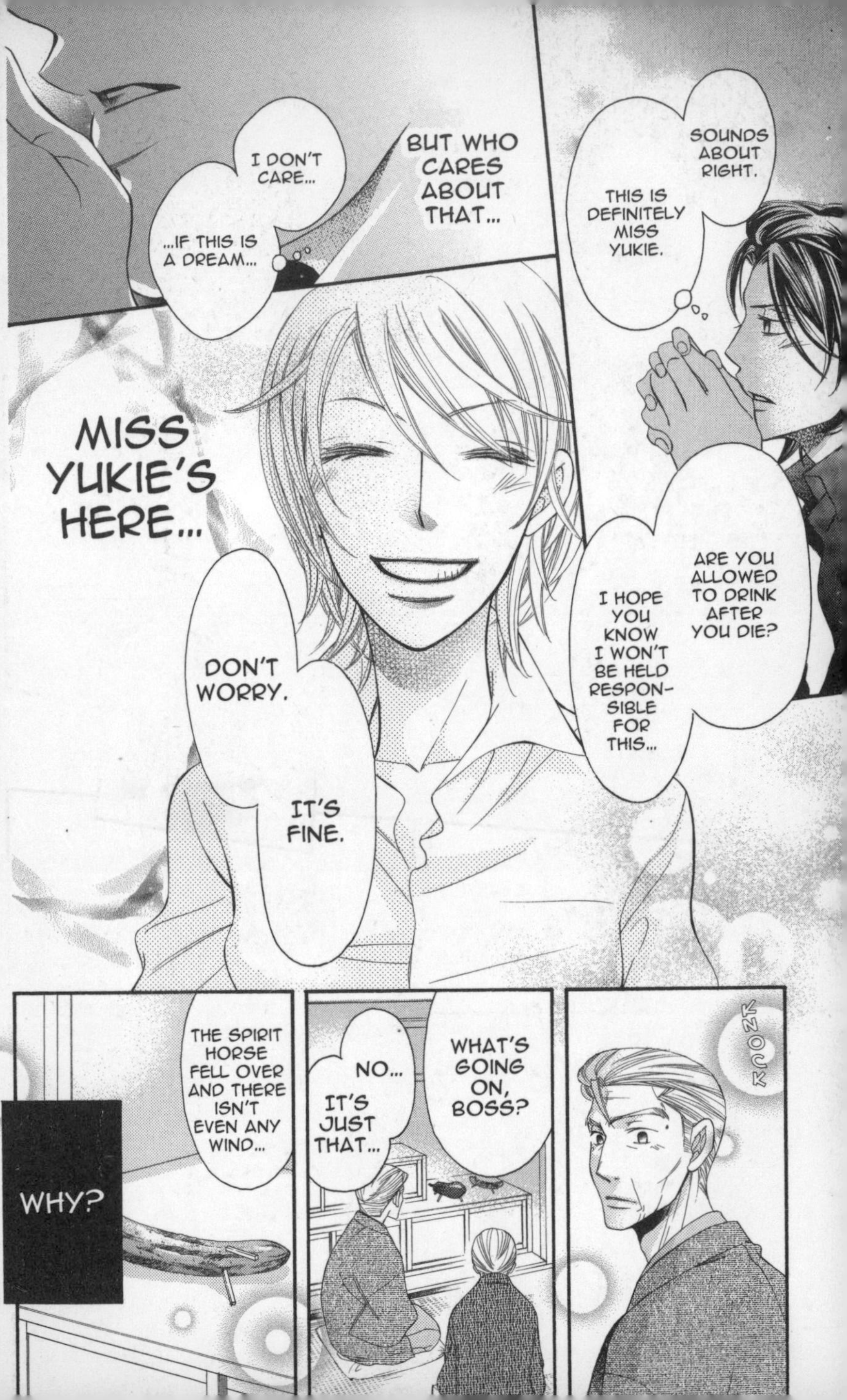
SOUNDS ABOUT RIGHT.
THIS IS DEFINITELY MISS YUKIE.
BUT WHO CARES ABOUT THAT...
I DON'T CARE...
...IF THIS IS A DREAM...
ARE YOU ALLOWED TO DRINK AFTER YOU DIE?
I HOPE YOU KNOW I WON'T BE HELD RESPONSIBLE FOR THIS...
MISS YUKIE'S HERE...
DON'T WORRY.
IT'S FINE.
KNOCK
WHAT'S GOING ON, BOSS?
NO...
IT'S JUST THAT...
THE SPIRIT HORSE FELL OVER AND THERE ISN'T EVEN ANY WIND...
WHY?

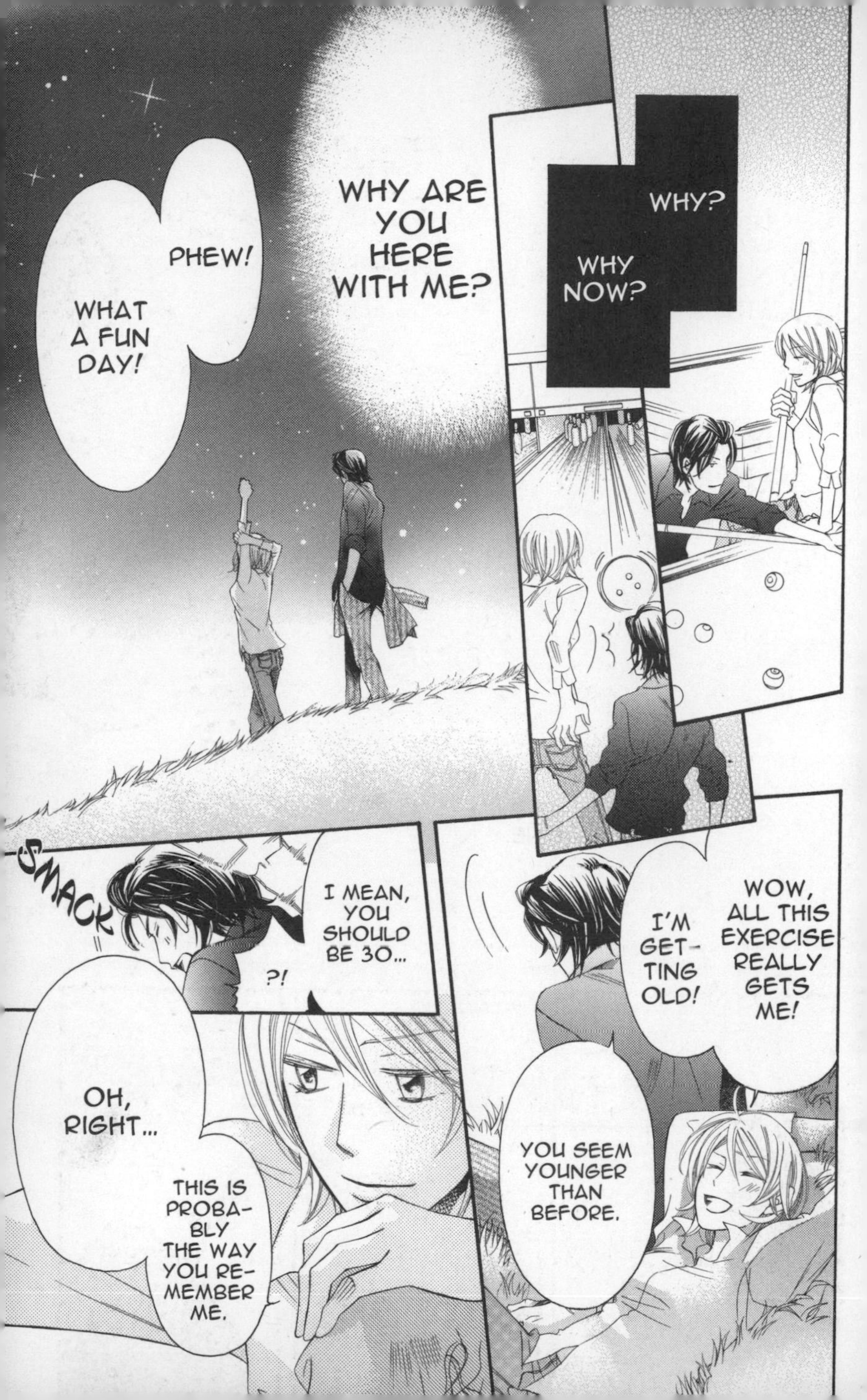
WHY?
WHY NOW?
WHY ARE YOU HERE WITH ME?
PHEW!
WHAT A FUN DAY!
WOW, ALL THIS EXERCISE REALLY GETS ME!
I'M GET-TING OLD!
I MEAN, YOU SHOULD BE 30...
SMACK
?!
YOU SEEM YOUNGER THAN BEFORE.
OH, RIGHT...
THIS IS PROBA-BLY THE WAY YOU RE-MEMBER ME.

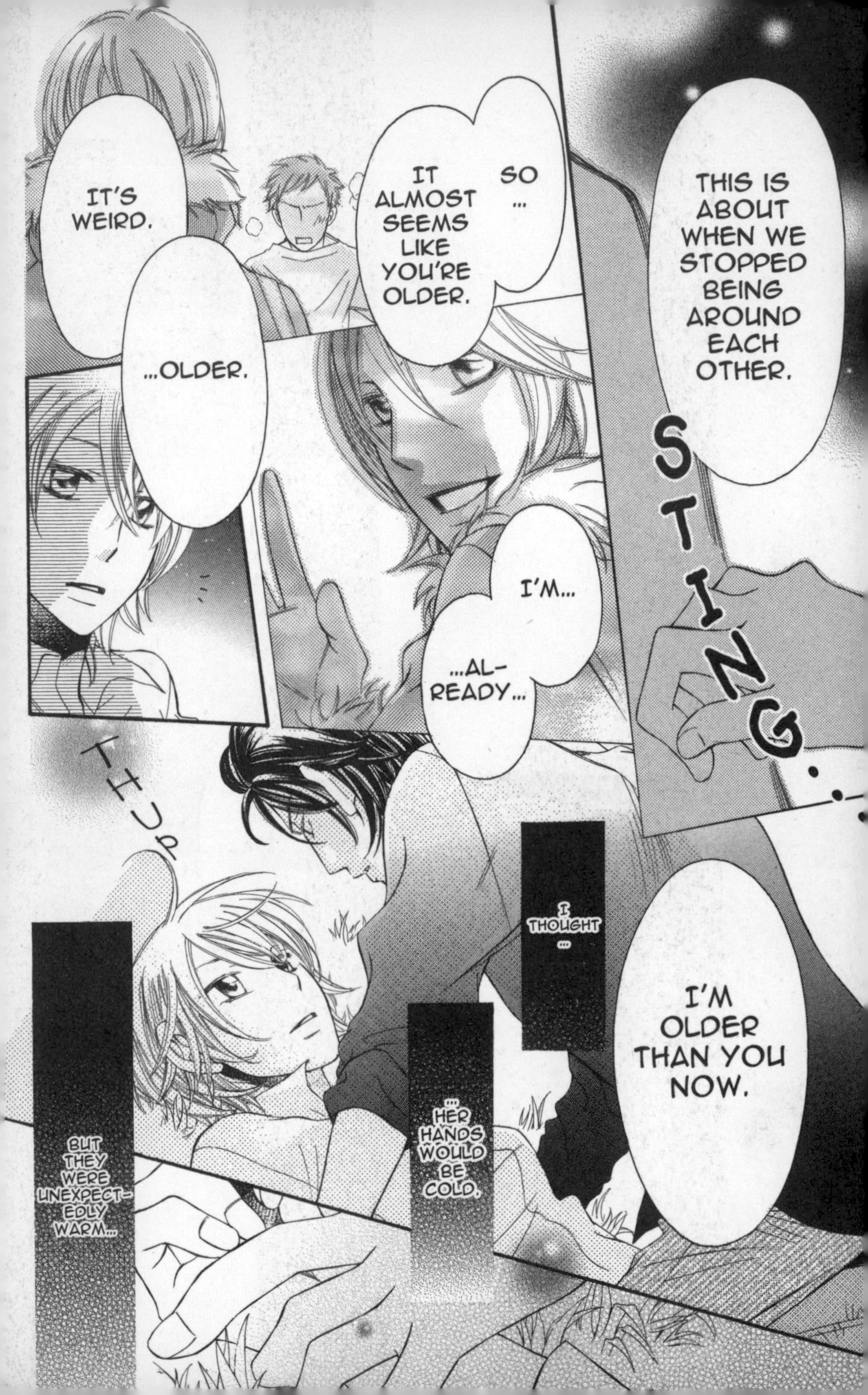
THIS IS ABOUT WHEN WE STOPPED BEING AROUND EACH OTHER.
STING..!
IT'S WEIRD.
SO ... IT ALMOST SEEMS LIKE YOU'RE OLDER.
...OLDER.
I'M...
...AL-READY...
THUP
I'M OLDER THAN YOU NOW.
I THOUGHT ...
... HER HANDS WOULD BE COLD.
BUT THEY WERE UNEXPECT-EDLY WARM...

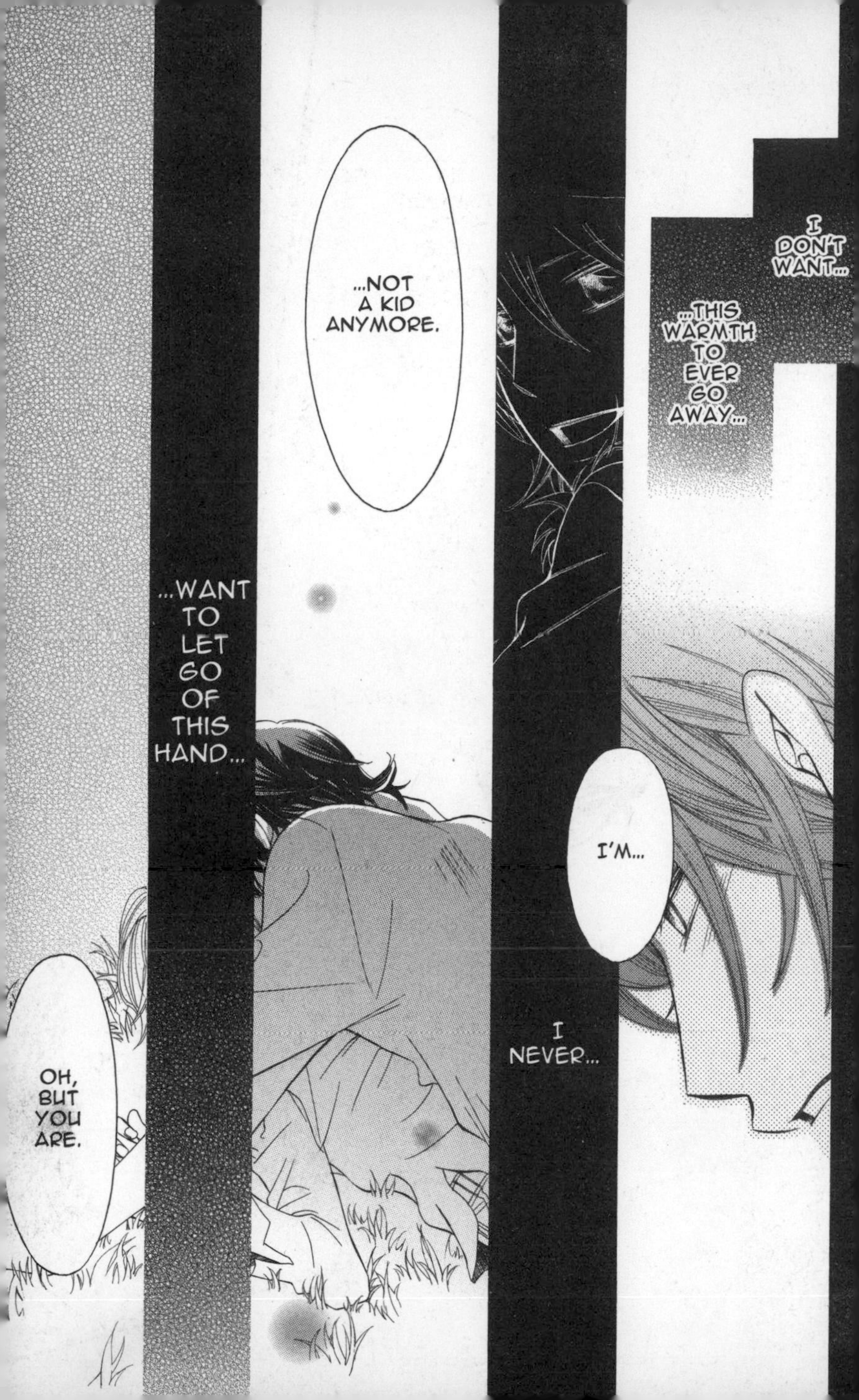
I DON'T WANT...
...THIS WARMTH TO EVER GO AWAY...
I'M...
I NEVER...
...NOT A KID ANYMORE.
...WANT TO LET GO OF THIS HAND...
OH, BUT YOU ARE.

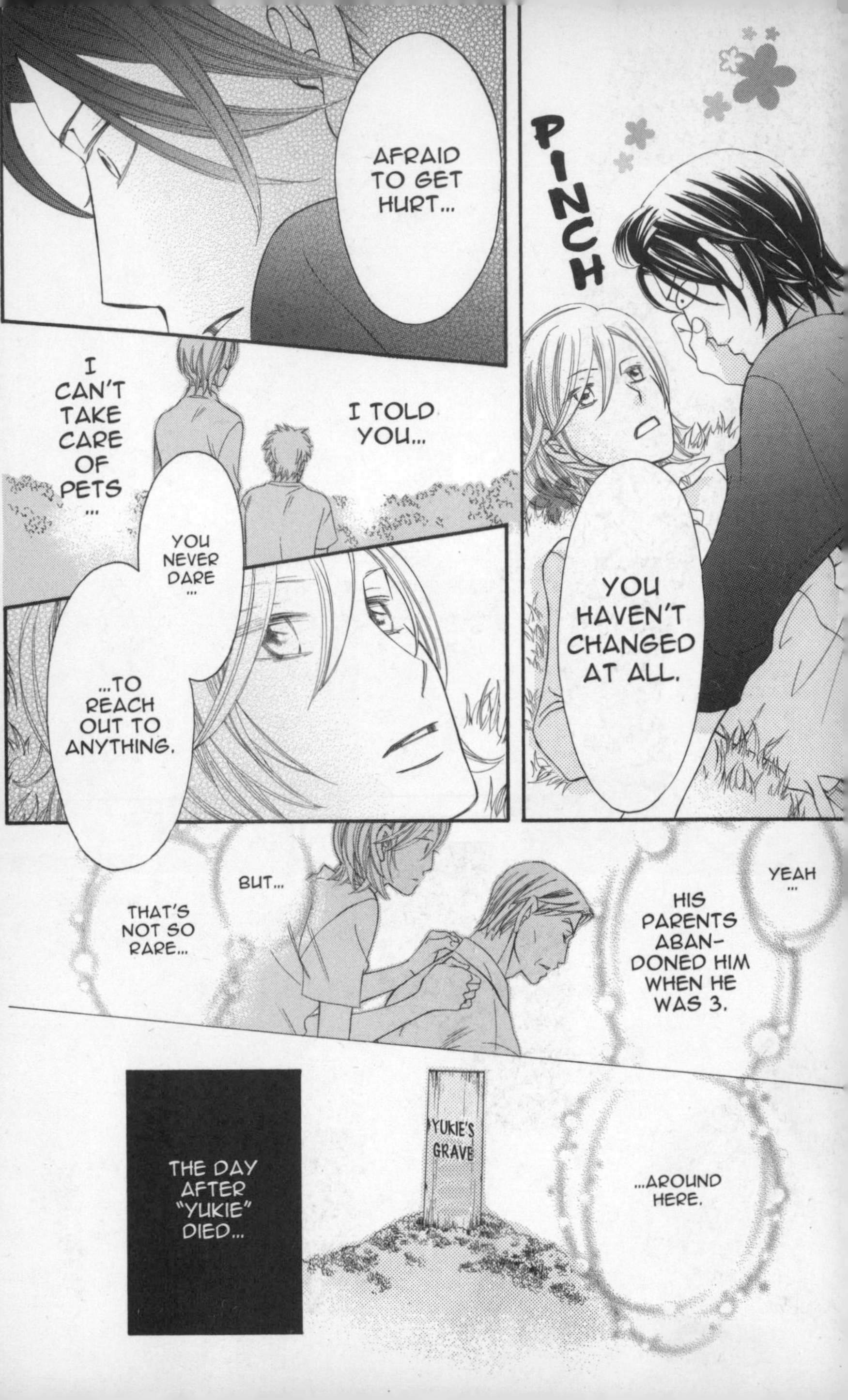
PINCH
YOU HAVEN'T CHANGED AT ALL.
AFRAID TO GET HURT...
I TOLD YOU...
I CAN'T TAKE CARE OF PETS ...
YOU NEVER DARE ...
...TO REACH OUT TO ANYTHING.
YEAH ...
HIS PARENTS ABAN-DONED HIM WHEN HE WAS 3.
BUT...
THAT'S NOT SO RARE...
...AROUND HERE.
YUKIE'S GRAVE
THE DAY AFTER "YUKIE" DIED...

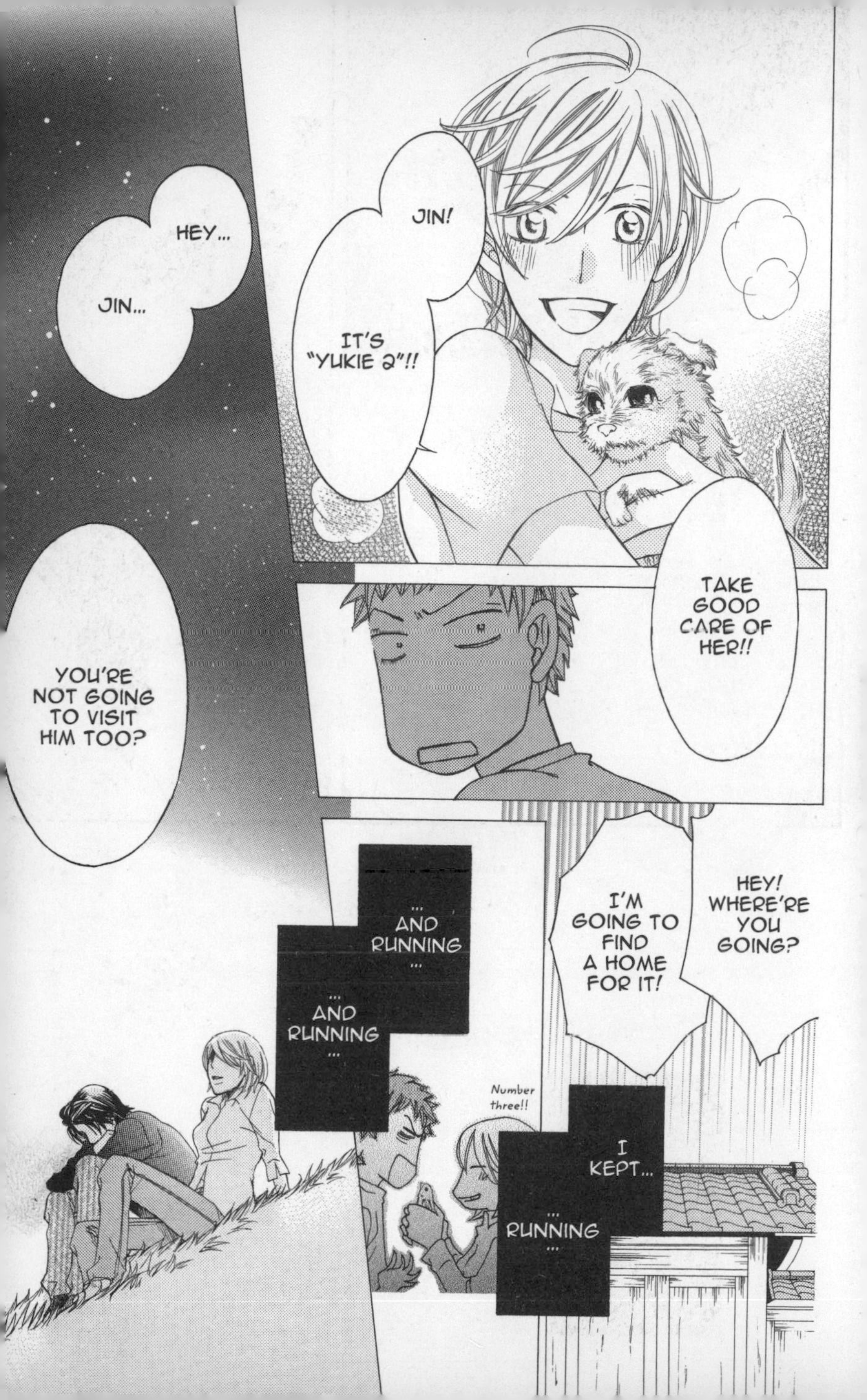
JIN!
IT'S "YUKIE 2"!!
TAKE GOOD CARE OF HER!!
HEY! WHERE'RE YOU GOING?
I'M GOING TO FIND A HOME FOR IT!
Number three!!
I KEPT...
... RUNNING ...
... AND RUNNING ...
... AND RUNNING ...
HEY...
JIN...
YOU'RE NOT GOING TO VISIT HIM TOO?

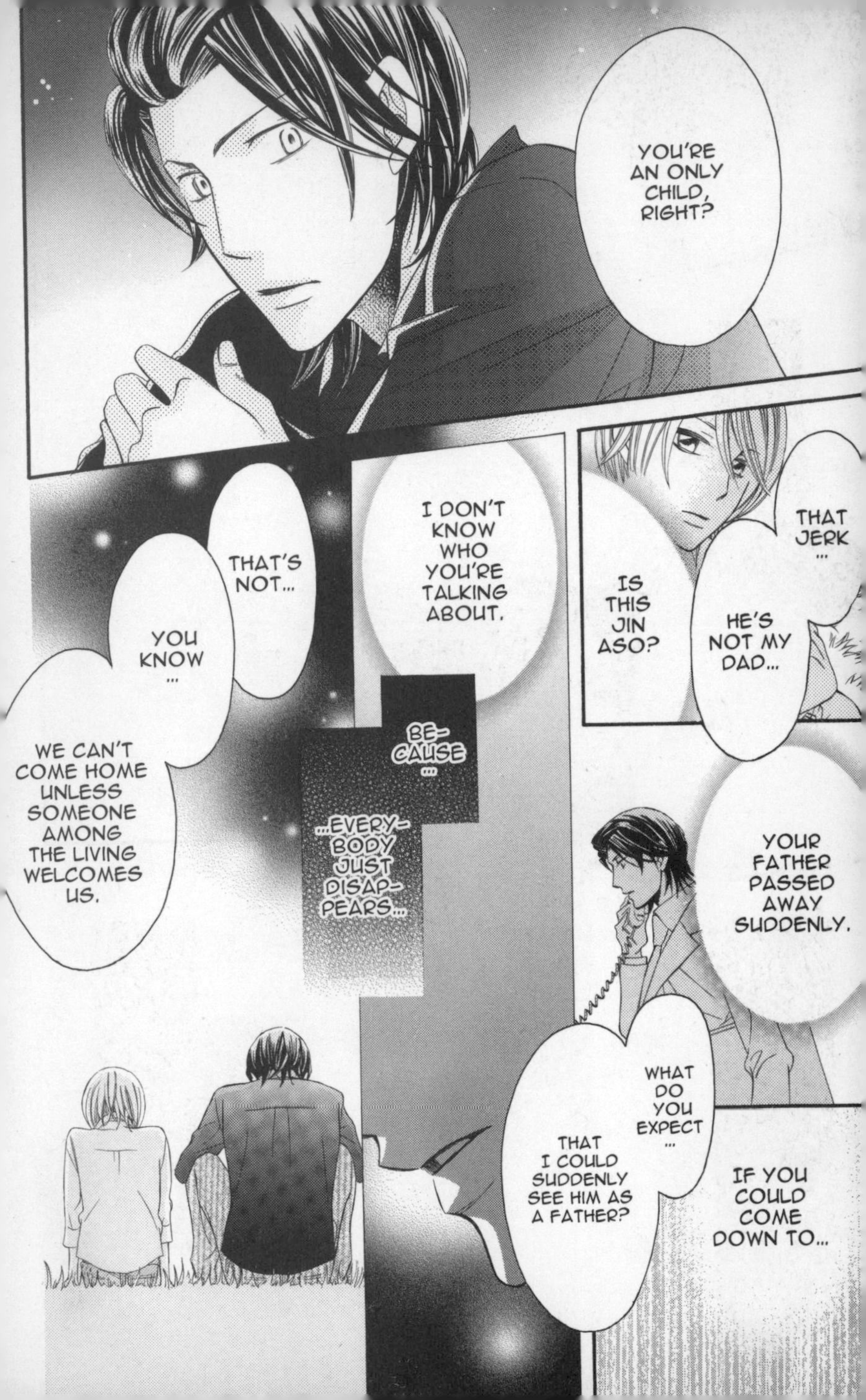
YOU'RE AN ONLY CHILD, RIGHT?
THAT JERK...
HE'S NOT MY DAD...
IS THIS JIN ASO?
I DON'T KNOW WHO YOU'RE TALKING ABOUT.
YOUR FATHER PASSED AWAY SUDDENLY.
IF YOU COULD COME DOWN TO...
WHAT DO YOU EXPECT...
THAT I COULD SUDDENLY SEE HIM AS A FATHER?
BE-CAUSE...
...EVERY-BODY JUST DISAP-PEARS...
THAT'S NOT...
YOU KNOW...
WE CAN'T COME HOME UNLESS SOMEONE AMONG THE LIVING WELCOMES US.

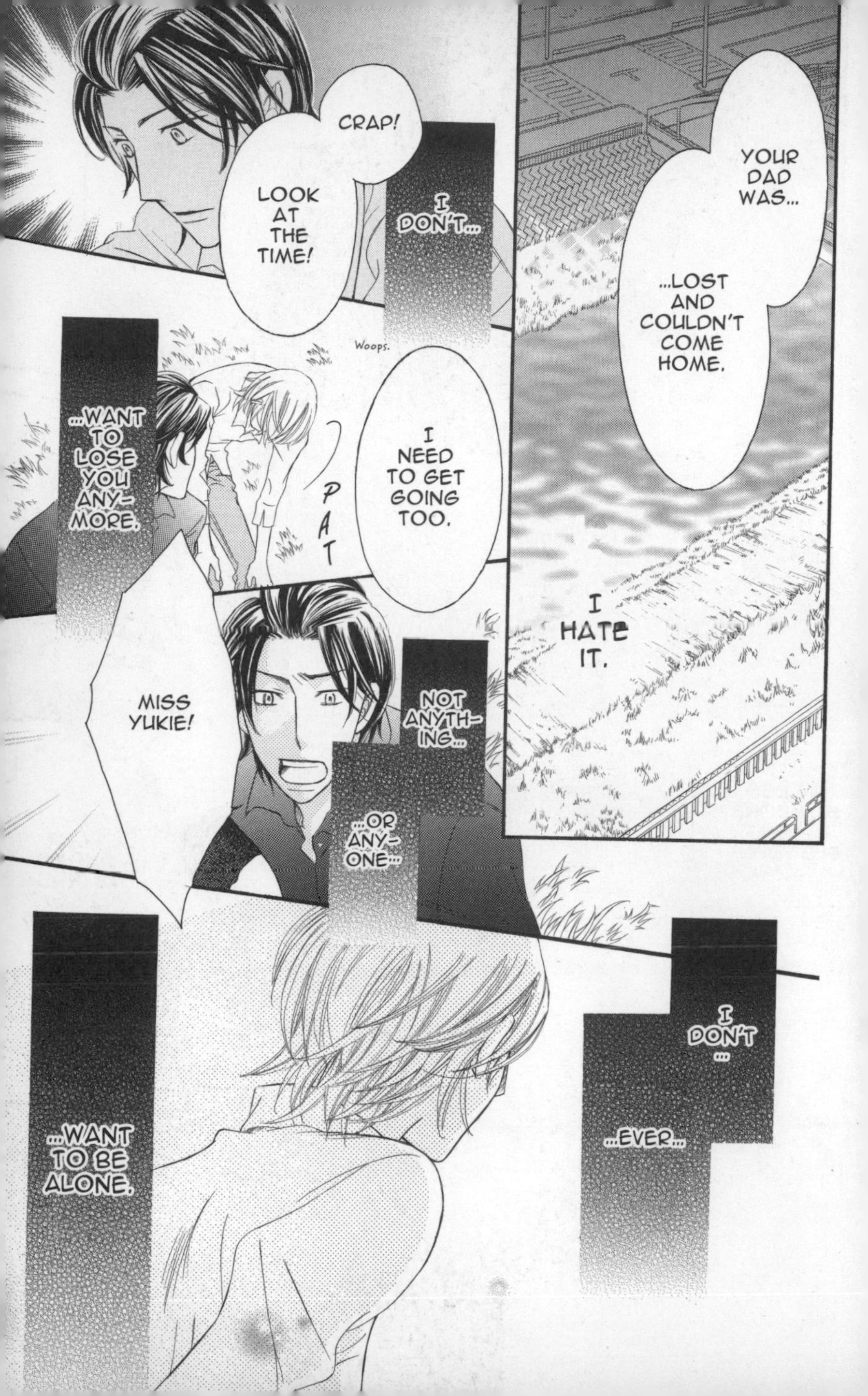
YOUR DAD WAS...
...LOST AND COULDN'T COME HOME.
I HATE IT.
CRAP!
LOOK AT THE TIME!
I DON'T...
Woops.
I NEED TO GET GOING TOO.
PAT
...WANT TO LOSE YOU ANY-MORE.
NOT ANYTHING...
MISS YUKIE!
...OR ANY-ONE...
I DON'T ...
...EVER...
...WANT TO BE ALONE.

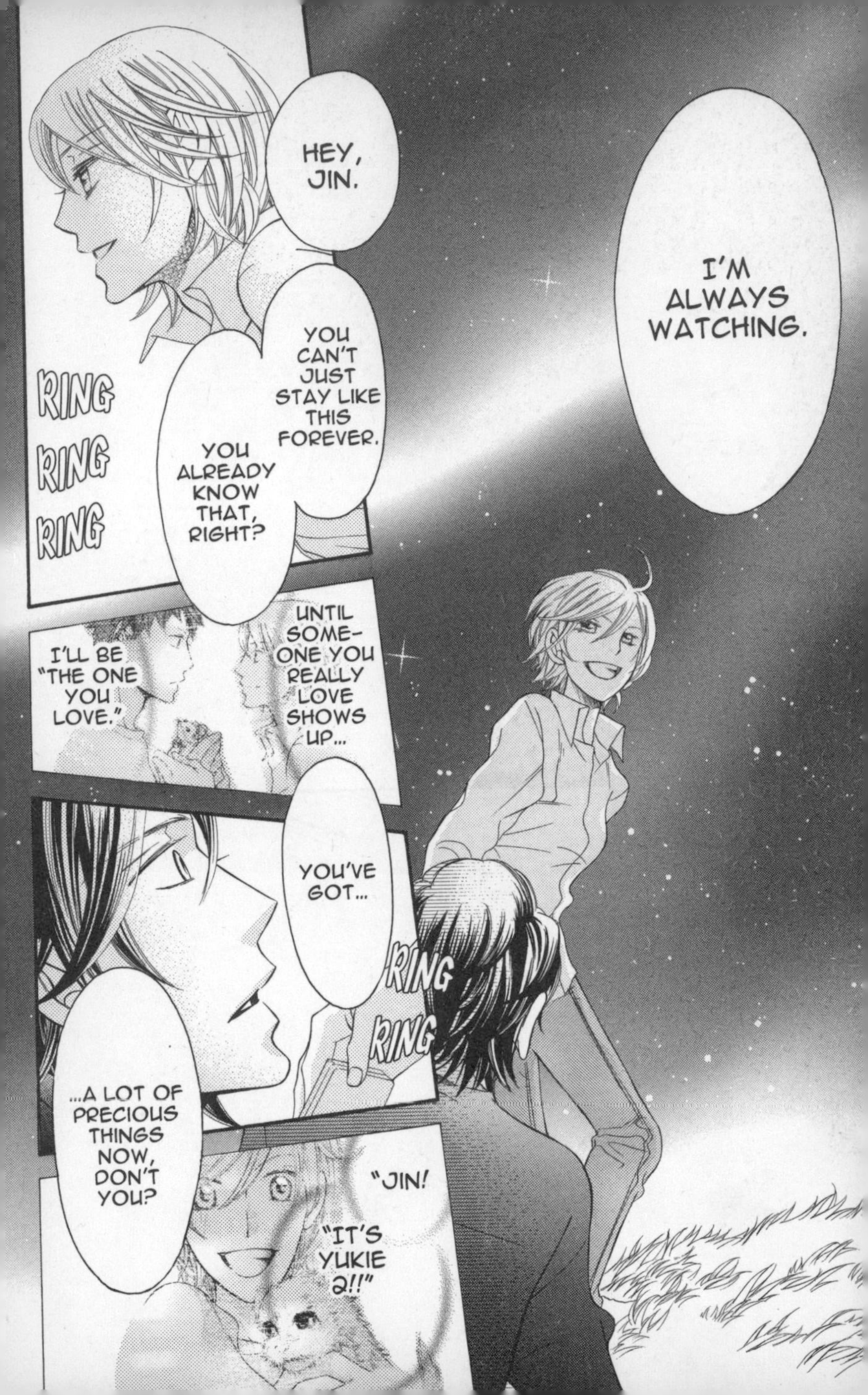
I'M ALWAYS WATCHING.
HEY, JIN.
YOU CAN'T JUST STAY LIKE THIS FOREVER.
YOU ALREADY KNOW THAT, RIGHT?
RING
RING
RING
UNTIL SOME-ONE YOU REALLY LOVE SHOWS UP...
I'LL BE "THE ONE YOU LOVE."
YOU'VE GOT...
RING
RING
...A LOT OF PRECIOUS THINGS NOW, DON'T YOU?
"JIN!
"IT'S YUKIE 2!!"

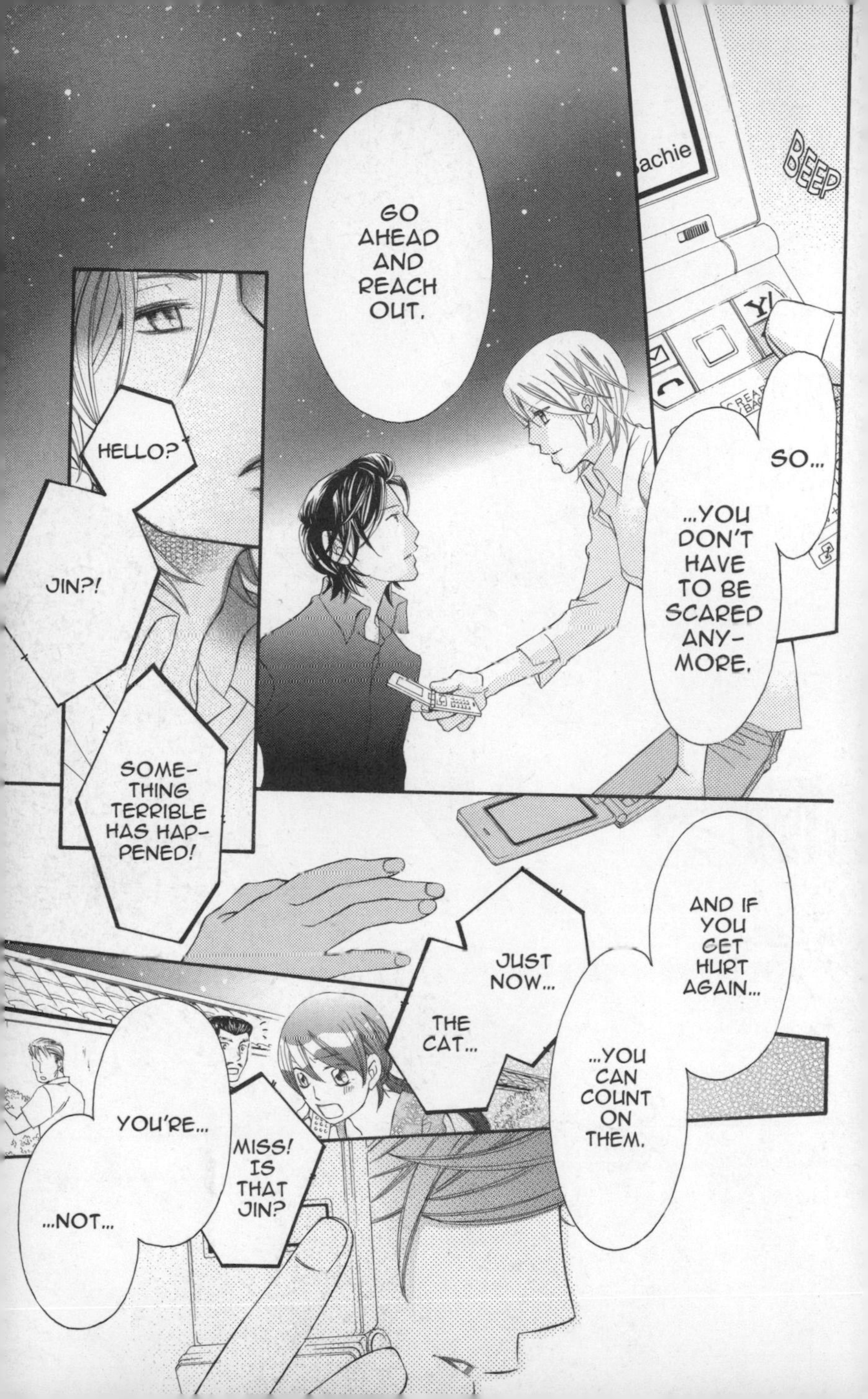
BEEP
Sachie
SO...
...YOU DON'T HAVE TO BE SCARED ANYMORE.
GO AHEAD AND REACH OUT.
HELLO?
JIN?!
SOMETHING TERRIBLE HAS HAPPENED!
AND IF YOU GET HURT AGAIN...
...YOU CAN COUNT ON THEM.
JUST NOW...
THE CAT...
MISS! IS THAT JIN?
YOU'RE...
...NOT...

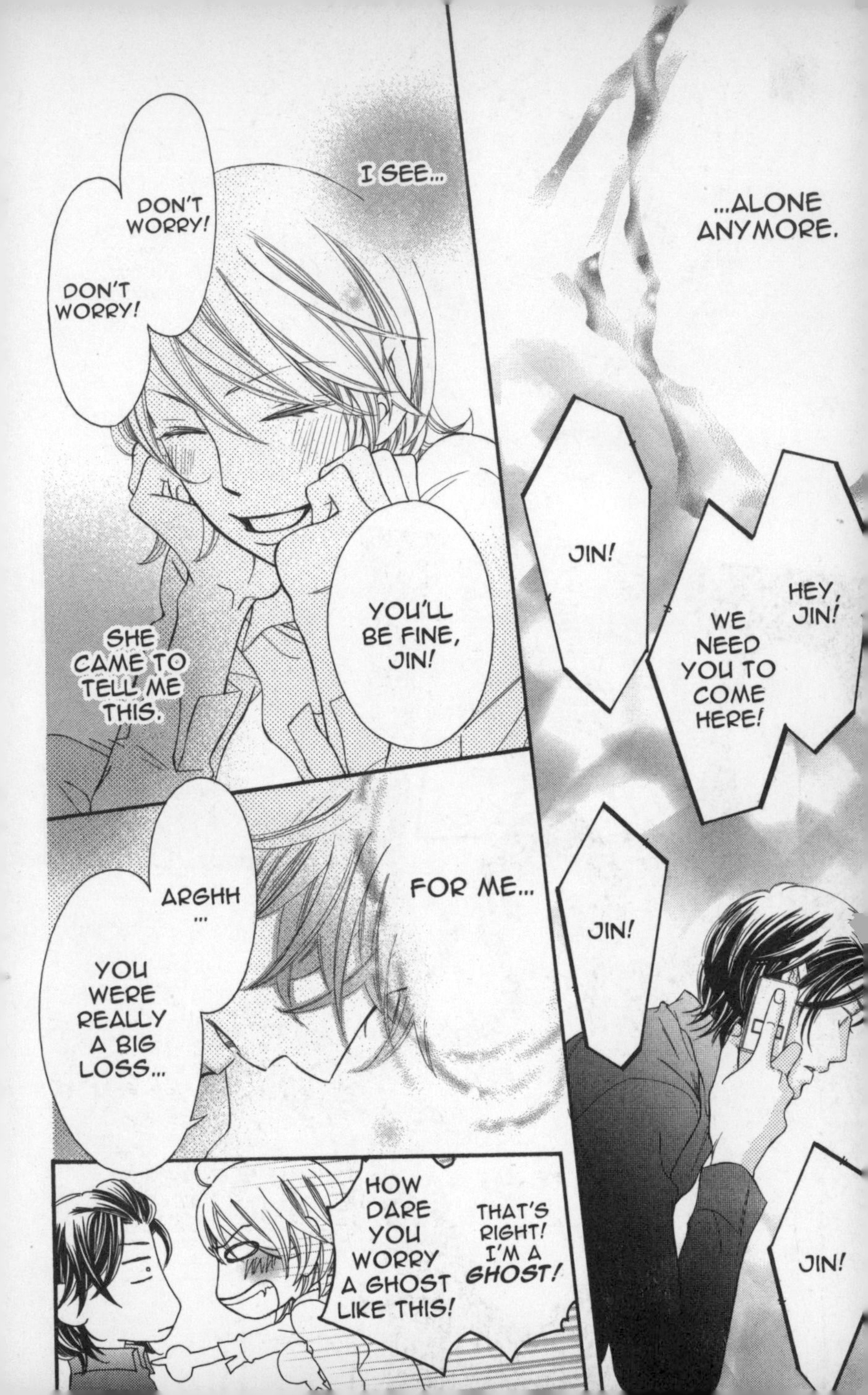
...ALONE ANYMORE.
HEY, JIN! WE NEED YOU TO COME HERE!
JIN!
JIN!
JIN!
I SEE...
YOU'LL BE FINE, JIN!
DON'T WORRY! DON'T WORRY!
SHE CAME TO TELL ME THIS.
FOR ME...
ARGHH... YOU WERE REALLY A BIG LOSS...
THAT'S RIGHT! I'M A *GHOST*!
HOW DARE YOU WORRY A GHOST LIKE THIS!

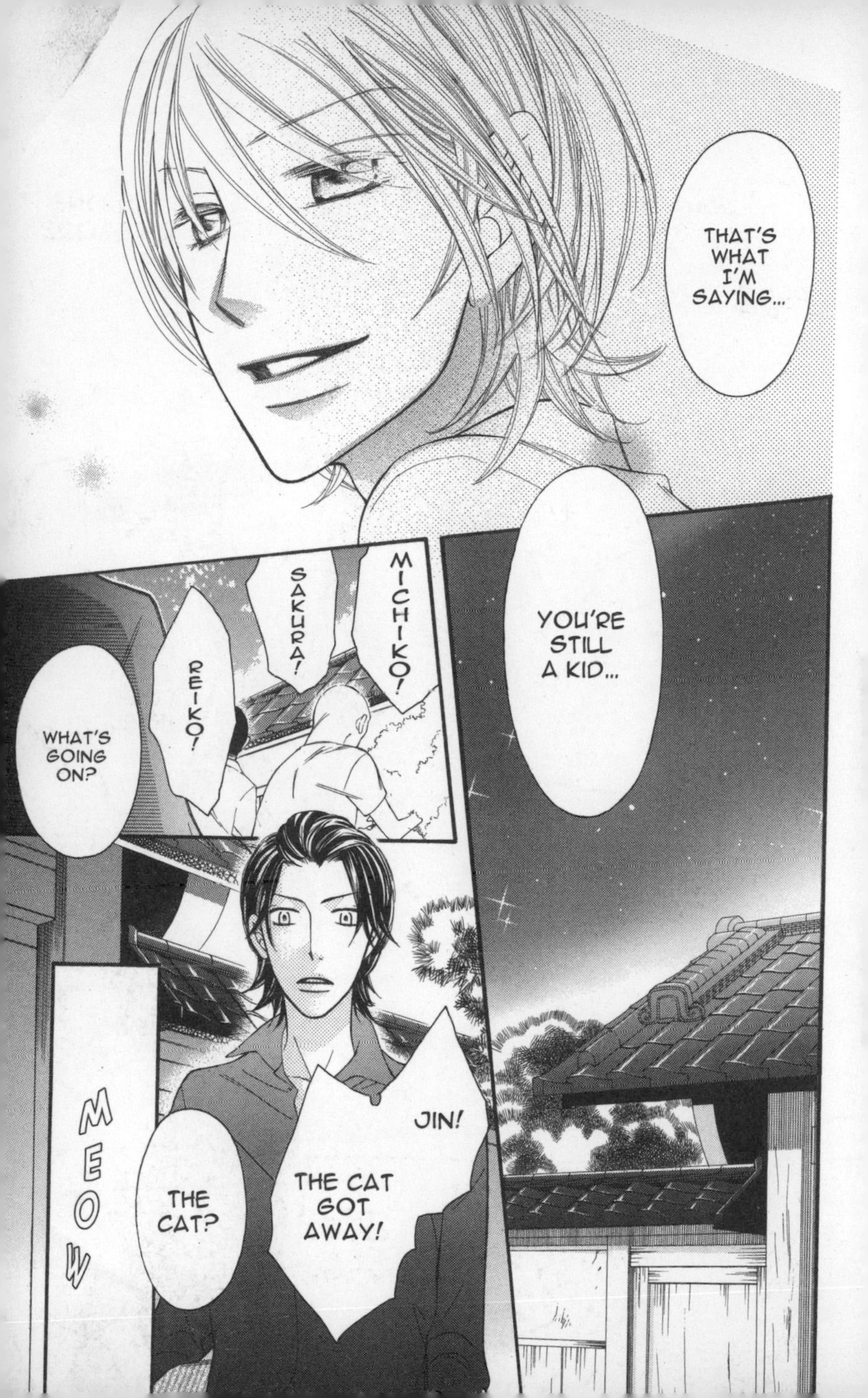
THAT'S WHAT I'M SAYING...
YOU'RE STILL A KID...
MICHIKO!
SAKURA!
REIKO!
WHAT'S GOING ON?
JIN!
THE CAT GOT AWAY!
THE CAT?
MEOW

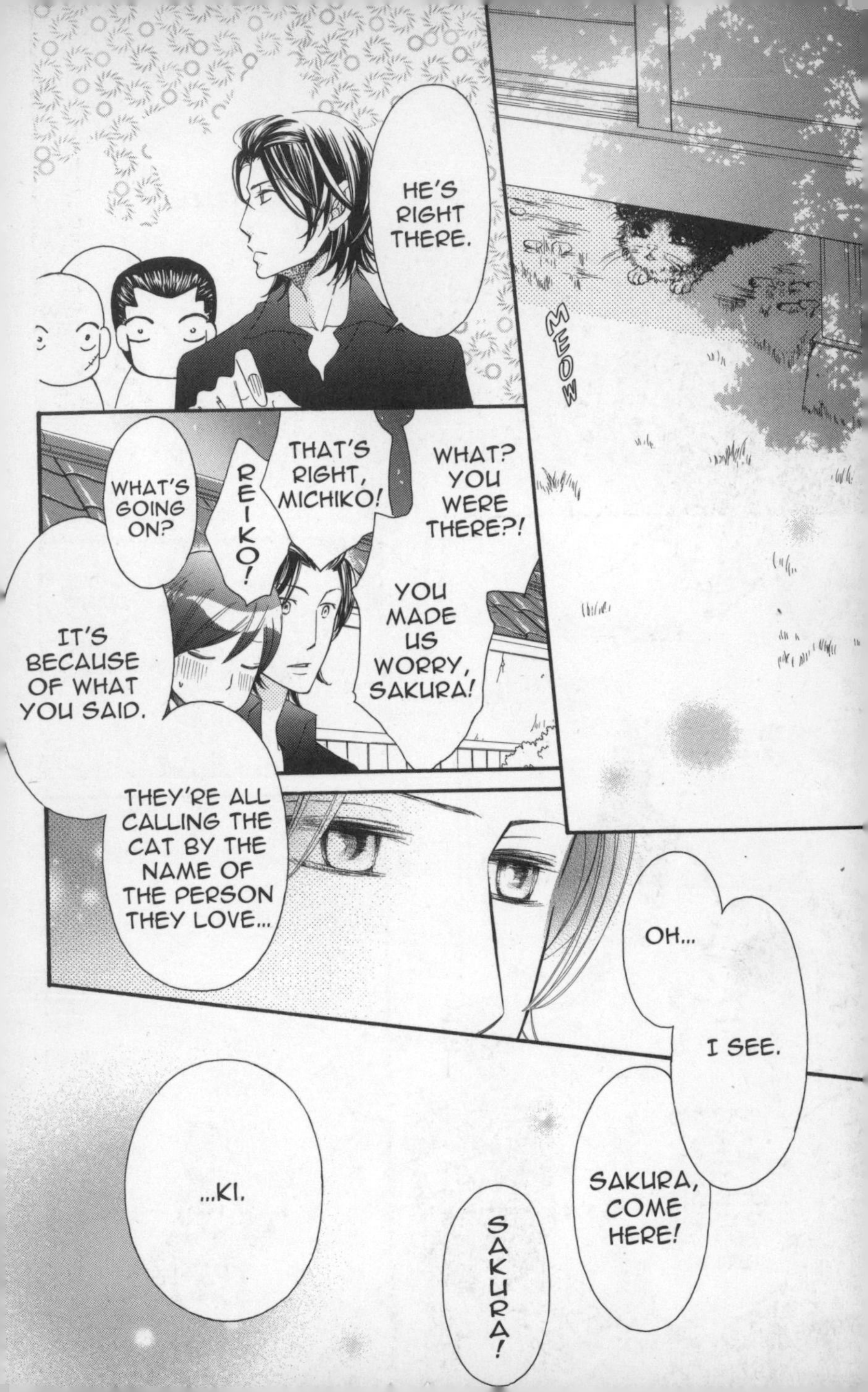
MEOW
HE'S RIGHT THERE.
WHAT? YOU WERE THERE?!
THAT'S RIGHT, MICHIKO!
REIKO!
WHAT'S GOING ON?
YOU MADE US WORRY, SAKURA!
IT'S BECAUSE OF WHAT YOU SAID.
THEY'RE ALL CALLING THE CAT BY THE NAME OF THE PERSON THEY LOVE...
OH...
I SEE.
SAKURA, COME HERE!
SAKURA!
...KI.

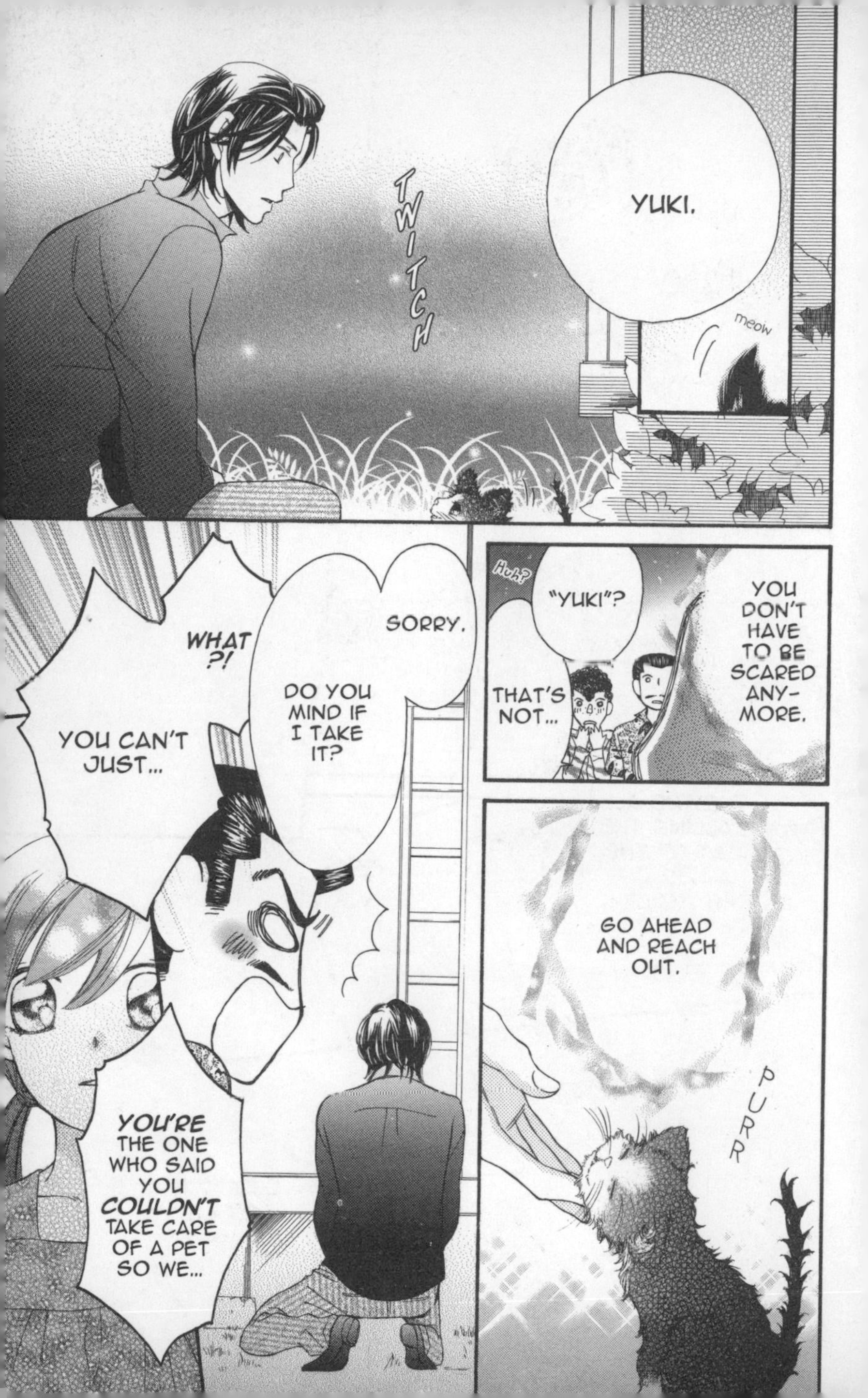
YUKI.
meow
TWITCH
YOU DON'T HAVE TO BE SCARED ANY-MORE.
"YUKI"?
Huh?
THAT'S NOT...
GO AHEAD AND REACH OUT.
PURR
SORRY.
DO YOU MIND IF I TAKE IT?
WHAT?!
YOU CAN'T JUST...
YOU'RE THE ONE WHO SAID YOU COULDN'T TAKE CARE OF A PET SO WE...

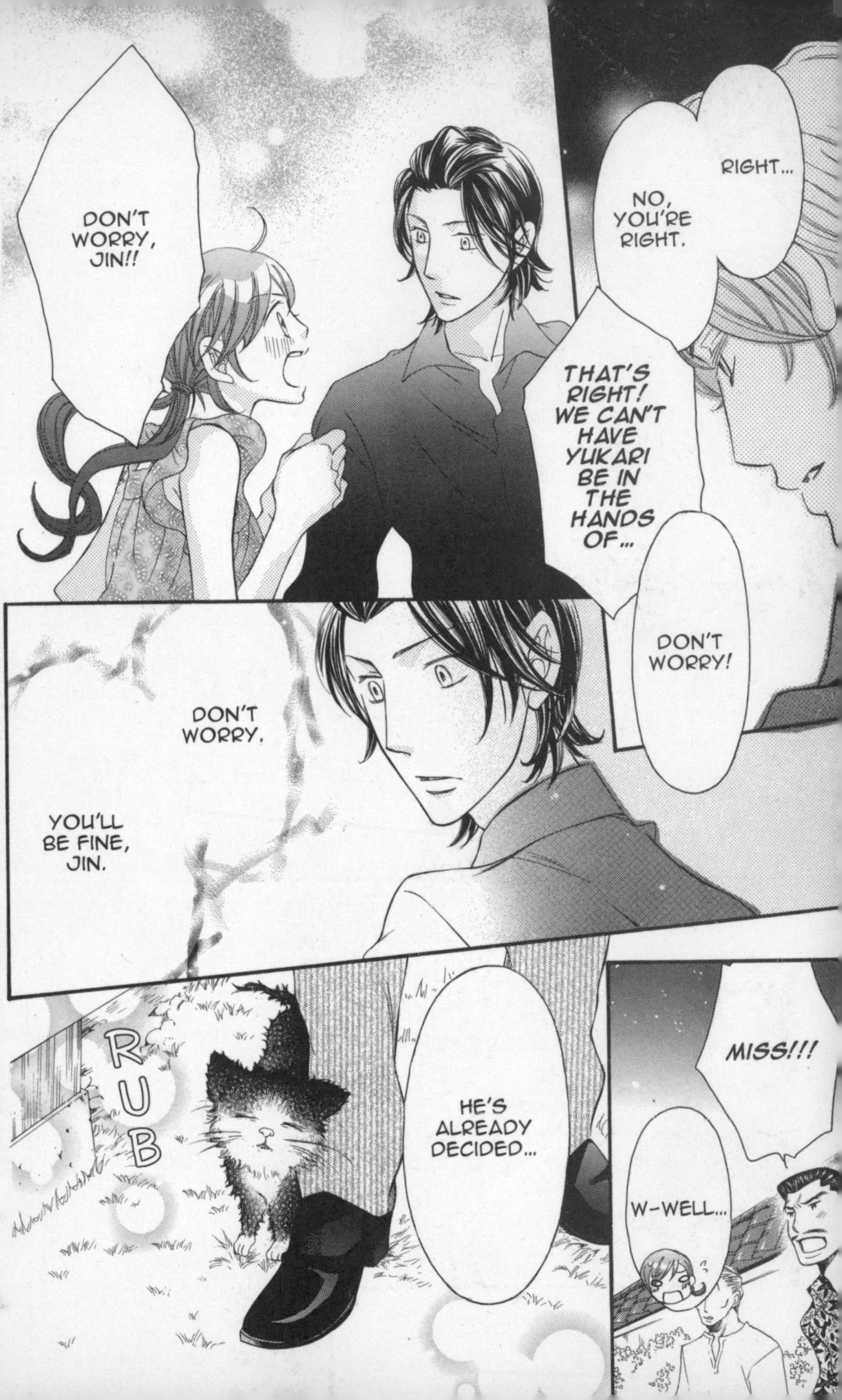
RIGHT...
NO, YOU'RE RIGHT.
THAT'S RIGHT! WE CAN'T HAVE YUKARI BE IN THE HANDS OF...
DON'T WORRY!
DON'T WORRY, JIN!!
DON'T WORRY.
YOU'LL BE FINE, JIN.
MISS!!!
W-WELL...
HE'S ALREADY DECIDED...
RUB

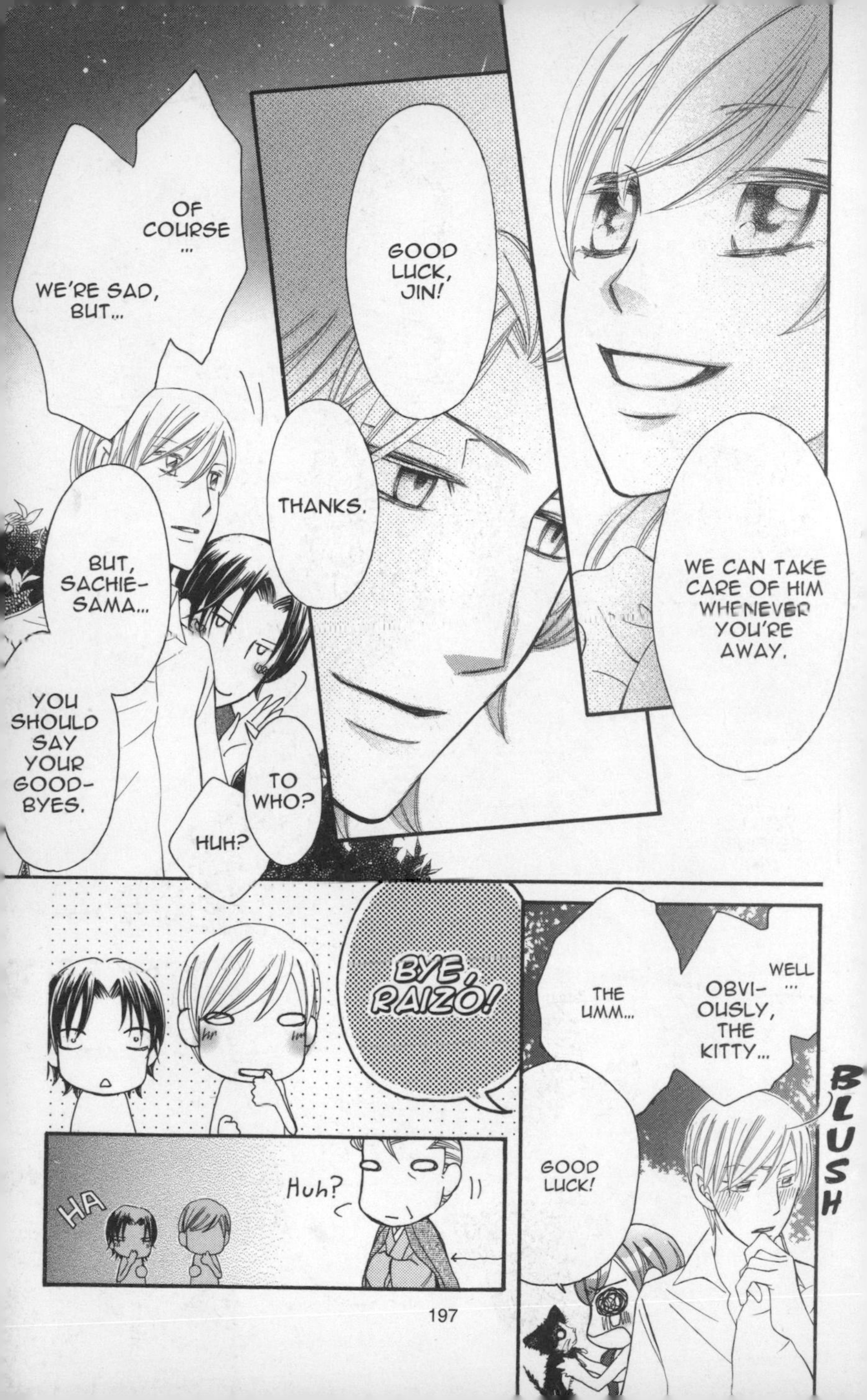
WE CAN TAKE CARE OF HIM WHENEVER YOU'RE AWAY.
GOOD LUCK, JIN!
THANKS.
OF COURSE ...
WE'RE SAD, BUT...
BUT, SACHIÉ-SAMA...
YOU SHOULD SAY YOUR GOOD-BYES.
TO WHO?
HUH?
WELL ...
OBVI-OUSLY, THE KITTY...
THE UMM...
BLUSH
GOOD LUCK!
BYE, RAIZŌ!
Huh?
HA

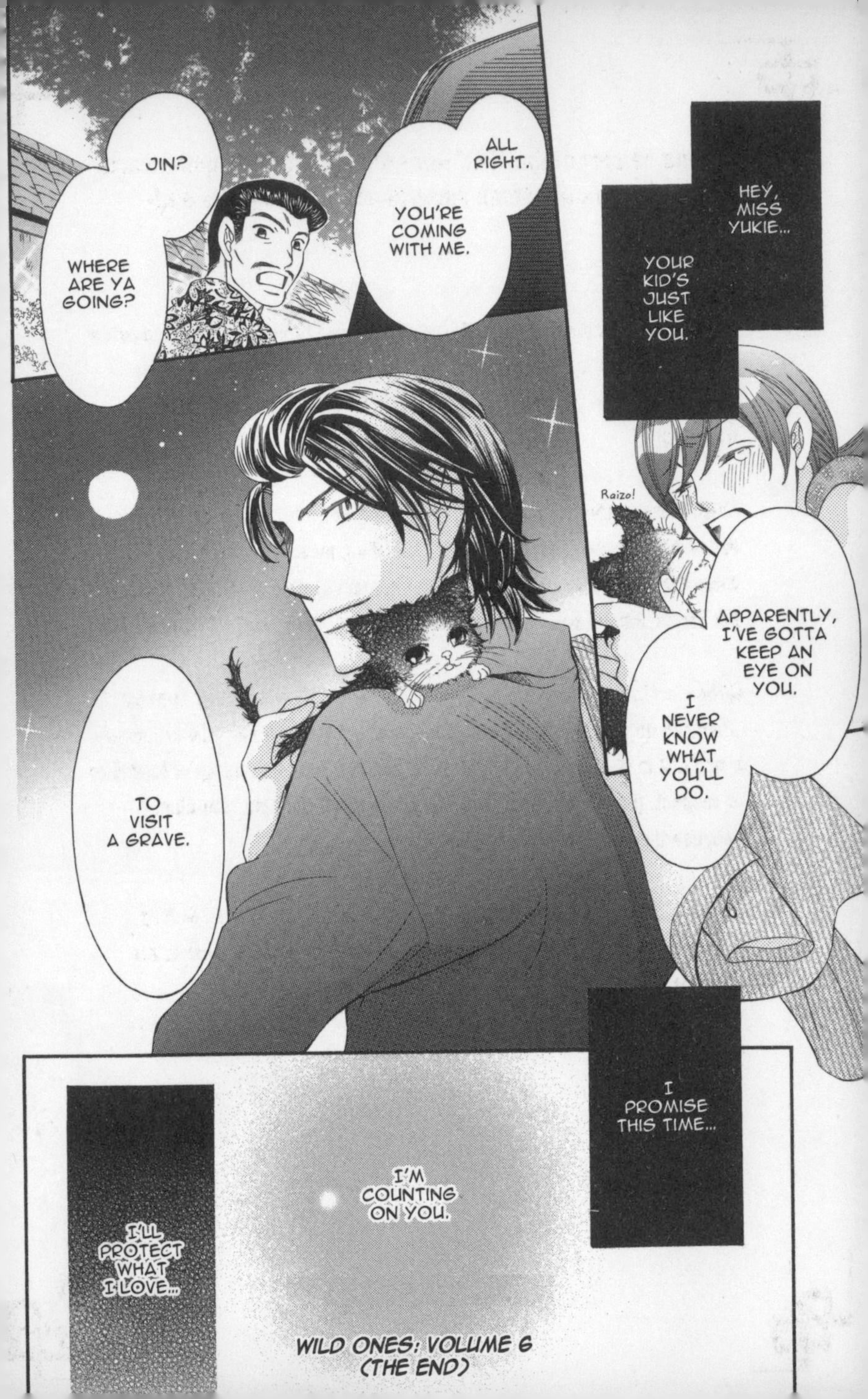
JIN?
WHERE ARE YA GOING?
ALL RIGHT.
YOU'RE COMING WITH ME.
TO VISIT A GRAVE.
HEY, MISS YUKIE...
YOUR KID'S JUST LIKE YOU.
Raizo!
APPARENTLY, I'VE GOTTA KEEP AN EYE ON YOU.
I NEVER KNOW WHAT YOU'LL DO.
I PROMISE THIS TIME...
I'LL PROTECT WHAT I LOVE...
I'M COUNTING ON YOU.
WILD ONES: VOLUME 6
(THE END)

Wanna be part of the *Wild Ones* gang? Then you gotta learn the lingo! Here are some cultural notes to help you out!

HONORIFICS

San – the most common honorific title; it is used to address people outside one's immediate family and close friends. (On page 9, Rakuto refers to Chigusa as "-san," because he is trying to be formal and distant, not friendly.)

Sama – the formal version of *san*; this honorific title is used primarily in addressing persons much higher in rank than oneself. *Sama* is also used when the speaker wants to show great respect or deference. (For most of the series, Rakuto calls Sachie "Sachie-sama" in addition to "princess.")

Chan – an informal version of *san* used to address children and females. *Chan* can be used as a term of endearment between women who are good friends. It is also used as a diminutive, to show a complete lack of formality or respect. (Sachie and the other classmates call Chigusa "Chi-chan," because they think of him as a kid. This angers him.)

Sensei – honorific title of respect, used to address teachers as well as professionals such as doctors, lawyers and artists. (Chigusa insists the students call him "sensei," which is a teacher's proper title.)

NOTES

Page 11, panel 1 – Shitake
A dark Japanese mushroom considered a delicacy by adults but usually unpopular with small children. Children not being able to eat *shitake* in Japan are like children not being able to eat liver in the West.

Page 13, panel 2 – Sports Day
A national holiday devoted to sports and physical activity. On this day, many schools hold a sports festival, and members of each class are chosen (often unwillingly) to represent the class in various sporting events.

Page 20, panel 2 – The Godfather of Shimizu
Jirocho of Shimizu, a famous historical gangster-turned-lawman of the 19th century. He was made famous in a series of novels, movies and TV series.

Page 20, panel 2 – Onihei's Clan
A fictional yakuza Robin Hood-type character introduced in novels in the 1960s, later expanding to movies and television.

Page 20, panel 5 – 893 = YA-KU-ZA
The numbers 8-9-3 can be pronounced YA-KU-ZA, and are thus code for Japanese gangsters.

Page 27, panel 1 – The stench of kendo
With long hours of hard training wearing heavy armor, kendo practice is associated with being extremely stinky. The armor is made of organic materials that absorb body odors and cannot be cleaned.

Page 145, panel 1 – Kanpai
A formal or festive toast, like the English "Cheers!" No party has officially started until every makes the first *kanpai* together.

Kiyo Fujiwara made her manga debut in 2000 in *Hana to Yume* magazine with *Bokuwane*. Her other works include *Hard Romantic-ker*, *Help!!* and *Gold Rush 21*. She comes from Akashi-shi in Hyogo Prefecture but currently lives in Tokyo. Her hobbies include playing drums and bass guitar and wearing kimono.

WILD ONES
VOL. 6
The Shojo Beat Manga Edition

STORY AND ART BY
KIYO FUJIWARA

Translation & Adaptation/Mai Ihara
Touch-up Art & Lettering/HudsonYards
Cover Design/Hidemi Dunn
Interior Design/Yuki Ameda
Editor/Jonathan Tarbox

Editor in Chief, Books/Alvin Lu
Editor in Chief, Magazines/Marc Weidenbaum
VP, Publishing Licensing/Rika Inouye
VP, Sales & Product Marketing/Gonzalo Ferreyra
VP, Creative/Linda Espinosa
Publisher/Hyoe Narita

Arakure by Kiyo Fujiwara
© Kiyo Fujiwara 2007
All rights reserved.
First published in Japan in 2007 by HAKUSENSHA, Inc., Tokyo.
English language translation rights arranged with HAKUSENSHA, Inc., Tokyo. The
stories, characters and incidents mentioned in this publication are entirely fictional.

Printed in Canada

Published by VIZ Media, LLC
P.O. Box 77010
San Francisco, CA 94107

Shojo Beat Manga Edition
10 9 8 7 6 5 4 3 2 1
First printing, March 2009

PARENTAL ADVISORY
WILD ONES is rated T for Teen
and is recommended for ages
13 and up. This volume contains
suggestive themes.
ratings.viz.com

www.viz.com
store.viz.com

Tell us what you think about Shojo Beat Manga!

Our survey is now available online. Go to:

shojobeat.com/mangasurvey

Help us make our product offerings better!

THE REAL DRAMA BEGINS IN...

Save OVER 50% off

Shojo Beat

The Shojo Manga Authority

This monthly magazine is injected with the most **ADDICTIVE** shojo manga stories from Japan. PLUS, unique editorial coverage on the arts, music, culture, fashion, and much more!

YES! Please enter my one-year subscription (12 GIANT issues) to *Shojo Beat* at the LOW SUBSCRIPTION RATE of **$34.99!**

Over **300 pages** per issue!

NAME

ADDRESS

CITY   STATE   ZIP

E-MAIL ADDRESS   P7GNC1

☐ MY CHECK IS ENCLOSED (PAYABLE TO *Shojo Beat*)   ☐ BILL ME LATER

CREDIT CARD: ☐ VISA   ☐ MASTERCARD

ACCOUNT #   EXP. DATE

SIGNATURE

CLIP AND MAIL TO

SHOJO BEAT
Subscriptions Service Dept.
P.O. Box 438
Mount Morris, IL 61054-0438